FINANCIAL INSTITUTIONS AND MARKETS IN SOUTHEAST ASIA

One of the more interesting aspects of the 1970s was the growth and development of financial institutions and markets within the Asia and Pacific region. Early in the decade few countries had financial markets of any significance: commercial banks dominated the domestic financial sectors and, in some cases, were virtually the only institutions. Today the capitalist countries of Southeast Asia have the beginnings of, if not developed, money, securities and foreign-exchange markets, as well as a wide range of specialized financial institutions which compete with and complement the services of the commercial banks.

Financial Institutions and Markets in Southeast Asia presents an in-depth, country-by-country coverage of these developments in Brunei, Indonesia, Malaysia, Philippines, Singapore and Thailand. Each chapter includes an introduction to the country and its financial sector; an examination of the development and operations of each type of financial institution, as well as the local money market, stock exchange and foreign-exchange markets; an analysis of the financial sector's overall performance; and finally some speculation on future developments that might occur. The endnotes for each chapter and the bibliography provide details for further research.

The book should prove a valuable reference for researchers in development and financial economics as well as international business, and for advanced graduate or undergraduate seminars. For the businessman, the book provides background on the financial sectors and is a handy financial guidebook to the region.

FINANCIAL INSTITUTIONS AND MARKETS IN SOUTHEAST ASIA

A Study of Brunei, Indonesia, Malaysia, Philippines, Singapore and Thailand

Edited by

Michael T. Skully
Senior Lecturer in Finance
University of New South Wales

St. Martin's Press   New York

Library of Congress Cataloging in Publication Data

Main entry under title:

Financial institutions and markets in Southeast Asia.

  Bibliography: p.
  Includes index.
  1. Financial institutions—Asia, Southeastern—
Addresses, essays, lectures. 2. Finance—Asia, South-
eastern—Addresses, essays, lectures. I. Skully,
Michael T.
HG187.A789F56 1984   332.1′0959   83–13892
ISBN 0–312–28964–2

Contents

List of Figures

List of Maps

List of Tables

ix

Preface

One of the more interesting aspects of the 1970s was the growth and development of financial institutions and markets within the Asian and Pacific region. Early in the decade, few countries had financial markets of any significance: commercial banks dominated the domestic financial sectors and, in some cases, were virtually the only institutions. Today the capitalist countries of this region have embryonic, if not developed, money, securities and foreign exchange markets, as well as a wide range of specialised financial institutions which compete with (and complement) the services of the commercial banks. This book represents the second of a series of titles which aim to provide an in-depth, country-by-country coverage of these developments, and the financial institutions and markets as they exist today.

In this volume, it was tempting to use the word ASEAN[1] rather than Southeast Asia to describe the region, as five of the six countries covered are ASEAN members and the sixth, Brunei, will probably join ASEAN in 1984. This, however, would have meant deviating from the major purpose of this series: the study of financial institutions and markets on a country-by-country basis. While ASEAN is often mentioned within the text – particularly within the chapter on Singapore – specific details of ASEAN itself and its related private sector bodies can well be found elsewhere.[2]

The information presented, unless otherwise noted, is derived from interviews and correspondence with government officials, academic researchers and business leaders within each financial sector. The use of local contributors also enabled more comprehensive coverage of each country than a sole researcher might hope to accomplish. Wherever possible, references published in English have been included within the Notes section at the end of each chapter, and should provide the reader with a worthwhile starting point for further study.

The task of constructing such a publication is considerable, and could not have been accomplished without the assistance of a multitude of people. The willingness of the contributors to devote their time in preparing the articles; the co-operation of the numerous financial executives and government officials contacted; and the assistance of the administrative personnel and my colleagues at the University of New South Wales are particularly appreciated. Special thanks must also go to the Research Departments and Libraries of Bank Indonesia; Bank Negara Malaysia; the Central Bank of the Philippines; the Monetary Authority of Singapore; the Oversea–Chinese Banking Corporation; the Bangkok Bank; the Siam Commercial Bank; the Bank of America; the Hongkong and Shanghai Banking Corporation; the Westpac Banking Corporation; the Brunei State Chamber of Commerce; the Bangkok Insurance Company; and the Bank of Thailand.

M.T.S.

NOTES

1. ASEAN (the Association of South East Asian Nations) was formed in August 1967 by Indonesia, Malaysia, Philippines, Singapore, and Thailand. However, it was not until after the February 1976 Bali Summit that it became a significant force within the region.
2. See A. Broinowski (ed.), *Understanding ASEAN* (London: Macmillan, 1982); Ross Garnaut (ed.), *ASEAN in a Changing Pacific and World Economy* (Canberra: Australian National University Press, 1981); Michael T. Skully, *ASEAN Regional Financial Cooperation: Developments in Banking and Finance* (Singapore: Institute of Southeast Asian Studies, 1979); T. W. Allen, *The ASEAN Report* (Hong Kong: Dow Jones, 1979); and *10 Years, ASEAN* (Jakarta: Association of South East Asian Nations, 1978).

Notes on the Contributors

Michael T. Skully is Senior Lecturer in Finance at the University of New South Wales and is known for his research in the financial institutions and markets of the Asia and Pacific countries. He has served as a consultant for the World Bank and other financial bodies and has published widely in the areas of international finance and business. His books include *Financial Institutions and Markets in the Far East, Merchant Banking in the Far East, ASEAN Regional Financial Cooperation: Developments in Banking and Finance,* and *A Multinational Look at the Transnational Corporation.*

Zeti Akhtar Aziz is a Research Economist at the South-East Asian Central Banks (SEACEN) Research and Training Centre in Malaysia. She is a graduate of the Universities of Malaya and Pennsylvania. She is known for her research in the areas of economics, interest-rate structures, and monetary policy within the SEACEN countries and is the author of *Commercial Bank Portfolio Behaviour in an Open Developing Economy: the Malaysian Case.*

Ross McLeod is a Lecturer in Economics at the Australian National University. He is a graduate of the University of Melbourne and ANU and prior to joining the university he worked both as a civil engineer and as a consultant to Bank Indonesia. He is known for his research in business finance and the informal credit markets in Indonesia and is author of *Finance and Entrepreneurship in the Small Business Sector in Indonesia.*

Alfredo E. Pascual is the American Express Foundation Professor of Financial Management at the Asian Institute of Management in the Philippines and Director of the Institute's Advanced Bank Management Program. He is a graduate of the University of the Philippines, and prior to joining the Institute held a number of senior financial positions within the Philippines' investment banking industry and private industry.

Lee Sheng-Yi is an Associate Professor in Business Administration at the National University of Singapore. He is known for research and consulting work in ASEAN economic matters and he has written many articles on money, banking and public finance in both business and international academic journals. His books include *Money and Banking Development of Malaysia and Singapore, Public Finance and Public Investment in Singapore* and *Financial Structures and Monetary Policies in Southeast Asia* (co-author).

1 Financial Institutions and Markets in Brunei

MICHAEL T. SKULLY

INTRODUCTION

(a) The Setting

Brunei is located on the northwest coast of the Island of Borneo and – due to its major oil and gas reserves – is one of the richest countries for its size in the world.[1] Its land area of 5765 square kilometres is divided between an eastern and a somewhat larger western portion, separated from each other by the Bay of Brunei and the Malaysian state of Sarawak.

This area is all that remains of what was up to the sixteenth century a major empire, covering not only the Island of Borneo but parts of mainland Malaysia and the southern Philippines as well. In the first decade of the fifteenth century, the then Sultan of Brunei, Sultan Bolkiah, even seized (and for a short time controlled) Manila. The arrival of the Western powers in the region soon reduced Brunei's standing, and slowly but surely the Portugese, Spanish, Dutch and English gradually acquired parts of Brunei's empire for their own.

Brunei nevertheless maintained nominal control of most North and West Borneo until the 1800s, when the Brooke family – the so called 'White Rajahs' – in the south, and the British North Borneo Company in the north, gradually began to acquire even those possessions, areas which now comprise respectively the Malaysian states of Sarawak and Sabah. Brunei's first contact with British government itself came on 18 December 1846, when Brunei was forced to cede Labuan Island to the Royal Navy. On 17 September 1888, Brunei became a British protectorate, and in 1906 accepted its first British resident to 'advise' the Sultan.

2

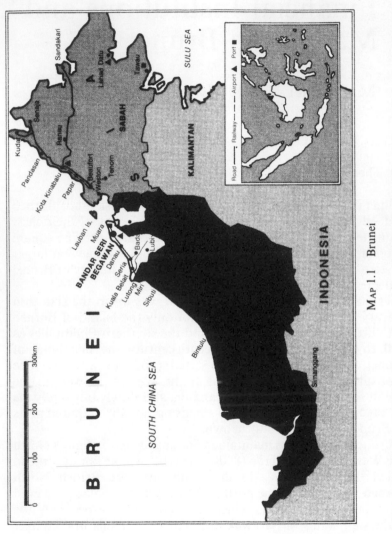

MAP 1.1   Brunei

Source: Department of Trade and Resources, *Guide to the Market: Brunei* (Australian Government Publishing Service, 1982).

Brunei's return to an independent nation has been a slow process, officially starting in 1959; under the Anglo–Brunei Treaty of Friendship and Co-operation 1979, the country will as of 31 December 1983 again have full control of its domestic and international affairs.

Economically, Brunei is well placed, and faces few of the problems of most newly independent nations. As the government itself once stated:

Brunei . . . is free from the pressing problems of foreign exchange shortages resulting from unfavourable balances of payments, and free from the limitation and restraints arising from unbalanced budgets. On the contrary, the accumulation of surpluses invested abroad, plus the favourable balance of payments, enables Brunei to finance a development programme from its own budgetary resources.[2]

This position is largely a function of the country's oil and gas fields, a resource which at current usage and reserve levels is expected to last at least another 20 years.

Brunei's heavy dependence on oil and oil related industries (as shown in Table 1.1) has 'nevertheless bothered government planners, and through a series of 5 Year National Development Plans the government hopes to broaden the country's economic base. The 1975–9 Plan tried to encourage private sector investment in forestry based industries; oil and gas related products; other mineral development; and various agricultural business.

TABLE 1.1   Brunei gross domestic product by economic activity (figures as at end year, at current prices, as a percentage share)

	1973	75	79
Agriculture, forestry & fishing	2.4	1.0	0.9
Mining & quarrying	77.7	75.4⎫	82.4
Manufacturing	3.7	11.8⎭	
Electricity, gas, water	0.1	0.2	0.0
Construction	2.6	2.1	1.8
Commerce	3.6	2.6	8.0
Transport & communications	0.8	0.8	0.9
Services	9.1	6.0	6.0
Total GDP	100.0	100.0	100.0

Source: *Brunei Statistical Yearbook* (Kuala Belait: Government Printer, 1980).

The 1980–4 Plan is similarly orientated, but oil and gas will probably continue to dominate Brunei's economy for many years to come.

(b) An Overview of the Financial Sector

Brunei's small physical size and population of only 200000 is a slender foundation on which to develop a financial sector, and perhaps not surprisingly it is the least developed of Southeast Asian capitalist countries. This has been exacerbated by the Brunei economy's comparable underdevelopment. With the loss of its empire, Brunei's trade with the outside world declined and prior to the discovery of oil was at best nominal. Even with oil, the economy retained a local agricultural orientation, causing one guide book to suggest that until recently Brunei's largest import had been the foreign films shown in local cinemas, and the largest export (other than oil) the return of empty beer bottles to Singapore![3]

While these comments no doubt overstated the position then – and are certainly not true today – they do nevertheless give some insight into why Brunei's financial sector has taken so long to develop. Even so basic an institution as a Post Office Savings Bank (POSB) did not appear until 1935, and was not until after the Second World War that the foreign commercial banks even considered opening a local office.

A number of commercial banks and finance companies now operate in Brunei, and more recently some local insurance companies have been established, but otherwise Brunei lacks the mix of financial institutions one normally finds in Southeast Asia – even the normal government and development finance institutions are missing. Furthermore (for the present at least) there seems no plan to change this position: any changes in the financial sector will have to wait till after Brunei's post-independence administration is well established. For the immediate future, the affairs of the financial sector will rate a rather low priority within the government.

FINANCIAL INSTITUTIONS

Brunei lacks a central bank; its equivalent functions are performed by two bodies – the Treasury Department and the

Currency Board. These two institutions will be discussed first, followed by the banks and other private sector institutions, and finally those government departments active in local lending or other financially related matters.

(a) The Brunei Treasury Department

The Treasury Department of the Brunei government is headed by the State Financial Officer (SFO), and is directly responsible for the regulation of most financial matters within the country. As shown in Figure 1.1, the department comprises three major divisions – Finance, Accounts and Currency – each with distinct functions. The Finance Division is the budgetary area of the department, and is basically responsible for the collection and expenditure of government monies. The Accounts Division handles the government's actual banking business; the investment of its surplus funds (a fiscal surplus of B$5.3 billion was expected for 1982);[4] the administration of housing and car loans to government employees; the payment of government pensions and other gratuities; and the fiscal supervision of Brunei's overseas agencies, leave passages and educational allowances. The Currency Division is responsible for the department's Ministry of Finance role – it collects the banking and finance company statutory reports, and assists the SFO in administering the various banking and finance company ordinances. It also administers the Exchange Control Enactment 1965 and (through the Currency Board) is responsible for the issue of notes and coin.

The relationship between the Currency Board and the department's Currency Division is an interesting one, since the administrative staff hold positions in both bodies. The head of the division (the Currency and Banking Officer) is also the Currency Board manager; his assistant similarly wears two hats. Given the need to handle both the currency issue and the Currency Divisions function, the division's regulation of the banks and finance companies is confined almost entirely to statistical collection. Any problems or other discussions between the government and the institutions are generally handled personally by the SFO.

The present SFO (an English expatriate, John Lee) has held the position for many years, and is well respected within both the government and the financial community. His position in the Brunei government is, however, much more important than just

6

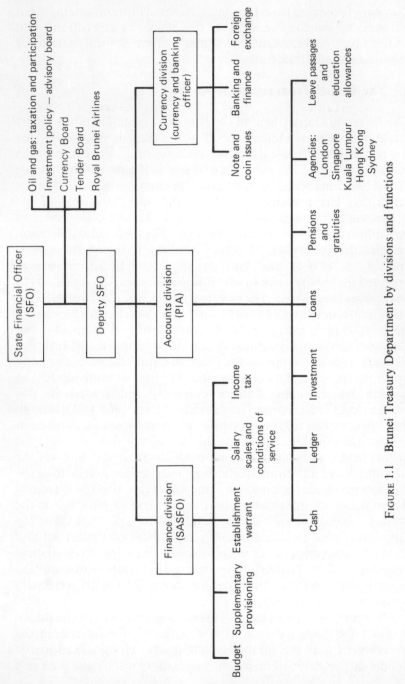

Figure 1.1 Brunei Treasury Department by divisions and functions

Source: Brunei Treasury Department, 1982.

that of a Treasurer for he (together with the State Secretary and Attorney General) effectively runs the country. They in turn are responsible to the Mentri Besar (or Chief Minister) and, of course, to the Sultan himself.

(b) The Brunei Currency Board

The Brunei Currency Board was founded on 12 June 1967, under the Currency Enactment 1967, to issue currency for legal tender within the state. Previously this role had been performed by the Board of Commissioners of Currency for Malaya and British Borneo; after 1967, the Brunei dollar replaced North Borneo notes in local circulation.

In June 1967, when the Brunei dollar was first issued, it had a parity of 0.290299 grams of gold to each dollar, and it still maintained this position in 1982. Initially, this parity was the same as that of the Malaysian and Singapore dollars and, by special arrangement, each of the currencies was interchangeable in the other countries. This relationship between Brunei and Malaysia was discontinued in May 1973, but parity with the Singapore dollar has remained.

Officially the Brunei dollar is designated the only legal tender within the state (the amount on issue is shown in Table 1.2) but under the interchangeability at par agreement between Brunei and Singapore, Singapore currency is considered as a 'customary' tender within Brunei, and at the request of the Board banks in Brunei exchange without charge Singapore dollars into Brunei dollars at face value.

Under the agreement, when the Currency Board collects the Singapore dollars from the banks it then repatriates them to Singapore where the settlement is made. As shown by Figure 1.2, the flow of currency is very one sided and often little if any Singapore dollars are repatriated. The reasons for this are numerous; one is that as Singapore supplies most of Brunei's consumer imports, many purchases are done in cash. Some traders may not trust the banking system, nor wish records kept of their transactions. Many Brunei workers are also frequent visitors to Singapore, and spend in cash.

Besides the issue and redemption of paper currency, the Board is also responsible for handling coins and numismatic items and the investment of the foreign exchange reserves (a breakdown of the latter is shown in Table 1.3). In practice, however, the Crown

TABLE 1.2 Brunei money supply and quasi-money (figures in $million)

End of year	Money supply & quasi-money	Money supply			Quasi-money private sector's fixed savings and other deposits		
		Total	Currency in circulation	Demand deposits of private sector	Total	Fixed (time) deposits	Savings & other deposits
1977	744.2	269.9	90.1	179.8	474.3	362.6	111.7
1978	779.8	360.5	100.5	260.0	419.3	295.8	123.5
1979	948.6	559.1	126.8	432.3	389.5	240.5	159.0
1980	1262.1	679.5	151.8	527.7	582.6	372.4	210.2

Source: Brunei Currency Board, Annual Report 1982.

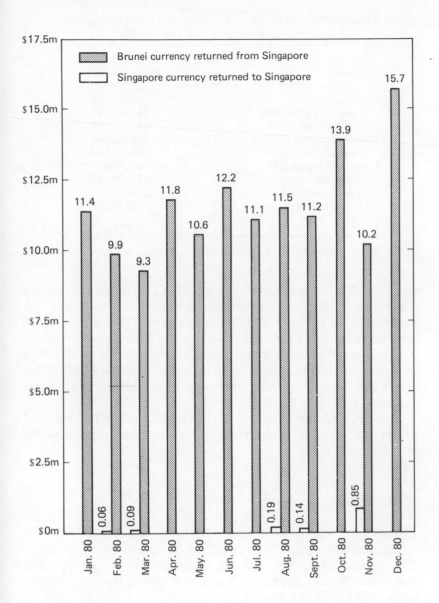

FIGURE 1.2   Brunei currency from Singapore and Singapore currency
returned to Singapore, 1980

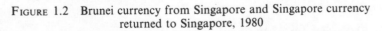

Source: Brunei Currency Board, *Annual Report 1980*, p. 36.

TABLE 1.3   Brunei Currency Board external assets by type and currency (figures as at end 1980, in B$)

Type of investment	Market value
Singapore currency	58677.00
Call deposits in sterling	1816615.56
Deposits at call in S$	13807937.95
Fixed deposits in sterling	3163520.00
Fixed deposits in US$	38360034.89
Fixed deposits in DM	11793.38
Sterling debt securities	51243789.37
US$ debt securities	22836785.90
DM debt securities	20064500.23
Total	151363654.28

Source: Brunei Currency Board, *Annual Report 1980*, p. 32.

Agents in the UK – in conjunction with a UK based investment committee – manages these investments. The Crown Agents also arrange for the printing of currency; the production of coins; and the overseas sale of numismatic items. This Crown Agents' connection reflects the importance of UK officials in Brunei's financial affairs, and even in 1982 under the Currency Ordinance the Board was obliged to exchange its notes for sterling on demand.

In early 1982, the Currency Board had a staff of 12 – most of whom were involved with the counting and physical distribution of the currency.

(c) The Banks

The banks are the oldest as well as the most important of Brunei's financial institutions, and as such deserve detailed consideration. This section first examines the development of the banking industry in Brunei, then its regulation, deposits, lending, interest rates, and finally the market's structure.

(i) *Development of the banking industry*

The banking industry in Brunei differs from those of its ASEAN neighbours, first in that it was established by the local government rather than foreign bankers, and second that it developed in the twentieth rather than the nineteenth century.

The impetus for the banking industry came with the discovery of oil in 1929; prior to that time Brunei's small trade and financial dealings were adequately served 'long distance' by banks in Singapore and what is now Malaysia. Oil exploration and development brought a substantial number of foreign workers to the country, and created a demand for local banking services. As most foreign workers were employed by what was then the British Malayan Petroleum Company, it is not surprising that this firm was heavily involved in developing local banking. Initially, the company provided some of these services itself, by having its employees establish accounts in Singapore and then arranging from them to draw against these accounts through the company's Brunei offices.

These arrangements proved inadequate, and in conjunction with a growing demand for local banking services among the domestic population the Brunei government in May 1935 opened the first banking institution, the Post-Office Savings Bank (POSB).

The POSB accepted deposits from the public, the security of which were guaranteed in full by the Brunei government. However, rather than reloan the funds locally, the POSB invested these monies overseas in sterling denominated securities. It did not offer cheque services as such, but through an arrangement with the government's Treasury Department customers could buy third party cheques drawn against the Brunei government's accounts in Singapore.

The Japanese occupation in 1942 brought Brunei's first foreign bank, when a branch of the Yokohama Specie Bank (since reconstituted as the Bank of Tokyo) was established to serve the needs of the Japanese Occupation Forces and the local economy. As elsewhere in Japanese controlled Southeast Asia, the Yokohama Specie Bank was responsible for the issue of the local occupation currency, and served as the bankers for the local Japanese established government.

The surrender of the Japanese forces in 1945 also brought an end to the Yokohama Specie Bank's operations in Brunei, and it took some time for the local banking industry to re-establish itself. During the occupation, the Post Office had been destroyed and with it most of the POSB's records. When the POSB finally reopened (on 15 November 1946) it therefore restricted its operations to 'new transactions' only. The effective loss of savings, despite the government guarantee, dampened local enthusiasm for this institution, for by the end of 1947 it had a total of only 57 customers and deposits of B$5914.[5] The business gradually grew, but the POSB's importance soon began to be eclipsed by the private banks. In 1976, the government reported that:

> As the number of depositors had dwindled to less than 2000 with an average holding of but $90 per passbook and with many accounts of less than $10 it was recommended that the bank should be closed.[6]

The bank ceased accepting new business on 1 January 1976, and ceased operations entirely on 31 December 1976.

The first private bank in Brunei came on 2 January 1947, when the Hongkong and Shanghai Banking Corporation established a branch office in Brunei's capital city, Bandar Seri Begawan (then known as Brunei Town). Later in 1947 it also opened an office in the country's other major city, Kuala Belait.

As shown in Table 1.4, the next bank to establish locally (the Chartered Bank) did not come until 1958. Three more came in the 1960s; a further three in the 1970s; The Island Development Bank was established only in late 1980.

TABLE 1.4 Brunei licensed banks by establishment date and country of incorporation

Bank	Country of incorporation	Local establishment date
Hongkong and Shanghai Banking Corporation	Hongkong	2 Jan. 1947
Chartered Bank	UK	1958
Malayan Banking Berhad	Malaysia	1960
United Malayan Banking Corporation Berhad	Malaysia	1963
National Bank of Brunei Ltd	Brunei	1965
Citibank NA	USA	Mar. 1972
Bank of America NT & SA	USA	Nov. 1972
Overseas Union Bank Ltd	Singapore	28 Dec. 1973
Island Development Bank Ltd	Brunei	18 Dec. 1980

(ii) *Bank regulation*

The banking industry in Brunei is regulated under the Banking Enactment 1956, which came into force on 1 January 1957. This Enactment limits the banking business within Brunei to companies which have an authorised capital of at least B$1000000, of which B$500000 is fully paid. The licensed local banks are also required to maintain a reserve fund equal to their paid-up capital and to transfer 20 per cent of the net profits each year to this fund until the reserve requirement is fulfilled. The Brunei branch operations of the foreign banks, however, are exempted from these requirements. All banks are also subject to a B$1000 annual licensing fee.

Under the reporting requirement section of the Enactment, each bank must file three types of reports on its Brunei operations. The First Schedule states that the bank's assets and liabilities within Brunei should be filed every 6 months; the Second Schedule provides an analysis of the type of advances and bills discounted, again every 6 months; the Third Schedule is much like the First, in that it refers to bank's assets and liabilities, but is less detailed and requires data to be filed monthly. In addition to those specific reports to government, the banks must also file copies of their overall annual reports with the SFO, and make copies of these available at all branches. As foreign banks release only their consolidated parent bank statements, no statistics on their respective Brunei operations are publicly available.

Other than paid-up capital and reserve funds, local banks are subject to no other reserve ratios or gearing requirements. This lack of potential monetary control, however, has not presented a major problem for the Brunei government. As a Bank of America study concluded 'the government can control the money supply through regulating its expenditures and deciding whether to take payment of the royalties and dividends from Shell abroad or in Brunei'.[7]

(iii) *Bank deposits or funding operations*

The banks in Brunei have set guidelines on their deposit taking business, and may accept funds for up to 12 months only at rates set by the Association of Banks for all members (see Table 1.7). As shown in Table 1.5, these deposits may come in the form of

TABLE 1.5   Brunei total assets and liabilities, 1981 (figures as at 31 December 1981, in B$)

Liabilities		
Deposits		
(a) Demand	732598228.74	
(b) Time	773305004.67	
(c) Savings	188134033.49	
(d) Deposit at call	21401320.10	
		1715438587.00
Balance due to		
(a) Other banks in the state		
(i) in respect of		
current transactions		23099237.66
(ii) in respect of		
loans & advances		—
(b) Banks abroad		
(i) in respect of current		
transactions		
1. UK	101077.97	
2. USA	1738176.05	
3. Hongkong/Canada	39478.54	
		1878732.56
4. Elsewhere		
Sterling Area		100066428.81
Non-sterling Area		1.14
(ii) in respect of		
loans & advances		—
Other Liabilities		736746968.70
Total		2577229955.87

Assets		
Cash		15474815.18
Balance due from Banks in the States:		
(a) in respect of current transactions		10357531.42
(b) in respect of loans & advances		—
(c) in respect of deposit		20000000.00
Balance due from Banks abroad		
(a) in respect of current transactions		
1. UK	70687693.50	
2. USA	7054981.04	
3. Canada	125523.37	
4. Hongkong	1430015.94	
5. Elsewhere		
Formerly Sterling Area	649230951.21	
Non-sterling Area	306352.53	
(b) in respect of current bills discounted		728835517.59
1. UK	211712.92	
2. USA	3092472.43	
3. Canada	18858.20	
4. Elsewhere		
Formerly sterling Area	374711.09	
Non-sterling Area	1547.14	
(c) in respect of deposit		3699301.78
(d) in respect of loans & advances		—
Loans and advances		
(to customers other than banks)		
(a) Primary productions	3996395.89	
(b) Other industries	159751161.32	
(c) Other advances	524890057.35	688637614.56
Investments		
(a) Local	31493004.00	
(b) Others	109310711.98	140803715.98
Other assets		
(a) Bills discounted	49336889.44	
(b) Bills receivable	4778203.14	
(c) Others	915306366.78	969421459.36
		2577229955.87

Source: Brunei Currency Board, *Annual Report 1982*.

demand (42.7 per cent); time or fixed (45.1 per cent); savings account (11 per cent); and at call (1.2 per cent). Demand and time deposits are traditionally the most important, but their significance at any one time is a function of the government's funds placements: it is the single major source of deposits. Table 1.5's value is also marred by a lack of consistency among the reporting banks – what one bank will call a time deposit another may call a demand deposit, and yet pay interest on these 'demand' balances. All government and Brunei Shell Petroleum Group[8] deposits accrue interest at a rate of 2 per cent below the current prime lending rate, even though they may be held at call.

Despite these inconsistencies within the sub-totals, an examination of the total deposits and total asset figures nevertheless provides some insight into the growth of the banking system. A comparison between the figures in Table 1.5 and the historical quarterly date in Table 1.6 indicates the banking system's substantial growth during 1981.

The government deposits funds with only three of Brunei's banks to meet its own operational requirements (paying and receiving) and for investment purposes. In the former case, the normal government bank business has traditionally been shared between the country's two oldest banks – the Hongkong and Shanghai Banking Corporation and the Chartered Bank: this is also true in the case of the country's major private customer, the Brunei Shell Petroleum Group. However, the spread of government banking business has since widened, with the National Bank of Brunei also assuming an important role. The government's placement of its time deposits was once available to any bank in Brunei by the way of competitive tender: the government set the amount and terms available, and the banks bid as to the interest rate paid. Recently, however, it seems that such bids are requested only from the government's bankers, and the other banks no longer have access to these funds: government monies comprise the bulk of the bank's 'deposits at call' funds.

Despite the effect of these government deposits, the figures in Table 1.5 probably still reflect the importance of demand and time deposits to most Brunei banks. As only the Hongkong and Shanghai Banking Corporation, the Chartered Bank and the National Bank have developed branch systems within the country, they together account for the bulk of savings deposits.

In contrast to the 'Big Three', the other banks – particularly the more recent entrants – suffer from the lack of a local deposit base,

TABLE 1.6 Brunei total bank assets and liabilities, 1977–80 (figures as at end of period, in B$ million)

Quarter	Assets						Liabilities		
	Cash	Amounts due from banks	Loans & advances	Investments	Other assets	Assets/ liabilities	Deposits	Amounts due to banks	Other liabilities
1977 1st	5.85	388.52	296.59	122.35	387.87	1191.18	786.17	89.77	315.24
2nd	5.35	293.25	325.50	112.35	391.90	1128.35	667.25	70.42	390.68
3rd	7.76	366.95	346.39	112.35	331.63	1165.08	705.44	128.48	331.16
4th	7.72	307.83	376.06	122.41	229.24	1043.26	654.19	138.44	250.63
1978 1st	6.24	354.44	387.59	145.88	190.60	1084.77	720.53	121.21	243.03
2nd	5.89	331.96	423.17	122.49	274.35	1157.88	680.11	123.86	353.90
3rd	7.62	565.98	399.87	124.23	275.56	1173.27	755.94	132.06	285.26
4th	6.51	373.99	396.53	124.12	240.97	1142.12	679.34	143.40	319.38
1979 1st	7.96	445.48	440.87	124.12	303.60	1322.04	870.95	115.64	355.47
2nd	7.71	520.00	476.54	124.12	413.74	1542.12	985.99	108.74	447.39
3rd	7.47	480.76	479.71	128.17	453.51	1549.63	1028.28	125.10	396.24
4th	11.40	304.60	474.62	128.17	591.50	1510.29	821.90	142.18	546.21
1980 1st	11.29	343.78	539.45	138.21	548.07	1575.80	913.43	135.21	527.16
2nd	10.85	413.13	585.20	129.96	572.25	1711.40	1077.06	106.51	527.83
3rd	11.33	308.84	610.39	111.48	694.24	1736.28	942.73	128.21	665.34
4th	13.74	498.41	638.16	111.76	665.27	1297.35	1110.34	139.14	677.87

Source: Brunei Currency Board, *Annual Report 1982.*

and must either bid the big local depositors away from the other banks or borrow on the Singapore interbank market in order to fund their local lending. As a rule, most of the smaller banks do both, and thus have a much higher cost of funds than the Big Three. No interbank market exists in Brunei; this is because (due to the parity between the B$ and S$) the larger banks are able to redeposit their surplus funds in Singapore, and prefer to do so rather than lend locally to their competitors.

(iv) *Bank lending activities*

There are no restrictions on bank lending within Brunei, and loans can be made for any maturity and in any currency. In practice, however, there is little demand for foreign denominated loans, and as of June 1982 there were no foreign borrowings. Most loans are thus made in Brunei dollars.

The Third Schedule of the Banking Enactment requires the banks to provide the Brunei government with details of their lending (both the total number of loans, and the amounts) in the following categories: the government; credit and financial institutions; primary production; manufacturing; construction; general commerce; miscellaneous. This would seem a logical way to discuss local bank lending, but (with the exception of the three divisions shown in Table 1.5) these details are not available to the public, and the government has in any case apparently never borrowed from the local banking system. There are few primary producers of any size, and even fewer manufacturers: the Brunei Shell Petroleum Group[8] does not borrow, but rather trades with related companies on credit terms. With the exception of some lending to finance companies (usually to affiliated ones), most bank loans are to the construction, general commerce and miscellaneous sectors, the latter including personal and most housing finance.

The construction industry is the most active of the bank lending areas, and is also probably the most profitable and competitive. Fortunately for the banks, Brunei has experienced an extended construction boom, and there has been a considerable and continuing demand for funds. Much of these advances – particularly to contractors on government or Brunei Shell Petroleum projects – are by way of term loans, but as much of the building materials come from overseas the banks generally provide the necessary import finance by letters of credit and meet any working capital requirements by way of overdraft: in aggregate, overdraft loans are still the most important form of domestic lending.

Most of Brunei's consumer and business requirements like her building materials are also met by imports, and as a result all the banks are active in letters of credit, foreign exchange, remittances, and other import finance work. These activities – together with overdrafts, guarantees, and other forms of small business finance – represent the basic business of the Brunei banks. These activities are conducted along normal banking lines, but two more specific areas of their miscellaneous business – consumer lending and housing finance – require more detailed discussion.

Consumer lending. The importance of consumer lending varies from bank to bank, with those banks without an affiliated finance company being the most active. Overseas Union, for example, has suggested that this accounts for some 30 per cent of its business,[9] and Citibank relies even more heavily on these types of advances. Such consumer lending includes car loans; boat loans; instalment credit; hire purchase; and other forms of personal loans (housing loans are discussed elsewhere).

In such lending, repayment ability (cash flow) is considered as important as loan security, and there is some competition among the banks to lend to such low risk groups as government and Brunei Shell Petroleum group employees. As the former group already have an excellent, highly subsidised car and housing loan programme, their borrowings are usually for other purposes.

The banks' emphasis on repayment ability (cash flow lending) rather than loan security (asset lending) is understandable when the local legal system is considered, and is the major reason why some banks limit their exposure in this area. Brunei's legal system has traditionally taken a fairly lenient view toward debt collection and loan foreclosures, possibly because the banks are either foreign owned or controlled. There is also the matter of time involved even when a successful judgement is obtained: adjournments are easily granted, and the trial calendar backlogged.

Another problem area in personal lending has been with bank credit cards – primarily VISA cards – which were issued locally in the mid-1970s by many of the banks. Some, like Overseas Union, later discontinued local card issue completely and in spring 1982 only the Bank of America actively promoted this service locally.

The Bank of America, Malayan Banking, the Chartered Bank and the Hongkong and Shanghai Banking Corporation (the Bank of America also acts as VISA's local merchant services agent) will selectively issue regional or international VISA cards, but the numbers outstanding in Brunei are not significant. The National Bank is also involved in credit cards as local merchant services agent for American Express.

Housing loans. The banks in Brunei will normally extend housing finance for up to 70 per cent of a property's value over periods of 5–7 years. In February 1982, these interest rates charges ranged from 12–14 per cent per annum. As with personal lending, the importance of housing loans varies from bank to bank, and must compete with the heavily subsidised government housing and resettlement loan schemes and also face various legal complications.

The basic legal problem (with this and other types of mortgage secured lending) is the structure of Brunei's Land Code. Perhaps in response to Brunei's past history of selling off most of its Borneo land holdings, the transfer of land in any form to a non-citizen or company now requires the specific approval of the Sultan in Council. As a mortgage constitutes a transfer of interest, it too must be so approved. While this requirement may protect the population against exploitation, as the Council meets only monthly and many other matters are usually discussed, there are long delays in approval; 3 years is not uncommon, and a delay of 5–6 years may often be involved.

Given these delays, not many mortgages are actually taken over Brunei property; instead, the banks rely on their physical possession of the title or deed to the property and an irrevocable power of attorney from the borrower to sell the property in the case of default: the resulting sale of property presents no problem as long as it is to another Brunei citizen. As further protection, the bank also sends a letter of notice to the Land Office, in effect registering the power of attorney and having a caveat indicating its existence placed in the property records. This arrangement should prove adequate security, but in the past some owners – apparently claiming to have lost or otherwise destroyed the title – have succeeded in having a new title issued and then selling the property without the bank's consent. Thus (as with personal lending) the banks' emphasis is on the borrower's ability to repay, and on his local credit standing.

(v) *Bank interest rate charges*

In theory, both bank deposit and lending rates are controlled by an interbank agreement administered by the Brunei State Association of Banks (the local industry body). In practice, however, this cartel is becoming more flexible. Before January 1981, the agreed rates applied to all transactions of B$500000 or less; it now covers business of only B$150000 or less, and there is talk of reducing this ceiling further to B$100000 by 1983.[10] These rates are shown in Table 1.7; larger amounts are subject to negotiation. Prior to January 1982, the Association changed the agreed rates only when the majority of its members agreed to do so; now rates are adjusted automatically at the end of each month by a formula based on the adjusted average rates of each bank's Singapore prime rate. As neither the National nor the Island Development Banks have Singapore branches, the rates of their correspondents there – respectively the Banque National de Paris and Morgan Guaranty – are used.

TABLE 1.7   Brunei agreed bank deposit rates for deposits of B$250000 or less,[a] August 1982

Term	Effective rate per annum (%)
Call on government funds	N/A
At call savings accounts deposits	6.00
1–3 month deposits	5.75
3–6 month deposits	6.50
6–12 month deposits	7.00
12 month deposits	7.50

[a]   Deposits from the Brunei Shell Petroleum Co. Ltd (and its affiliates) are exempt from this agreement.

This calculation is also used as the basis for adjusting Brunei's prime lending rate, a rate which – like that for deposits – is subject to an interbank agreement. Most commercial loans are made on a margin over prime; the specific margin is for each bank to determine, but a 2–3 per cent margin seems the most common. From January–August 1982, Brunei's prime lending rate stood at 10.0 per cent – down from 12 per cent in December 1981.

The use of a Singapore base rate reflects the importance of that market to Brunei's financial system – the parity between the Singapore and Brunei dollar and the lack of major foreign exchange controls has meant that, in terms of banking, the two countries are almost one market; at least, this is so from Brunei's standpoint. With effectively no local interbank market, the banks in Brunei must cover or place their temporary shortages and surpluses in the Singapore market (the 'Elsewhere: Formerly Sterling area' category in Table 1.5 would be predominantly Singapore transactions). As most smaller banks in Brunei lack a sufficient Brunei dollar deposit base, they are also forced to borrow on the Singapore market to finance local lending. The banks' local customers generally have good business connections in Singapore, and will borrow or deposit their funds directly if the rates between the two markets differ sufficiently.

To win or maintain local deposits, Brunei banks must thus be willing to negotiate their larger deposit and loan rates as close to those of Singapore – a position which affects both local interest rates and bank profitability. The lack of reserve ratio requirements in Brunei normally allows the Brunei banks some competitive advantage; nevertheless, the overall bank rates in Brunei seem slightly higher than their Singapore equivalents.

Besides the lending and deposit rates, the Brunei State Association of Banks is responsible for setting the general rules and conditions for the local banking industry – including banking hours; collection fees; and other procedures. The Association is also responsible for running the country's clearing house operations, a service for which its members pay on a pro rata cost basis. The facility is located in the Hongkong and Shanghai Banking Corporation's main office building, and this bank (which was for 1982 also the Chairman bank of the Association – the position rotates annually) provides the clearing house manager. The banks settle their local positions in the clearing house daily through their accounts in Singapore, but for some minor amounts the Hongkong and Shanghai will cover an overnight shortage at close to the prime rate (in spring 1982 10 per cent) while any surplus balances earn only 3 per cent.

(vi) *Bank market structure*

As shown in Table 1.8, the National Bank of Brunei has the largest number both of local offices and of staff; however, this

TABLE 1.8   Brunei licensed banks by no. of local branches and staff, 1982

Bank	No. of offices	No. of staff	(*Expatriates*)
Bank of America NT & SA	1	32	(1)
Chartered Bank	7	150	(6)
Citibank NA	2	35	(1)
Hongkong and Shanghai Banking Corporation	7	200	(9)
Island Development Bank	1	16	
Malayan Banking Berhad	1	35	(7)
National Bank of Brunei Ltd	10	260	(26)
Overseas Union Bank	1	20	(1)
United Malayan Banking	1	25	(2)

does not mean that it is the largest in terms of local business. The Hongkong and Shanghai and Chartered Banks dominate local banking and (in conjunction with the National Bank) conduct the banking business of the Brunei government. The two older banks are also at something of an advantage in dealing with Brunei's other major customer, Brunei Shell Petroleum. As one Brunei Shell executive explained 'we deal with most of the major banks although the bulk of our transactions are handled by the Chartered Bank and the Hongkong and Shanghai Banking Corporation'.[11] As these comprise a major portion of Brunei's local banking and bank deposit business, this already assures them a leading role. The historical and ethnic background, however, is just as important, for the big British trading houses – still significant in Brunei's imports and wholesaling – are probably the next biggest single customer group, firms which would possibly prefer a British run institution. These banks are also well represented in all of Brunei's major trading partners.

The other foreign banks in Brunei can also offer good regional connections, but as latecomers they have had to win business away from the 'establishment' and of course lack the British connection. The Malaysian and Singapore based banks may also gain some ethnic advantages with local – particularly small Malay and Chinese – business, but the two American banks have no such advantage. They have had to work even harder, and today are probably among the most competitive of the local banks. They have not always been successful; Citibank, which initially expanded its Brunei operations to four local branches and a finance company in an attempt to gain business, now operates only two Brunei offices.

In contrast to the later foreign banks' experience, both locally incorporated banks – the National Bank of Brunei and the Island Development Bank – commenced business with some inbuilt advantages. The National Bank had the advantage of being the first locally incorporated bank, and although being primarily Singaporean Chinese owned has placed great emphasis on being Brunei's 'national bank' and of 'actively fulfilling the banking needs of the Government of His Highness the Sultan and Yang Di-Pertuan of Brunei and his subjects'.[12] This Brunei connection is particularly strong as two princes of the Brunei Royal Family, brothers of the present Sultan (Prince Mohamed Bolkiah and Prince Hagi Sufri Bolkiah) serve respectively as the Bank's President and Deputy President; an indication of their importance is that the former is rumoured as prospective Foreign Minister and perhaps 'Chief' or Prime Minister after independence, while the latter is expected to become Brunei's Minister of Finance upon the retirement of the present SFO. There is little question that this government connection has been important in the National Bank's growth, but it is a relationship that has worked both ways. Although the National Bank has become one of the government's three bankers, and its finance company subsidiary appointed to handle the government's special colour television loan scheme, it has opened branches in all commercial centres within the country (an expensive investment which will take a long time to recoup); conducted the first public offering of a Brunei company; and provided a number of innovations to local – particularly retail – banking services. In addition to the bank itself, the National's controlling shareholder (with an estimated 85 per cent of the shares) Mr Khoo Teck Puat (formerly the Chairman of the Malayan Banking Corporation and presently Chairman of the Goodwood Park Hotel Group) has also been actively involved on Brunei's behalf.

The other locally incorporated bank, the Island Development Bank, is a joint venture between the Brunei government and the Ayala Group – 50 per cent Brunei government, 25 per cent Ayala Corporation, and 25 per cent (Ayala controlled) Bank of the Philippines Islands. It is also Brunei's newest bank. As the name implies, Island Development is not intended as a retail bank, and unlike its competitors does not have a street level office. It instead hopes to utilise the knowledge and expertise of its Filippino shareholders, the Ayala Group, to finance major private and public sector real estate and construction projects, as well as other areas of development finance within the state; the Ayala Group is a major factor in Philippine real estate development, banking, merchant banking and insurance. Some of these Brunei projects may well involve other Ayala Group companies and already one such firm (Ayala International) has the main contract for the construction of the Sultan's new B$500 million palace,[13] undoubtedly the largest single construction project within the country. Many other small projects are also anticipated, as Brunei's forthcoming independence (and the resulting embassies that will be established) is expected to cause a further construction boom.

(d) The Finance Companies

The finance companies are the second largest type of financial institution in Brunei. Unlike the banks the present firms are all locally incorporated, but are nevertheless overseas controlled. This section first examines the finance companies' regulation, then their operation, and finally the industry's market structure.

(i) *Finance company regulation*

Finance companies are the most regulated of Brunei's financial institutions. This has been the case since 1973, when the Finance Companies Enactment 1972 came into effect. The Enactment requires licensing and a variety of other conditions, and gives the SFO overall responsibility for their supervision. In practice, however, he delegates most day to day work to the Currency Division of the State Treasury.

The Enactment defines the financing business as the 'borrowing and lending of money from the public'; it defines each of these terms as follows:

> *borrowing* money from the public, by acceptance of deposits and issuing certificates or other documents acknowledging or evidencing indebtedness to the public and undertaking to repay the money at call or after an agreed maturity period . . . and

. . . *lending* money to the public or to a company on the basis that the public or the company undertakes to repay the money, whether within an agreed period of time or not, or by instalments, and shall include the business of financing hire-purchase transactions arising out of hire-purchase agreements, where the money used, or to be used, for such business is borrowed from the public.[14]

The companies operating such businesses (unless otherwise covered under Brunei's banking, moneylender or pawnshop legislation) require a valid licence from the SFO. In considering the company's application, the SFO must be satisfied as to the firm's financial conditions (a minimum paid-up capital of B$500000); quality of management; capital structure; earning prospects; overall objectives; convenience and needs of the community; and general public interest.

Once approved, a company must maintain shareholders' funds in excess of B$500000; obtain approval for opening or closing branches, agencies or offices; and submit any proposed changes to its Memorandum or Articles of Association to the SFO for approval. Licensed companies are also precluded from paying dividends until all capitalised expenses are fully written off, and must publish their annual Balance Sheet in the daily press and display copies in all offices.

Within their business operations, finance companies are specifically precluded from accepting demand deposits, foreign exchange or bullion dealing; making unsecured loans totalling more than 10 per cent of shareholders' funds or individual unsecured loans of more than B$5000; making loans, advances, or guarantees to any customer of more than an amount equivalent to 60 per cent of shareholders' funds (on special approval the SFO may increase this to 100 per cent); and holding more than 25 per cent of aggregate paid-up capital in the form of shares of other companies.

If successful in their activities, finance companies must also maintain a special statutory reserve fund, and increase it annually through transfers from after tax profits. If the firm has a paid-up capital of B$2 million or more, the transfer required varies with the firm's existing reserves. If the reserve is less than half of paid-up capital 30 per cent of net profits; if the reserve is 50 per cent or more (but less than 100 per cent) of paid-up capital 15 per cent of net profits; if the reserve is equal or greater than the paid-up capital 5 per cent of net profits only. Companies with a paid-up capital of less than B$2 million have the same conditions, but must transfer greater percentages – respectively 50 per cent, 25 per cent and 10 per cent.

In addition to the rules now in effect, the Finance Company Enactment gives the SFO a wide range of powers to call in the books and records of licensed companies; qualify or refuse annual licence renewals; prescribe lending and deposit interest rate ceilings; direct the types and relative importance of investments; specify the down payments and maturities of certain loans; and set a liquid asset requirement. Except for obtaining the records of some unsuccessful companies, these powers have yet to be utilised; they nevertheless give the SFO substantial moral suasion powers over the industry.

(ii) *Finance company operation*

The finance companies' main lending activity is the hire purchase finance of motor and commercial vehicles. Borrowers generally must have one-third of the purchase price as a down payment, and can pay off the remainder over a 1–3 year period. Most hire purchase contracts involve flat interest rates of 12–16 per cent, or effective per annum rates ranging from 24–32 per cent. Most firms will loan on both new and used cars, but generally require both higher interest (and quicker repayment) for the latter. The average loan is for approximately $10000–12000, payable over 36 months – generally to purchase a new Japanese car. Most lending is apparently on a referral basis from car dealers, and although advances are usually between the borrower and the finance company, at least some advances are made within recourse to dealers: this is common for potentially more risky borrowers.

The bulk of finance company monies are raised in the form of fixed time deposits, with individuals and businesses generally being of equal importance as depositors. Amounts are accepted with a minimum of $500–1000, and interest paid according to a posted rate schedule. The rate on deposits for more than 1 year, or on amounts of over B$50000, are generally subject to negotiation. The Credit Corporation, for example, advertises for 24 month and 36 month deposits in the local press offering 'negotiable' rates. In February 1982, most finance companies were offering rates similar to those for Industrial Resources shown in Table 1.9; the marked difference between these rates and those for United

TABLE 1.9   Brunei finance company fixed deposit rates,
1982

Term	Industrial Resourses (%)	United National Finance (%)
1 month	—	11.5
3	7.75	11.5
6	8.25	11.0
9	8.50	11.0
12 months	8.75	11.0
Savings account	—	10.0

Source: Industrial Resources and United National Finance
(Feburary 1982).

National is the fact that United National has no direct affiliation
with any other major firm in Brunei. Brunei's other two non-
affiliated finance companies (Mahattan Borneo Finance and
Trust Corporation and Investment and Finance Kalimantan Ltd)
crashed respectively in 1976 and 1977, and no doubt today's
depositors are well aware of United National's relatively independent position.

(iii) *Finance company market structure*

The finance industry in February 1982 consisted of the five
operating companies shown in Table 1.10. Their individual
operations, however, differ considerably. Mortgage and Finance
Ltd and Credit Corporation (Brunei) Ltd are the most similar, as
they are both affiliated with a major bank—Mortgage and
Finance is a wholly owned Brunei subsidiary of the Hongkong
and Shanghai Banking Corporation, and Credit Corporation is a
51 per cent Chartered Bank owned joint venture with the
Australian Guarantee Corporation. These companies obtain
virtually all of their money from public deposits, and devote the
bulk of their lending to vehicle hire purchase with some trucks
and heavy equipment financing. Industrial Resources' lending
activities are similar to the other two, but due to their mutual
Inchcape group parentage it gives particular support to Borneo
Motors, until recently Brunei's largest Toyota dealer. Industrial
Resources, however, relies primarily on unsecured bank loans for
its financing.

TABLE 1.10   Brunei licensed finance companies by total assets (figures as at 31 December 1980, in B$)

Industry assets (%)	Company	
13.0	Credit Corporation (Brunei) Ltd [a]	26710942
11.7	Industrial Resources Ltd	24009981
20.0	Mortgage and Finance Ltd	41229411
49.0	National Finance Ltd	100875654
6.3	United National Finance Ltd	12969413
100.0		205795401

[a] Also known in Malaya as Sharikat Kredit (Brunei) Berhad.

Source: Finance Companies' *Annual Reports 1980*.

The good relations between Industrial Resources and its main bankers the National Bank of Brunei have influenced the operations of the Bank's own finance company subsidiary, National Finance Ltd. Unlike the other three, National Finance does very little vehicle hire purchase and in some cases even directs this business to Industrial Resources. National Finance instead concentrates on personal and housing loans. The former business was greatly expanded when National Finance was selected to administer the government's colour TV loan programme which followed the introduction of television within Brunei on 9 July 1974. The scheme was designed to place colour TV ownership within means of all Brunei citizens as well as those non-citizens employed by the government. The government placed interest free deposits with National Finance to enable it to grant applicants up to a B$3000 loan payable over 3 years at 2 per cent interest; initially B$10 million was provided by way of deposit, and in all some B$26.5 million (or over 10000 television sets) were purchased under the plan. When the plan was discontinued in 1980, many of the loans were still outstanding, and on 31 December 1980, National Finance still had B$6.26 million in government deposits: some 6 per cent of its total funding. National Finance's other major area of operation is housing finance, and here, like United National, its major competitive advantage is not its rates or terms but rather the fact that the finance company will lend at a slightly higher percentage of valuations than the banks. National Finance, for example, will extend loans for up to 80 per cent of the property's valuation.

The final company under discussion – United National Finance – differs from its counterparts, for despite having a trademark similar to United Malayan Banking there is no direct linkage between the two companies; only some shareholders and directors are the same. Unlike the other finance companies, it thus obtains a large portion of funds through its savings accounts programme as well as through normal fixed deposits. Much of its lending is also different, as it has strong orientation toward housing finance, and has extended some loans for periods as long as 20 years; these, however, are probably exceptional. Also unlike the other finance companies, United National has some small involvement in import/export finance.

A brief consideration of United National's background is appropriate, as its position results for the same reason that Malayan Finance, a wholly owned subsidiary of Malayan Banking, no longer operates within Brunei. The regulations of Malaysia's central bank – Bank Negara Malaysia – preclude licensed borrowing companies from operating overseas branches. To operate in Brunei, Malaysian licensed firms require a separate company. United National was incorporated in Brunei as a result of this ruling, and was to have been a wholly owned subsidiary of the bank. Bank Negara Malaysia, however, apparently disapproved, and a separate company (using the same shareholders and directors as United Malayan Banking) was formed. Later, however, when the bank's shareholdings changed, the finance company's ownership remained as before: it is at present indirectly affiliated with the Hong Kong based Overseas Trust Bank.[15] Thus although some directors and shareholders are the same, there is no longer a direct connection. Malayan Finance is still nominally licensed in Brunei, but under Malaysian regulation cannot operate there; it has yet to use a local subsidiary to resolve the impasse, but interviews suggest this is still considered a possibility.[16] Citibank, which operated a finance company subsidiary in Brunei in the mid-1970s, may also still have a nominal finance company but at present does not seem interested in re-entering this business.

(e) General Insurance

The general insurance industry in Brunei is largely unregulated and subject to government control only in respect to third party motor vehicle coverage. Since 28 February 1950, companies wishing to sell such policies must be licensed annually under the Motor Vehicles Insurance (Third Party Risks) Enactment 1950. To qualify, a company must place a B$250000 deposit with the government; present copies of its Memorandum and Articles of Association and the policies themselves; and notify the government of any local agent arrangements.

At one time, these matters were handled by the State Secretariat, but since mid-1981 insurance and insurance regulation has been an additional duty of the government's Economic Development Board. In February 1982, as shown in Table 1.11, there were 17 registered insurance companies, three of which were locally incorporated.

TABLE 1.11   Brunei licensed third party motor vehicle insurers, 1982

Firm	No. of licensed agents
Borneo Insurance Ltd[a]	(50)
Motor & General Insurance (Pty) Ltd[a]	(18)
AUA Insurance Ltd[a]	(17)
The New Zealand Insurance Co. Ltd	(16)
QBE Insurance Co. Ltd	(12)
Royal Insurance	(11)
National Employees' Mutual General Insurance Association Ltd	(7)
Straits & Island Insurance Sdn Berhad	(4)
The Netherlands Insurance Co. Ltd	(4)
American International Assurance Co. Ltd	(3)
Norwich Winterthur Insurance (Far East) Pty Ltd	(3)
The Asia Insurance Co. Ltd	(2)
Provincial Insurance Co. Ltd	(2)
Union Insurance of Canton Ltd	(2)
General Accident Fire & Assurance Corpn Ltd	(1)
The American Insurance Co.	(1)
Phoenix Assurance Co. Ltd	(1)

[a] Locally incorporated company.

Source: Economic Development Board (February 1982).

Besides establishing a local insurance company (either as a wholly owned subsidiary or as a joint venture with local interests), a foreign insurer may operate locally as a branch office, through locally appointed agents, or on an occasional basis via local insurance brokers. As shown in Tables 1.12–15, five foreign companies operate through local branches while eight have locally appointed agents. There are also 12 locally incorporated insurers and four local insurance brokers. In addition, many local general insurance agents (such as car dealers, local shops and real estate agents) sell insurance as a sideline to their normal business.

TABLE 1.12   Brunei foreign insurance companies with full branches, 1982

QBE Insurance Co. Ltd
New Zealand Insurance Ltd
Phoenix Assurance Co. Ltd
American Insurance Co.
South East Asian Insurance Ltd

Source: QBE Insurance (February 1982).

TABLE 1.13   Foreign insurance companies represented by Brunei agents, 1982

Royal Insurance Co.
Provincial Insurance Co.
General Accident, Fire & Life Assurance Corpn Ltd
Commercial Union Assurance
Norwich Winterthur Insurance (Far East) Pty Ltd
Netherlands Insurance Co.
National Employers Mutual Insurance
United Malayan Insurance Ltd

Source: QBE Insurance (February 1982).

TABLE 1.14   Brunei locally incorporated insurers, 1982

AUA Insurance Ltd
Motor & General Insurance Pty Ltd
Worldwide Insurance Corpn Ltd
Borneo Insurance Ltd
National Insurance Ltd
Prime International (Brunei) Ltd
Meridian Insurance
Fidelity Insurance
London Far East Insurance Corpn Ltd
Marine & General Insurance
Ace Insurance Co. Ltd
Steinhouse Insurance Services Ltd

Source: QBE Insurance (February 1982).

TABLE 1.15   Brunei local insurance brokers, 1982

Alliance Insurance Brokers
A & S Associates Insurance
City Insurance Brokers
A & F Insurance Brokers

Source: QBE Insurance (February 1982).

The general insurance business in Brunei covers the range of policies found in most countries; general fire insurance and workman compensation are the most common. Personal accident is also popular, although free medical care limits its appeal to Brunei citizens. There is little call for marine coverage outside of the local fishing industry, as most imports are covered from their country of origin and there are few exports other than oil and gas; the insurance coverage for these are arranged overseas by Shell. The construction boom has been quite favourable for the industry, as contractor insurance produce substantial premiums and there is much business available. To the extent these new buildings and businesses require coverage, construction adds to the market's potential.

Another advantage of Brunei is that companies fix most general premium levels under the General Insurance Association of Singapore's tariff agreement: an overseas tariff cartel. In terms of investment policy, Brunei also differs from its Southeast Asian neighbours in that the companies can freely remit their premiums for investment overseas; however, given that Brunei has no government securities, few corporate shares, and a prohibition on foreign land investment, the companies have no real alternative but to do so.

In this peaceful environment, the only competitive problems have come from the local insurance companies. As there are no minimum capital and deposit requirements (except for third party motor cover), many local companies were established specifically to undercut the foreign operators. In many cases, the local companies simply took a few foreign company policies and wrote their own versions – often omitting some coverage in the process – and then undercut the foreigners' rates. These companies' financial stability, investment policies, and coverage of risk exposure through reinsurance are all unanswered questions for the Brunei consumer.

Perhaps the most interesting development among the local companies is the recent reactivation of the National Insurance Company Ltd. National Insurance was formed on 24 December 1969 as a wholly owned subsidiary of the National Bank of Brunei, but after only 3 months of trading the firm suspended operations due to inadequately trained staff. By 1981, however, the Bank and its finance company subsidiary's operations had grown sufficiently for an insurance affiliate to be desired, and new staff were obtained from overseas. To expand the company's financial footing a public share offering of B$1.5 million – the second local equity issue by a Brunei company – was held on 31 July 1981. The issue (underwritten and marketed by the National Bank) was fully subscribed and the Bank now holds around only 25 per cent of the insurer's shares. With new capital and management, as well as National Bank and National Finance support, National Insurance will no doubt soon rank with Borneo Insurance and Motor & General Insurance as the leading locally incorporated insurer, and become a strong competitor with New Zealand Insurance and other more active foreign companies.

The growing number of local companies is viewed with concern by foreign insurers, and as yet the government has no controls on other than third party insurance. However, the Economic Development Board has indicated that new insurance company applications now require the Board's concurrence before the Registrar of Companies will approve the incorporation.[17] The Board realises a need for regulation, but as yet not even draft legislation has been prepared. Soon, however, the government may be forced into action as even the present Motor Vehicle Enactment is now inadequate, and a recent settlement of B$400000 on just one claim greatly exceeded the present B$250000 deposit requirement. The Board now feels that least B$500000 deposit should be required, but again no action has been taken.[18] It feels that Brunei's insurance agents should also be more professional, and would like to restrict local agencies to operating in proper business premises rather than as a sideline of another business or from the agent's residence.[19]

With the government's attention devoted to foreign affairs and the defence problems that Brunei's independence on 31 December 1983 presents, insurance legislation has a low priority. Unless a major insurance company failure forces action, insurance will probably continue unregulated until at least 1984.

(f) Life Insurance

As with most general insurance, there are no controls on life insurance operations within the State of Brunei. Few companies have in fact been active in this field; for a long time Great Eastern Life Assurance Co. Ltd (a Singapore based firm) was the only company seriously engaged in local life insurance sales. During 1978–80, however, American International Assurance commenced operations by aggressively marketing mortgage reducing term policies to government employees which would pay off their outstanding housing mortgages in the case of death. These sales proved successful, and gave the company access to Brunei's important middle class. Asia Insurance Corporation of Singapore and Prudential have also recently been more active in life sales, primarily through local agents. It is expected that (as elsewhere in Asia) endowment policies will probably prove the best selling type of life insurance. Most sales involve policies of B$10000–100000, and in some cases whole life policies may be in excess of B$100000. As with general policies, most Brunei premium income is forwarded overseas (often Singapore or Hong Kong) for reinvestment.

(g) Pawnshops

As with moneylenders, pawnshop operations are subject to government control, and since 1 January 1920 have been licensed under the Pawnbroker Enactment 1920. The licence for each office is non-transferable, and is issued (on request) by the Sultan in Council. Although not specifically stated, a favourable recommendation must be made by the Police Department and Attorney General before approval is granted.

The Enactment give the police substantial powers in respect to stolen articles, and there are many penalties for improper operation; the government also has power to set the rates and terms under which the loans are granted.

In February 1982, there were four pawnshops in operation, two in the Brunei district and two in Kuala Belait.

(h) Moneylenders

Since 1 January 1972, moneylenders in Brunei must register with the government under the Moneylenders Enactment 1972. The licences are issued by the State Secretariat, and are renewable quarterly. The Enactment places strict controls on the lenders' operations, and sets a maximum per annum lending rate of 15 per cent on secured lending and 24 per cent on unsecured loans. As finance companies earn an effective 25–30 per cent per annum on their own secured advances, these moneylenders' interest rate ceilings are relatively unattractive, and in February 1982 there were only three licensed moneylenders in Brunei – although there may well be many more moneylenders operating outside the Act.

(i) Co-operative Societies

Co-operative societies are formed under the Co-operative Societies Enactment 1975, and administered by (and subject to an annual audit from) the government's Co-operative Development Department. The first society (Kampong Lumapas) was organised under the Enactment on 25 February 1976; in February 1982 some 64 co-operative societies had been formed and were operating within the State. As yet, none of these societies are credit co-operatives; the bulk are small retail store co-operatives – generally operating in the smaller villages. There are also two petrol station co-operatives, three fisheries and a couple of agricultural related societies. As most societies provide services on 30 day terms, they are of some minor importance as a source of credit. One society (Sharikat Kerjasama Kakitagan) formed in 1978, actually has the power to grant loans to members (as a normal credit co-operative) but by February 1982 had yet to exercise this power. The first active credit union or credit co-operative is likely to be an outgrowth of an existing government department retail co-operative, or possibly formed by the Brunei Shell Petroleum Group as a fringe benefit. As the credit co-operative movement is relatively successful in both Malaysia and Indonesia, it is surprising there are no similar institutions within Brunei.

(j) Other Government Institutions and Departments

Though there are no government financial institutions as such, many bodies in addition to the Currency Board have an interest (or involvement) in the country's financial affairs. Of these the Economic Development Board, the Treasury Department's Government Employee Loan Schemes and the Resettlement

Department are probably the most important, as they actually make loans to the private sector. Of equal importance are the government's Development Fund – which finances public sector projects – and the Economic Planning Unit (EPU) – which helps direct both planning and the government's general economic policy.

(i) *Economic Development Board (EDB)*

The Brunei government's EDB was established on 1 January 1976, to assist the industrial sector's growth under the country's 5 Year National Development Plan. The EDB is managed by its own Board of Directors (one of which is traditionally the local Hongkong and Shanghai Bank manager) and operates under the provisions of the Brunei Economic Development Board Enactment 1975 and under the nominal supervision of the State Secretariat. In addition to administering a special loan scheme and the Investment Incentives Enactment 1975, the EDB also has responsibility for licensing travel agents and tourist promotion as well as licensing and administering the State's third party motor vehicle legislation.

Loan scheme for small and medium business. The EDB's legislation gives it a wide range of powers, including those 'to establish a bank or financial institution' and underwrite securities; advance loans; and make guarantees. While no such institution has been established, the EDB (through its Loan Scheme for Small and Medium Business) has been an important lender since August 1977. This programme is essentially a government 'soft' loan scheme to encourage bumiputras to establish their own businesses and hence take an active part in the otherwise largely Brunei Chinese or foreign controlled private sector.

The scheme advances funds from B\$10000–500000 at a rate of 6 per cent per annum on the reducing monthly balance for periods as long as 10 years. In some cases – such as with new construction or substantial physical site modification – a grace period on repayments of up to 1 year is also provided. As a rule, the EDB lends up to 90 per cent of the proposal's appraised value, and in special cases may even provide 100 per cent of the fixed and working capital required. The amounts and terms naturally vary with the project: a loan to establish a small retail shop, for example, might require only B\$10000 and involve a 2–3 year repayment; a service station would need B$200000–250000, and could be repaid over 6 years. Another source of major longer term funding is the financing of rental property construction – usually two or three houses or shops. Overall, the EDB's loans average around B$40000 and primarily finance the service industry – trucking, taxies, buses and some agro businesses.

The Loan Scheme initially received a budget allocation of some B$15 million; with additional grants and loan repayments and interest it now stands at B$23 million. Up to 1982, some B$8 million was available for lending, but despite the highly concessional interest rates, by February 1982 most remained unlent. This, however, reflects more the way the loans are processed than a lack of demand. All loans are handled by the EDB's one office in the capital, Bandar Seri Begawan; unlike most development banks, the EDB has no field staff to promote or explain the scheme, or assist in processing applications. In effect, the borrower has to come to the capital, make the application, and then wait until the EDB's employees can check the proposal and value any collateral or personal guarantees involved. Some bankers interviewed felt that they could administer the scheme more effectively, and this is a common practice in some countries.[20] Some felt the government's desire to handle the money directly perhaps reflected the EDB's intention eventually to establish its own commercial or development bank: a position denied by all government officials interviewed.[21]

Investment incentives. In discussing the EDB, some mention should be made of the Investment Incentives Enactment 1975, and its potential benefits. This Enactment was designed to assist the development of any industry 'not being carried on in Brunei on a commercial scale suitable to . . . [its] economic requirements or development'[22] where there are favourable prospects for such an industry, and it is in the public interest to develop it.

On application, the EDB may make a Statutory Order declaring that industry a 'pioneer industry' and its products 'pioneer products'. This makes the company eligible for extended tax relief depending on its capital investment: where the fixed capital is below B$250000 a 2 year tax period is provided; between B$250000 and 500000 3 years; B$500000–1000000 4 years; over B$1000000 5 years. Import duty exemptions are also provided on any machinery, equipment, or raw materials required provided these are not otherwise available within Brunei.

(ii) *Government employee loan schemes*

As the Brunei government is the largest employer in the country, the government employee housing and car loan schemes (administered by a special loans section of the Treasury Accounts Division) are an important source of finance, and make it impossible for private sector institutions to compete in these areas.

Housing loans. Housing loans may be granted to all permanent government employees, generally after 3 years of service. The loans are repayable over 15 years, and may be granted in two ways. There is normal scheme under which an employee receives a loan equal to up to three times his annual salary, charged at a per annum interest rate of only 0.5 per cent. A second scheme allows for a further loan, the equivalent of an additional year's salary to be granted (4 years in all), but charged at 3 per cent per annum interest rate. Most government employees can therefore borrow three times their annual salary at 0.5 per cent, and one year's salary at 3 per cent, with the entire amount payable over 15 years. If both husband and wife work for the government, their salaries can be combined for calculation purposes, and a joint loan granted.

Car loans. Car loans also relate to salary levels, but are sufficient for most employees to own a new vehicle. There is no interest charge associated with these advances, and an employee is entitled to one loan every 3 years (or if already heavily committed in the housing loan scheme, every 4 years).

(iii) *Resettlement Department*

Although not a financial institution as such, the government's Resettlement Department is an important source of housing and housing finance for bumiputras and other Brunei permanent residents. Its resettlement schemes originally concentrated on moving bumiputras from the river stilted kampong villages to agricultural land. Participants received a 'reasonable' house, the land surrounding the house, and another piece of land suitable for agriculture. No cash down payments were required, and the cost could be paid over up to 20 years at no interest charge.

A rush of applicants might have been expected, but although a number of bumiputra did participate the planners discovered that those citizens desiring work preferred government employment. Today most local 'cash crop' agriculture is done by Taiwanese, Japanese and South Korean market gardeners who migrated to Brunei for this purpose, and the concept of transforming Brunei's kampong residents into farmers has since been replaced with a satellite village programme. This is still in the feasibility and planning phase, with the construction of houses for the first of five villages commencing in 1983. When the plan is completed, eight new villages – each consisting of 1500–3000 residences and related infrastructure – will have been constructed. Each village includes both flats and houses with the prices ranging from B$20000 for a timber built 'kiplock' galvanised iron roof dwelling, to a B$90000 brick and tile structure (the four major styles are expected to be priced respectively at B$20000, B$45000, B$60000 and B$90000). The type of house depends on the buyer's income level, and financing, employment and ethnic status.

Those buyers working for the government are expected to utilise the government's normal housing finance scheme, but given the quality and price of the residence it is intended that only junior officers (Division III and below) should apply. The availability of reasonable priced housing, rather than the financing, is the attraction for this group.

The second type of purchaser is the (non-government employee) bumiputra. For these buyers, housing finance is provided at a highly concessional interest rate – around 3 per cent – with up to 20 years to repay. At the end of this period, the purchaser owns both the house and the land it occupies.

The third alternative is that available to permanent residents i.e. most of Brunei's Chinese population. In early 1982, the exact terms and conditions available were unclear. Due to the 1959 Land Code, non-citizens cannot own land; whether they could buy a residence still seems undecided. In discussing the matter with departmental officers, some felt that permanent residents could acquire the residence on similar terms as citizens, but not the land.[23] Others suggested that non-citizens could only rent – not buy – their home: it would be a permanent rental, but a rental all the same. The specifics should be determined some time in 1983.

(iv) *Development Fund*

The Brunei government's Development Fund is also not strictly a financial institution, but rather the means by which the government finances the bulk of public sector projects contained in its series of 5 Year National Development Plans. Allocations to the Fund represent an important segment of the government annual budget, and in 1980 some B$250.1 million (or 20 per cent of the year's budget) was so allocated. Through the Fund the 1980–4 5 Year National Development Plan (Brunei's fourth), will finance some B$2000 million in public sector projects.

(v) *Economic Planning Unit (EPU)*

Though neither a financial institution nor a regulatory body, some mention must be made of the government's EPU, as this agency is responsible for drawing up the country's 5 Year National Development Plan, and for monitoring its economic health. It is also heavily involved (in conjunction with the Treasury), in structuring the government budget.

FINANCIAL MARKETS

Brunei has the distinction among the Southeast Asian capitalist economies of having no financial markets at all. These functions are served almost totally by overseas markets, and due to the interchangeability of the Brunei and Singapore dollar. Singapore's financial sector fulfils most of these requirements.

There is not even a local interbank market, as Brunei's banks conduct even their local settlements through accounts in Singapore, and any substantial surpluses or deficits are placed or covered on the Singapore interbank market – it has more participants, a greater range of borrowing and lending opportunities, and usually better rates. As one Brunei banker commented, 'why lend money to a local competitor when you can place it offshore for more'.[24]

The position is similar in respect to foreign exchange, where the banks again rely almost totally on the Singapore market. Most banks set a fixed rate twice daily, based on a small margin over that available in Singapore. Small to medium transactions are thus handled immediately; the Hongkong and Shanghai Bank, for example, does this in as many as 10 currencies. For amounts of over B$100 000, or for less usual currencies, the transactions are usually placed directly by the bank on the Singapore market. Besides the small administrative lending in respect to clearing house operations, there is only one exception to this position. This is in respect of some very small foreign exchange and Brunei dollar transactions between the Island Development Bank and Citibank in Brunei. As the former does not have a Singapore branch, Citibank's offshore connections can sometimes be to Island Development's advantage. At present, however, the arrangement seems more a function of Island Development's relatively small size and newness in the local market, than the start of a local interbank/foreign exchange market.

Besides the banks, there is a substantial flow of investment monies from Brunei to the offshore financial markets – particularly Hong Kong and Singapore. Most of these funds are placed directly by investors in the markets concerned, but the Overseas Union (and probably the other banks too) will arrange to buy and sell shares on the Singapore or other market as well as providing investment advice to their clients. Both the Hongkong and Shanghai Banking Corporation and the National Bank of Brunei also buy and sell gold within Brunei, and all banks will handle such transactions for their clients on the overseas markets.

In 1981, however, the commodity business expanded to include non-banks as well when in August 1981 the first of four commodity brokers established offices in Bandar Seri Begawan. These included Trivest Commodities Traders Ltd, Jasra International Commodity Ltd, Commwell Commodity, and Global Commodities. Jasra is a Brunei–Japanese joint venture; Global involves local and Hong Kong interests; Trivest and Commwell are primarily Hong Kong owned companies. All four specialise in commodities futures and (in the case of Jasra) require deposits from B$7000–100000 before handling a transaction – the latter is most common. Global also handles the sale of Australian property, and to a lesser extent overseas securities transactions.

As Brunei has no securities or commodities industry regulations, the only government approval required is to register with the Registrar of Companies either as a foreign or a newly formed local company and obtain (if non-residents are employed) an expatriate worker 'labour quota' from the government's EPU.

Once established, these firms are subject to no other regulation, and one at least attracted substantial business with promises of 50–60 per cent returns. These proved unrealistic; as the local press reported '17 investors, mostly Chinese, claim to have lost about $1 million through dealings',[25] and complained to the police. One firm, Trivest, now has a notice posted on its door: 'this office will be temporarily closed pending police investigations'.

This is certainly not the first time that Brunei investors have had difficulties with outside investment sales groups. Such celebrated financial experts as Bernie Cornfield of Overseas Investor Services felt Brunei worth visiting, as did Amos Dodd. The local business community has not attempted to tap these risk orientated investors, and as yet the National Bank and National Insurance share offers have been the only public flotations in the country.

ANALYSIS

Given its general state of underdevelopment, Brunei's financial system offers little to the analyst. The government has so far taken a fairly casual approach to the sector's development and regulation, and to a large extent left the industry to its own devices. This section will examine some of the reasons for, and consequences of, these attitudes.

(a) Lack of Regulation

The life insurance and brokerage industry in Brunei are subject to no specific government regulation. The general insurers are regulated only to the extent that they write third party liability business; otherwise, they are free to do what they like. While these business were conducted only by the major international insurers, the need for local regulation was perhaps not important; with the incorporation of a number of local companies, some financial standards are required.

The presence of government regulations will not in themselves, however, be sufficient to prevent a major financial crisis; they must also be enforced. The finance companies are a good example of this problem. The Finance Company Enactment (adapted from earlier Singapore legislation) was passed in 1972, and thus had been in operation for some 4 years when in October 1976 one

of Brunei's major financial crashes – that of the Mahattan
Borneo Finance and Trust Corporation – took place. This failure
occurred in spite of the extensive powers given the government
under the Enactment, and the losses to Brunei investors as a result
were estimated at B$21 million. One might have thought that new
regulations – or a change in the enforcement policies – would
have resulted, but in the following year yet another crash – that of
Investment and Finance Kalimantan Ltd – occurred; as of early
1982, the finance company legislation still remained unchanged.

Such difficulties are not confined to the finance companies, and
even the National Bank of Brunei has had its problems. In both
1973 and 1977 it was subject to a flood of withdrawals; in 1977 the
Bank even received special government support through the
Currency Board. Despite these experiences, there has still been no
expansion of the banking legislation to provide for minimum
liquidity requirements.

(b) Lack of Government Involvement

The Brunei government, owing to its oil revenues, is in the happy
position of not having to raise funds on the local markets; no
change in this position is expected in the near future, there are still
many years of oil and gas supplies remaining. While fortunate for
the government, this has meant that there are no government
securities issued on which the local money market and securities
markets can build – nor are any expected.

Brunei is probably none the worse off as a result. Singapore's
financial markets service its needs fairly well, and the interchangeability between the Singapore and Brunei dollar seems likely to
continue long after Brunei's independence. If the Brunei government simply limited local participation to Singapore licensed
companies it might in fact completely avoid the expense of
regulating the local market and rely wholly on the Singapore
authorities for this purpose. Instead, it has allowed a variety of
local financial institutions to be established, but has not as yet
expanded its regulatory operations accordingly.

One can argue that this will come after independence, and that
in time a Ministry of Finance will be established and the Currency
Board eventually transformed into a Central Bank. This may
result, but the impression gained in early 1982 was that most post-
independence changes in the finance area – if any in fact occur –
will be of a very minor nature.

There are probably many good reasons not to change the existing system. It would mean expanding the already heavy responsibilities of the SFO and Treasury staff; there seems little political pressure to change the existing system; and there appears little private sector interest in change – most of the existing institutions operate quite profitably under the present system.

THE FUTURE

Much can be written about Brunei's future, but in 1982 most discussion centred on what will happen to the country after it obtains full independence. This section will concentrate on three potential problems – regional affairs, government capabilities, and the economy.

(a) Regional Affairs

Independence means that Brunei will again control its own foreign affairs; good relations with its neighbours will become very important, but until fairly recently Brunei's relationship with Malaysia and Indonesia had not been very warm. Indonesia under Sukarno had indirectly helped support the 1963 rebellion in Brunei, and later granted asylum to its leader, A. M. Azahari. With Malaysia, relations were soured over Brunei's treatment in its 1962–3 negotiations to join the Federation of Malaysia: in the end, Brunei chose to stay out. Relations were not helped in 1975–7 when Indonesia joined Malaysia in supporting UN resolutions calling for Britain to hold free elections in Brunei and leave the country. Relations have since improved, and in June 1978 President Suharto of Indonesia asked Singapore's Prime Minister Lee Kuan Yew (who has good relations with Brunei), to convey the Sultan a message that ASEAN would welcome Brunei as a member. This marked a considerable change in Brunei's regional relationships, and the Sultan has since officially visited both Malaysia and Indonesia, and has been officially visited in return. Brunei has also sent an official delegation as observers to the ASEAN Foreign Ministers' meetings.

There now seems little question that Brunei will become ASEAN's sixth member state. This should mean good relations with Malaysia and Indonesia in the future, and reduce Brunei's need for maintaining a battalion of British Army Gurkhas in addition to its own defence forces.

(b) Government Capabilities

The present group of long serving expatriates will probably stay on after independence, but there is already an active programme to replace foreign staff where possible with suitably trained Brunei citizens.

Brunei has invested substantial monies in overseas education, but it is only now that these foreign trained officers are gaining sufficient experience to assume their future roles: there is already a greater emphasis on improving government efficiency. Perhaps most important, the Sultan himself is very much interested in the day to day affairs of state and will hopefully ensure a smooth transition to full local administration. Brunei is fortunate that its oil revenues should allow an extended period in which to adjust to these changes.

(c) The Economy

Brunei's oil and gas based economy seems well set for at least the next two decades, but one of the responsibilities of independence is to plan and restructure the economy in preparation for the day when the oil revenues become insufficient for the country's needs. At present, these efforts are directed in three major areas: first to broaden Brunei's trading links through membership of ASEAN, the Commonwealth, the UN and other international bodies – at present Japan takes 84 per cent of Brunei's exports as well as being its largest source of imports; second, there is the investment of the government's present revenue surplus into tangible, overseas income producing assets – its recent A$5.8 million purchase of the Willeroo Cattle Station in Australia's Northern Territories (a ranch larger than Brunei itself) is a good example; third, there is the government's programme to develop new local industries – Brunei's size limits its manufacturing potential, but more can be done to utilise its existing resources.

Brunei thus appears well placed to assume full independence; it has already had many years of full local self-government. Its relationship with its immediate neighbours seems good, and there are substantial areas in which to increase trade, particularly with Malaysia. Its economy, although dependent on oil revenues, is strong and should allow the government considerable scope in implementing its various development policies. Brunei's financial institutions will, of course, benefit in the process through the increased business but, due to the public sector's funding activities, will probably play less an important role in financing these changes than elsewhere in ASEAN.

NOTES

1. Brunei had an estimated *per capita* income of US$22000 in 1982, *Asian Wall Street Journal* (28 September 1982) p. 11.
2. *National Development Plan 1962-6* (Kuala Belait: Government Printer, 1962) p. 19.
3. David Jenkins, *Student Guide to Asia* (London: Student Travel Australia, 1979) pp. 42-3. Energy related exports accounted for 98.99 per cent of Brunei's exports in 1981.
4. Bank of America, *Brunei: Economic Update* (7 July 1982) p. 3.
5. Brunei State Chamber of Commerce, *Chamber Journal 1980-1: Jubilee Edition* (1981), p. 43.
6. Brunei Information Section, State Secretariat, State of Brunei *Annual Report 1976*, p. 371.
7. Bank of America, *Brunei: Economic Update* (7 July 1982) p. 3.
8. The Brunei Shell group of companies comprises four major firms: Brunei Shell Petroleum Co. Ltd is the main firm and the largest industrial concern in the country, it is owned equally by Shell and the Brunei government; the Brunei Shell Marketing Co. Ltd, (also owned equally by Shell and the government) distributes petroleum products throughout Brunei; Brunei LNG Ltd, (which is owned jointly by Shell, Mitsubishi and the government) operates Brunei's LNG facilities; and Brunei Coldgas (also owned by Shell, Mitsubishi and the government) markets and transports Brunei's LNG to Japan. Brunei State Chamber of Commerce, *Chamber Journal 1980-1*, pp. 57-62.
9. Interview, 1982.
10. Interview, 1982.
11. I. B. J. Ross (Public Affairs Adviser, Brunei Shell Petroleum Ltd): correspondence (9 August 1982) p. 1.
12. National Bank of Brunei Ltd, *Annual Report 1980*, p. 2.
13. Barry Wain, 'In Brunei, Sultan's New Palace Recalls Days of Glory', *Asian Wall Street Journal* (10 October 1982) p. 1.
14. Finance Companies Enactment 1975, Part 2, paras. (a), (b) (mimeograph of the Enactment).
15. Until 1976, the late Chang Ming Thien owned approximately 65 per cent of the United Malayan Banking Corporation. The Malaysians who acquired much of this interest did also not acquire his United Finance holdings. Until his death (in mid-1982) Chang's financial interests then centred around the Overseas Trust Bank in Hong Kong. See Gary Coull, 'A giant spiderless web', *Far Eastern Economic Review* (11 June 1982) pp. 105-8.

16. Interview, 1982.
17. Interview, 1982.
18. Interview, 1982.
19. Interview, 1982.
20. Interview, 1982.
21. Interview, 1982.
22. Investment Incentives Enactment 1975, Part II, Chap. 1, 3 (1) (a), p. 5a.
23. Interview, 1982.
24. Interview, 1982.
25. Han Ling, 'Police Probe Commodities Firm', *Borneo Bulletin* (30 January 1982) p. 1.

2 Financial Institutions and Markets in Indonesia

ROSS McLEOD

INTRODUCTION

(a) The Setting

The Indonesian archipelago comprises thousands of islands strewn along a 5000 kilometre stretch of the equator from just west of peninsular Malaysia at the western extremity to the border with Papua New Guinea in the east. The three largest islands – Kalimantan (formerly Borneo), Sumatra and Irian Jaya (formerly West New Guinea) – account for about three-quarters of its nearly 2 million square kilometre land mass. Most others are little more than dots on the ocean. Indonesia's population of about 150 million is the largest of the ASEAN nations, and fifth largest in the world. About two-thirds of this population are concentrated in Java, southern Sumatra and Bali.

Despite Indonesia's wealth of natural resources, *per capita* income is the lowest of the ASEAN countries, standing at about $US521 in 1981. This is because the transition from a traditional agricultural society to a modern economy has not progressed very far. About two-thirds of the workforce still earns its income from traditional farming – the agricultural sector (including estate crops, forestry and fisheries) accounts for 32 per cent of GDP, whereas manufacturing provides only 13 per cent. There is a relatively large mining and quarrying sector (dominated by oil) which contributes nearly 10 per cent of GDP. Of the other sectors, only wholesale and retail trade (17 per cent) and public administration and defence (9 per cent) are important.

To understand present day Indonesia and its economic policies, it is helpful to know a little of Indonesia's history. The

49

archipelago was colonised by the Dutch for some 350 years, during which time their main aim was to exploit the islands for their own benefit. Indonesia was occupied by the Japanese during the latter half of the Second World War, but on their surrender the Indonesians' anti-Dutch feelings and desire for independence was such that the Dutch never regained full authority. After several years of struggle at both the military and diplomatic levels, the Dutch formally relinquished authority in 1949, but so far as Indonesians are concerned, independence dates from 17 August 1945.

One far-reaching Dutch legacy was a lack of sufficiently trained or experienced personnel to assume the Dutch managerial and administrative roles in both the government and private sectors. This deficiency has plagued Indonesia's post-independence development, and will continue to do so for several years to come.

A second legacy is more psychological in nature. The economy that existed under the Dutch became equated with capitalism, and so it was natural that hostility toward the Dutch would be reflected in hostility towards capitalism. The constitution (adopted the day after the Proclamation of Independence) required that the economy be based on co-operative effort, and that production of 'essential' goods and services and natural resources be controlled by the government for the greater good of the people. The economic system under the Dutch was in fact the antithesis of capitalism, since its policy of enforced monopoly was quite contrary to the basic principles of capitalism; it is unfortunate that Indonesia's broad economic philosophy has been so influenced by this misunderstanding.

Another important aspect of Indonesia's recent history is the long period of Chinese immigration. This ended many years ago, and the proportion of ethnic Chinese in the population (about 2 per cent) is small by comparison with neighbours such as Singapore and Malaysia. Nevertheless, their predominance in the modern sector of the economy is very pronounced. As in other countries, this is resented, and a second prominent feature of economic policy is conscious discrimination in favour of pribumi (indigenous population) businesses. Since, however, virtually all big Chinese firms enjoy the patronage of various civil and military officials, they have maintained their position despite the government's pro-pribumi policies.

Indonesia's first 20 years of independence were marked by great political instability. The late President Sukarno had little

51

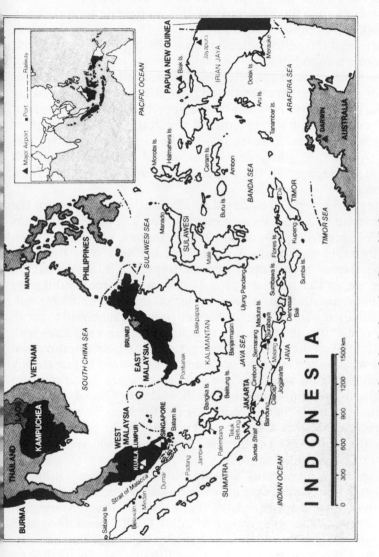

MAP 2.1   Indonesia – General Infrastructure

Source: Department of Trade and Resources, *Guide to the Market: Indonesia* (Australian Government Publishing Service, 1982).

interest in economics, and government spending became increasingly financed by money creation rather than by taxation or borrowing. By 1965, the country was experiencing hyperinflation which (combined with direct price and other controls) brought chaos to the monetised sector of the economy. A failed coup attempt led eventually to Sukarno's replacement by President Suharto and the period since has seen comparative political and economic tranquility.

The most profound development affecting Indonesia's recent economic performance was the oil price rise in 1974. Crude oil, oil products and LNG now constitute approximately two-thirds of total exports, and the tax on oil amounts to 71 per cent of government domestic revenues. In this sense the country has recently been extremely dependent on oil and LNG, although only a tiny segment of the population earns its livelihood from this sector.

The rapid growth of oil based revenues has made it easy for the government to finance its own expenditure. The public sector has therefore grown rapidly since 1975. Economic growth has been equally rapid – averaging 7.6 per cent per year over the same period. Nevertheless, the recent faltering of international oil prices means that greater austerity may well be required during the 1980s, and this was already reflected in the 1982/83 budget.

In discussing Indonesian economic policy, it is helpful to recall two points: first, the tendency to equate free market forces with the economy of the Dutch era; second, ethnic Chinese domination of the modern sector of the economy. The two are in fact closely related, partly because the Chinese enjoyed a privileged position (relative to pribumi) under the Dutch, and partly because pribumi in general tend to have a poor regard for their own ability to compete with ethnic Chinese. There is therefore a tendency to think that a free market oriented economy would lead to even greater Chinese domination.

Despite the important liberalisation and rationalisation in economic policy making following Sukarno's demise, the tendency has thus been towards increasingly pervasive government intervention. The private sector finds itself constrained and buffeted more and more by a powerful government bureaucracy. Although this bureaucracy has great faith in its ability to allocate productive resources for the good of the people, the lack of a well educated or otherwise trained élite has meant that this bureaucracy lacks an appreciation of the realities of private business. Few civil servants have private sector experience, and as a result, government development policies are often built on very shaky foundations.

(b) An Overview of the Financial Sector

Some idea of the relative importance of Indonesia's various financial institutions can be gained by comparing their total assets, as shown in Table 2.1. The financial sector is clearly dominated by the commercial banks and the central bank (Bank Indonesia). In very rough terms, the commercial banks as a whole and Bank Indonesia each had total assets (at the end of 1980) of the order of Rp10000 billion, whereas total assets of all other institutions combined amounted to only about Rp1200 billion.

TABLE 2.1   Indonesia financial institutions total assets (figures as at end 1980, in Rp billion)[a]

Institution	Amount
Commercial banks[b]	10852
Central Bank	9805
Insurance companies	362[c]
Investment Finance Corpns	324
State Development Bank	276
State Savings Bank	129
Development Finance Corpns	76
Government pawnshop service	30
National Investment Trust	24
Market banks	7

[a] The figures shown should be regarded as indicators of order of magnitude, rather than precise values.
[b] Including Regional development banks.
[c] At December 1979; the coverage is incomplete.

Source: Bank of Indonesia, 1982.

A second striking feature is the very marked government ownership of financial institutions. Five State and 26 Provincial government banks account for most commercial banking business; there are no private savings or development banks of significance; the majority of merchant banks (or investment finance corporations) have State owned banks as major shareholders; the development finance corporations are basically government institutions (although one has a substantial private sector shareholding); government firms operate more than two-thirds of all insurance business; the State has a monopoly on pawnshop operations; and there is a large State owned investment trust.

In order to have a balanced picture of the finance sector, it is necessary to recognise that a very large proportion of financial transactions are of an informal nature. These are very diverse, encompassing loans by specialised moneylenders, loans between business acquaintances, friends and family members, trade credit, hire purchase arrangements and so on. One of the few things that they have in common is that none is recorded in any official statistics. There is therefore no way of knowing the extent of informal finance. There can be no doubt, however, that it is extremely important – especially to poorer individuals and small enterprises. Few of the former, and a large proportion of the latter, even have a bank account. Virtually their only exposure to formal sector finance is their use of the national currency.

Given this overview, the remainder of this paper considers the financial sector in more detail and consists of three sections. The first concerns the various kinds of bank and non-bank financial institution. The second is devoted to the money market, the Stock Exchange and the National Investment Trust. Finally, there is a summary of development of finance in Indonesia and the government policies which affect it, together with some predictions for the future.

FINANCIAL INSTITUTIONS

(a) Banks

Banking in Indonesia is controlled under Law No. 14 1967. This law defines kinds of banks – the Central Bank; 'general' or commercial banks; savings banks; and development banks. In regard to the last three, four kinds of ownership are distinguished – government (national or provincial); co-operative; private; and foreign. Co-operative ownership in reality is restricted to commercial banks and is negligible. Savings banks may not be owned by foreigners, and Provincial governments are permitted to own only development banks.

This discussion first considers the Central Bank, and then the commercial banks. Since the Provincial government development banks in practice differ little from the commercial banks, they are also included in this section. The State owned savings bank and development bank (there being no private institutions of significance) are then considered, and finally the other banking institutions, the most important of which are the tiny privately or co-operatively owned market banks.

(i) *Central Bank (Bank Indonesia)*

During the colonial era, a Dutch commercial bank (De Javasche Bank) issued Indonesia's currency, but 'it did not perform other central-banking functions such as controlling credit expansion, holding the reserves of banks, or serving as a lender of last resort'.[1] This bank was nationalised in 1951, and became Bank Indonesia. The main focus of the present discussion will be the period since December 1968, when a series of major banking reforms began to be implemented.[2]

Bank Indonesia's responsibilities come under three broad headings – the promotion of government economic objectives; the development of the financial sector; and the maintenance of price stability.

In promoting government economic objectives, Bank Indonesia is perhaps more active than most central banks. It tries to influence both the direction and the cost of bank lending to favour priority sectors and borrowers.

These influences and priority rankings have several dimensions. By industry, small scale agriculture, fisheries and the like take precedence over manufacturing, manufacturing over construction, and construction over commerce. Exports are favoured over imports, 'essentials' over 'luxuries', the public sector over the private. By size, small firms are favoured over medium, and medium over large. By ethnic group, pribumi are very strongly favoured over non-pribumi. Certain concessional loans are available only to pribumi firms, but it should also be noted that pribumi borrowers are relatively more strongly represented amongst smaller firms and in sectors such as small scale agriculture, fisheries and so on. Perhaps the most important ranking is therefore that of pribumi over non-pribumi – whether this be explicit or implicit.

Bank Indonesia's efforts to develop the financial sector have been mainly concerned with banking (which dominates the financial sector) and, to a much lesser extent, with the non-bank financial institutions (merchant banks and development finance companies. These policies are invariably directed – nominally – at strengthening these institutions and their performance, and in making them more responsive to policy requirements. Such control can often be inimical to these institutions' effectiveness in meeting the public's financial requirements, however, and this is especially important in the case of the bank sector.

While it is difficult to evaluate the success of Bank Indonesia's broad economic and financial policies and financial development in particular, evidence regarding price stability or the absence thereof is substantial. The New Order (Suharto) government did reduce the inflation rate to as little as 2 per cent per annum in 1971 – an enviable performance given that the rate for 1966 was officially 636 per cent. This low rate has not been maintained: it rose to 33 per cent in 1974, fell, then peaked again at 24 per cent in 1979, before subsequently returning to around 7 per cent in 1981.

High inflation throughout most of the 1970s resulted from failure to control the growth of the money supply. This was largely the consequence of exchange rate policies adopted during the period. Foreign exchange earnings increased dramatically following the oil price rises in 1973–4, but the authorities chose not to revalue the rupiah to relieve the payments surplus thus

TABLE 2.2   Indonesia classification of commercial banks (figures as at 31 March, 1982)

Sector	Group	Description	No. of banks	No. of branches
Public	National	State[a]	5	712
	Provincial	RDB[b]	26	174
Private	Foreign	Foreign[c]	11	20
	Domestic[d]	Private	71	297
	Foreign exchange		(10)	N/A
	Non-foreign exchange[d]		(61)	N/A
Total			113	1203

[a]   All the State banks have a foreign exchange licence.
[b]   The RDBs do not have foreign exchange licences.
[c]   Includes one joint venture bank (i.e. with some Indonesian shareholders).
[d]   Includes five banks owned by co-operatives.

Source: Bank of Indonesia, 1982.

generated. On the contrary, the currency was deliberately devalued late in 1978 (in an attempt to stimulate the manufacturing
sector by artificially improving its international competitiveness).
Foreign exchange reserves thus rose in all but one year during
1970–80, causing the money supply to grow rapidly.

Throughout this period, Bank Indonesia eschewed the use of
open market operations as a technique of monetary control, and
the rapid growth of bank reserves (because of balance of
payments surpluses) rendered control by varying the banks'
minimum reserve ratios virtually impotent. It is therefore not
surprising that the Central Bank fell back on a system of more
direct controls. A new system of credit ceilings was introduced in
1974, under which each bank was allocated a share of the total
credit expansion allowed for that year. For the State banks, limits
were also set for each priority sector and for non-priority loans.
Although this system appears to have reduced money growth and
inflation below the otherwise expected levels, there has been a
very substantial cost in the form of 'almost complete subordi-
nation of the [State] commercial banks to discretionary central
bank control'.[3]

(ii) *Commercial banks*

It is useful to begin by classifying the commercial banks and their
regional development bank (RDB) colleagues according to their
significant characteristics. The major divisions are first, between
the public and private sector institutions; second, whether the
former have provincial or national and the latter domestic or
foreign ownership; finally, whether the domestic owned private
banks have a foreign exchange licence.

As shown in Table 2.2, the private banks are by far the most
numerous, with 71 (or some 62.8 per cent) of Indonesia's 113
licensed commercial and provincial banks. A very different
picture emerges, however, if the categories are instead compared
in terms of asset size. Then the state commercial banks (as shown
in Table 2.3) become the dominant grouping with 81 per cent of
the industry total:[4] in contrast, the private domestic banks as a
group hold only 8.6 per cent.

There are also substantial differences in terms of the average
assets per bank in each group. The average assets per State bank
at the end of 1980 for example, were Rp1749 billion. The foreign
and private foreign exchange (FE) banks are similar to each other

TABLE 2.3 Indonesia commercial bank size indicators (figures as at end 1980 in Rp billion)

Bank	No. of banks	Assets			Offices			Assets per office
		Total	(%)	Average	No.	(%)	Average	
State	5	8743	80.6	1749	700	61.0	140.0	12.5
Foreign	11	752	6.9	68	22	1.9	2.0	34.2
Private	66[a]	934	8.6	12	275	24.0	4.2	3.4
FE	10	(550)	(5.1)	55	(114)	(9.9)	11.4	4.8
Non-FE	56[a]	(384)	(3.5)	6	(161)	(14.0)	2.9	2.4
RDBs	26	423	3.9	16	150	13.1	5.8	2.8
Total	108[a]	10852	100.0	100	1147	100.0	10.6	9.5

[a] Data unavailable for the nine smallest private banks. None of them, however, had assets exceeding Rp1 billion at end 1980.

Source: SGV–Utomo, A Study of Commercial Banks in Indonesia 1980 (Manila: SGV Group, 1980); Bank Indonesia, Indonesian Financial Statistics (May 1981), and Annual Report 1979–80; Annual Reports of State banks and Bapindo; author's estimates.

in size, with average assets respectively of Rp68 billion and Rp55 billion – only about one-thirtieth the size of the State banks. The RDBs are much smaller again (Rp16 billion), and the private non-FE banks are tiny (Rp6 billion). A listing of the larger institutions in each of these groups is shown in Table 2.4. In addition to these firms, some foreign banks not licensed in Indonesia nevertheless have a local presence through shareholdings in a number of non-banking financial institutions. Also (as shown in Table 2.5) many foreign banks maintain representative offices in Jakarta.

In terms of branches, the State banks have a wider coverage than the other groups, with 140 branches each. The foreign banks are at the other end of the spectrum, with only two branches each on average. The private non-FE banks average three branches each, the RDBs six and the private FE banks more than 11. The geographic dispersion of bank offices also differs greatly between the groups. The foreign banks' offices are entirely located in Jakarta, by government decree. The private banks also have a strong big city orientation, with 70 per cent of their branches located in the five biggest cities, though many other cities are served by at least one or two banks. At the other extreme, the RDBs are much more oriented towards smaller towns, with 68 per cent of their offices in places other than the national and provincial capitals. The State banks have a locational pattern intermediate between that of the private banks and the RDBs, though closer to the latter.

Prior to independence, there were seven major commercial banks operating; all were foreign, and the three largest were Dutch. A few other foreign banks had a lesser presence, but there appears to have been only a handful of Indonesian ones – each very small. Following independence the Dutch banks began to be nationalised – a process which was completed in 1960. Four of the present five State banks can trace their beginnings to these Dutch institutions.[5] Toward the end of the Sukarno era, the non-Dutch foreign banks also began to lose their operating licences and have their assets distributed amongst the Indonesian banks. Foreign banks therefore became virtually non-existent by the mid-1960s, and it was not until the New Order regime undertook new initiatives – reflected in the Basic Banking Law 1967 and the Foreign Bank Law 1968 – that they could return. Thus the 10 foreign banks now operating in Indonesia commenced operations during 1968–9 (the eleventh, Bank Perdania – the sole joint venture bank – was founded in 1956).

60

TABLE 2.4   Indonesian individual banks' total assets
(figures as at end 1980, in Rp billion)

State banks	
Bank Dagang Negara	2339
Bank Bumi Daya	1996
Bank Negara Indonesia 1946	1847
Bank Rakyat Indonesia	1541
Bank Ekspor Impor Indonesia	1019
Private foreign exchange banks	
Pan Indonesia Bank	112
Bank Central Asia	110
Bank Umum Nasional	60
Bank Buana Indonesia	58
Bank Niaga	46
Bank Pacific	44
Bank Bali	38
Overseas Express Bank	37
Bank Duta Ekonomi	33
Bank Dagang Nasional Indonesia	10
Private non-foreign exchange banks (10 largest)	
United City Bank	26
Bank Agung Asia	23
Bank NISP	23
Bank Arta Pusara	20
South East Asia Bank	17
Sejahtera Bank Umum	16
Bank International Indonesia	12
Bank Amerta	12
Bank Danamon	11
Bank Perniagaan Indonesia	11
Licenced foreign banks	
Citibank	151
Bank of Tokyo	114
Chase Manhattan Bank	103
European Asian Bank	73
Bank of America	68
Bank Perdania	53
Bangkok Bank	47
Algemene Bank Nederland	45
American Express International	37
Hong Kong and Shanghai Bank	36
Chartered Bank	26

Source: SGV–Utomo, *A Study of Commercial Banks in Indonesia* (Manila: SGV Group, 1980).

TABLE 2.5   Indonesia bank representative offices

Amsterdam–Rotterdam Bank NV
Arbuthnot Latham & Co. Ltd
Asia Commercial Banking Corpn Ltd
Bank of Credit & Commerce International SA
Bank of India
Bank of Montreal
The Bank of Nova Scotia
Bankers Trust Company
Banque de Paris et des Pays-Bas
Banque de l'Indochine et de Suez
Banque de l'Union Européene
Banque Francaise du Commerce Exterieur
Banque Nationale de Paris
Barclays Bank International Ltd
Chemical Bank
Commerzbank AG
Continental Illinois National Bank
Credit Industrial et Commercial
Credit Lyonnais
The Dai–Ichi Kangyo Bank Ltd
Donner Bank
Dresdner Bank
European Banks International
The Export–Import Bank of Japan
The First National Bank of Chicago
The Fuji Bank, Ltd
Habib Bank Ltd
NV De Indonesische Overzeese Bank
Industrial Bank of Japan
International Bank of Singapore
M. M. Warburg-Brinckmann, Wirtz & Co.
Manufacturers' Hanover Trust Co.
Marine Midland Bank
The Mitsubishi Bank Ltd
The Mitsui Bank
Morgan Guaranty Trust Co.
The National Australia Bank
Philippine National Bank
Pierson, Heldring & Pierson NV
The Sanwa Bank Ltd
Société Generale
The Sumitomo Bank Ltd
The Tokai Bank Ltd
Tat Lee Bank Ltd
Toronto Dominion Bank
United California Bank
Wells Fargo Bank
Westpac Banking Corpn

Source: Bank of Indonesia, 1982.

Indonesia's private banks began to emerge during the 1950s. Several were military related, but many more were closely related to various business enterprises, mainly owned by ethnic Chinese. These banks were established primarily to serve the requirements of these common interest groups and enterprises, but by the end of the decade few had developed into significant banks. The rapid growth in private bank numbers and the relative frequency of their bankruptcies finally led the government in 1955 to introduce measures for their control and supervision. Further entry was stopped in 1959, and although this prohibition was slightly relaxed in 1964, no new licences have been issued since 1971.

The RDBs for the most part were established during the early 1960s. They are owned by the respective Provincial governments, and act as their fiscal agents, collecting and disbursing government funds. Although intended to specialise in the provision of long term investment loans and to accept only time and savings deposits from the public, they have in fact always been more involved with short term loans financed mainly by demand deposits. The growth of these institutions, however, has been hampered because each must operate only within its respective province. As a result, only those RDBs based in the five largest cities – Jakarta, Surabaya, Medan, Bandung, Semarang – have been able to grow to a size comparable with that of the private FE banks and the foreign banks.

It is widely acknowledged that, in general, much better service is provided by the foreign banks and the better private ones. A few RDBs have also managed to build good reputations. The State banks tend to fare poorly by comparison in regard to deposit rates, the speed with which transfers can be completed and loans approved, opening hours of cash windows, attitude of staff and so on. Nevertheless, the State banks' share of banking business (as shown in Table 2.6) is fairly constant. The explanation for this is twofold. First, the government has placed severe obstacles on the private (including foreign) banks' and RDBs' expansion. Second, there are a number of important subsidies, both explicit and implicit, which are available (with a few minor exceptions) only to the State banks.

No new foreign bank licences have been issued since 1969,[7] nor any for private banks since 1971, and there is virtually no scope for new RDBs, since all but one province already has one. More important, there is an almost total prohibition on

TABLE 2.6   Indonesia share of bank groups in total bank assets (figures as at end of March for selected years)

Group	1971	75	78	79	80	81
State[a]	79.8	82.7	77.7	78.7	79.0	79.6
Private			9.7	9.3	8.9	9.9
	10.4[b]	7.4[b]	(12.8)	(12.6)	(12.4)	(13.5)
RDBs			3.1	3.3	3.5	3.6
Foreign	9.8	9.9	9.5	8.7	8.6	6.9
Total	100.0	100.0	100.0	100.0	100.0	100.0

[a]   Includes Bapindo. For this reason, and because of the use of different source material, the data here are not directly comparable with those in Table 2.2.

[b]   Separate figures for the private banks and RDBs were not provided in Bank Indonesia's *Annual Reports* until 1978–9.

Source: Bank Indonesia, *Annual Reports*.

opening new branch offices. The foreign banks are not permitted offices anywhere but in Jakarta;[8] indeed, they are not even allowed to lend to companies headquartered there if the project being financed is located elsewhere.[9] The private banks, by contrast, are not constrained to operate only in Jakarta; they are prevented (except in special circumstances) from opening new branches there or in any of the other large cities. They are allowed to open new branches in the smaller towns to help reduce the alleged urban–rural imbalance in banking services, but since the demand in small towns is quite modest, this is not a very meaningful option. In practice, then, the physical (branch) structure of the private bank sector is very nearly frozen.

A further restriction on the private banks is their ability to obtain FE licences. Although this is not an outright prohibition – one new licence was issued in 1980, bringing the total to 10 – it is now almost impossible to fulfil the necessary conditions. The inability of the non-FE banks (including the RDBs) to offer foreign currency facilities effectively precludes them from providing the banking services required by larger corporate clients, whose custom could otherwise provide a sound foundation for those banks' expansion.

A third control on the private banks' expansion is Bank Indonesia's practice of setting ceilings for the expansion of each bank's lending, in order to control the growth of the money supply. A side effect at the micro level is for the ceilings to constrain the expansion of well managed banks, and to preserve the share of those banks not so well managed. This disadvantage is present both within and between the various sectors. Although it appears that the ceilings for the private banks have been generous enough so as not to constrain their expansion, the reverse is true of the foreign banks (no information is available on this aspect regarding the RDBs.)

The second reason for the State banks' relatively constant market share is the various subsidies from which they benefit. The first is the subsidy on time deposits: the total interest paid to depositors' is only partly paid by the bank concerned, the remainder is contributed by the Central Bank. When introduced in the late 1960s, the subsidy was substantial. The rates paid on 6 and 12 month deposits were respectively 5 per cent and 6 per cent per month, with Bank Indonesia contributing one-third of the interest. Since then, the subsidies have at various times been abolished, reinstated at different levels, and applied to deposits of differing maturities. In 1982 only deposits of 2 year maturity attracted a subsidy – $4\frac{1}{2}$ per cent per annum for amounts up to Rp2.5 million, but only $1\frac{1}{2}$ per cent for any excess. The deposit rates are respectively 15 per cent and 12 per cent. Deposit rates on shorter maturities are no longer attractive, so that the majority of time deposits are for 2 years. State bank lending is also subsidised: in general, for any given loan, the bank concerned can refinance a specified proportion with Bank Indonesia at a relatively low interest rate. As can be seen in Table 2.7, both the refinance rate and proportion varies with the loan category, as does the lending rate to the borrower[10] (the loan category depends on the priority accorded to the activity or borrower in question). Since the refinance proportion in most cases is quite large – even as high as 100 per cent – this constitutes a very important source of funds for the State banks.

Deposit guarantees by the government are another kind of State bank subsidy. Both their savings and time deposits are explicitly guaranteed, but it also appears that there is an implied guarantee on demand deposits as well. The generally accepted notion is that the government could hardly allow one of its own institutions to fail at the expense of its depositors and others. One of the largest State banks (Bank Bumi Daya), which had massive bad debts problems in the mid-1970s, would almost certainly have collapsed had it been privately owned.[11] In the event, the government stepped in, installed a new Board of Directors, and

TABLE 2.7 Indonesia State bank lending rates and subsidies

Group	Short term credits (< 1 year)	Investment credits (> 1 year)	%\nper annum	%\nper annum	%\nper annum
1.	Supply and distribution of rice, paddy & corn by co-operatives		1.00[a]	3[b]	9.0[c]
2.	Special agricultural programmes		1.00	3	12.0
3.	Salt, wheat flour	KIK,[d] KI[e] (up to Rp75m)	0.80	3	10.5
4.	Smallholders' agriculture, animal husbandry, poultry farming, fisheries & handicrafts	KMKP[f]	0.75	4	12.0
	Export & production of export goods				
	Aid financed imports; distribution of non-food commodities				
	Production, import and distribution of fertilisers and insecticides for use by smallholders	KI (Rp75m–Rp200m)			
5.	Manufacturing, service rendering, sugar stock	KI (Rp200m–Rp500m)	0.70	4	13.5
6.	Domestic trade, import & distribution of supervised goods	KI (Rp500m–Rp1500m)	0.65	4	13.5
7.	Contractors to public sector		0.70	6	13.5
8.	Contractors to private sector		0.60	6	13.5
9.	Imports & distribution of other import goods		0.40	6	18.0
10.	Others (not included elsewhere)		0.25	6	21.0

[a] Refinance proportion.
[b] Refinance rate.
[c] Lending rate.
[d] Kredit Investasi Kecil (small investment loan).
[e] Kredit Investasi (investment loan).
[f] Kredit Modal Kerja Permanen (Permanent working capital loan).

Source: Bank Indonesia *Annual Report, 1979–80.*

made sure that the Bank had sufficient funds to continue operation – no matter how large the necessary write-offs.

The other major implicit subsidy enjoyed by the State banks results from the policy that State owned enterprises may not place their deposits elsewhere. Since the latter are both numerous and in many cases very large, this provides an important 'captive' source of funds.

Perhaps the most striking aspect revealed by this discussion is the enormous difference between the State banks' operations on the one hand, and those of the private sector banks and RDBs on the other. This difference is in the restrained way in which the State banks respond to market forces; the government expects them to be 'agents of development', which means that they should allocate their funds to the sectors and borrower categories accorded a high priority by Indonesia's policymakers. Thus their entire lending rate structure is determined by the government; the same is true of most of their time deposit rates and the savings deposit rate. These five giants of Indonesian banking are therefore left with little scope for following their own initiative. Because of the various controls on the other bank groups, the spur of competition has little chance to make itself felt, and it is hardly surprising that the State banks' performance leaves something to be desired.

(iii) *State Savings Bank*

The State Savings Bank, Bank Tabungan Negara (BTN) was established by the Dutch in 1898. It appears always to have utilised Post Office facilities for transactions with its depositors, and indeed was once known as the Postal Savings Bank, Bank Tabungan Pos. Its present legal form was set out in Law No. 20 1968.

By 1967, Indonesia had 13 private savings banks, with a total of 14 branches. Many also maintained agencies to receive payments from their borrowers. A decade later the number of private savings banks had fallen to seven, and each had only one office. By March 1980 only two were still operating, and their combined total assets were negligible by comparison with those of BTN.

The demise of the private savings banks since 1970 is largely attributable to banking policies of the New Order government. An essential feature of its drive to curtail money supply growth was the October 1968 interest rate reform. The substantial increase in interest rates that resulted understandably gave the state banks – including BTN – a much greater ability to attract deposits. But in 1971, the private savings banks were further affected by the introduction of the National Development Savings Scheme (Tabanas). Under this scheme, savings deposits attracted a rate of 18 per cent per annum. The banks permitted to participate included the BTN, the five state commercial banks, several RDBs and the private commercial banks; only one of the private savings banks was included. Since inflation had been largely brought under control by this time, the deposit rate proved very attractive, and the non-participating savings banks found it very difficult to compete.

About a year after its introduction, the Tabanas rate was reduced to 12 per cent per annum for balances in excess of Rp100000. There have been several changes since then, but this two tier rate structure (favouring smaller depositors) has endured. At present, Tabanas deposits of up to Rp200000 attract 15 per cent per annum interest, while any excess earns only 6 per cent. In practice, however, Tabanas some 9.2 million accounts have a much lower average balance: about Rp36000 in mid-1981.

The Tabanas programme has grown rapidly. Over the 9 years to December 1981, the number of accounts increased at an annual average rate of 16.1 per cent, while the amount outstanding grew at around 12 per cent in real terms. More recently, growth has been appreciably slower. For the 4 years to December 1981, the rates were respectively 7.6 and 5.6 per cent.

The growth of BTN, as indicated by increases in its total assets, has been considerably more rapid than the increases in its savings deposits (as Table 2.8 shows). The average growth rates during the period December 1977 – September 1981 were respectively about 67 and 33 per cent. The rapid expansion in total assets can mainly be attributed to a policy decision in 1974, requiring BTN to finance relatively poor individuals' purchases of low cost housing. The new programme remained fairly insignificant for some time, but began to grow rapidly in 1978 following the reduction of the lending rates to 9 per cent per annum for privately constructed houses, and to only 5 per cent for those built by the State housing construction company, Perumnas. Loans provided by BTN (presumably all within this programme) have risen at an annual rate of 109 per cent over the 15 quarters to September

TABLE 2.8   Bank Tabungan Negara recent growth performance
(figures in Rp billion)

	December 1977		September 81		Growth rate % per annum
		% of total funds		% of total funds	
Total assets	30.0	100.0	206.0	100.0	67.2
Loans	9.1	30.3	144.9	70.3	109.2
Savings deposits	12.6	42.0	36.4	17.7	32.7
Loans received	6.1	20.3	91.3	44.3	105.8
Capital	6.3	21.0	46.6	22.6	70.5
Other liabilities	—	—	25.1	12.2	—

Source: BTN, *Annual Reports.*

1981, and now comprise some 70 per cent of its total assets. Given the much slower growth in savings deposits, BTN has had to fund these loans through concessional borrowings from the government; such loans have risen commensurately – at about 106 per cent per annum – so that at September 1981 they constituted about 44 per cent of BTN's total liabilities, as compared with only 20 per cent in December 1979. Savings deposits as a proportion of total liabilities fell correspondingly during this period, from 42 to 18 per cent.

Between 1968 and 1976, there was little change in BTN's physical structure: it had seven branches and approximately 180 Post Office agencies, although the Post Office sub-branches and auxiliaries grew respectively from 79 and 760 in 1967 to 132 and 883 in 1976. The increased business generated by home loan activities, however, created the opportunity for physical expansion of BTN itself. The first new branch was opened in Denpasar (Bali) in 1977, and four more branches have opened since. There have also been further increases in the various Post Office outlets.

The name 'State Savings Bank' is thus rapidly becoming more and more of a misnomer. Under the law by which it was established, BTN was to collect individuals' savings, and to direct these funds to general development purposes. It has now largely become an administrative instrument by which the government channels its subsidised loan funds for low cost housing, and is now hardly at all subject to those commercial pressures which promote efficiency and innovation.

(iv) *Indonesian Development Bank*

The Indonesian Development Bank, Bank Pembangunan Indonesia (Bapindo) is the only significant bank specialising in long term lending. It is wholly owned by the Indonesian government, and was established on 25 May 1960 from the merger of two government owned banks: the State Industrial Bank (Bank Industri Negara) and the Universal Development Bank (Bank Pembangunan Semesta).

Emery observed that neither Bapindo nor the State Industrial Bank were particularly successful in attracting private savings (domestic or foreign), or converting these into long term credits or investments.[12] A decade later (as shown in Table 2.9) Bapindo still attracts only a relatively small amount of savings. Its major funds still come from the government (including the central bank and the State commercial banks). It now also obtains some funding from the large international aid oriented institutions – the World Bank, the Asian Development Bank, Kreditanstalt für Wiederaufbau, and the International Development Association. Today, however, Bapindo's portfolio is no longer dominated by short term credits: on the contrary, these amounted to less than 2 per cent of assets in 1980.

Bapindo's growth has accelerated rapidly since the mid-1970s, and Table 2.10 shows its yearly increase in assets over 1976–80.[13] Growth was negligible in money terms – and negative in real terms – during 1977, but nominal growth has considerably outstripped inflation since.

Bapindo's financing activities have undergone several significant changes since 1960. The Bank began by specialising in equity investments using funds from the State budget. In 1966, it was instructed to extend only short term loans due to the rapid inflation rates. According to Emery, these were used mainly for working capital purposes rather than for financing the purchase of equipment.[14]

By the end of 1980, however, most Bapindo loans were 'long term', and of the remainder, most were 'medium term'. 'Long term' refers to Kredit Investasi loans. These are charged interest rates ranging from $10\frac{1}{2}$–$12\frac{1}{2}$ per cent per annum, increasing with loan size. Bapindo is the only bank permitted to provide loans exceeding Rp$2\frac{1}{2}$ billion. Its loans can be for up to 15 years, with a 6 year grace period, whereas the corresponding limits for other

TABLE 2.9 Bapindo sources of funds, 1976–80ᵃ (figures in Rp billion)

Year	Total liabilities/assets	Bank Indonesia and government loans	Paid-up capital + contributed reserves	Retained earnings	Special deposits (pension fund)	State banks	Total government contribution	World Bank	IDA ADB KfW	Total international institutions	Demand and time deposits
1976	124.9	37.9	44.0	1.5	—	10.0	93.4	8.9	3.9	12.8	7.7
(%)	100.0	30.3	35.2	1.2	—	8.0	74.8	7.1	3.1	10.2	6.2
1977	126.3	12.1	59.5	2.4	3.0	9.9	86.9	17.5	3.7	21.2	14.5
(%)	100.0	9.6	47.1	1.9	2.4	7.8	68.8	13.9	2.9	16.8	11.5
1979	196.9	48.0	60.0	4.8	18.0	4.9	135.7	28.7	6.9	35.6	10.1
(%)	100.0	24.4	30.5	2.4	9.1	2.5	68.9	14.6	3.5	18.1	5.1
1980	275.7	53.4	70.0	5.8	32.0	9.6	170.8	40.7	10.9	51.6	30.6
(%)	100.0	19.4	25.4	2.1	11.6	3.5	62.0	14.8	4.0	18.7	11.1

KfW = Kreditarstalt fur Weideraufban;   IDA = International Development Agency;   ADB = Asian Development Bank.
ᵃ Figures for 1978 not available.

Source: Bapindo, Annual Reports.

TABLE 2.10 Bapindo growth of total assets and managed funds, 1976–80
(figures as at 31 December, in Rp billion)

Year	Total assets	% increase	Managed funds	Assets + managed funds	% increase
76	124.9		—	124.9	
77	126.3	1.1	30.6	156.9	25.6
78	144.8	14.6	89.8	234.6	49.5
79	196.9	36.0	123.5	320.4	36.6
80	275.7	40.0	109.6	385.3	20.3

Source: Bapindo, *Annual Reports*.

banks are respectively 10 and 4 years. No information is provided in its reports about the typical duration of 'long term' loans, but it is suggested that most are in excess of 5 years. So far as size distribution is concerned, the only figures provided relate to cumulative totals rather than to loans outstanding, but given the rapid expansion of Bapindo's portfolio in recent years, these are probably fairly representative of current lending practice. By far the largest proportion of long term loans are over Rp500 million – no less than 89 per cent at the end of 1980. Loans from Rp200–500 million account for 7 per cent; those of less than Rp200 million comprise less than 4 per cent.

Whereas long term loans are of the fixed instalment type (with the interest rate depending on the sum borrowed), medium term loans finance working capital requirements associated with the investments funded by long term loans. Medium term working capital loans are thus provided as part of a package together with long term investment loans. The interest rate ranges from 9–21 per cent per annum, depending on the sector of the economy in which the borrower operates (see Table 2.4). The duration of these 'medium term' loans is not clear; in official banking terminology, 'medium term' extends from 1–3 years.

The precise distribution of Bapindo's lending as between long, medium, and short term is difficult to discern because of inconsistencies in its reports, but long term loans seemingly account for some three-quarters of the total. Medium term loans comprise about 15 per cent, while short term loans and equity financing each amount to about only 2 per cent. KIK/KMKP loans are also small, less than 3 per cent. Short term loans and marketable securities (mainly short term promissory notes issued by investment finance corporations and negotiable certificates of deposit) total some 8.2 per cent.

About 88 per cent of Bapindo's long term loans (and presumably a similar proportion of medium term ones) as at the end of 1980 were to the private sector. It should be noted also that all Bapindo loans must be directed to pribumi firms, although the purchase of marketable securities of course allows non-pribumi firms indirect access to the Bank's funds, albeit at higher interest rates. There is also an obligation for Bapindo to promote (through its lending policies) other government objectives, such as creating employment opportunities with low investment cost per worker, developing the country's foreign exchange earning ability, promoting small businesses and so on.

With respect to the Bank's direct financing activities (loans plus equity participation), some two-thirds were (as at the end of 1980) directed to industry, with the largest single concentration of funds to shipping, especially for financing log carriers.

In September 1967, Bapindo had some 865 head office staff and 525 more in its 20 branches.[15] Since then, a shift in lending (from small, short term working capital loans to large, long term investment financing), together with the diminished importance of demand and time deposit funding allowed the Bank to reduce its staff. By December 1981, these had declined to 811, 487 located at the head office and 324 at 18 branch offices.

Besides its other banking business, Bapindo handles the banking for several major government aid projects. Funds for these are channelled through the Bank, but since they are considered government behest loans – for which the latter apparently accepts full responsibility – they are not included in the Bank's assets and liabilities. Instead, they are recorded as an 'off balance sheet' item, 'Managed Funds'. Bapindo receives a small administrative fee for this service, which amounted to Rp280 million in 1980. The volume of Managed Funds is large – Rp110 billion at the end of 1980 (or 40 per cent of Bapindo's total assets). When these funds (which were non-existent in 1976) are taken into account, the recent growth of Bapindo becomes even more impressive (Table 2.10).

(v) *Other banking institutions*

The remaining banking institutions to be considered are those officially described as 'village and rural banks', although a good many of these are actually located in the larger cities.

Such banks are of minor importance in the financial market as a whole. They have therefore attracted very little attention from either researchers or the authorities, so it is very difficult to discuss their activities.[16] It appears that the majority are closely associated with the thousands of traditional markets found all over Indonesia (dealing in agricultural produce, fish, meat and other culinary requirements, household wares, clothing, farm tools and so on). Their depositors and borrowers are mainly the traders who earn their livelihood in these markets. Amounts deposited and borrowed tend to be very small, and the time scale short. As collectors of funds, the 'market' banks (as they are popularly known) are more akin to savings banks than to commercial banks, since they do not offer cheque account facilities. As lenders of funds, some at least are similar to pawnshops, in that they hold the borrower's physical assets (such as crockery, radios, bicycles and so on) in their possession until the loan is repaid, or sell them in the case of default.

There is very little official control of the market banks; they are free to set their own interest rates – which, of course, need to be quite high in order to cover the high administrative costs involved in small transactions. They may be owned privately, by co-operatives, or by government bodies. It would appear that none of them has more than a single office.

There were 3537 'village banks' in March 1980,[17] although the number of such banks which were 'active' is said to be only 3264.[18] The volume of outstanding credit was put at Rp6.3 billion in December 1981.

There is one other kind of rural bank deserving mention – the so called 'paddy banks'. These accept deposits and make loans in rice, rather than money. There were 2143 such banks in March 1980, but apparently only five were active.[19] If these figures are correct, they suggest that this form of banking, once quite popular, is now virtually extinct. The exact reasons will have to await detailed study by historians, but one possibility might be that rice had many advantages over money as an asset during the inflation of the 1960s.

(b) The Non-bank Financial Institutions

In accordance with its desire to improve the money and capital markets, the government has encouraged the establishment of a number of new financial institutions outside of banking and insurance. A preliminary decree was promulgated in December 1970, and subsequently amended and supplemented in January 1972. The institutions encompassed by these decrees are of two types: Development Finance Corporations (DFCs), and Investment Finance Corporations (IFCs).

(i) *Development Finance Corporations (DFCs)*

Indonesia has three DFCs: PT Indonesian Development Finance Company (IDFC, established in 1972); PT Private Development Finance Company of Indonesia; (PDFCI, 1973); and PT Bahana Pembinaan Usaha Indonesia (Bahana, 1973). Since the latter is much smaller than the other two, and its function somewhat different, it will be considered separately.

IDFC is purely a public sector institution. Its shareholders are Bank Indonesia (75 per cent) and the Netherlands Finance Company for Developing Countries (the Nederlandse Financierings Maatschappij voor Ontwikkelingslanden NV (FMO)) as trustee for the government of the Netherlands (25 per cent). Bahana is also a public sector corporation owned 80 per cent by the Ministry of Finance and 20 per cent by Bank Indonesia. By contrast, PDFCI has a large number of private sector shareholders, both local and overseas; the public sector is represented by Bank Indonesia and the RDB of Jakarta. A breakdown of these firms and their shareholdings is shown in Table 2.11.

IDFC's total assets at the end of 1980 were Rp26 billion, while PDFCI's amounted to Rp39 billion. The former closely reflects the kind of financial institution the government intended the DFCs to be – institutions engaged principally in granting medium and long term loans to, and participating in the capital of, Indonesian enterprises. All IDFC's loans are long term (greater than 5 years), and constitute 57 per cent of its assets; equities account for a further $11\frac{1}{2}$ per cent. By contrast, PDFCI's asset structure is more short term oriented. Loans amount to only 47 per cent of assets, and more than a quarter of these are classified as medium rather than long term. Investment in equities is very small – less than 4 per cent. What is more interesting is that no less than 42 per cent of PDFCI's assets are in short term promissory notes. At IDFC, current assets (promissory notes and certificates of deposit) amount to 23 per cent. One last point of

TABLE 2.11 PT Private Development Finance Co. of
Indonesia shareholders and relative holdings, 1982

Shareholder	(%)
Indonesia	
Bank Indonesia	21.93
AJB Bumiputera 1912	14.60
Pan Indonesia Bank Ltd	12.25
All Truba Inter	7.02
Gading Mas	4.32
Intrada	2.15
Julius Tahija	1.61
Metropolitan Kencana	1.61
BPD Jakarta Raya	1.61
Achmad Bakrie	0.58
Samudera Indonesia	0.58
Foreign	
The Nippon Credit Bank Ltd	5.37
The Bank of Nova Scotia	4.02
DEG	4.02
Irving International Financing Corpn	2.88
Schroder, Darling & Co. Ltd	2.16
International Finance Corpn	2.16
Lloyds Bank International Ltd	2.01
Credit Lyonnais	2.01
Banco di Roma Holdings SA	2.01
Westdeutsche Landesbank Girozentrale	2.01
Deutsche Genossenschafts Banks	2.01
Union d'Etudes et d'Investissements	1.08
	100.00

Source: PDFCI, 1982.

interest concerning the two companies' assets is that although
PDFCI is half as large again as IDFC, its direct financing
(through loans and equity funding) is very little different: Rp20
billion compared with Rp18 billion. This is due to PDFCI's
greater emphasis on short term money market activities.

The degree of enthusiasm for money market activity is
evidenced and explained in Table 2.12. In the year to 1980, both
companies increased their short term assets by some 80 per cent;
as a result, net interest income rose by around 70 per cent. After
tax profit rose by 69 per cent at IDFC, and by no less than 105 per
cent at PDFCI.

Turning to the two companies' liabilities, the most striking

TABLE 2.12 Indonesia Development Finance Co. and PT Private Development Finance Co. of Indonesia short term money market activities (figures in Rp billion)

	IDFC			PDFCI		
	1979	80	Increase %	1979	80	Increase %
Short term assets[a]	3.21	5.87	82.9	9.67	17.03	76.1
Gross interest income	1.441	2.470	71.4	2.513	4.670	85.8
Borrowing costs	0.393	0.736	87.3	1.348	2.646	96.3
Net interest income	1.048	1.734	65.0	1.165	2.024	73.7
Profit (after tax)	0.210	0.355	69.0	0.290	0.594	104.8
Shareholders' funds[a]	7.15	7.50	4.9	4.62	5.03	8.9

[a] End of year.

Source: IDFC; PDFCI, Annual Reports 1980.

aspect is the almost complete dependence on government and international aid orientated institution long term funds. There is no private sector participation of this kind, except for the non-government shareholdings in PDFCI. The Indonesian government – either directly, or through the central bank – emerges as the most important source of funds for the institutions' long term lending activities – although the World Bank group's long term loans to PDFCI (Rp10.1 billion) is only a little less than the government/Bank Indonesia contribution (Rp10.9 billion). IDFC has no private sector funding at all. Both capital and long term borrowing derives from Bank Indonesia and FMD; its only short term borrowing at the end of 1980 was a single promissory note (Rp1 billion) payable to the State-owned Bank Rakyat Indonesia. PDFCI does have substantial private sector borrowings, reflecting its active money market role. By the issue of promissory notes it raised short term funds equivalent to over 30 per cent of its total liabilities at the end of 1980.

Both firms are permitted to lend to pribumi, non-pribumi and joint venture enterprises but, in accordance with official policy, there is an increasing tendency to concentrate on the former. As with Bapindo, lending policy is expected to pay attention not only to commercial viability, but also to the job creation and balance of payments effects as well as to location.

IDFC is more concerned with small and medium scale projects than is PDFCI. It is involved in a co-financing programme with some of the RDBs which appears to be strongly oriented towards relatively small firms. It also has a subsidiary company, PT Bina Wiraswasta Konsultan (Enterpreneurial Guidance Consultant Company), to provide management and technical assistance to small businesses – including IDFC borrowers and non-borrowers. The number of IDFC's 'small projects' (undefined) has been increasing relative to 'medium' and 'large' ones since the late 1970s. These are presumably the main explanation for the relatively high staff (relative to total assets) at IDFC (102) by comparison with PDFCI (84).

The third and smallest DFC, Bahana, is owned by the government and Bank Indonesia and is specifically intended to assist small and medium pribumi enterprises. In contrast to PDFCI and IDFC, its financial assistance must incorporate equity participation, but may also include Kredit Investasi loans on a medium or long term basis.[20] The intention is that when the firm progresses sufficiently, Bahana will sell its shares (which must be less than half the total) either to other shareholders or to a third party. It also prepares feasibility studies, deals with various official regulatory bodies, advises on financial administration, technology and marketing and so on.

Bahana's total assets at the end of 1980 were around Rp7 billion.[21] Other than shareholders' funds, it appears funded solely by refinancing its loans with Bank Indonesia – presumably under the same conditions as those which apply at the banks. By the beginning of 1982, the company was financing some 36 projects, 20 of which were in Java. Of total funds provided to clients, about 80 per cent were in loans and the remainder in equity participation.

Loans generally fall between Rp30 million–Rp200 million, corresponding respectively to the top of the KIK/KMKP and the bottom of the Category III range for Kredit Investasi. The limit on equity funding was Rp150 million per firm, so that the maximum loan/equity finance package was Rp350 million. By early 1982, further expansion had been hampered by lack of additional funding, and an application had been made for a doubling of paid-up capital to Rp5 billion to overcome this difficulty.

Though not a DFC in the normal sense, the PT Papan Sejahtera or National Housing Finance Company (NHFC) is often included with the three other DFCs for government administrative purposes. The NHFC was established in April 1980 in conjunction with the World Bank's Group to assist Indonesians to obtain their housing requirements. A number of local insurance companies and Bank Indonesia are also major shareholders. A listing of these, and their relative holdings, is shown in Table 2.13.

(ii) *Investment Finance Corporations (IFCs)*

Indonesia's IFCs (or merchant banks) are governed by the same decrees as the DFCs, although the distinction between the two institutions was made only by subsequent amendments and additions. In framing the decrees, the government clearly intended the IFCs to tap both foreign capital and financial expertise. Although the decrees permit IFCs to be wholly Indonesian owned, this was seemingly intended to accommodate the prior existence of PT Indonesian Financing and Investment Company (IFI), as no other purely Indonesian IFCs have been permitted.

TABLE 2.13   National Housing Finance Co. list of shareholders and relative holdings, 1981

Shareholder	(%)
Bank Indonesia	15.0
PT PDFCI	15.0
PT Asuransi Pensiun Bumiputra 1974	12.5
PT Asuransi Jiwasraya	12.5
PT Asuransi Jasa Indonesia	5.0
PT Ree Seidendhie	5.0
Dewan Ekonomi Veteran Indonesia	2.5
Dewan Ekonomi Islam Indonesia	2.5
International Finance Corporation	15.0
Friesch Groningsche Hypotheek Bank	15.0

Source: Michael T. Skully, *Merchant banking in ASEAN: A Regional Examination of its Development and Operations* (Kuala Lumpur: Oxford University Press, 1982) p. 107.

Joint venture IFCs required at least three foreign partners – each from a different country. From the outset, at least 50 per cent of executive staff below board level had to be Indonesian nationals; all administrative staff had to be Indonesian, and staff were expected to be given special training overseas. Within 10 years of commencing operations, 51 per cent of the voting stock of each IFC had to be held by Indonesian individuals or organisations.

IFCs which are fully Indonesian owned must have paid-up capital of Rp150 million and a credit line of Rp350 million, while joint ventures require respectively Rp300 million and Rp200 million. In terms of operational regulations, the IFCs' gearing ratio of total plus contingent liabilities: shareholders' funds and subordinated loans may not exceed 15:1. Subordinated loans may not exceed three times paid-up capital and earned surplus. It should be noted, however, that the IFCs are not subject to loan ceilings (in contrast with the banks), nor are they restricted to operating in Jakarta (which is the case with the foreign banks).

With the exception of IFI[22], all the IFCs were established during 1973–4 (details of shareholders are shown in Table 2.14). Other than IFI (a subsidiary of the largest private life insurance company), all IFCs have Indonesian banks or companies closely associated with such banks as their local partners. The Central Bank is the major shareholder in the largest IFC, Ficorinvest (Bapindo also has a minor holding in this company). Each of the five State commercial banks has an associated IFC, as do the two largest private banks – Bank Central Asia and Pan Indonesia Bank. The smallest IFC (MIFC) is indirectly associated with a smaller private bank – Sejahtera Bank Umum.

Based on total assets, the smallest IFC is MIFC (with Rp13.5 billion in assets at the end of 1980) and the largest Ficorinvest (Rp69.1 billion). The latter company plus the five firms in the State bank group account for 78 per cent of total industry assets (Table 2.15). IFCs with local private sector partners are placed towards the small end of the spectrum, although there is some overlap with the smallest members of the State bank group.

Officially, their principal function is to act as an intermediary in issuing and underwriting business; in reality, this is a minor part of their activities since there have been few issues to date. The IFCs' main income is from financing the working capital requirements of joint venture firms and the largest and most reputable Indonesian companies.[23] This is usually effected by the purchase of promissory notes (typically of 1 month maturity) issued by the firms concerned. In turn, the IFCs generally raise the required funds in the money market by the issue of their own notes.

The composition of the IFCs' assets is shown in Table 2.9; these institutions are not permitted to accept deposits nor to provide loans. The State banks apparently feared competition with the new non-bank institutions, and these prohibitions were to placate them. In practice, of course, similar intermediation activities are carried out, but using different terminology. One of the IFCs – Aseam – has not been deterred from calling a loan a loan, however, and such assets make up a large part (58 per cent) of its portfolio. MIFC makes a distinction between commercial and bank securities on the one hand, and 'investments' on the other: it has been assumed that 'investments' means 'loans' for the purpose of constructing Table 2.9.

With these two exceptions, it can be seen that debt securities (predominantly promissory notes) account for by far the larger part of IFCs' assets: the range varies from 91.5–96.0 per cent. Even with Aseam and MIFC included, debt securities amount to 84 per cent of total industry assets; loans held by Aseam and MIFC account for a further 10 per cent. The remaining asset categories are necessarily very small. Equities are of very little significance relative to debt securities, comprising only 1.1 per cent. This is a clear reflection of the embryonic state of the Jakarta

TABLE 2.14   Indonesia Investment Finance Corporations' list of shareholders and relative holdings (figures as of 30 June 1982)

IFC and Shareholders	(%)
1. PT First Indonesian Finance and Investment Corpn (Ficorinvest)	
(a) Bank Indonesia	69.45
(b) Bancom International Ltd*a*	25.00
(c) PT Bina Usaha Indonesia	5.55
	100.00
2. PT Finconesia	
(a) Bank Negara Indonesia 1946	51.0
(b) The Nomura Securities Co. Ltd	12.0
(c) Barclays Bank International Ltd	9.0
(d) Manufacturers Hanover Holding (Delaware) Inc.	9.0
(e) The Mitsui Bank Ltd	9.0
(f) Banque Française du Commerce Exterieur	5.0
(g) Commerzbank AG	5.0
	100.0
3. PT Indonesian Investments International (Indovest)	
(a) Bank Dagang Negara	42.3
(b) First Chicago International Finance Corpn	26.9
(c) The Mitsubishi Bank Ltd	15.4
(d) The National Australia Bank	7.7
(e) The Nikko Securities Co. Ltd	7.7
	100.0
4. PT Multinational Finance Corpn (Multicor)	
(a) Bank Central Asia	27.50
(b) Chemical Bank International	23.75
(c) The Long-term Credit Bank of Japan Ltd	23.75
(d) The Royal Bank of Scotland	15.00
(e) Jardine Fleming & Co. Ltd	10.00
	100.00

a The shares owned by Bancom International Ltd are being transferred to Bank Indonesia (Ficorinvest *Annual Report 1981*).

Stock Exchange: a large part of the industry's equity holdings are in fact in unlisted companies.

Turning to sources of funds, IFC promissory notes dominate, accounting for 78 per cent of total industry liabilities. Other short and long term borrowing accounts for a further 12 per cent, but

TABLE 2.14   *(contd.)*

IFC and Shareholders	(%)
5. PT Merchant Investment Corpn (Merincorp)	
(a) Bank Ekspor–Impor Indonesia	38.0
(b) Morgan Guaranty International Finance Corpn	24.8
(c) The Sumitomo Bank Ltd	23.4
(d) Mees & Hope Finanzgesellschaft AG	13.8
	100.0
6. PT Indonesian Financing and Investment Co. (IFI)	
(a) PT Ustraindo	61.7
(b) Asuransi Jiwa Bersama Bumi Putera 1912	38.3
	100.0
7. PT Aseam Indonesia	
(a) Bank Bumi Daya	50.0
(b) Banque de Paris et des Pays-Bas	10.0
(c) The Dai–Ichi Kangyo Bank Ltd	10.0
(d) Dresdner Bank AG	10.0
(e) Kleinwort, Benson Ltd	10.0
(f) Union Bank of Switzerland	10.0
	100.0
8. PT Inter-Pacific Financial Corpn (Inter-Pacific)	
(a) Bank Rakyat Indonesia	65.4
(b) The Sanwa Bank Ltd	29.1
(c) Credit Commercial de France SA	5.5
	100.0
9. PT Mutual International Finance Corpn (MIFC)	
(a) PT Mutual Promotion Corpn Ltd	34.5
(b) Fuji Bank (Schweiz) AG	20.0
(c) Crocker International Investment Corpn	17.0
(d) Westpac Banking Corpn	15.0
(e) PT Pan Indonesia Bank Ltd	7.5
(f) The Fuji Bank Ltd	6.0
	100.0

Source: PT Finconesia, 1982.

here there is considerable variation across firms. Ficorinvest and IFI report no such borrowing, whereas at Aseam, Finconesia and Indovest, they account for about a fifth to a quarter of liabilities.[24]

Table 2.15 Indonesia Investment Finance Corporations' assets and liabilities (figures as at end 1980, in Rp billion)

	Ficoinvest	Aseam	Finconesia	Indovest	Merincorp	Inter-Pacific	Multicor	IFI	MIFC	Total	(%)
Assets											
Debt securities	66007	20452	38798	34627	30246	20726	30698	21898	9962	273414	84.4[a]
Banks/Financial institutions	(1236)	(2249)	(4193)	(28902)	N/A	N/A	N/A	N/A	(2035)		
Commercial	(64771)	(18203)	(34605)	(5725)	N/A	N/A	N/A	N/A	(7927)		
% of total assets	(93.8)	(38.2)	(95.2)	(96.0)	(94.0)	(92.4)	(94.9)	(91.5)	(73.6)		
Loans	—	30885	—	—	—	—	—	—	2924	33809	10.4
Short term	—	(13670)	—	—	—	—	—	—	(2077)		
Medium term	—	(17215)	—	—	—	—	—	—	(847)		
Equities	12	787	782	324	89	771	713	98	—	3576	1.1
Marketable (listed)	(12)	(52)	(2)	N/A	(89)	N/A	(83)	(63)	—		
Investments (unlisted)	(—)	(735)	(780)	N/A	(—)	N/A	(630)	(35)	—		
Fixed assets	79	45	61	194	164	47	57	522	54	1223	0.4
Other assets	2955	1321	1131	911	1663	891	892	1424	591	11779	3.6
Total assets	69054	53492	40772	36056	32161	22436	32360	23943	13532	323806	100.0
Share of industry total (%)	21.3	16.5	12.6	11.1	9.9	6.9	10.0	7.4	4.2	100.0	

[a] Excluding Aseam and MIFC: 94.6 per cent.

TABLE 2.15 (contd.)

Liabilities	Ficoinvest	Aseam	Finconesia	Indovest	Merincorp	Inter-Pacific	Multicor	IFI	MIFC	Total	(%)
Notes/securities issued	61661	36770	27697	26380	27909	19398	21827	21298	8832	251772	77.8
Long term borrowing	—		780				7213	—	—	37722	11.6
Short term borrowing	—	12477	8351	5255	895	376	—	—	2375		
Subordinated loans	1083	2127	1143	1791	1002	449	1137	130	625	9487	2.9
Shareholders' funds	4392	1196	2178	1950	1714	1428	1488	1721	886	16953	5.2
Other liabilities	1918	923	619	681	642	786	696	794	815	7874	2.4
Total liabilities	69054	53492	40772	36056	32161	22436	32360	23943	13532	323808	100.0

Source: respective annual reports, 1980.

One item of particular interest is subordinated loans. These are special loans from the shareholders over which other loans take precedence. If the IFCs' losses accumulate to 75 per cent of paid-up capital, these loans are automatically converted to equity. The two items combined contribute about 8 per cent of industry liabilities.

Although equity financing by IFCs has been of little significance as yet, increasing numbers of firms have gone public, and the process is likely to continue, probably at an increasing pace. It has not been uncommon for all IFCs to be jointly involved with the public offerings made so far – if not as lead manager, then perhaps as one of several underwriters or sub-underwriters to each issue. In this way they acquire useful experience and help to bring their name to public attention.

Another kind of equity participation involves joint venture companies where foreign firms desire to operate in Indonesia but are not yet ready for a permanent local partner. In this context, IFCs are regarded as Indonesian companies, and are permitted a stake of up to 25 per cent of paid-up capital of the companies concerned, for a period not normally exceeding 5 years. During this time, the foreign partner obtains a deeper understanding of local business conditions, and can search for a suitable Indonesian partner or arrange for a Stock Exchange listing. The IFCs may also participate in domestic firms, and thus can be used to avoid the prohibition on foreigners owning shares in such firms (by way of trusteeships or portfolio management arrangements); of course, there is no readily available information on this matter.

Another activity of importance is loan syndication. IFCs faced with a very large borrowing requirement from a particular firm may prefer to fulfil a certain proportion themselves, then turn to their shareholders and other institutions. In its 1980 report, Ficorinvest mentions total syndicated loans of Rp41 billion (of which it retained Rp12 billion)[25] while Multicor noted syndications amounting to more than Rp16 billion.[26] Little additional information on syndications is available, but most IFCs advertise this as one of their services.

Besides the IFCs' money market activities, lending, equity participation and loan syndications, they also earn significant income in the form of fees and commissions for the provision of various financial services including underwriting; brokerage; furnishing guarantees; client advice on mergers, acquisitions and issues and so on. For five of the seven firms for which this information is available, the proportion exceeds 30 per cent, so it is clear that these activities are of considerable significance.

(iii) *The insurance industry*

Despite Indonesia's large population, it ranked only 38th in world national premium volume in 1979.[27] On another measure – premiums as percentage of gross national product – it ranked 45th, and on the measure premiums per head of population, 48th. Although Indonesia ranks well behind its ASEAN partners (see Table 2.16) on these latter measures, it is still nevertheless ahead of Singapore and Thailand in turnover, and should rival Malaysia and the Philippines by the mid-1980s.

TABLE 2.16   Insurance in ASEAN: regional comparisons (figures in US$ million)

	Total premiums	*Premiums: GNP (%)*	*Premiums per head*
Indonesia	265	0.57	1.8
Malaysia	478	2.47	35.9
Philippines	445	1.49	9.6
Singapore	248	2.74	105.1
Thailand	240	0.88	5.2

Source: *Sigma*, no. 5 (May 1981).

The insurance industry's backward state can largely be traced to its operating environment under the Old Order government.[28] In the early years of independence, there were no locally incorporated and financed insurance companies; by mid-1955, there were 20, in competition with 115 foreign (especially Dutch) firms. During the next decade, however, foreign companies either discontinued their operations or were nationalised. Political uncertainty and inflation also had their effect, and life insurance soon became impractical and therefore unprofitable. By 1967, only 89 companies remained: five were state owned, and of the private firms only three were foreign companies.

With the emergence of the New Order government inflation and political instability subsided and the government's attitude toward the insurance industry became more positive. Foreign companies, which had previously served their multinational clients through local agency arrangements, began to establish a more tangible presence. Several foreign insurers established branch offices, but the government's preference has clearly been for joint ventures. By 1980, only one foreign insurer remained; the others had set up Indonesian joint venture companies with local partners.

The number of firms in each sector of the industry at the end of 1979, classified by ownership, is shown in Table 2.17. The only foreign company still operating was in the non-life (general) insurance sector, and seemed likely to follow the general trend by seeking a joint venture partner; in the subsequent discussion, it will be treated as a joint venture firm. There were also three representative offices of foreign non-life firms, two of which were also partners in joint ventures. Foreign presence until mid-1982 was restricted solely to the non-life sector. Although there was only one wholly State owned non-life company, the State also had an interest in at least one national private firm and two joint ventures.

TABLE 2.17   Indonesia insurance firms by sector and ownership (figures as at end 1979)

	Life	Non-life	Reinsurance	Social
State	1	1	2	5
National private	11	42	1	—
Joint venture	—	11[a]	—	—
Foreign	—	1[b]	—	—
Total	12	55	3	5

[a]   Two joint venture companies have a State owned company as the local partner.
[b]   There were also three representative offices of foreign firms, two of which were also partners in joint venture companies.

Source: Ministry of Finance, 1982.

The absolute and relative importance of these firms and sectors is shown in Table 2.18. The most important sector 'social insurance' has the least information available. It comprises five State owned bodies, but there is no data available for two of them – Astek or Askes. Astek is involved mainly with workers' compensation insurance, and Askes with health insurance. Since both activities are still in their infancy, it will be assumed in the following discussion that these are of negligible quantitative significance.

TABLE 2.18   Indonesia total insurance industry assets by sector and ownership
(figures as at end 1979 in Rp billion)

	Assets	% of Sector assets	% of Industry assets
Life	79.5	100.0	22.0
State (Jiwasraya)	30.7	38.6	
National Private	48.8	61.4	
Bumiputera 1912	(37.7)	(47.4)	
Others (10)	(11.0)	(13.8)	
Non-life	98.0	100.0	27.1
State (Jasa Indonesia)	46.1	47.0	
National Private	31.1	31.7	
Indrapura	(3.1)	(3.2)	
Others (40)	(28.0)	(28.6)	
Joint ventures	20.9	21.3	
Jayasraya	(5.7)	(5.8)	
Insindo Taisho	(3.1)	(3.2)	
Others (10)	(12.0)	(12.3)	
Reinsurance	47.4	100.0	13.1
State			
Umum Re	26.4	55.7	
Askrindo	20.4	43.0	
Private (Marein)	0.6	1.3	
Social	136.8	100.0	37.8
Taspen	108.0	78.9	
Asabri	19.8	14.5	
Jasa Raharja	9.0	6.6	
Industry total	361.7		100.0

Source: Ministry of Finance, 1982.

It can be seen from Table 2.18 that the social insurance sector accounts for about 38 per cent of the industry, or Rp137 billion. This sector is dominated by Taspen (the State Corporation for Civil Servants' Savings and Insurance) with assets of Rp108 billion. All Indonesian civil servants contribute to this superannuation fund through compulsory deductions from their wages and salaries; there were about 1.9 million participants at the end of 1979.

The two other members of this sector for which data are available are Asabri and Jasa Raharja. Asabri is similar to Taspen, but is for military personnel rather than civil servants. Jasa Raharja operates both a road accident and a passenger accident fund (for passengers in motor vehicles, trains, ships and aeroplanes), and also obtains income from guaranteeing bonds related to bids; performance; supply; advance payments; customs and excise duties and the like. As with Taspen and Asabri, most of its premium income is from compulsory contributions. Asabri accounts for 14.5 per cent of sector assets, and Jasa Raharja 6.6 per cent.

The next most important sector is non-life insurance with about 27 per cent of total assets, or Rp98 billion. It is dominated by a single State owned firm, Jasa Indonesia, with Rp46 billion in assets – no less than 47 per cent of the sector.[29] Of the remainder, 32 per cent is held by the national private companies, and 21 per cent by joint venture firms. Within these two groups there are large numbers of firms of roughly similar size, with the two government affiliated joint venture firms ranking first and second amongst the so called private sector firms.

The largest truly private firm (Indrapura) has assets of only Rp3.1 billion. Several other local joint venture partners still operate separately on their own account – presumably servicing different sections of the market. Not all national private firms are completely independent, as many have extensive interlocking directorships.[30] Thus, the small size of many insurers, and the government's apparent preference for a relatively small number of competitors in regulated industries, suggests that mergers or takeovers may become relatively common within the near future.

It can be seen that the life sector is somewhat smaller than the non-life business, and again the sole State owned company plays a very important role. In this case, however, one private sector firm is even larger. Bumiputera 1912 has 46.2 per cent of the sector's total assets, while Jiwasraya – the State owned firm – has 38.9 per cent. The remaining firms are quite small; their names and relative importance are shown in Table 2.19.

Indonesia's local reinsurance industry was once operated as a state monopoly. As Emery commented, Umum Re (the Indonesian General Reinsurance Company) 'had a monopoly on reinsurance [in 1967] as a result of special government regulation'.[31] Although there is now one private reinsurance firm, it is tiny by comparison with Umum Re: the two firms have respectively Rp26.4 billion and Rp0.6 billion in total assets. Nevertheless, Umum Re now also has another State owned firm as a competitor – Askrindo (the Indonesian Loan Insurance Company). It was established in 1971, mainly to insure banks

TABLE 2.19   Indonesia life companies by total assets (figures as at 31 December 1980, in thousand Rp)

% of total	Firm	Amount
1.5	PT Asuransi Jiwa Buana Putra	1507671
3.5	PT Asuransi Jiwa Bumi Asih Jaya	3653007
46.2	AJB Bumiputera 1912	48186755
1.7	PT Asuransi Pensiun Bumiputera 1974	1810762
0.4	PT Asuransi Jiwa Central Asia Raya	403898
0.6	PT Asuransi Jiwa Ikrar Abadi	654212
0.2	PT Asuransi Jiwa Iman Adi	186032
0.5	PT Pertanggungan Jiwa Jaminan	469264
38.9	PT Asuransi Jiwasraya	40571479
0.3	PT Asuransi Jiwa Mahkota Jaya Abadi	359460
3.5	PT Asuransi Jiwa Panin Putra	3696159
2.1	PT Asuransi Jiwa Pura Nusantara	2225057
0.6	Koperasi Assuransji Indonesia	604848
100.0	Total	104328604

Source: Bumiputera 1912 Mutual Life Co., 1982.

against default risks on loans to small and medium sized firms, and a very large part of its operations is in insuring KIK/KMKP loans to small pribumi firms.[32] Total assets of Askrindo stood at Rp20 billion at the end of 1979 – 43 per cent of the reinsurance sector. Askrindo is now also very much involved in general reinsurance. It is widely believed to lose consistently on KIK/KMKP business, but to survive by virtue of income from reinsurance activities and investments (mainly in time deposits).

It is thus evident that Indonesia's insurance industry is dominated by a number of large firms – most of which are State owned. The nine largest companies comprise some 84 per cent of the industry's total assets. Of these firms, only the life company Bumiputera 1912 is completely private owned. One other, a joint venture company, has a State owned firm as its local partner, and the seven remaining institutions all have direct state ownership. Together, these seven account for 72 per cent of industry assets and dominate all but the life insurance sector.

The insurance industry has grown rapidly since 1975, with total industry assets increasing at a real rate of around 17.1 per cent per annum during 1975–9. Although all sectors indicated positive real growth, there was considerable variation. The non-life and reinsurance sectors grew respectively at 6.6 and 7.6 per cent in real terms – a little slower than the economy as a whole. At the other extreme, the social insurance sector companies Taspen and Jasa Raharja grew very rapidly indeed – respectively 33.3 and 32.2 per cent per annum. The third company in this sector for which data are available – Asabri – increased its total assets in real terms at the rate of 19.5 per cent during the period, while the life sector somewhat exceeded this, growing at 23.5 per cent.

In regard to the assets held by insurers, little information is available. It appears that by far the largest part comprises demand and time deposits as well as short term money market assets, but it is not possible to be more precise. Long term debt (greater than 1-year) and equities are clearly of little importance. The sole exception is Asabri, which – astonishingly – increased its holdings of shares from zero in 1978 to some Rp7.6 billion in 1979; no further details are available. Another matter of interest is that joint venture companies are not permitted to own shares in Indonesian firms; this is somewhat paradoxical, given the government attempts to promote the development of an active Stock Market and the very limited availability of other kinds of assets for investment. The rationale is apparently that Indonesia does not want foreigners to own local firms and as joint venture companies are part foreign owned, their purchase of shares would indirectly increase the overall level of foreign ownership within the country.

The industry as a whole has been otherwise relatively free of government regulation. So far, in contrast with many other countries, Indonesia has not set any official solvency standards or other ratio controls; new firms are still permitted (both domestic and joint ventures) with the approval of the Department of Finance. They are required to have paid up capital of at least Rp1½ billion, of which 20 per cent must be deposited at Bank Indonesia (these statutory deposits attract interest, but at a fairly low rate). The paid-up capital requirement is much less stringent for existing firms, which must increase their paid-up capital to at least Rp½ billion by the end of 1985 (if they have not already done so). It seems doubtful whether many will achieve this, as many (national private) firms are barely solvent at present. If so, it seems likely the government will push for mergers or takeovers, as it has done in the banking sector.

One area which the government has recently begun to regulate concerns the tariffs of the non-life sector. As in other countries, the insurers have set a common tariff (a schedule of rates for different kinds of risk), so as to eliminate or reduce price competition amongst themselves. Competition between firms then centres on better service to customers. As with all cartels (whatever their objective), the problem is enforcement of the common pricing agreement; in the insurance industry, this is usually undertaken by industry associations, with varying degrees of success. In Indonesia, however, the government itself has begun to take on the enforcement role, using its power to revoke operating licences as a threat to firms not upholding the tariff. So far, this control is restricted to fire insurance only, but it would not be surprising for it to extend into other areas such as marine and hull insurance tariffs.

One problem with expanding its regulatory involvement in the insurance industry is the relative lack of insurance expertise within both the Department of Finance and within the industry. Until fairly recently, this has meant that insurance firms have been relatively free of controls, but this situation has already begun to change. New legislation for the industry is presently being drafted – probably similar to that in Malaysia and Singapore (there a good deal of interaction between the ASEAN countries in this field). There can be little doubt that, with this legislation, the industry will find itself subject to much more stringent requirements, particularly in relation to solvency standards.

(iv) *Leasing companies*

Like the investment finance corporations, leasing companies in Indonesia were selected as an area where joint ventures were permitted with foreign firms. They are regulated by the Ministry of Finance under the Leasing Operations Licence(s) Decree issued on 7 February 1974. Five firms were eventually licensed and commenced operations in 1975–6; two were joint ventures with foreign firms.

Leasing, however, never became an important source of financing, and prior to 1980 little business was written. In 1980–1, however, this position began to change as the Ministry of Finance sought to expand leasing as an alternative source for capital equipment finance and began accepting new joint venture applications. Such firms must have a minimum paid-up capital of Rp3 billion, and local companies Rp1 billion: they are both then subject to a 33:1 liabilities to capital ratio in their operations.

Besides direct access to an otherwise closed market, the leasing companies have advantages over both foreign bank branches and IFCs; leasing companies may establish branches and conduct business with companies outside the Jakarta area, and, as yet, their lease activity is also independent of Bank Indonesia credit ceilings.

The lease contracts may be written in US dollars or rupiah, depending on the currency of the leasee's income. These leases are funded by the leasor both locally and offshore, depending on the contract. As the leasing companies cannot accept deposits, their main source of outside rupiah funding has been from the local NBFIs and some of the non-state commercial banks. The foreign monies, primarily US dollars, are borrowed from the international banks in the offshore capital markets, often from (or through) their foreign parents.

The leasing companies, like the insurance industry, are regulated by the Directorate of Financial Institutions under the Director General of Monetary Affairs. There is indeed some similarity in these two institutions' development, for both have been relatively dormant for many years and have only recently begun to expand. Their resurgence has been spearheaded in both cases by joint venture companies, bringing foreign expertise and capital, and exploiting the domestic partners' local knowledge and business/political ties. In both cases, new regulations are being developed to cater to this new expansion.

As of July 1982, there were 13 leasing companies established. Many more firms have also filed applications with the Ministry of Finance and further approvals should result. A listing of the currently licensed firms, as well as some joint ventures known to be seeking approval, is shown in Table 2.20.

TABLE 2.20 Indonesia leasing companies by establishment date and shareholders, 1982

Company	Establishment date	Shareholders[a]
PT Pengembangan Armada Niaga Nasional (PT Pann)	15 Jan. 75	Indonesian Government Bapindo
PT Indonesia Lease Corpn (PT Indo Lease)	1 May 75	F. G. Leimena R. M. Kusmulyono A. Syahbudin B. M. A. Pardede

TABLE 2.20 (*contd.*)

Company	Establishment date	Shareholders[a]
PT Orient Bina Usaha Leasing (PT Obul)	30 Aug. 75	PT Bina Usaha Indonesia Orient Lease Co. Ltd
(PT Nusa Lease Corpn (PT Nusa Lease)	29 Jan. 76	J. A. Sumendap Ny. E. Sumendap R. Sumendap J. Sumendap
PT Perjahl Leasing Indonesia	19 Mar. 76	Pertamina Japan Overseas Leasing Co.
PT Indo American Leasing (PT IAL)	24 Aug. 81	PT Inter Pionir Nasional Bank America
PT Indo Ayala Leasing Corpn (PT ISPLC)	24 Aug. 81	Ayala Finance
PT Central Sari Metropolitan Leasing Corpn (CSML)	17 Sep. 81	PT Bank Central Asia Japan Lease Corpn
PT Wardley-Summa Leasing	Nov. 1981	Wardley Ltd PT United Tractors Summa
PT Clipan Leasing	Nov. 1982	Credit Lyonnais France Pan Indonesian Bank
PT Jakarta Tokyo Lease	Nov. 1982	Lim Sin Seng
PT Batu Mas Murni Leasing Corpn	N/A	
PT Bangkok Bank Lease Corpn	N/A	Bangkok Bank
PT Oey and Lim	N/A	N/A
PT Bumiputera-B of T Lease Co.[b]	N/A	PT Asuransi Bumiputera Bank of Tokyo
PT Citicorp Leasing Indonesia	N/A	Citibank PT Sumber Daya-Keluarga
PT Saseka Gelova Leasing	N/A	Lloyds Bank International Finance Corpn Ficorinvest Bank Niaga
PT Chemco Graha Sejahtera leasing	N/A	Chemco Leasing

[a] Where available, major shareholders have been shown. Note that all foreign affiliated companies have local shareholders, even if not listed.
[b] Licensed firms as of July 1982.

Source: Table 2.20 has been compiled from a variety of sources which are believed to be accurate.

(v) *Other Non-bank finance*

Government pawnshop service. The government has a legal monopoly on pawnbroking operations, and owns about 460 pawnshops[33]: illegal private pawnbrokers also exist, but of course there are no available data concerning their operations. Total funds outstanding at the end of 1981 amounted to Rp42 billion, which suggests that the pawnshop service is much more important than the market banks, despite having far fewer offices.

Little information on the pawnshop service is available other than that in Table 2.21, but it appears that the government has been reluctant to provide it with much additional funding. Lending has been held at the relatively low rate of 4 per cent per month. Nevertheless, its growth has been impressive since 1975, with loans outstanding increasing at an average rate around 32 per cent per annum during 1976–81, well in excess of the average inflation rate. The pawn redemption rate is said to be as high as 99 per cent, and unredeemed pawns are auctioned without delay. In this respect, at least, the pawnshop service is more effective in providing the poor with access to institutional credit than some of the programmes administered by State banks. These programmes are plagued by bad debt problems, which are exacerbated by the extreme difficulties faced in liquidating assets pledged as security.[34] This process is so time consuming and costly that it is undertaken with great reluctance. The banks are forced to respond by being much more selective when deciding upon loan applications than the pawnshop service. On the other hand, however, lending activities which require physical assets to be kept in the possession of the lender are not feasible except for very small loans.

TABLE 2.21   Indonesia pawnshop activity (figures in Rp billion)

Particulars	1975	76	77	78	79	80	81
No. of offices[a]	441	441	441	446	448	450	463
Total loans extended	31	38	46	59	90	110	156
Redemption	29	35	44	56	83	103	144
Loans outstanding	8	11	13	16	23	30	42

[a] In units.

Source: Pawnshop Service, 1982.

Private moneylenders. It is illegal to be in the business of moneylending in Indonesia without a licence. Such licences are issued only to the banks and non-bank institutions already discussed. Nevertheless, it would appear that many private moneylenders operate illegally. For the most part, they lend very small sums to individuals, mainly to finance consumption expenditures. There is considerable demand for such loans – even though the interest rates are relatively high – presumably because in other respects they are very attractive: lenders usually visit borrowers (rather than the reverse); documentation is almost non-existent; collateral not insisted on; and repayments easily rescheduled if necessary. Sometimes loans are made in kind – in the form of consumer goods – thus saving the borrower the time and money cost otherwise incurred in actually expending the loan.[35] It is difficult to say much more than this, however, owing to the lack of relevant published data or research.

There is also a great deal of informal financing of business activity, but it is doubtful that much of it is done by specialised moneylenders. It is more useful to imagine business persons ranged along a continuum: at one extreme, some conduct a large volume of lending alongside their other business interests; at the other, no lending is undertaken. Particular individuals are sometimes lenders but at other times borrowers, since it is common for businessmen to borrow and lend amongst their circle of family and friends according to their current need for (or surplus of) funds. At least some lending in the informal market uses 'hot money' – money obtained illegally (a product of tax avoidance) or borrowed at subsidised rates from the State banks, ostensibly for other (approved) purposes.[36]

Rotating credit groups. Like the private moneylenders, the rotating credit groups or arisan are an important part of Indonesia's informal financial sector. Typically an arisan consists of about 10 individuals who meet at regular intervals (usually weekly or monthly) and contribute a fixed sum of money to the fund. This fund is then distributed to one of the members at that meeting. Arisan exist at all levels of the community, from the richest to the poorest. Their popularity is due to a number of factors. First (and probably most important) is their social function of bringing the members together at regular intervals: the group often consists of housewives, and normally meets at the house of the organiser. Second there is a gambling element involved. Although the member foregoes interest by saving through an arisan, the fund's recipient at each meeting is often determined by lot; those lucky enough to receive their payout at an early meeting effectively borrow from the others at no interest cost. As a rule, these social arisans cease after one full round of contribution and payout has been completed.

In some arisan, however, no meetings are held and the payouts are made in a predetermined sequence. In these cases, the arisan is an ongoing arrangement and an agent is appointed to collect the members' contributions and make the payouts. Presumably the participants perceive some benefit from the discipline and convenience this form of savings provides.

The arisan are certainly widespread within Indonesia, but their very nature makes it impossible to determine their overall monetary importance. They do, however, appear to act more in the nature of social clubs than true financial institutions.

FINANCIAL MARKETS

(a) The Money Market

A highly developed formal money market presupposes the availability of very high quality negotiable debt instruments. This condition is not met in Indonesia, largely due to the government's unwillingness to borrow from the public (or to allow State enterprises to do so). To the extent that revenue has been insufficient to cover cash outflow, it has instead preferred to borrow from the central bank. There are many instances of the government wanting to subsidise or finance certain activities, in which it has relied on Bank Indonesia to supply the funds rather than making a budgetary allocation.[37] The market is thus denied the largest single potential source of high quality paper. In addition, the number of large private companies widely regarded as a sound credit risk is very small.

For these reasons, the most active part of the formal money market is the interbank market – which should be taken to include the IFCs and DFCs, with their strong local and foreign banking affiliations. The market for commercial paper, on the other hand, is extremely limited. The very top companies (or those with particularly close ties to certain banks) are able to call on the financial institutions for additional short term funds when needed, but even so there is very little secondary trading in the paper. Such trading as does occur is largely confined to re-purchases by the issuer.

The major net lenders to the money market are the State commercial banks, RDBs, larger insurance companies and pension funds, Bapindo and DFCs. The major net borrowers are the private FE banks and a few of the more reputable non-FE banks. The IFCs perform an intermediation role, raising funds by the issue of promissory notes and using these funds to purchase promissory notes issued by other institutions and the corporate sector. It is interesting to note that despite its 'development' role, PDFCI is heavily involved in this same intermediation activity; 42 per cent of its total assets comprised short term instruments (at the end of 1980), about three-quarters of which were financed by the issue of its own short term debt.

Bank Indonesia provides something like a lender of last resort facility for the IFCs which enables them to rediscount promissory notes. The importance of this facility is probably in fact not great, as several IFCs have arranged formal standby credit facilities with their foreign shareholders, and there are almost certainly similar informal arrangements at the others. For Ficorinvest, in which Bank Indonesia itself holds nearly 70 per cent of the shares, the rediscount facility is presumably of no practical significance. The five IFCs with State bank local partners – which themselves have access to emergency liquidity credits at the central bank – can probably rely on those partners for unexpected short term funding requirements.

If rupiah funds are especially scarce, the IFCs are also able to utilise a currency swap facility at the Central Bank. Dollars are first borrowed offshore, then sold to Bank Indonesia with a guarantee of repurchase at the same price after a stated interval – usually 1, 3 or 6 months. Each IFC is limited in the extent to which it can draw on this facility: a typical ceiling seems to be $US20 million. Bank Indonesia's charge for assuming the exchange rate fluctution risk is around $2\frac{1}{4}$ per cent per annum. This, together with a 10 per cent withholding tax on interest paid overseas, makes such funds quite costly to the ultimate borrower, since the total cost to the IFC itself would be about 4 points over the Singapore Interbank Offered Rate (SIBOR).

Although the formal money market is as yet very limited in scope, there is nevertheless an active informal intercompany and interpersonal market serving the needs of medium and small scale enterprises – which of course represent the major share of economic activity in Indonesia. Trade credit, for example, constitutes intercompany lending – albeit only between firms which have an established trading relationship. Businessmen who are temporarily short of funds commonly borrow from acquaintances for short periods – often by issuing post-dated cheques. Equity funds are often made available to enterprises by family and friends of their owners.

(b) The Stock Exchange and the National Investment Trust

The Stock Exchange Building in central Jakarta epitomises the stock market in Indonesia. Opened in 1981, it is a modern and impressive edifice but almost entirely devoid of activity. The boards, desks and telephones are all in place on the spacious trading floor, but the buyers and sellers are conspicuous by their absence.

In the colonial era, there was an active stock market serving Dutch businesses and individuals. Because of the Japanese occupation and the independence struggle it was closed during 1942–52, and although reopened during 1952–8, the progressive nationalisation of Dutch firms and the departure of Dutch nationals meant that it became nearly dormant in the latter years. As the result of the Suharto government's efforts, however, the Jakarta Stock Exchange (JSE) again commenced operations on 10 August 1977.

This second reopening followed a Presidential Decree in December 1976, which provided for the establishment of a 'Capital Market Development Council' to advise the government regarding the stock market; a 'Capital Market Executive Agency' (Bapepam) for controlling and running the market in conformity with government policy, and for evaluating companies wanting to go public; a National Investment Trust (PT Danareksa) to purchase shares on the JSE for resale in small lots to the public; and various kinds of tax relief to companies obtaining JSE listing and to the purchasers of shares in such companies.

Listings have been slowly achieved. The reopening of the JSE coincided with the first such listing – PT Semen Cibinong, a joint venture cement manufacturer in which the government was the local partner. Plans were well advanced for other firms to go public late in 1978 or early the following year, but the large devaluation of the rupiah threw these plans awry: it was not until May 1979 that the next listing was made. Details of other listings are provided in Table 2.22. The biggest so far has been that of Unilever Indonesia; the value of this issue was Rp29.2 billion. No debenture issues have been made as of mid–1982. Various factors have contributed to the slow progress of the JSE. In respect of domestic companies, there is usually a strong desire to avoid the dilution of ownership that results from a public issue – all the listings to date have been foreign or joint venture firms. Second, although there is an official requirement for at least 50 per cent of joint venture companies to be in Indonesian hands by 1985, this does not imply that such companies are forced to seek listings. 'Indonesianisation' can also be met by private placements, the existing local partner expanding its holding, or the foreign partner converting part of its equity to loans. Third, many companies are encouraged to rely on State bank finance rather than equity funding, because of the low interest rates. Fourth, finance is also available from other sources (such as the IFCs and DFCs, and suppliers of plant and equipment); nor should the significance of profit re-investment be underrated. Fifth, the public disclosure requirements associated with listing are a

TABLE 2.22   Companies listed on the Jakarta Stock Exchange (figures in Rp million)

Company	Listing date	Amount of issue
Semen Cibinong		
Primary issue	Aug. 77	1787.5
Secondary issue	May 82	3600.9
Centex	May 79	638.0
BAT Indonesia	Dec. 79	16500.0
Tificorp	Feb. 80	7975.0
Richardson Vicks Indonesia	Apr. 80	840.0
Goodyear Indonesia	Dec. 80	7687.5
Merck Indonesia	Jul. 81	3192.0
Multi Bintang Indonesia	Dec. 81	4964.3
Unilever Indonesia	Jan. 82	29210.0
Sepatu Bata	Mar. 82	1530.0
Unitex	Jun. 82	1081.9
Sucaco	Jul. 82	5280.0
Bayer Indonesia	Aug. 82	3079.4

Source: PT Danareksa (September 1982).

decided disadvantage for companies which traditionally negotiate their tax liabilities with taxation officials, as is often the case
in Indonesia. Finally, the existence of competing investments
should be stressed. As well as reasonably attractive time and
savings deposits, individuals commonly invest in real assets such
as gold and real estate, not to mention their own small enterprises
or those owned by others within their circle of family and friends.

The main function of a stock exchange is to facilitate
secondary trading in financial assets, especially corporate stock.
If there is an active market, this implies that such assets are highly
liquid, and in turn companies can issue shares at a higher price
than would be otherwise possible. Another measure of the
government's success in promoting the JSE is the volume of
business transacted, and to date secondary trading has been on a
very small scale. Although there are many registered stockbrokers, few bother to attend the JSE on all trading days. What
business there is can usually be completed within a very short
space of time, and the value of shares sold in a typical day's
trading is absurdly small by comparison with the facilities made
available for this purpose.

Paradoxically, it is the government itself which, by its own
actions, could do much more to stimulate stock market activity.
It has not been prepared to borrow from the public by issuing
bonds; as the owner of a very large number of companies, it could
easily increase the number of listings quite dramatically. This was
the hope of at least some foreign advisors at the time the reactivation of the JSE was planned. One can only speculate as to
why the government does not see this as an option, but perhaps it
is not only private sector company directors who would prefer not
to have their firms exposed to public scrutiny.

One of the most important government initiatives concerning
the JSE was the creation of Danareksa. This company has the
option to take up at least 50 per cent of newly issued shares of
companies going public. It may do so with any of three objectives
in mind. First, it may create back to back certificates for shares in
those companies, which are then sold to the public (in lots which
may be smaller than marketable parcels allowed on the JSE)
through a network of agents (mainly the State banks) and sub-
agents throughout the country. The buyers of these certificates
receive dividends equal to those paid on the shares they represent,
and can resell their holdings to Danareksa at any time (at the
current price) through the same network. Second, it may place the

shares in a mutual fund and then sell certificates in this fund to the public in the same manner. The return to certificate holders is then the sum of dividends paid on all shares held by the fund. Third, it may hold the shares in its own portfolio, partly as a source of income, and partly to buy and sell shares in order to stabilise their price.

The practice of issuing back to back certificates is being phased out in favour of the mutual fund concept. The latter has taken longer to implement, of course, because of the lack of listed companies. Certificates in the first mutual fund (Series A) were offered to the public during April–June 1981. The fund was valued at Rp15 billion, and comprised shares in five listed companies, as well as a substantial (Rp4.25 billion) investment in short term money market assets. There are two surprising features of this fund. The first is that Danareksa promises to repurchase its certificates at any time at a price based on the current value of the portfolio, but in any case not less than the nominal issue price of the certificates; the second is that Danareksa guarantees to pay a dividend not less than the interest rate on State bank time deposits of 12 months' maturity. These provisions mean that the fund certificates are almost as liquid as demand deposits, and yet carry a return at least as high as time deposits; in addition the risk is borne by Danareksa.

Danareksa has paid-up capital of no less than Rp24 billion. Its buying power – combined with the fact that it is not an ordinary profit orientated institution – means that it is an important factor in the stock market. Danareksa is committed to the development of the JSE, for which it is essential that there be more listings. In this context, Danareksa plays a very important role in determining the issue price for new shares – both because of its close relationship with Bapepam, and because of its role as joint underwriter with first option to take up 50 per cent of each issue. Since the explicit (tax) benefits to companies going public are perhaps not great in relation to the disadvantages of doing so, there is probably a bias towards setting a somewhat generous price for the issue as an added inducement. Thus the bargaining position of the companies is strengthened by the knowledge that the government desires more listing). At the same time, however, Danareksa is committed to avoiding potential investor losses since (it is argued) this would lead to a decline in confidence and hence be detrimental to the market's development. This implies that there should be little difficulty finding buyers for shares not taken up by Danareksa, because such buyers can reasonably expect the latter to use its funds to support the share price initially determined.

ANALYSIS

(a) State of Development

The Indonesian financial sector is still in an early phase of development. Perhaps the most important manifestation of this is the very significant role played by informal finance – financial transactions not directly involving specialised financial institutions. The importance of the informal finance sector is a reflection of the economy as a whole. Peasant agriculture still accounts for a large proportion of both output and employment; much economic activity outside agriculture is undertaken by very small enterprises; only a small proportion of the population lives in large cities; average income and educational attainment is still low; the demand for insurance of most kinds is limited. All these characteristics tend to favour informal rather than institutional forms of finance for the funding both of personal consumption and business enterprise.

One important constraint on the development of formal sector finance is the fact that the private sector is still quite backward, in the sense that the separation of ownership from control has not yet progressed very far. With the exception of the nationalised Dutch and other foreign enterprises, almost all Indonesian companies have been established since independence – or even since Sukarno. Their ownership has continued to be highly concentrated, usually restricted to a sole owner (plus one or two nominal shareholders), a family group, or a small number of entrepreneurs. The concept of corporations as economic entities which bring together relatively small amounts of capital from large numbers of individuals (who delegate the task of putting that capital to work to a team of managers) is not yet widely appreciated in Indonesia.

Another way of examining Indonesia's slow financial development is to highlight the community's relatively strong preference for holding real (rather than financial) assets. For longer term investment, land is very popular, but there is also a strong demand for gold as a liquid asset. Its importance as a competitor for financial assets cannot be overrated; an extremely high proportion of Indonesian households invest in gold (in the form of jewellery). There is a well developed system for transferring gold between individuals, which ensures high liquidity. A person (or family) with a surplus of cash is very likely to visit a gold shop and purchase a bracelet, chain or ring. When later there is a need for cash, the item can readily be sold through the same shop. Gold thus serves the same function as, for example, a savings bank deposit. No interest is earned but, on the other hand, gold is historically a good hedge against inflation. Another advantage of gold jewellery over bank deposits is, of course, that it can be worn as an adornment.

The popularity of gold relative to financial assets such as savings deposits is clear. Whereas the number of savings deposit accounts is of the order of 10 million – say one for every three families – casual observation suggests that perhaps four out of five families own at least some gold. The number of gold shops throughout Indonesia could be measured in thousands, and exceed bank offices and agencies by a wide margin. The strength of this market, and its accessibility and usefulness to the wider community, makes it an interesting contrast with the JSE.

Money is the only financial asset as yet widely understood and accepted by the community as a whole. It is not surprising, then, that the commercial banks predominate amongst financial institutions. Since relatively few individuals and firms maintain cheque accounts, cash still rates almost equally with demand deposits – which means that the central bank (the issuer of currency) is also bound to be large by comparison with other kinds of financial institutions.[38]

(b) Government Policies

The major policies adopted by the government in respect of the financial sector have already been touched upon; it will suffice here to provide a brief summary.

The most important restrictions apply to commercial banking. They include prohibition of new firms; strict control of new branches; tight restriction on the allocation of foreign exchange licences;ceilings on the credit provided by individual banks; and a complex set of subsidies and controls on the direction of lending by the State banks, combined with very extensive controls on their interest rate structure.

By contrast, some other sectors have remained relatively free of government regulation – the IFCs; the insurance industry; and the rural or market banks. Even so, one important control has been placed on joint venture insurance firms – the prohibition on purchasing shares in Indonesian companies. Each segment of the formal finance sector is characterised by restrictions on entry of new firms by means of licensing. It is difficult to perceive any benefit to the community from these restrictions, but on the other hand they probably do not do much harm at present: the market for the services of the IFCs and the insurance companies is still very limited, while close substitutes provided by the market banks are readily available.

In most other major segments of the formal finance sector, restrictions on entry would be redundant, since the activities appear insufficiently profitable to support privately owned institutions of any significance. Fully or partly State owned institutions have their respective markets virtually to themselves. This is true of Bapindo; the State Savings Bank; the development finance corporations (PDFCI, IDFC and Bahana); the specialised reinsurance companies (Umum Re and Askrindo); the so called 'social insurance' institutions (Taspen, Asabri and Jasa Raharja); and Danareksa. Perhaps all that needs to be said in regard to these institutions is that their combined assets indicate the length to which the government has been prepared to go in order to cater for largely non-existent demands for the services they provide.

One other State institution which appears to have a market to itself is the pawnshop service. This is true only in the legal sense, however; in practice, the monopolisation of pawnshop operations is probably of little consequence because close substitute services are readily available from unlicensed pawnshops and moneylenders, as well as the market banks.

Finally, it should be re-emphasised that a very large part of the finance market is constituted by informal finance, which is amorphous, unrecorded, and virtually incapable of being directed by government policy in any way. It is important to realise that its very existence tends to neutralise many of the policies applied to the formal sector, for example, the virtual impossibility of enforcing an effective monopoly of pawnshop operations. A more telling example concerns subsidising bank loans to promote particular kinds of activity. Consider a pribumi borrower who obtains a State bank (KMKP) loan at 1 per cent per month for financing working capital. Even if the bank ensured that the loan was used initially to build up the firm's inventories (of materials, work in progress and finished goods), it would not be feasible to prevent these being run down to pre-existing levels and then lending the funds to a non-pribumi borrower at 3–4 per cent per month interest. The efficacy of promoting particular kinds of activity by subsidised credit is therefore seriously open to question.[39]

TRENDS AND PREDICTIONS

In contrast with the first two decades of Indonesia's independence, the economic and political environment within which the financial sector has operated during the Suharto era has been remarkably stable. There have been no major changes in the direction of government generally, nor in the kinds of policies adopted concerning money and finance. It seems unlikely that there will be any major change in the underlying philosophy of government for many years to come; mistrust of the capitalist system, and faith in the ability of the bureaucracy to promote efficiency and distributional objectives can be expected to remain the guiding principles of economic policy.

Nevertheless, the constraints within which government must operate appear to have altered significantly since 1982. The rapid growth of oil revenue which swelled government coffers for most of the 1970s suddenly seems unlikely to be sustained because of the apparent inability of the OPEC cartel to restrain output sufficiently to keep oil prices high. This has already had some impact, with President Suharto's surprise reduction in the hitherto enormous subsidy to domestic fuel consumption and a freeze in civil servants' salaries.[40]

Whether slower or negative growth in oil revenues and taxes will have a major impact on the financial sector seems purely a matter for speculation. It is possible that reduced tax revenues from oil might induce the government at last to borrow directly or indirectly from the public to finance part of its expenditure; this would have a substantial impact on the securities market's development. Alternatively, it might increase taxes of other kinds, or reduce its own spending. It might be argued that the authorities will have more incentive in the future to control inflation – and, therefore, the money supply – since inflation would lead to balance of payments disequilibrium (by causing deficits) rather than induce a movement towards equilibrium (by reducing surpluses, as in the 1970s). This in turn might also lead to a greater willingness by the government to borrow from the public. On the other hand, there has in recent months been a tendency to allow the exchange rate to move in line with market forces;[41] if flexibility becomes acceptable to the policymakers, the monetary discipline which sometimes accompanies commitment to a fixed exchange rate would be lost.

Many State enterprises, large and small, appear to generate very little revenue for the government; indeed they almost certainly constitute a drain on the public purse. To speculate almost into the realm of fantasy, divestment of these enterprises by their sale to the public through the stock exchange or by other means would be an event of considerable moment in the finance market. Few think such a move likely (but by the same token, few thought it likely that fuel prices would be increased so dramatically only a few months prior to the 1982 elections). The argument used to justify that decision – the need to conserve the State's resources for high priority development projects in the face of falling oil tax revenues – would be equally valid in this context.

The safest prediction for the financial sector insofar as policy is concerned, seems to be that there will be 'more of the same'. The ubiquitous restrictions on entry to the formal financial market are likely to be maintained and intensified; the more detailed interventions (such as those placed on commercial banks) can be expected to be extended elsewhere, as is evident already in the case of the insurance industry.

The major growth areas are likely to be life and non-life insurance and merchant banking. Such growth will reflect the increasing sophistication of the Indonesian economy and in particular the growth of the modern, large scale business sector. Development finance institutions, on the other hand, probably have much more limited prospects. The scope for such institutions seems small, even in the more developed countries, and usually relies on concessional loans from governments or international institutions such as the World Bank and the Asian Development Bank. The latter are finding it more and more difficult to obtain grant or aid funds themselves, and the flow of revenue to the Indonesian government is likely to stagnate (or even fall) in the next few years. Regardless of these considerations, however, the commercial banks and the Central Bank will maintain their dominant position amongst financial institutions for many years to come. Nor is there any reason for believing that the State will relinquish its role as 'Mr Big' in the financial sector in the foreseeable future.

NOTES

1. Robert F. Emery, *The Financial Institutions of Southeast Asia: A Country by Country Study* New York: Praeger (1970) p. 167.
2. H. W. Arndt, 'Banking in Hyper inflation', *Bulletin of Indonesian Economic Studies* (October 1966).
3. H. W. Arndt, 'Monetary Policy Instruments in Indonesia', *Bulletin of Indonesian Economic Studies* (November 1979) p. 115.
4. The figures presented here are slightly inaccurate, due to the unavailability of data for the nine smallest private banks. The inaccuracies are greatest for the private bank group – particularly the average figures – but do not invalidate the broad picture suggested in the discussion.
5. The fifth, Bank Negara Indonesia 1946, was established in that year to serve as the newly proclaimed republic's central bank. In 1953, it reverted to a normal commercial/development banking role.
6. H. W. Arndt, 'Banking in Hyper inflation', p. 47.
7. Apart from the 11 foreign banks with branches in Indonesia, there are many more with representative offices. Such lending as is undertaken by the latter must be offshore – usually in Singapore – and although this is inconvenient, there is certainly still a good deal of business done in this way. No data are available on this point.
8. There is also a limit of two offices per bank.
9. This particularly stringent interpretation of the regulations has only recently been made. A number of foreign banks which had been working on a more liberal interpretation were heavily fined late in 1981. This episode came as a shock to the foreign banks, as no prior warning had been given. In early 1982, talks were still being held with Bank Indonesia on the subject, with a view to further clarification and (presumably) to softening the latter's stance.
10. For an analysis of this method of loan subsidisation, see R. H. McLeod, 'Finance and Entrepreneurship in the Small-Business Sector in Indonesia', PhD thesis at Australian National University, 1980, ch. 6.
11. David Jenkins, 'Creditworthy Credit Limits', *Far Eastern Economic Review* (8 April 1977).
12. Robert F. Emery, *Financial Institutions*, p. 190.
13. The item 'Managed Funds' is discussed on p. 72.
14. Robert F. Emery, *Financial Institutions*, p. 189.
15. Robert F. Emery, *Financial Institutions*, p. 188.
16. R. H. McLeod, 'Finance and Entrepreneurship', pp. 31–2 provides a case study of a co-operative market bank.
17. Bank Indonesia, *Annual Report 1980*.
18. Bank Indonesia, *Indonesian Financial Statistics* (May, 1981).

19. Interview, 1982.
20. See Table 2.7, p. 65.
21. This is the author's estimate, based on the published figures for all the other DFCs and IFCs, together with Bank Indonesia's published figure for these institutions as a whole. Bahana does not publish its financial statements.
22. IFI was established on 2 March 1956.
23. There are also some cases in which less well known companies have a close relationship with a particular IFC, which allows them access to funding by the latter.
24. Interview, 1982.
25. Interview, 1982.
26. Interview, 1982.
27. *Sigma*, no. 5 (May 1981) pp. 8–11: *Sigma* is the journal of the Swiss Reinsurance Co, Zurich.
28. Based on Robert F. Emery, *Financial Institutions*, pp. 205–7.
29. One reason for this is that government and quasi-government bodies comprise such a large part of the market in Indonesia.
30. See J. D. Legye, *Indonesia,* and etc (Sydney: Prentice-Hall, 1977) pp. 14–28.
31. Robert F. Emery, *Financial Institutions*, p. 206.
32. R. H. McLeod, 'Finance and Entrepreneurship', Ch. 6.
33. Bank Indonesia, *Indonesian Financial Statistics* (May 1981).
34. This problem is discussed in detail in R. H. McLeod, Ch. 7.
35. R. H. McLeod, 'Finance and Entrepreneurship', Appendix A, p. 228 provides a case study of this kind of consumer finance.
36. R. H. McLeod, 'Finance and Entrepreneurship', Appendix A, p. 228.
37. H. W. Arndt, 'Monetary Policy Instruments', p. 11 refers to the practice of concealing budget deficits 'by shifting certain expenditures out of the budget, to be financed by central bank credit'.
38. During 1981, currency in circulation constituted about 43 per cent of the money supply (currency + demand deposits).
39. See also R. H. McLeod, 'Finance and Entrepreneurship', Ch. 6.
40. Government statement on the draft State Budget for 1982–3 to the House of the Peoples' Representatives (5 January 1982) pp. 22–3.
41. After being held steady at about Rp625 = US$1 for 3 years, the rate rose to about Rp650 in the first 4 months of 1982.

3 Financial Institutions and Markets in Malaysia

ZETI AKHTAR AZIZ

INTRODUCTION

(a) The Setting

There are two main regions in Malaysia, peninsular Malaysia (West Malaysia), located south of Thailand; and Sabah and Sarawak (East Malaysia), located across the South China Sea in the northern part of the island of Borneo. Its total land area is approximately 331000 square kilometres. The population of Malaysia (based on 1980 estimates) is 14261200, with the major part (some 11849000) living in West Malaysia. Sabah and Sarawak's populations are respectively 1097800 and 1314400. Of the people in peninsular Malaysia, 53.9 per cent are Malay, 34.9 per cent Chinese and 10.5 per cent Indian. Another important feature of the population structure is that a high proportion are young. In 1980, for example, 71.8 per cent of the labour force fell within the age group 15–39 years. While a greater proportion has become urbanised, 65 per cent in 1980 still lived in rural areas.

Malaysia's economic performance over the past decade has been impressive, a high economic growth rate accompanied by stable prices. Malaysia is the world's leading producer and exporter of tin and rubber, in addition to being a principal exporter of palm oil, tropical hardwoods and pepper. While there has been a distinct movement towards diversification, Malaysia continues to be a very open economy. This fact can be observed in the high average ratio of exports and imports to GNP respectively of 44 and 41 per cent over the period 1970–80. The export sector is thus an important factor influencing the country's economy.

In addition to real economic growth and price stability, a major

111

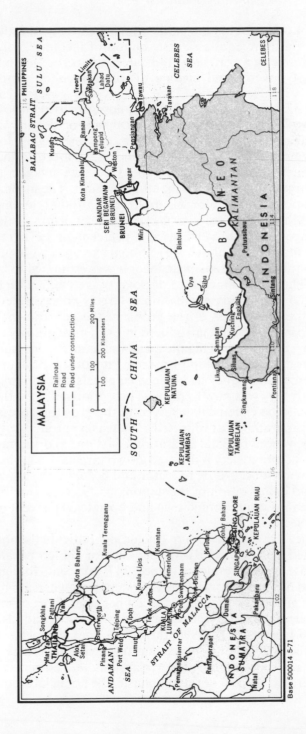

Base 500014 5-71

Map 3.1 Malaysia

Malaysian economic goal is the eradication of poverty and the achievement of a more equitable distribution of income. While the macroeconomic aggregates may indicate a prosperous nation, the problem of poverty and income distribution is of major concern. In 1976, for example, the Malaysian government estimated that 37.7 per cent of total households were living below minimum subsistence standards.[1] The incidence of poverty is lower for peninsular Malaysia at 35.1 per cent and higher for Sabah and Sarawak respectively (at 51.2 and 51.7 per cent). This situation is further complicated by the fact that income is unevenly distributed among different ethnic groups. The income *per capita* among Malays, for example, is half that among Chinese. The Malay mean income, taken as a proportion of the national average, was estimated at 67.3 per cent in 1979; the Chinese mean income was above the national average at 144 per cent, and the equivalent Indian mean income was estimated to be 102 per cent. The highest incidence of poverty is in agricultural areas, where the indigenous population is largely concentrated.

In view of the seriousness of the problem, the government's New Economic Policy (NEP), introduced in 1971, gave priority to eradicating poverty and reducing the racial imbalance in income, employment and the ownership of assets. Previously, development programmes and policy had placed emphasis on economic growth. The strategy was now to provide an opportunity for the poorest groups to be effectively involved in the growth process. Development programmes are directed at increasing productivity and income by a more optimal utilisation of labour and capital; the aim to restructure society is directed at two targets. First, that by 1990 employment according to sector and occupation should reflect the racial composition of the nation; and second, that by 1990 the indigenous group should own and operate 30 per cent of the corporate sector.

In 1971, the indigenous group (including individuals and agencies) owned and controlled 4.3 per cent of the corporate sector; other Malaysian residents owned 34.0 per cent; foreign interests owned 61.7 per cent. In 1980 the estimated ownership by the indigenous group had increased to 12.4 per cent (short of the target of 16 per cent) and other Malaysian ownership had also increased to 40.1 per cent. By 1990, the NEP's goal is to achieve ownership in the proportions: 30 per cent ownership by indigenous Malaysians, 40 per cent by other Malaysians, and 30 per cent by foreign interests. In view of this emphasis, the financial sector has an important role to play in achieving these ends.

Although agriculture represents the main sector in the economy, its relative importance has declined. Rubber planting is the most important activity in terms of employment, export earnings and government revenue. In 1970, agriculture represented 32.0 per cent of GDP; by 1980, it had decreased to 23.6 per cent. With efforts to industrialise the economy, the relative importance of the manufacturing sector has increased; manufacturing output as a proportion of GDP, for example, increased from 12.2 per cent in 1970 to 19.4 per cent in 1980. During the period covered by the Fourth Malaysia Plan 1980–5, the agricultural sector is projected to grow at 3 per cent per annum, while the manufacturing sector should grow at an annual rate of 11 per cent, thereby becoming increasingly important in generating income and employment.[2] At the end of the Plan, the relative importance of agriculture is expected to have declined to 17.8 per cent of GDP, and the manufacturing sector to have increased to 23.9 per cent. Agricultural policy during the Plan is based on the objective of augmenting food production to fulfil the needs of the population, as well as to accelerate export growth.

In view of the openness of the economy, Malaysia is significantly affected by movements in international commodity prices. Malaysia's major exports include rubber, tin, sawn logs and timber, palm oil and petroleum; these combined comprise approximately three-quarters of total exports. Petroleum has increased in significance only during the 1970s as a major foreign exchange earner for the country. The export of manufactured goods has also increased in importance; they comprise mainly electronics; textiles; rubber; and wood products. There have also been significant changes in the structure of imports; with the growth of the manufacturing sector, the import of intermediate inputs and investment goods has increased, while there has been a declining trend in the import of food and consumption goods.

As in many primary commodity exporting countries, Malaysia's external position is subject to wide fluctuations. Notwithstanding this, it has continued to experience a surplus on its trade account since the 1950s. However, as a result of the prolonged recession in the major industrialised countries, Malaysia experienced for the first time a deficit in its trade account in 1981. This was largely due to the depressed commodity prices in international markets, and the sharp increase in import prices and global inflation. Its current account position, however, had generally been in deficit, largely reflecting increased payments for services and outflows on payments of investment income. The overall balance of payments position, however, had consistently been in surplus until 1981 (prior to this, the current account position had been offset by capital inflow from abroad).

Another feature of the Malaysian economy is its ability to maintain relatively stable prices. The average rate of inflation over the period, 1970–80 was 5.6 per cent, with the highest rates recorded in 1973 and 1974 (respectively 10.5 and 17.4 per cent); this reflected the global inflation resulting from the sharp increase in oil prices. The rise in domestic prices is not attributable only to the sharp increase in import prices, but is also the result of domestic factors – domestic prices also increased as a consequence of the rapid rise in aggregate demand and shortages in supply. Nevertheless, the rate of inflation in Malaysia compares favourably with those experienced in Southeast Asia. The government of Malaysia has not incurred the inflationary deficit financing which has been a major contributory factor to the inflationary process in many developing countries.

While the economic system in Malaysia is market orientated, the government has an important role. Public sector consumption and investment increased at an average rate of 19.1 per cent over the 1970's. This expansion in the government sector was intended to achieve stable economic growth and to assist in the attainment of the objectives of the NEP. Government participation in the economy and in the financial system has largely been in areas which the market system has been unable adequately to provide. Within the economic system, the government has established a number of wholly or partially owned corporations and financial institutions. These corporations and financial institutions are generally specialised, and were established to fill specific gaps in the economic and financial system.

(b) An Overview of the Financial Sector

The financial sector of Malaysia experienced rapid growth in the 1970's. In terms of total assets, the financial system grew at the rate of 20.3 per cent per annum; this growth has taken the form not only of expansion of existing institutions, but also the emergence of new institutions and new instruments to meet the changing needs of the economy.

The financial system in Malaysia is expected to play an important role in economic development. During the period of the Fourth Malaysian Plan (1981–5), private savings are projected to increase at the rate of 26 per cent per annum, to amount to 17.9 per cent of GNP at the end of the period. Private sector investment, on the other hand, is expected to increase at a rate of 19.2 per cent, to amount to 20.3 per cent of GNP in 1985. Foreign savings is expected to finance the difference.

The financial sector is thus faced with the task of mobilising resources for the efficient allocation of investment. Domestic private resources are estimated to provide 70.6 per cent of the funds required for private investment; public sector financing of the private sector investment and other transfers are expected to account for another 16 per cent. Net private long term capital inflow is intended to account for the remainder, reflecting the expected continued importance of foreign investment in the economic development of Malaysia. The mobilisation of saving in a form that can be drawn on for financing investment will largely be influenced by the extent to which the financial system in Malaysia is adequate and responsive.

Table 3.1 shows the growth of financial assets of the financial system in Malaysia during the period 1960–80. An important feature is the rapid growth of the commercial banks. The relative importance of the commercial banking system has increased in significance, from 35 per cent in 1960 to 43 per cent at the end of 1980. In the 1960s, the commercial banks were largely dominated by foreign owned banking institutions, but in the 1970s there was a change in the composition of ownership of commercial banks. During this period, domestic banks increased significantly, especially in terms of branch expansion.

The 1970s also witnessed an increase in the sophistication of Malaysia's financial system. In the 1960s, it comprised mainly the Central Bank, commercial banks, the National Savings Bank (NSB) and provident and pension funds. These institutions made up 91.1 per cent of its total assets. Their relative share, however, declined to 85.1 per cent in 1970, and to 77.8 per cent in 1980. This was largely the result of the rapid expansion of finance companies, and the emergence of new institutions such as merchant banks, development banks, discount houses and other specialised financial institutions.

While the commercial banks dominate in the mobilisation of savings, deposits placed with finance companies and merchant

TABLE 3.1   Malaysia financial system by total assets, 1960–80 (figures in million Ringgit)

Financial institutions	1960 Amount	1960 (%)	As at end of 1970 Amount	1970 (%)	1980 Amount	1980 (%)
Banking institutions	*2504*	*70.5*	*7305.7*	*62.9*	*48338.0*	*65.6*
Central Bank[a]	1114	31.4	2415.9	20.8	12994.1	17.6
Commercial banks	1232	34.7	4460.2	38.4	31971.7	43.4
Savings banks	157	4.4	296.0	2.5	1235.1	1.7
Development banks	1	0.0	133.6	1.2	2137.1	2.9
Non-bank financial institutions	*1049*	*29.5*	*4308.8*	*37.1*	*25392.1*	*34.4*
Merchant banks	—	—	—	—	2228.4	3.0
Finance companies	10	0.3	531.0	4.6	5635.4	7.6
Insurance companies	103	2.9	436.8	3.8	2385.2	3.2
Provident & pension funds	733	20.6	2717.0	23.4	11129.4	15.1
Co-operative societies[b]	110	3.1	349.0	3.0	1142.3	1.6
Building societies	93	2.6	203.0	1.7	1031.8	1.4
Other non-bank financial institutions	—	—	72.0	0.6	1839.6	2.5
Total	3553	100.0	11614.5	100.0	73730.1	100.0

[a] Includes Malaysia's estimated share of the residual assets of the Board of Commissioners of Currency, Malaya and British Borneo.
[b] Includes Bank Rakyat and the Co-operative Central Bank.

Source: Bank Negara Malaysia, *Annual Report 1981*.

banks have increased at a higher rate. This reflects the competitive situation in which higher rates of return are paid on these deposits. The commercial banks are also the main source of credit to the non-bank private sector. As can be observed in Table 3.2, at the end of 1981, the commercial banks provided 66.4 per cent of the total credit extended to the non-bank private sector. This credit is largely short term; medium and longer term credit is largely provided by finance companies, merchant banks and other development finance institutions. The relative significance of the commercial banks can also be seen in terms of their role in the domestic money market. The commercial banks are the main depositors for short term funds at the discount houses. The commercial banks also dominate the Treasury bill market and are important participants in the market for longer term government

TABLE 3.2 Malaysia financial sector credit to non-financial private sector (figures as at end 1981, in $ million)

Source and maturity[a]	Amount	(%)
Commercial banks	*23865*	*66.4*
Short term	15457	43.0
Medium term	1511	4.2
Long term	6897	19.2
Finance companies	*4558*	*12.6*
Short term	232	0.6
Medium term	3024	8.4
Long term	1302	3.6
Others[b]	*7534*	*21.0*
Short term	1880	5.2
Medium term	1286	3.6
Long term	4368	12.2
Total	35957	100.0

[a] Breakdown by original maturity: Short term is up to 1 year; medium term more than 1 year – 4 years; long-term over 4 years.
[b] Includes merchant banks; housing credit institutions; industrial development finance institutions; urban credit institutions; rural credit institutions; insurance companies; provident funds; unit trusts; Pilgrims Management and Fund Board; and NSB.

Source: Bank Negara Malaysia, *Annual Report 1981*, p. 43.

securities. This market is, however, dominated by 'captive' buyers – pension funds and the NSB.

The financial system experienced a number of reforms in the 1970s. One major change was the liberalisation of interest rates in October 1978. Prior to October 1978, the Central Bank, in consultation with the Association of Banks in Malaysia, determined the deposits and lending rates charged by the commercial banks. With effect from October 1978, banks were permitted to determine their own deposit and lending rates. The Central Bank, however, continues to set the maximum lending rates to the priority sectors.

Two new instruments were introduced in May 1979 – negotiable certificates of deposits (NCDs) and bankers' acceptances (BAs). The NCDs are an attractive instrument for the corporate sector in view of their liquidity and high rate of return. To develop a secondary market for BAs, the Central Bank has allowed the instrument to be included up to a specified limit into the computation of most liquidity requirements; the Central Bank also offers rediscounting facilities for BAs that have a maturity of less than 21 days.

Fiscal incentives were also introduced in 1981 to induce stability of deposits. Interest earned on all saving deposits at the NSB are exempt from tax; fixed deposits with commercial banks and finance companies with maturities exceeding 12 months are also exempted from tax. This is largely to encourage longer term saving. Commercial banks and merchant banks are also permitted to accept foreign currency deposits from non-residents. The banks are also exempt from the 15 per cent withholding tax on interest paid to non-residents. Commercial banks and merchant banks are also allowed to lend loans in foreign currency to residents in Malaysia.

An important feature of the role of the Central Bank is in ensuring that priority sectors have access to funds at reasonable rate of interest. The Central Bank has prescribed a number of guidelines for lending by commercial banks and finance companies for this purpose. These guidelines aim at allocating credit to agricultural food production; manufacturing; small scale enterprises; individuals for housing; and the bumiputera community. Commercial banks and finance companies are required to extend a specific proportion of their total loans outstanding to the respective priority sectors.

In addition to directing credit to priority sectors, the Central Bank has played an important role in establishing development financial institutions to finance those areas not met by the private sector. For the most part, development finance institutions are government owned, and are established to provide funds that existing financial institutions are not able to provide. These institutions generally mobilise funds from other financial institutions and the government, rather than from the non-bank private sector.

The government also participates in the ownership of a number of other financial institutions, for example, it has major shareholdings in three of the larger domestic banks and also owns the Development Bank of Malaysia; the Industrial Development Bank of Malaysia; the Agricultural Bank of Malaysia; and Komplex Kewangan Malaysia Berhad. In addition, the government and the Central Bank have shares in the Malaysian Industrial Development Finance Berhad. The government also has shares in the Malaysian Building Society and Malaysia

Export Credit Insurance. Still other development finance institutions are owned by the State Governments; these include the Borneo Development Corporation owned by the State of Sabah and Sarawak, the Sabah Development Bank and the Sabah Credit Corporation owned by the State of Sabah.

The policy of the Central Bank has developed largely in response to domestic and international pressures. The 1970s and the 1980s have witnessed the Central Bank expanding the financial structure and instituting reforms to induce a more efficient financial system. Steps were taken not only to develop the domestic financial and capital markets, but also to improve the links between the Malaysian financial system and the international capital market. This was not only in response to the more diversified and complex needs of the economy, but also to provide a system conducive to an effective implementation of monetary policy. Stabilisation policy by the Central Bank during the 1970s and early 1980s has largely been directed towards dealing with inflationary pressures and disequilibrium in the balance of payments; for the main part, traditional Central Bank policy instruments were applied to influence the cost and availability of credit. Another important emphasis of Central Bank policy is to ensure (by regular inspection and close monitoring of the financial institutions) a high degree of professionalism in the financial service.

FINANCIAL INSTITUTIONS

The financial institutions in Malaysia can be classified into two main groups: banks and non-bank financial institutions. As a single group, the commercial banks represent the largest and most significant financial institution in the country. The other banking institutions include the NSB and the development banks. Within this group the development banks (which are relatively new in the financial system) have expanded at the most rapid rate. At the centre of the financial system is, of course, Bank Negara Malaysia, the Central Bank of Malaysia.

The non-bank financial institutions include the merchant banks; finance companies; insurance companies; provident and pension funds; discount houses; building societies; unit trusts;

urban credit co-operative societies; rural credit institutions and other specialised non-bank financial institutions; Malaysia Export Credit Insurance; and the Pilgrims Management and Fund Board. Within this group (in terms of total resources) finance companies and merchant banks have expanded at a significantly higher rate than the rate of growth of the financial system as a whole.

(a) The Banking Institutions

(i) *Bank Negara Malaysia*

Bank Negara Malaysia was established under the Central Bank Ordinance 1958, and commenced operations on 26 January 1959. It is responsible for formulating and implementing monetary and credit policies within the structure of the country's overall financial and economic objectives.

Amongst its primary objectives are to issue currency; to protect the value of the currency; to promote an effective and efficient monetary system in line with the requirements of the developing economy; and to ensure monetary stability. It also acts as banker and financial advisor to the government as well as undertaking to influence the credit situation of the country so that credit volume is adequate to meet demand. In view of the expansion of the Malaysian economy, the Bank has the specific task of promoting an efficient means by which funds can be mobilised to finance development, as well as the broader task of dealing with the major economic problems of inflation, balance of payments disequilibria and the eradication of poverty.

Bank Negara Malaysia is the sole currency issuing authority in the country. The Bank assumed this function in June 1967; prior to this, currency was issued by the Currency Board which was the sole issuer of currency for the Malaysian – Singapore – Brunei region.[3] In June 1967, when the Bank began issuing currency, the Currency Board ceased operation and Malaysia had a separate currency from Singapore and Brunei. However, during this period under a special agreement the Malaysian dollar was made interchangeable at par with the Singapore and Brunei dollar. As under the Currency Board system, the Malaysian dollar was defined in terms of gold (M\$1 = 0.290299 grammes of fine gold). The statutory regulations under which the Board functioned required it to provide upon demand local currency for pounds sterling at a specified rate of exchange. When the Bank effectively replaced the Currency Board, it continued to purchase and sell Malaysian currency to maintain the official parity exchange rate against the pound sterling, and the pound sterling was used as the official intervention currency.

Although there was a legislative provision that required the Bank to maintain a minimum of 80.59 per cent of reserves against its currency liabilities, it generally exceeded 100 per cent by a substantial margin.[4] In November 1967, sterling was devalued by 14.3 per cent in terms of gold. The Malaysian dollar did not follow the devaluation, but maintained its gold parity. However, in June 1972 (with the floating of the pound sterling) Malaysia began using the US dollar as the intervention currency. A year later, in June 1973, the Malaysian dollar was permitted to float freely. During this period, the interchangeability agreement between the Malaysian and Singapore dollar was also terminated.

As a result of large fluctuations in the Malaysian dollar in terms of the US dollar – mainly due to conditions in the USA – the Bank considered it more appropriate to determine the value of the Malaysian currency in terms of a group of countries that were significant trading partners with Malaysia. This means that intervention by the Bank now reflects changes in the weighted average of a group of currencies, rather than changes in the US dollar alone. As shown in Table 3.3, gold and foreign exchange holdings comprised the bulk of Bank Negara Malaysia's assets, and at the end of 1981 these stood at M$9172.3 million.

Bank Negara Malaysia has several means by which it can achieve its objectives of monetary stability and other economic goals. These are mainly directed at bank reserves, and thereby affect the cost and availability of money and credit. In Malaysia, the main instruments used include variations in the reserve requirements and interest rates. These have been supplemented by selective credit controls, discounting arrangements and moral suasion.

The commercial banks in Malaysia must fulfil three types of reserve requirements. First, they must maintain with Bank Negara Malaysia a portion of their total deposit liabilities as a statutory reserve. A statutory reserve requirement was also introduced for finance companies and merchant banks, respectively in 1972 and 1975. Second, the banks are required to keep a liquidity requirement against total deposits less savings deposits. In 1972, a minimum liquidity requirement was introduced

TABLE 3.3　Bank Negara Malaysia assets and liabilities, 1981 (figures as of 31 December 1981, in $)

Liabilities	
Paid-up capital	100000000
General reserve fund	869645003
Currency in circulation	5492924762
Deposits:	
Commercial banks, finance companies and merchant banks	1586089549
Other financial institutions	47287538
Federal government	1204596512
State governments	288955920
Other	169288613
Allocation of SDRs	363069516
Other Liabilities	1580512684
	11702370097
Assets	
Gold and foreign exchange	9172281976
IMF reserve position	304199207
Holdings of SDRs	328502262
Federal government securities (including Treasury bills)	707726650
Other assets	1189660002
	11702370097

Source: Bank Negara Malaysia, *Annual Report 1981*, pp. 128–9.

for finance companies. A wide range of assets are eligible for liquidity purposes and include cash; short term money market instruments; trade bills; Treasury bills; government securities; housing loans; and cheques purchased. Half of this liquidity requirement must be held in specific liquid terms, and banks must also maintain 50 per cent of their savings deposits in government securities as well as in loans under the Credit Guarantee Scheme. Since February 1982, the Bank could also impose separate and individual reserve requirements on different deposit categories.[5] This includes foreign currency deposits at commercial banks and merchant banks.

As an instrument of monetary policy, the reserve requirement has been used to influence the credit situation. There have, however, been infrequent changes in the reserve requirement. Besides their monetary role, these restrictions are also used to channel commercial bank funds into specific financial instruments to finance development.

Until October 1978, when they were liberalised, interest rates in Malaysia were subject to direct control. Bank Negara Malaysia set the maximum interest rate paid on deposits by the commercial banks, as well as the minimum rate charged on bank loans and advances. The Central Bank also prescribed the maximum interest rate which the commercial banks could charge on loans to priority sectors. In October 1978, commercial banks were permitted to determine their own deposit rate, as well as the prime lending rate. The Central Bank, however, continued to set the maximum lending rate for the priority loans – those to small scale enterprises for loans not exceeding M$200000; to the bumiputera community for loans not exceeding M$500000, and housing loans where the cost of the house and land did not exceed M$100000.

With the liberalisation of interest rates, there was an upward adjustment in interest rates. Despite the high inflation during 1979 and 1980, the real rate of return on fixed deposits during this period was positive. This is in contrast to the inflationary period in 1973 and 1974, when the real rate of return on time deposits was negative; over this period, the market response to interest rate adjustment was prompt. The Central Bank influence on interest rate adjustment is mainly through the money market; this intervention, however, has been largely to smooth out variations in interest rate movements, rather than significantly to attempt to influence the underlying trend. The Central Bank's concern has mainly been that sharp increases in interest rates undermine business confidence and adversely affect private investment. At the same time, the Bank recognised the need to encourage savings, and to ensure that the domestic interest rates were not out of line with foreign rates, which might result in destabilising capital outflows.

While open market operations have increased in importance with the liberalisation in interest rates, the Bank has recently placed greater emphasis on foreign exchange swap facilities as a means of improving liquidity conditions. These swaps also help offset the effects of short term capital flows. The Central Bank also acts as lender of the last resort to commercial banks, merchant banks and discount houses; borrowing may be in the form of rediscounting of Treasury bills or other eligible short term bills, or alternatively in the form of an advance against government securities as collateral. There is, however, no bank rate as such. The Treasury bill rate is used as a reference rate when determining the rate for rediscounting other bills.

Bank Negara Malaysia also directly affects the allocation of credit and uses selective credit policy measures to channel credit to priority sectors. Initially, this selective credit policy (implemented in 1975, and made more specific in October 1976) was based on the new loans extended by commercial banks and finance companies. From October 1976, commercial banks were required to channel a specified minimum proportion of their increase in credit to agricultural food production; the manufacturing sector; and the indigenous community. Finance companies were also required to channel specified minimum proportions of their new loans to agriculture; manufacturing; construction and real estate development; housing; and the indigenous community.[6] New guidelines based on total loans outstanding were introduced in June 1979. Commercial banks were additionally also required to extend at least 20 per cent of total loans to small scale enterprises.[7] These sets of guidelines were further revised in March 1981.

'Moral suasion' has also been used by the Central Bank to influence the activities of the financial sector. Commercial banks were induced to hold a larger proportion of their portfolio in domestic (as opposed to foreign) assets. Banks were also urged to discourage the extension of credit for speculative, rather than for productive, purposes; they were encouraged to extend credit to finance development and to undertake increased medium and longer term financing.

From time to time, the Bank also reviews the banking legislation, introducing amendments so as to respond to developments in the financial system. In October 1981, a number of amendments and new provisions were introduced to the Central Bank of Malaysia Ordinance 1958, with a view to ensuring that adequate provisions were made in the law to promote a sound and modern banking structure as well as to facilitate more effective supervision and control of banks operating in Malaysia.[8]

(ii) *Commercial banks*

Malaysia is served by a network of 38 commercial banks, of which 21 are locally incorporated. The foreign banks include five incorporated in Singapore, three in the USA, two in Hong Kong and one each in the UK, Japan, Canada, Thailand, the Netherlands and West Germany. Until the 1970s, commercial banking was largely dominated by foreign banks. At the end of

1964, for example, foreign banks accounted for 74 per cent of the banking system's total assets. Among the major foreign banks were the British banks that were initially established to finance trade. Although the British banks remain important, there are now (as a result of mergers) only two remaining. The banks' ownership and size in terms of total assets at the end of 1980 is shown in Table 3.4.

Due to their rapid deposit growth and expanded activities, the domestic banks by the end of 1980 accounted for 62.0 per cent of the banking system's total assets. Expansion in the domestic banks has also been in terms of bank branches; by the end of 1980, the domestic banks had a total number of 399 branches, concentrated among the three major banks – Malayan Banking Berhad (126), Bank Bumiputra Malaysia Berhad (74) and United Malayan Banking Corporation (40). Bank Bumiputra Malaysia Berhad is the largest commercial bank, and is wholly owned by the Malaysian government.[9] The government is also a major shareholder in the other two: it acquired its interest in Malayan Banking Berhad in 1969, and in the United Malayan Banking Corporation in 1976.

While the relative importance of foreign banks in Malaysia has declined, they continue to play an important role in the economy. At the end of 1980, there were 147 foreign banking offices; the two British banks dominated, the Chartered Bank having 35 and the Hongkong and Shanghai Banking Corporation (incorporated in Hong Kong) also having 35 branches. The third and fourth largest banks are incorporated in Singapore. It has been government policy not to encourage more foreign branches in Malaysia; in view of the heterogenous nature of the banks in the Malaysian financial system, the classification of the banks according to domestic and foreign may be too simplistic. However, some distinct characteristics can be discerned in the manner in which foreign and domestic incorporated banks manage their portfolios.[10] This can be attributed partly to the different clientele of the two groups. Domestic banks have expanded particularly in smaller towns and non-urban areas not previously serviced by banks; it is likely that such banks experience different deposit as well as loan demand due to the particular economic activities in these areas.

Sources of commercial bank funds. As shown in Table 3.5, deposits comprise the main part of the resources of the commer-

TABLE 3.4   Malaysia commercial banks (figures as at end 1980, in M$ million)

	Year of Commence-ment in Malaysia	Total assets in Malaysia
Malaysian banks		
Ban Hin Lee Bank Berhad (7)[a]	1935	273.2
Bank Bumiputra Malaysia Berhad (74)	1966	12015.8
Bank Buruh (Malaysia) Berhad (1)	1975	81.8
Bank of Commerce Berhad (2)	1956	215.2
Bank Utama (Malaysia) Berhad (1)	1977	84.8
Development and Commercial Bank Berhad (21)	1966	997.1
Hock Hua Bank Berhad (8)	1951	435.7
Hock Hua Bank (Sabah) Berhad (4)	1961	183.1
Kong Ming Bank Berhad (5)	1964	164.3
Kwong Lee Bank Berhad (9)	1923	322.4
Kwong Yik Bank Berhad (11)	1913	379.7
Malayan Banking Berhad (126)	1960	7972.6
Oriental Bank Berhad (10)	1936	419.5
The Pacific Bank Berhad (6)	1963	334.9
Perwira Habib Bank Malaysia Berhad (15)	1976	1128.2
Public Bank Berhad (16)	1966	1192.9
Sabah Bank Berhad (1)	1979	340.9
Southern Banking Berhad (10)	1965	362.0
United Asian Bank Berhad (30)[b]	1973	2191.7
United Malayan Banking Corporation Berhad (40)	1960	2708.4
Wah Tat Bank Berhad (2)	1955	77.2

[a]   Figures in parenthesis show no. of bank branches.
[b]   The United Asian Bank was the result of the merger of three Indian Banks. The Indian Bank (1941); The Indian Overseas Bank (1937); and The United Commercial (1948).

cial banks. The banks accept four main types of deposits – demand deposits; fixed deposits; savings deposits; and NCDs. The relative importance of each is shown in Table 3.6. Demand deposits earn no interest, but a service charge is imposed on such accounts. These charges are however, waived for accounts with balances above a certain minimum level. Fixed deposits earn interest according to their maturity; the terms range from 1–60 months, and a penalty is charged for withdrawals before maturity. A minimum of M$500 is required for the acceptance of fixed deposits. Savings deposits, on the other hand, operate on a pass book system. Limited amounts of such deposits can be

TABLE 3.4 *(contd.)*

	Year of Commence- ment in Malaysia	Country of incorpora- tion	Total assets in Malaysia
Foreign Banks			
Algemene Bank Nederland NV (2)	1888	Holland	449.3
Bangkok Bank Ltd (1)	1959	Thailand	475.0
Bank of America NT and SA (1)	1959	USA	762.3
The Bank of Canton Ltd (1)	1957	Hong Kong	91.8
The Bank of Nova Scotia (1)	1973	Canada	95.7
The Bank of Tokyo Ltd (1)	1959	Japan	1466.1
Banque de L'Indochine et de Sues (2)	1958	France	480.5
The Chartered Bank (35)[a]	1875	UK	3395.6
The Chase Manhanttan Bank NA (1)	1964	USA	526.2
Chung Khiaw Ltd (16)	1951	Singapore	1060.7
Citibank NA (3)	1959	USA	1203.6
European Asian Bank (1)	1968	Germany	345.0
The Hongkong and Shanghai Banking Corporation (35)[b]	1884	Hong Kong	3488.5
Lee Wah Bank Ltd (9)	1956	Singapore	441.5
Oversea–Chinese Banking Corporation (25)	1932	Singapore	1477.7
Overseas Union Bank Ltd (12)	1958	Singapore	558.9
United Overseas Bank (1)	1966	Singapore	49.3

[a] In July 1971, the Eastern Bank was merged into the Chartered Bank.
[b] In July 1973, the Mercantile Bank was merged into the Hongkong and Shanghai Banking Corporation. The Hongkong and Shanghai Banking Corporation is a British bank incorporated in Hong Kong.

Source: *A Study of Commercial Banks in Malaysia 1980* (Kuala Lumpur: SGV–Kassim Chan Sdn Berhad, 1981).

withdrawn on demand, but the interest paid is generally lower than for fixed deposits.

Since 1960, bank deposits have grown at an average annual rate of 16.6 per cent. There has, however, been a change in the structure of deposits. In 1960, demand deposit comprised 49.1 per cent of total deposits; at the end of 1981 they accounted for only 20.8 per cent. This reflects the tendency for the non-bank private sector to economise on current account balances, as a wider spectrum of instruments (with more attractive rate of return) became available. Fixed deposits at commercial banks have increased significantly, at the rate of 19.4 per cent per annum over

TABLE 3.5 Malaysia sources of commercial bank funds by type (figures as at end 1981, in M$ million)

Sources	
Domestic:	
Capital & reserves	1594.7
Deposits	28106.5
Public sector[a]	(4976.1)
Private sector	(23130.4)
NCDs issued	1784.5
Amounts due to financial institutions[b]	1418.6
Banker's Acceptances	1159.2
Other	3129.4
Total domestic sources	37192.9
Foreign:	
Amounts due to financial institutions[c]	3319.6
Other	215.9
Total foreign sources	3535.5
Total	40723.4

[a] Refers to the Malaysian government, State governments, statutory authorities and local governments.
[b] Refers to other commercial banks, merchant banks, or finance companies.
[c] Refers to head offices and branches, other commercial banks, and other financial institutions.

Source: Bank Negara Malaysia, *Annual Report 1981*, p. 53.

the period 1960–80. At the end of 1960, fixed deposits comprised only 37.2 per cent of total deposits; at the end of 1981, they comprised 59.1 per cent.

This partly reflects the response to higher yields of such deposits, as well as the wider range in maturity available. Prior to 1971, only deposits with maturity of up to 1 year were offered; since then, the banks have offered longer maturities, and their respective interest rates have become more differentiated. The higher rates of return also attracted savers into deposits of longer maturity. Saving deposits, on the other hand, have expanded at the rate of 18.4 per cent per annum over the period 1960–80.

TABLE 3.6   Malaysia deposits with commercial banks by type of deposit, 1979–81 (figures in M$ million)

	As at end					
	1979		1980		1981	
	Amount	(%)	Amount	(%)	Amount	(%)
Current	4548.9	23.5	5326.2	22.0	6234.8	20.8
Fixed	11025.9	57.0	13816.8	57.0	17657.5	59.1
Savings	3566.5	18.4	4183.3	17.2	4214.2	14.1
NCDs	200.3	1.1	931.1	3.8	1784.5	6.0
Total	19341.6	100.0	24257.4	100.0	29891.0	100.0

Source: Bank Negara Malaysia, *Annual Report 1981*, p. 54.

Their relative share in total deposits also increased, from 13.2 per cent in 1960 to 17.9 in 1980. Savings deposits are largely mobilised from small savers, and the expansion in the numbers of bank branches was an important factor in mobilising such deposits.

Negotiable Certificates of Deposits (NCDs), which were introduced in May 1979, have also expanded rapidly. Such deposits have maturities ranging from 3–36 months. The minimum deposit is M$50000, and the maximum M$1 million; the interest rate paid on such deposits is negotiable. As a result of the flexibility in rates, and their marketability, NCDs are an attractive instrument; at the end of 1981, there were M$1784.4 million NCDs outstanding. The 6 month NCD tended to be the most important, and at the end of 1981 accounting for 75 per cent of the total. A general tax exemption for the 1982 tax year on interest from fixed deposits and NCDs exceeding 12 months in maturity may increase the overall importance of longer term deposits.

Borrowing is also an important source of funds for the banks, and liability management is particularly important to the foreign banks. These banks (concentrated mainly in urban areas), have less access to deposits, and thus must borrow from both the domestic and foreign money markets. Foreign liabilities are in the form of deposits placed by foreign banks, as well as borrowing from abroad. In 1970–80, foreign liabilities ranged between 1.4–5.6 per cent of total resources.

Capital and reserves as a source of funds has not increased substantially; this has been regarded by Bank Negara Malaysia with some concern, and to ensure that the banks' capital is adequate for their overall operations, and in order to 'strengthen the basic structure of the banking industry on a uniform basis' new capital adequacy requirements were introduced in September 1981.[11] Domestic banks are required to maintain a minimum capital ratio of 4 per cent against total assets (not including long term investment). Foreign banks in contrast, must maintain a ratio of 6 per cent of net working funds: total assets in Malaysia (not including long term investment).

Uses of commercial bank funds. As shown in Table 3.7, loans and advances are the main use of resources of the commercial banks. During the period 1960–80, loans and advances expanded at the rate 20.2 per cent per annum. In 1960, loans and advances accounted for 34.1 per cent of total assets; by the end of 1981, they accounted for 64.9 per cent. As a result of the growth of bank loans, the loan deposit ratio of the commercial banks has increased significantly, from 69 per cent in 1970 to 85 per cent in 1981. A large proportion of bank lending is in the form of overdrafts and loans of 1 year or less. At the end of 1981, 61 per cent of total loans outstanding were in the form of such overdrafts and loans. The proportion of loans of more than 4 years has also increased significantly over the period 1970–81; while in 1970 the proportion in total of such loans outstanding was only 5 per cent, by the end of 1981 the proportion had increased to 32 per cent. This can partially be attributed to the change in the structure of deposits to those with longer maturities.

The commercial banks, which were originally established to finance foreign trade, have undergone significant changes in the structure of their lending activities. With the increased diversification of the economy, loan demand has become correspondingly more diversified. In 1967, loans for general commerce accounted for the major share of total loans (35 per cent). As shown in Table 3.8, however, by 1981 they comprised only 21.9 per cent. With increased industrial activity, loans to the manufacturing sector increased from 15 per cent in 1967 to 23.3 per cent of total loans at the end of 1981. Loans for building and construction, real estate activity and housing have also increased significantly, reflecting the increased activity of this sector; its share of total loans increased from 10 per cent in 1970 to 28.2 per cent at the end of 1981. Loans to the agricultural sector declined from 9 per cent in 1967 to 7.5 per cent of total loans at the end of 1981, again reflecting the diversification of the economy.

TABLE 3.7 Malaysia commercial banks uses of funds (figures as at 31 December 1981, in M$ million)

Uses	
Domestic	
Cash[a]	458.9
Statutory reserves	1374.5
Money at call	1027.8
Amounts due from financial institutions[b]	2774.6
Investments	5619.5
Treasury bills	(1401.5)
Government securities	(3817.1)
Private securities	(400.9)
Loans	25514.7
Overdrafts	(13091.1)
Term loans	(9213.0)
Trade bills[c]	(3210.6)
Fixed assets	493.7
Other	2068.8
	39332.5
Foreign	
Amounts due from financial institutions[d]	1291.8
Trade bills	6.7
Investments	39.1
Other	58.3
	1395.9
Total	40728.4

[a] Includes balances with Central Bank.
[b] Refers to amounts due to and due from other commercial banks, merchant banks and finance companies.
[c] Includes bankers' acceptances.
[d] Refers to amounts due to and due from head office and branches, other commercial banks and other financial institutions.

Source: Bank Negara Malaysia, *Annual Report 1981*, p. 53.

In view of the selective credit policies of the Central Bank, the direction of bank lending has been significantly influenced by the guidelines introduced, to extend loans to the priority sectors – agricultural food production; housing to the bumiputra community; and small scale enterprises including those loans guaran-

TABLE 3.8   Malaysia commercial bank lending by type of industry, 1981 (figures as at 31 December 1981, in M$ million)

Industry	Amount
Agriculture	1910.2
Of which	
Forestry & logging	673.0
Oil palm	452.8
Cocoa	258.2
Rubber	181.8
Mining & quarrying	276.5
Of which	
Tin	180.6
Quarrying	58.7
Manufacturing	5947.1
Of which	
Processing	731.1
Textiles & wearing apparel	613.7
Wood & wood products	554.2
Food	549.5
Petroleum products	471.7
Transport equipment	383.2
Electrical machinery,	
apparatus & appliances	372.8
Basic metal industries	353.0
Metal products	296.5
Electricity	169.6
Real estate & construction	4398.4
General commerce	5594.3
Transport & storage	623.7
Financing, insurance & business services	2198.1
Individual housing loans	2810.9
Other	1592.6
Total loans and advances	25521.4

Source: Bank Negara Malaysia, Annual Report 1981, p. 59.

teed by the Credit Guarantee Corporation.[12] At the end of 1981, the commercial banking sector as a whole had complied with these guidelines on priority sector lending.

(iii) *National Savings Bank (NSB)*

The Bank Simpanan Nasional Malaysia (NSB) (which took over the operations of the POSB) was established in December 1974.[13] The NSB mobilises savings from small savers, particularly in small towns and rural areas, through a wide network of Post Offices in addition to its own branches. At the end of 1981, there were nine branches and 688 Post Offices with savings bank facilities.

The primary source of funds of the NSB is savings deposits based on a pass book system. Interest rates on the deposits are prescribed. The NSB faces substantial competition from the savings departments of the commercial banks and finance companies; attempts have been made to maintain rates comparable, if not higher than, those paid by the commercial banks and finance companies. To attract savings with the NSB, the government granted tax exemption on interest earned on funds deposited at the bank up to a maximum amount of M$1400 (a maximum of M$600 would be tax exempt on interest earned from savings deposits at commercial banks). There were also substantial withdrawals from the bank to purchase trust units from the National Unit Trust Scheme that was set up in April 1981.[14] In the 1982 Budget, tax exemption for deposits with the bank covered all interest earned on funds deposited at the bank. Despite these incentives, growth in deposits with the NSB has been relatively slow.

While the POSB was required to invest solely in government securities, the NSB is permitted to invest a maximum of 30 per cent in specified assets, and the remaining 70 per cent in government securities. Among the assets permitted are trustee securities and housing loans, as well as approved loans and advances, securities and investments. Given this diversification potential, the NSB has reduced its government securities holdings in an attempt to improve its overall return on assets. At the end of 1981, government securities comprised 72 per cent of its total portfolio; other investments include trustee securities and fixed deposits with other financial institutions. The NSB has yet to invest in the other assets permitted in its portfolio, including the issue of housing loans.

(iv) *Development banks*

The development banks in Malaysia are mainly public sector established institutions aimed at financing specific areas of the economy not serviced by existing types of institution. They specialise in encouraging investment in key industries and priority sectors by providing medium and long term development finance. They are distinguished from other development institutions in that the latter perform financing activities only as a subsidiary component of their other activities.

The development banks play a significant role in the Malaysian financial system in that they provide funds and financial services in areas of the economy that do not otherwise have access to such funds. These institutions are mainly funded by other financial institutions or by the government. These banks include the Malaysian Industrial Development Finance Berhad, the Development Bank of Malaysia, the Industrial Development Bank of Malaysia, the Sabah Development Bank, Agricultural Bank of Malaysia, and the Borneo Development Corporation.

Malaysian Industrial Development Finance Berhad. The MIDF was incorporated in 1960, with participation by the government commercial banks, insurance companies and other (including foreign) financial institutions. The Malaysian government in March 1982 held 4.04 per cent of the equity in MIDF, with foreign shareholdings in the company at 28.98 per cent. MIDF was established as the country's first development financing institution to promote the growth of the manufacturing sector through financial assistance in the form of medium and long term loans or by direct equity participation, and by providing financing, technical and managerial advice.

MIDF has three major financing schemes – project loans; machinery loans; and factory mortgages. The project loans scheme finances the whole venture, and the loans range from 5–15 years. Machinery loans are provided for 1–4 years, and are for up to 75 per cent of the CIF value of the machinery. Under the factory mortgage scheme, MIDF lends up to 80 per cent of the cost of acquiring the land and setting up the factory. At the end of 1981, project loans comprised 86.9 per cent of MIDF advances, machinery loans 9.8 per cent, and factory mortgage loans 3.3 per cent. A breakdown of MIDF loans outstanding by industry is shown in Table 3.9.

MIDF obtains its funds primarily from loans from the government and other domestic and foreign financial institutions.

TABLE 3.9   Malaysian Industrial Development Finance advances by type of industry, 1981 (figures in M$ million)

Type of business	No. of loans	Amount
Manufacturing	*743*	*282.1*
Food, beverages & tobacco	133	59.9
Textiles & wearing apparel	70	37.1
Wood products	87	43.4
Printing & publishing	78	14.9
Chemical & chemical products	102	20.5
Rubber products	45	23.7
Non-metallic mineral products	32	19.0
Basic metal & metal products	93	39.4
Machinery & transport equipment	73	16.1
Other	30	8.1
Non-manufacturing	*43*	*16.1*
Total	786	298.2

Source: Bank Negara Malaysia, *Annual Report 1980*, p. 7.

Shareholders' funds are also important, and at the end of 1981 accounted for 37.4 per cent of its M$406 million resources.

Development Bank of Malaysia. The DBM (Bank Pembangnnan Malaysia Berhad) with a paid-up capital wholly subscribed by Bank Bumiputra Berhad, was established in 1973 to finance industrial enterprises owned by bumiputra individuals or companies that are in turn majority owned by bumiputras. The DBM's objective was to increase indigenous community participation in the industrial and commercial sector. DBM provides assistance in the identification; evaluation; planning; financing; and implementation of industrial projects. This financial support is by way of medium or long term loans at special rates of interest, or by purchase of an equity interest which can later be sold back to the borrower or other bumiputras. DBM also guarantees industrial equipment loans extended by the supplier or foreign institution. A wide range of technical, managerial and advisory services are also provided throughout the various stages of planning and implementing the project. DBM has similar financing schemes to MIDF, including medium and long term loans for the purchase of fixed assets, and a factory mortgage scheme for the purchase of a factory and land on a long term basis.

In terms of funding, most DBM resources are by way of long term loans from the Federal government, as well as from the Bank's own capital.

Industrial Development Bank. The IDB (Bank Kemajuan Perusahaan Malaysia Berhad) was established in August 1979, to help finance industrial development. In particular, its function is to promote and finance the growth of productive capacity in industries that are capital intensive as well as 'high technology'. Emphasis is given to export orientated industries and other ventures with long gestation periods identified as nationally desirable. Long term funds are provided by IDB at concessional rates where appropriate. The Bank's lending has so far been mainly directed to the shipping industry. The Bank is funded initially by long term loans from the Federal government, Treasury and the Central Bank. At the end of 1981, IDM had resources of some M$143.8 m.

Sabah Development Bank. The SDB was established by the State government of Sabah in 1977, to provide medium and long-term loans and equity participation to private and government sponsored projects contributing to the development of the State of Sabah. SDB provides medium and long term loans for fixed assets and development expenditure to both public and private enterprise. It also provides short term credit for working capital purposes and issues guarantees, opening letters of credit and other necessary forms of financial and non-financial assistance. In addition, it may also provide, equity participation, underwriting and syndication of loans as well as technical and managerial services. Other specialised services include general corporate advice and the identification and development of new projects. At the end of 1981, 21.5 per cent of its M$654.9 million outstanding loans were to manufacturing, 15.7 per cent to agriculture, and the remainder to a variety of other industries. Besides its development finance role, SDB also acts as the financial intermediary to the Sabah State government.

Agricultural Bank of Malaysia. The ABM (Bank Pertanian Malaysia) was established by the Federal government in 1969, to mobilise savings from the agricultural sector and to provide short and long term funds for developing the agricultural sector, including production and marketing. While initially the emphasis was on short-term loans, the Bank has now increased its long term loans for large scale agricultural development projects. The Bank has six loan schemes and eight project loan facilities, the largest being a credit programme for rice farmers. The next major programme is the financing scheme for the production of tobacco, and its marketing. The Bank's equipment loan scheme provides credit to small farmers for the purchase of power tillers, water pumps, tractors, sprayers and various other agricultural implements. Other areas of credit operations by the bank include loans for sugar planting and processing and for the cultivation and processing of oil palm. These credits are provided through its branches, and through a network of farmers' associations and co-operative societies that are agro based; at the end of 1981, the Bank had 38 branches. The main source of funds of the bank is fixed and savings deposits. Deposits from small savers are mobilised through its branches; in 1978, it introduced a Giro service facility. The bank also accepts short and medium term deposits from the government and other financial institutions. Total loans outstanding at the end of 1981 were M$265.1 million. Although loans by ABM have expanded significantly, its financing is still small when compared to total loans to the agricultural sector by the commercial banks and finance companies.

Borneo Development Corporation. The BDC was initially set up in 1958 as a subsidiary of the Commonwealth Development Corporation. It was, however, purchased by the Sabah and Sarawak government in 1975. Its main objective is to promote industrial and commercial development in the States of Sabah and Sarawak. Most recent lending has been to finance the purchase of BDC developed industrial buildings; of BDC's M$24.7 million loans outstanding at the end of 1981, 70 per cent were directed to manufacturing activities with transport and storage projects, general commerce and residential housing construction accounting for the remainder.

As with the other development banks, it obtains much of its funds in the form of State government loans, special deposits and its own shareholders' funds. Loans have also been received from other sources including the commercial banks.

(v) *Other banking institutions*

There are two Apex co-operative societies in Malaysia—the Co-operative Central Bank, CCB (the apex of the urban credit co-operative societies) and Bank Kerjasama Rakyat Malaysia, Bank Rakyat (the apex of the rural credit co-operative societies).

Co-operative Central Bank. The CCB was established in 1958 with the main objective of mobilising funds from individuals and co-operative societies and of directing these funds to viable co-operative enterprises. At the end of 1981, it had 13 branches throughout the country, and a membership of 186 societies and 119456 individuals. The bank accepts fixed and savings deposits; interest paid on these deposits has generally been higher than interest earned at deposits with the commercial banks. Deposits represent the main source of funds; the remaining source comprises shareholders' funds. Initially CCB granted loans only to member co-operative societies. In 1971, a personal loan scheme for individual members, as well as a hire purchase financing scheme for its member societies, was introduced. The bank also extends loans to member co-operatives, as well as mortgage loans for individual members. Remaining funds are generally placed in fixed deposit with various financial institutions, or invested in long term government securities.

Bank Rakyat. Bank Rakyat was established in 1954, as the Rural Co-operative Apex Bank. At the end of 1981, it had 18 branches and a membership of 890 rural co-operative societies and 27526 individuals. The bank is a major source of funds for the co-operative societies; it also provides loans directly to individual members. The total resources of the bank have expanded rapidly, mainly because of the growth of savings and fixed deposits resulting from attractive rates of return offered by the bank, and also the increase in the number of its branches. Loans provided by the bank have largely been for the financing of industry; agriculture and fishing; and housing. A major proportion of these loans are medium term. Total loans outstanding at the end of 1981 were M$166.8 million.

(b) The Non-banking Financial Institutions

(i) *Merchant banks*

The merchant banks in Malaysia were established to complement and supplement the services provided by the commercial banks and finance companies. The first merchant bank was established in 1970. At end of 1981, there are 12 merchant banks in Malaysia; their relative importance and establishment dates are shown in Table 3.10. Most of these were established as joint ventures between Malaysian and foreign interests; a list of their share-

TABLE 3.10 Malaysia merchant banks by assets, incorporation and establishment date (figures as at 31 December 1980, in M$ million)

Bank	Date of incorporation	Year of commencement	Total assets
Amanah–Chase Merchant Bankers (M) Berhad	28 December 1974	1975	268.4
Arab–Malaysian Development Bank Berhad	5 August 1975	1976	540.9
Aseam Bankers Malaysia Berhad	28 September 1973	1973	358.0
Asian International Merchant Bankers Berhad	5 July 1972	1973	180.5[a]
Asiavest Merchant Bankers Berhad	29 March 1975	1975	137.5[b]
Bumiputra Merchant Bankers Berhad	4 October 1972	1972	105.1
D & C Nomura Merchant Bankers Berhad	5 August 1974	1974	194.0
Malaysian International Merchant Bankers Berhad	3 December 1970	1971	280.4
Permata Chartered Merchant Bank Berhad	3 October 1970	1970	111.7
Pertanian Baring Sanwa Berhad	24 April 1974	1974	109.4
Rakyat First Merchant Bankers Berhad	8 April 1974	1974	111.3
UDA Merchant Bankers Berhad	22 July 1975	1975	133.1

[a] As at end of September 1980.
[b] As at end of May 1980.

Source: Merchant banks' *Annual Reports*.

holders is provided in Table 3.11. Until 1979 when they were
brought under the Banking Act 1973, merchant banks operated
under a broad set of guidelines instituted by the Central Bank
with the concurrence of the Ministry of Finance. With effect from
1 January 1979, the merchant banks were granted a licence under
the Banking Act 1973 to conduct banking business. However, due

TABLE 3.11 Malaysia merchant banks by shareholders and relative holdings (December 1981)

Name of bank	Local shareholder(s)			Foreign shareholder(s)	
	Name			Name	
1. Amanah-Chase Merchant Bank	(a) Komplek Kewangan Malaysia Berhad	B	72.4%	(a) Chase Manhattan Banking Corporation	20.0%
				(b) The Mitsubishi Bank Limited	5.8
				(c) Orion Royal Pacific Limited	1.8
				Total	27.6%
2. Arab-Malaysian Development Bank	Data Azam Hashim		100%		
3. ASEAM Bankers Malaysia	(a) Malayan Banking Berhad	B	46.0%	(a) B. A. Asia Limited	21.5%
	(b) Sarawak Foundation	B	5.0	(b) Banque de Paris et des Pays-Bas	5.5
				(c) The Dai-Ichi Kangyo Bank Ltd.	5.5
				(d) Dresdner Bank AG	5.5
				(e) Union Bank of Switzerland	5.5
				(f) Kleinwort Benson Ltd.	5.5
	Total		51.0%	Total	49.0%

	Local shareholders			Foreign shareholders	
4. Asian International Merchant Bankers	(a) United Malayan Banking Corp. Bhd. (b) Omariff Holdings Sdn. Bhd.		50.0% 7.5	(a) Grindlays Bank Limited (b) Fuji Bank Limited	27.5% 15.0
	Total		57.5%	Total	42.5%
5. Asiavest Merchant Bankers	(a) Asiavest Holdings (M) Sdn. Bhd.		100.0%		
6. Bumiputra Merchant Bankers	(a) Bank Bumiputra Malaysia Berhad	B	77.5%	(a) N. M. Rothschild and Sons Limited (b) The Bank of Tokyo Limited	15.0% 7.5
				Total	22.5%
7. Permata Chartered Merchant Bank Berhad	(a) Malaysian International Shipping Corporation Berhad (b) Lembaga Tabung Angkatan Tentera (c) Koperasi Pegawai Pegawai Melayu Malaysia Berhad (MOCCIS)	 B B	35.0% 30.0 5.0	(a) The Chartered Bank	30.0%
	Total		70.0%		
8. D & C Nomura	(a) Development & Commercial Bank		51.0%	(a) The Nomura Securities Co. Ltd. (b) The Mitsui Bank Ltd. (c) The National Australia Bank	30.0% 10.0 9.0
				Total	49.0%

TABLE 3.11 *(contd.)*

Name of bank	Local shareholder(s)		Foreign shareholder(s)	
	Name		Name	
9. Malaysian International Merchant Bankers Berhad	(a) Malaysian Industrial Development Finance Berhad	55.2%	(a) Barclays Bank International Limited	20.0%
	(b) Geh Ik Cheong	4.8	(b) Continental Illinois National Bank & Trust Co. of Chicago	20.0
	Total	60.0%	Total	40.0%
10. Pertanian Banking Sanwa Bhd.	(a) Bank Pertanian Malaysia	68.0%	(a) Baring Brothers & Co. Ltd.	16.0%
			(b) The Sanwa Bank Limited	16.0
			Total	32.0%
11. Rakyat First Merchant Bankers Bhd.	(a) Bank Kerjasama Rakyat Malaysia Berhad	B 55.0%	(a) Deutsche Genossenschafts bank	40.0%
			(b) Genossenshaftliche Zentral bank	5.0%
12. UDA Merchant Bankers Bhd.*	(a) Bank Utama	B 60.0%	(a) Wardley Ltd	30.0%
			(b) The Industrial Bank of Japan, Ltd.	10.0
			Total	40.0%

B – Bumiputra interests.

*Expected to be changed to Utama Wardley Merchant Bank Ltd.

Source: Permata Chartered Merchant Bank Berhad, 1982.

to the specialised nature of their activities, the merchant banks are exempted from certain provisions in the Banking Act.[15]

The merchant banks in Malaysia provide merchant banking services.[16] While their activities have been concentrated in money market and lending operations, the Central Bank has encouraged the merchant banks to place equal emphasis on the provision of fee based activities. These include corporate finance and advisory services relating to underwriting of share issues; loan syndications; corporate reconstructions; acquisitions; mergers; portfolio management; and investment feasibility studies. Due to the tendency of merchant banks to concentrate more on profitable money market and fund based operations, their new licences required that within 3 years, at least 30 per cent of income earned should be obtained from fee based operations. In 1978, fee based operations amounted to 24 per cent of total income; at the end of 1981, all merchant banks had complied with this condition and fee income for the industry as a whole accounted for 44.2 per cent of total income earned.

As shown in Table 3.12, the main source of funds for the merchant banks is from deposit liabilities. Initially, merchant banks could accept deposits only of at least M$250000 with a maturity of 1 month or more from other licensed banks and finance companies. In February 1975, this was extended to include insurance companies for deposits of 1 year or more. While the merchant banks could also accept deposits from other institutions and corporations, this was as determined from time to time by the Central Bank. A substantial proportion of their funds were thus deposits placed by the commercial banks and finance companies for short periods. As from March 1979, merchant banks were permitted to accept deposits of not less than M$1 million per deposit from the corporate sector at a market determined rate. Prior to 1979, merchant banks could participate in the money market and accept 7-day call money; such funds, however, had to be placed in government securities or other negotiable instruments approved by the Central Bank. With effect from January 1979, merchant banks could participate in the interbank money market without restriction. Borrowings from the interbank money market thus constituted another important source of funds. Since the introduction of bankers' acceptances (BAs) in May 1979, the merchant banks also have been active in rediscounting this instrument. At the end of 1981, rediscounting of their own BAs was the second major source of funds, (18.8 per

TABLE 3.12 Malaysia sources and uses of merchant bank funds (figures as at 31 December 1981, in M$ million)

Sources	
Capital & reserves	158.2
Deposits	1627.9
Amounts due to financial institutions[a]	426.8
Banker's Acceptances	546.4
Other	144.7
Total	2904.0
Uses	
Cash[b]	2.4
Statutory reserves	26.8
Money at call	2.0
Amounts due from financial institutions[a]	93.9
NCDs held	28.7
Investments	210.7
Treasury bills	—
Government securities	(179.8)
Private securities	(30.9)
Loans	2348.4
Short term loans[c]	(906.3)
Term loans	(676.9)
Trade bills[d]	(766.2)
Refinancing facilities	34.4
Fixed assets	6.8
Other	149.9
Total	2904.0

[a] Refers to amounts due to and due from other merchant banks, commercial banks and finance companies.
[b] Includes balances with Central Bank.
[c] Refers to loans with repayment periods of 1 year and less.
[d] Includes Banker's Acceptances.

Source: Bank Negara Malaysia, *Annual Report 1981*, p. 70.

cent of the total). Merchant banks are now also permitted to undertake foreign currency borrowing, and to accept foreign currency deposits from non-residents.

Prior to this, merchant bank lending was largely in the form of loans extended to business enterprises. Credit facilities of the merchant banks were largely in the form of short term loans and trade bills financing. These were largely for the financing of the manufacturing sector; real estate development; and general commerce. Other activities included loans for construction, and mining and quarrying. While there has been growth in short term loans of 1 year and less, as well as term loans of 1 year and more, there has been a tendency since 1979–81 for short term loans to increase more rapidly – particularly due to the growth in trade bill financing. The merchant banks also provided financing facilities in the form of block discounting for hire purchase papers. Prior to this, Bank Negara Malaysia was concerned about the merchant banks' tendency to borrow short and lend long;[17] loans by merchant banks have been increasing at a more rapid rate than deposits, thus resulting in high loan deposit ratios. At the end of 1981, the loan deposit ratio was 146.4 per cent.

In carrying out their operations, merchant banks are required to maintain two ratios: domestic borrowings should not exceed their shareholders' funds by more than 15 times, and domestic borrowings (together with contingent liabilities) should not exceed their shareholders' funds by more than 20 times. The merchant banks also maintain a statutory reserve requirement against their total eligible liabilities with the Central Bank, as well as a minimum liquidity requirement (introduced in 1979). There is also a minimum paid-up capital requirement. The merchant banks have access to lender of last resort facilities, subject to the Bank's terms and conditions.

(ii) *Finance companies*

At the end of 1981, there were 39 finance companies operating in Malaysia with a network of 230 offices. Finance companies in Malaysia were first established in the early 1960s; as can be observed in Table 3.13. Many finance companies are subsidiaries of commercial banks. At the end of 1980, bank affiliated finance companies accounted for 68.4 per cent of the total assets; it can also be observed that bank affiliated finance companies are among the larger companies in terms of total assets. The expansion of finance companies has been in terms of both size and number of banking offices. Finance companies, however, have generally concentrated in the larger towns and commercial centres.

Finance companies were brought under the control of the Central Bank only with the enactment of Finance Company Act 1969.[18] As shown in Table 3.14, the finance companies' main

TABLE 3.13   Malaysia finance companies (figures as at end 1980, in M$ million)

Bank	Total assets	Share (%)
Bank affiliated		
Arab–Malaysian Finance Berhad (1)[a]	224267	4.1
Asia Commercial Finance (M) Berhad (5)	64589	1.2
Chung Khiaw Finance (M) Berhad (1)	19527	0.4
Credit Corporation (M) Berhad (6)	740968	13.7
D & C Finance Berhad (6)	102645	1.9
Hock Thai Finance Corporation Berhad (6)	94846	1.8
Kewangan Bumiputra Berhad (9)	317643	5.9
Kong Ming Finance Corporation Berhad (5)	89518	1.7
Kwong Yik Finance Berhad (3)	80010	1.5
Magnum Finance Berhad (4)	59381	1.1
Malayan Finance Corporation Berhad (11)	248564	4.6
Malaysian International Finance Berhad (1)	8856	0.2
Mortgage and Finance (M) Berhad (4)	651369	12.0
Oversea–Chinese Finance Company Berhad (4)	227490	4.2
Overseas Union Trust (M) Berhad (6)	142999	2.6
Public Finance Berhad (21)	425925	7.9
Southern Finance Company Berhad (4)	40643	0.8
United National Finance Berhad (8)	164212	3.0
Total Bank affiliated companies	3703452	68.4

[a] Figures in parentheses show no. of branches.

source of funds are in the form of deposits. They may accept both fixed and savings varieties, but not deposits repayable on demand. Of the total deposits at the end of 1981, 94 per cent were in the form of fixed deposits. The finance companies accept deposits with a maturity ranging from 3–60 months. The 12 month deposit has generally been the most popular, accounting for more than half the total; however, at the end of 1981 its importance declined somewhat as there was an increase in the demand for deposits with a maturity of 3 months in view of the uncertainties experienced with respect to interest rates. Prior to August 1973, interest rates on deposits at finance companies were regulated, the maximum rate being generally 1 per cent higher than that offered by commercial banks. After 1973, the rates were determined by the finance companies. As the interest rate differential widened between the two institutions, finance com-

TABLE 3.13   *(contd.)*

Bank	Total assets	Share (%)
Non-bank affiliated		
Boon Siew Finance Berhad (1)	71919	1.3
Central Malaysian Finance Berhad (24)	126451	2.3
Chew Geok Lin Finance (M) Berhad (1)	29958	0.6
Delta Finance Company Berhad (3)	42340	0.8
Eu Finance Berhad (5)	94556	1.7
Hong Leong Finance Berhad (10)	216831	4.0
Interfinance Berhad (1)	28080	0.5
Keng Soon Finance Berhad (2)	111267	2.1
Kewangan Usaha Bersatu Berhad (1)	49838	0.9
Kuala Lumpur Finance Berhad (2)	77559	1.4
Leong Hin (M) Finance Company Berhad (2)	9306	0.2
Malayan United Finance Berhad (6)	89038	1.6
Malaysia Borneo Finance Corporation (M) Berhad (38)	426018	7.9
Malaysia Credit Finance Berhad (2)	61563	1.1
Overseas Credit Finance (M) Berhad (1)	19129	0.4
Pertama Malaysia Finance Berhad (2)	17767	0.3
Sabah Finance Berhad (3)	44921	0.8
Sim Lim Finance (M) Berhad (17)	172114	3.2
Tai Cheng Finance Berhad (3)	19843	0.4
Total non-bank affiliated companies	1708498	31.6
Total (all finance companies)	5411950	100.00

Source: *A Study of Licensed Finance Companies in Malaysia 1980* (Kuala Lumpur: SGV–Kassim Chan Sdn Berhad, 1981).

panies provided commercial banks with increased competition in the mobilisation of deposits. Borrowing from commercial banks represents another source of funds.

The main lending activity of the finance companies is in hire purchase finance, largely to finance consumer durables and motor vehicles. At the end of 1981, hire purchase finance amounted to 45 per cent of total credit outstanding; hire purchase loans are also provided for commercial vehicles, machinery and equipment. Other areas of financing include loans to individuals for the purchase of houses; at the end of 1981, loans for housing comprised 18.3 per cent of the total. Leasing finance is also

TABLE 3.14   Malaysia sources and uses of finance company
funds (figures as of 31 December 1981, in M$ million)

Sources	
Capital & reserves	331.6
Deposits	6422.8
Fixed	(6021.3)
Savings	(401.5)
Amounts due to financial institutions[a]	63.2
Refinancing obligations	6.0
Other	573.0
Total	**7396.6**
Uses	
Cash	6.2
Statutory reserves	115.8
Money at call	257.6
Amounts due from financial institutions[a]	1763.2
Investments	164.4
Treasury bills	(3.7)
Government securities	(151.4)
Private securities	(9.3)
Refinancing facilities	56.7
Loans	4583.6
Hire purchase finance	(2086.1)
Leasing finance	(400.3)
Housing loans	(839.6)
Other loans	(1257.6)
Fixed assets	37.5
Other	411.6
Total	**7396.6**

[a]   Refers to amounts due from other finance companies, commercial
banks and merchant banks.

Source: Bank Negara Malaysia, *Annual Report 1981*, p. 65.

important. While the loan deposit ratio of the finance companies
has increased significantly, the growth of lending by the finance
companies is limited by the risk asset ratio. Prior to 1977, it was
required that the ratio of risk assets to shareholders' funds should
not exceed 10 times.[19] In 1977, this ratio was increased to 15
times, to enable the finance companies to expand their loan
portfolio.

In April 1971, finance companies were subject to a liquidity requirement against their total deposit liabilities. In 1972, the finance companies were also required to maintain a statutory reserve with the Central Bank. The reserve ratio, which has been changed a number of times, has ranged from 2.5–7 per cent. The liquid assets of the finance companies comprise mainly deposits with commercial banks, merchant banks and government securities. Treasury bill holdings by finance companies have been small. In March 1979, new liquidity requirements were introduced to require finance companies to maintain a minimum level of liquid assets to eligible liabilities, as opposed to total deposits.[20]

Guidelines were introduced in 1975 to influence the direction of lending by the finance companies. It was required that 50 per cent of new loans be extended to the indigenous community; manufacturing (including food production); housing; and for the purchase of machinery and equipment. In 1976, these guidelines were respecified as a minimum proportion of total loans outstanding, and were revised again in March 1981. Under the newest guidelines, the finance companies were required to grant a minimum of 20 per cent of their total loans at the end of 1980 to the indigenous community, 25 per cent to small scale industries, and 20 per cent to housing; the finance companies as a group complied with these guidelines during the period. In terms of the total loans outstanding, loans to the indigenous community comprised 23.1 per cent, loans to small industry 24.6 per cent, and loans to housing 18.2 per cent. The breakdown of total loans, shown in Table 3.15, indicates that loans to individuals are the most important.

A set of rules has also been introduced by the Association of Finance Companies in Malaysia to standardise the operations of the finance companies, in particular relating to their operational activities. These rules relate to the charges incurred for services, with respect to achieving a standard method of calculation of interest rates on deposits and loans and introducing greater professionalism into the industry.

(iii) *Insurance companies*

There are 65 insurance companies operating in Malaysia – of five life, 47 general, and 13 composite life and general insurance. Although the insurance industry was initially dominated by foreign companies, since the 1970s domestic insurance companies

TABLE 3.15   Malaysia finance company lending by type of industry (figures as of 31 December 1981, in M$ million)

Total assets (%)		Amount
9.0	Agriculture	412.1
1.5	Mining & quarrying	70.6
4.9	Manufacturing	225.6
23.6	Real estate & construction	1083.5
5.6	Commerce	254.2
43.2	Private individuals	1977.4
(18.2)	Housing	(833.4)
(21.9)	Consumption credit	(1002.9)
(3.1)	Other purposes	(141.1)
12.2	Other	560.2
100.0	Total	4583.6

Source: Bank Negara Malaysia, *Annual Report 1981*, p. 68.

have increased significantly. Of the total as at the end of 1981, 41 are domestically incorporated. The operation of life insurance companies comes under the Insurance Act 1963, and life insurance companies account for about two-thirds of the total assets of the industry. Under the Insurance Act 1963, both types of insurance companies are required to invest a proportion of their total asset portfolio in the form of authorised Malaysian assets. The proportion (which was set at 25 per cent in 1963) has gradually been increased, to 80 per cent in 1975. As at the end of September 1981, the proportion of authorised Malaysian assets : total assets was 92.9 per cent for the industry as a whole, 91.9 per cent for life insurance companies, and 94.7 per cent for general insurance companies. The insurance companies are also required to invest a minimum proportion of their assets in government securities. This ratio (which was 10 per cent in 1970) has been raised gradually. Under the Insurance (Amendment) Act 1978, the insurance companies were required to maintain at least 24 per cent of their portfolio in government securities.

The life insurance companies offer a whole life policy as well as an endowment policy, the latter also acting as a form of saving in that it can be used as saving for retirement, for loans or mortgages on housing, or for education of children. There is also a group policy, which is offered to organisations for their employees. In view of the long term nature of the liabilities of the life insurance companies, a high proportion of their funds are invested in long term instruments such as long term government securities; corporate securities; loans to public corporations; and mortgage and policy loans. Motor insurance business is the most important among the general insurance companies. Others include marine, aviation and transit insurance, as well as insurance covering personal and commercial property. In view of the short-term nature of their liabilities, general insurance companies' investments tend to be more liquid; they include deposits with the commercial banks and other financial institutions; corporate securities; and government securities.

(iv) *Provident and pension funds*

Provident and pension funds in Malaysia are significant in the financial system in terms of total resources. Provident and pension funds have been so effective in the mobilisation of savings that they rank second, next to commercial banks. In Malaysia, the provident and pension funds include the Employees' Provident Fund, the Teachers' Provident Fund, the Social Security Organisation, the Armed Forces Fund (Tabung Angkatan Tentera), and other approved statutory and private provident and pension funds. Together at the end of 1981 these funds had a combined membership of 6.1 million.

The Employees' Provident Fund (EPF), the largest, covers more than 70 per cent of Malaysia's labour force, and represents an important source of finance for the government. The total membership at the end of 1981 was 3.9 million and total resources were M$11,363.6 million. The EPF was established in 1951, under the Employees' Provident Fund Ordinance. Employers and employees had to contribute 5 per cent each; these contributions were increased in 1975 to 13 per cent – 7 per cent by the employer, 6 per cent by the employee. This was subsequently increased to a total of 20 per cent in 1980 – 11 per cent by the employer, 9 per cent by the employee.

The employee's contributions are deducted by the employer. The principal source of funds are thus the net contributions and income from investment. The EPF must invest at least 70 per cent of its funds in Federal government securities; in practice, it is generally 90 per cent. Approximatley half the domestic debt is thus held by the EPF. The holdings of government securities are generally of long-term maturity, and the EPF therefore represents an important source of funds for the public sector in financing development.

(v) *Urban credit societies*

The urban credit societies in Malaysia are closely equivalent to credit unions overseas, and represent the more viable side of the local co-operative movement. As with their overseas counterparts, most of the funds come from members in the form of share subscriptions and deposits, and are lent out to members to finance their purchase of consumer durables (and, to a lesser extent, as housing loans). They also hold a portion of their assets in liquid form.

At the end of 1981, the 690 urban credit societies had assets totalling M$812 million and a combined membership of 656500. In terms of both numbers and assets, employees' credit societies are the most important, and comprise 53 per cent of the societies. Thrift and loan societies account for another 35 per cent, and housing credit and thrift and investment societies the remainder.

The Co-operative Central Bank has played a major role in the industry's success.

(vi) *Rural credit co-operative societies*

The rural credit co-operatives in Malaysia include farmers' organisations, agro based co-operatives, and fishermen societies, among others. Due to past problems, they have been subject to a number of government improvement programmes both through Bank Rakyat and more specialist organisations such as the Farmers' Organisation Authority and the Fisheries Development Authority. The goal of each of these programmes has been to make the individual co-operatives into strong and viable organisations.

(vii) *Malaysian Building Society*

The Malaysian Building Society Berhad was established to provide housing finance within penisular Malaysia; it specialises in financing the construction and purchase of low cost housing. This is accomplished by way of long term concessional loans.

It obtains its funds from deposits, loans and share capital. Of these, borrowings are the most important with two-thirds coming from Bank Negara Malaysia and the remainder from the EPF.

(viii) *Borneo Housing Mortgage Finance*

The BHMF (Borneo Housing Mortgage Finance Berhad) was established to provide housing finance within the states of Sabah and Sarawak. Besides its own share capital, it obtains its financing from long term borrowings from the EPF and from fixed deposits from statutory authorities, insurance companies, provident and pension funds, and the Sabah State government. At the end of 1981, it had resources of some M$261.9 million.

FINANCIAL MARKETS

The money market in Malaysia has experienced significant development since 1970, providing financial institutions with adjustment instruments to achieve their desired portfolio position. The interbank money market is the most active. Other instruments in the money market include Treasury bills, bankers' acceptances and NCDs. Despite its relatively higher rate of return, the market for trade bills in Malaysia has not become active largely due to the credit risk involved.[21] There is also a certain amount of intercompany lending, although this is not significant.

The capital market in Malaysia comprises government securities, corporate debt securities and shares. Government securities are almost entirely held by institutions, a number of which are 'captive' holders. Debt securities and shares, on the other hand, are held by a wide range of individual investors and institutions. The corporate securities market—while small relative to the government securities market—represents the more active market.

(a) The Money Market

(i) *Interbank funding*

The interbank market is an important source of short term funds for the banking system. It provides the banking system with such

funds to accommodate adjustments in their liquidity requirements, as well as to fund their loan activities. With the increased
importance of liability management among the Malaysian commercial banks, the interbank money market has grown rapidly.
The average monthly borrowing on the domestic inter-bank
market in 1967 was M$107 m; this had increased to M$430 m in
1978, and by 1981 the average monthly borrowing on the interbank
market had increased significantly, to M$6112.2 million.

In the interbank money market transactions are predominantly
for overnight and 7 day money. Funds are also placed on a 1
month, 2 month, 3 month and 6 month basis. Prior to the
introduction of liquidity requirements in March 1979, 8 day
money was the predominant maturity (under the new liquidity
requirement, deposits up to 7 days with the commercial banks are
no longer eligible for the liquid asset requirement) as it was not
required for banks to take the net position of borrowing of 8 days
or longer into the computation of liquid assets. In view of the
marked increase in their investments portfolio, commercial banks
have increasingly resorted to borrowing in the interbank money
market to accommodate temporary adjustments in their holdings.
Banks that do not have a wide deposit base also rely on the market
to fund their activities; this is particularly true for the foreign
owned banks. Money market conditions tend to reflect the
general liquidity position of the banks.

Merchant banks, the Agricultural Bank and Bank Rakyat are
also permitted to operate without restriction in the interbank
market. Merchant banks were initially permitted to accept only 7
day call money, with the restriction that the funds had to be
invested in government securities. After January 1979, when the
merchant banks were licensed under the Banking Act 1979, they
were permitted to participate fully in the market without
restriction. Borrowing in the interbank market has since become a
major source of funds for the merchant banks. In the general
market, deposits are also made among commercial banks, finance
companies and merchant banks.

An alternative to the interbank money market is to place funds
at the discount houses. These institutions were established in
1963, and as at the end of 1981 there are five discount houses in
Malaysia. The discount houses accept deposits from the general
public, commercial banks and non-bank financial institutions,
but do not lend funds in the domestic money market. The
regulations under which the discount house operate require that
they restrict their investments to government instruments up to a

maturity of 3 years. Their asset portfolio thus comprises mainly Treasury bills and government securities with a maturity of 1 year and less. With effect from May 1979, the discount houses were also permitted to purchase BAs and NCDs. Investment in these instruments, however, is limited to a maximum of 15 per cent of total assets.

The discount houses accept deposits overnight and up to 7 days. Funds may be placed at the end of the day for call the following day, and are made with a cheque drawn on balances at the Central Bank or with a cashier's cheque. The minimum amount accepted for deposit is M$50000. While the discount houses accept mainly deposits, they are also permitted to sell government instruments in the market – a discount house can obtain funds to meet deposit withdrawals by selling government instruments. Alternatively, it can borrow from the Central Bank against its holdings of these securities. The main depositors at the discount houses have been the commercial banks; at the end of 1981, commercial bank deposits with the discount houses comprised 77.9 per cent of the total.

The discount houses are thus influenced significantly by the liquidity position of the commercial banks. The average monthly volume of call money accepted by the discount houses at the end of 1981 was M$11400 million, while the average monthly deposits was M$11943 million.

(ii) *Treasury bills*

Treasury bills were initially issued on tap at rates prescribed by the monetary authorities. After August 1973, a tender system was introduced, with the rates determined by the market. Under this system the 3 month Treasury bill is issued weekly, the 6 month fortnightly and the 12 month, every 4 weeks. The 3 month Treasury bill, which had initially been significant, has since declined in importance and the 9 month Treasury bill discontinued. The issue of Treasury bills is, however, subject to a statutory limit which has been raised several times. In 1977, this stood at M$3000 million and remained unchanged up to the end of 1981.

A major factor contributing to the growth of the Treasury bill market is the fact that such bills are eligible as part of the liquidity assets structure of the commercial banks, finance companies and merchant banks. In 1965, commercial banks were required to maintain a minimum liquidity requirement comprising only domestic instruments; this resulted in a distinct shift from the holding of foreign instruments to the holding of domestic securities (mainly Treasury bills). In 1971, a Minimum liquidity requirement was also applied to finance companies, and in 1979, to merchant banks. With the marked increase in deposits at these institutions, demand for Treasury bills has significantly increased. The commercial banks, however, remain the main holder of Treasury bills, and at the end of 1981 they held 80.7 per cent of the Treasury bills outstanding. To encourage the development of the market for Treasury bills, the Central Bank provides rediscounting facilities for these securities.

(iii) *Bankers' acceptances (BAs)*

Introduced in 1979, BAs are an attractive money market instrument in view of their relatively high yield and marketability. The instrument represents a category of bills of exchange used to finance foreign and domestic trade. BAs issued represent an alternative liability instrument available to financial institutions. For the financial institutions that purchase the instrument, it represents an alternative short term investment.

The growth of BAs has been rapid. At the end of 1981, the volume outstanding at commercial banks was M$11642.8 million. Of this amount, 70.6 per cent was refinanced and comprised 51 per cent of trade bills outstanding. Foreign banks were more active in this market, accounting for 66.4 per cent of the BAs issued. The rediscounting of own BAs represents an important source of funds for the merchant banks; finance companies and discount houses are also active participants in this market. The holding of BAs and NCDs by discount houses are subject to a maximum limit of 15 per cent of total assets.

To encourage the development of an active secondary market for BAs, they are permitted in the computation of the minimum liquidity requirement. For commercial banks and merchant banks, inland bills of exchange (including BAs issued by other commercial banks or merchant banks eligible for rediscounting with the Central Bank) are permitted in the computation of the minimum liquidity requirement up to a maximum of 5 per cent of their eligible liabilities. The Central Bank also offered rediscounting facilities for BAs with a maturity of not more than 21 days. In 1981, the Central Bank purchased a gross volume of $4130 million from commercial banks, merchant banks, finance companies and discount houses.

(iv) *Negotiable certificates of deposits* (*NCDs*)

NCDs were also introduced to the Malaysian money market in 1979. NCDs are particularly attractive to the corporate sector, in view of their liquidity and relatively high rates of return. When the instrument was first introduced, their minimum duration was for 6 months, and the minimum denomination was M$100000. In December 1981, the minimum initial maturity was reduced to 3 months, and the minimum denomination to M$50000. At the end of 1981, the 6 month maturity accounted for 75 per cent of the total outstanding, the 12 month for 10.3 per cent.

At the end of 1979, of the total NCDs issued by the commercial banks, more than half were held by the banking system. At the end of 1981, the commercial banks, however, had utilised only 75 per cent of the limit set by the Central Bank. At the end of 1981, NCDs outstanding comprised 6 per cent of total bank deposits; of these, 87 per cent had been issued by the domestic banks.

(b) The Stock Market

The beginning of the Stock Exchange in Malaysia was initiated when the Malayan Stockholders' Association of 19 firms reconstituted itself into the Malayan Stock Exchange (MSE) on 21 March 1960, and established two trading rooms – one in Singapore and the other in Kuala Lumpur. A Sydney board system of trading was adopted – whereby the shares of the various companies were posted on boards in each trading room and bids and offers were entered into on a continuous auction basis. Direct telephone wires were installed between the two trading rooms in 1962.

When the Federation of Malaysia was formed in 1963 (with Singapore as a component state) the MSE was renamed the Stock Exchange of Malaysia (SEM). With the separation of Singapore from the Federation of Malaysia in 1965, the SEM was renamed the Stock Exchange of Malaysia and Singapore, and although the two countries were politically separated the Exchange and its two trading rooms remained a joint operation. Its split into the Kuala Lumpur Stock Exchange (KLSE) and the Stock Exchange of Singapore (SES) finally came on 8 May 1973, when the Malaysian government announced its intention of achieving greater control and flexibility in financial matters by establishing a separate Stock Exchange and discontinuing the interchangeability of currencies between the two countries.[22]

The KLSE has grown at a steady and substantial rate. As compared to the growth of total deposits at the commercial banks and the NSB (which increased from M$20225 million in 1979 to M$25987 million in 1981), the issued capital of KLSE listed companies increased from M$6400 million in 1979 to M$10900 million in 1981.

Although the KLSE is largely a self-regulatory body, with its own rules, by-laws, listing requirements and corporate disclosure policy, it is subject at present to the administrative controls of the Capital Issue Committee (CIC), a body established by the Central Bank to supervise the securities industry. New issues or offers for sale to the public – whether by public offering or private placing; right issue; reconstruction scheme; takeover; acquisition of assets; listing of shares and debentures on the KLSE – require CIC approval in addition to the sanction of KLSE. Bonus issues arising from the revaluation of plant and machinery or buildings and land also require CIC's scrutiny and approval.

The requirements for a public offering are contained in the Companies Act, and in the KLSE Listing Manual, and are designed to ensure the fullest disclosure of information necessary for a potential investor to assess the worth of the securities offered.

Under the Companies Act, a public offer of securities must be accompanied by a prospectus which complies with the Act and is duly registered with the Registrar of Companies. The contents of a prospectus include, details on share capital; minimum amount to be raised; nature of business of the issuing corporation, its directors and the nature and extent of their interest; auditors; underwriting commission; preliminary expenses; and general nature (including date and parties) of every material contract. The prospectus is also required to present a report by an approved company auditor on the accounts (Profit and Loss and Balance Sheet statement) of the issuing company (and of the guarantor corporation in the case of a guaranteed bond issue).

The Listing Manual supplements the requirement of the Companies Act. The clause on share capital states that the company shall not issue shares to transfer a controlling interest without prior approval of shareholders in a general meeting, and that the applicant company for listing must have a paid-up capital of at least M$2 million, of which 25 per cent is in the hands of not less than 500 shareholders holding not more than 10000, and not less than 500, shares each. The purpose of these requirements is to ensure that a company seeking listing is of sufficient size (and that its shareholding is reasonably spread out) to create a market.

One of the principal roles of a stock market is to raise capital for financing the development of the national economy, mobilising the available funds as effectively and efficiently as possible. An indicator of the importance of the capital market to the economy is the amount of funds raised through new issues relative to the value of GNP. The ratios for 1974 and 1981 were respectively 4.85 and 8.65 per cent;[23] the net funds raised in these two years were respectively M$803 million and M$4706 million. However, the Federal government dominates the new issues market, with the bulk of its securities going to 'captive' institutions such as provident and pension funds. The government's share of the new funds raised in 1974 and 1981 was respectively, for example, 90 and 81 per cent. Corporations on the KLSE raise only a fraction of their financing requirements by new securities issues; their funding is mainly from internally generated funds such as retained profits and depreciation allowances, and from bank borrowings.

Another major function of the Stock Exchange is to provide a central mechanism for the purchase and sale of securities. It is important that the 'trading process' be conducted efficiently, so that it does not discriminate between firms of comparable risk. As at the end of 1981, total paid-up capital of the 252 listed companies on the KLSE amounted to M$10014 million, with a total market capitalisation of M$48 billion. An indication of the listed firms by types of industry is shown in Table 3.16. Turnover on the KLSE increased from 391 million units, (having a total value of M$722 million) in 1974 to 1636 million units; (having a total value of M$8059 million) in 1981. Trading in industrials dominates the transaction volume, and in 1981 it accounted for 75.6 per cent of the total turnover. Next in importance were rubber, tin and palm oil shares, accounting for 10.6 per cent of total. Transactions in property and hotel shares together accounted for 10.7 per cent of total volume traded, while trading in shares of financial institutions accounted for the balance of 3.1 per cent. There was no significant difference from the above pattern in value terms.

Capital markets in developing countries are generally found to be underdeveloped – the markets are thin, with little or no trading and relatively few and insignificant amounts of new issues; the

TABLE 3.16   Kuala Lumpur Stock Exchange listings by industry and type of security (figures as of 29 October 1982, in M$)

Sector[a]	No. of companies	Market valuation		
		Ordinary capital	Preference capital	Loan/debenture capital (include convert)
Industrials	149	24275995378	9721392	41591362
Finance	16	10342567319	—	228202079
Hotels	11	2701309824	—	4515325
Properties	13	3633384190	—	81240187
Oil Palms	10	3273194449	—	—
Tins	29	2286802517	92500	—
		£588000	£100000	—
$Rubbers	30	3210236983	—	2813703
£Rubbers	2	100800000	—	—
Total	260	49824290660	9813892	358362656
		£588000	£100000	

[a]   Total market capitalisation M$50195189.796.

Source: Kuala Lumpur Stock Exchange, 1982.

securities market in Malaysia is one of the few exceptions to this generalisation.[24]

(c) The Kuala Lumpur Commodity Exchange (KLCE)

The KLCE was established on 23 October 1980, to trade commodity futures contracts within Malaysia, and to provide domestic palm oil producers with an opportunity to hedge their activities locally. The KLCE operates under the Commodity Trading Act 1980, and is supervised by the Commodities Trading Council.

At present the KLCE trades only in crude palm oil futures contracts, but if they prove successful it is eventually hoped to introduce other contracts as well – particularly tin and rubber. The contracts are handled by the Kuala Lumpur Commodity Clearing House Berhad which is owned jointly by the London based International Commodities Clearing House and seven commercial banks.

As of June 1981, the KLCE had 91 full members (27 are floor members) and 18 trade associates.

ANALYSIS

Deliberate efforts have been made by the monetary authorities to develop the financial infrastructure, not only to accommodate increased and more diversified financial needs but also to promote an efficient monetary policy. These efforts have been particularly intensified since 1970.

While the commercial banking system has expanded at a rapid rate since 1970, the non-bank financial institutions have grown at an even faster rate. Not only has there been an increase in the number of new institutions but also growth in the exisiting ones. A number of mergers have also taken place, strengthening the institutions. The growth in the network of commercial banks has been particularly in the smaller towns, providing increased access to savers and investors. There has also been a significant increase in domestic ownership in the financial institutions. Previously, the financial system in Malaysia was significantly dominated by foreign incorporated institutions, particularly commercial banks and insurance companies. The 1970s also witnessed increased government ownership of financial institutions.

Related to development orientation of the monetary authorities was the emergence in the 1970s of a number of specialised development finance institutions. As many of these institutions have been in operation for only a few years, it is difficult to evaluate their relative effectiveness in promoting the activities for which they were established. Such institutions should have comparative advantage in the evaluation of creditworthiness, as well as in the administration and servicing of loans granted to the specific priority sectors; however, the institutions need to expand in order to take advantage of economies of scale.

A number of reforms have been introduced into the financial system. Interest rates were liberalised during the period; this caused an upward shift in interest rates, and in spite of an increase in inflation, real rates have been positive. Demand for, and supply of, funds has shown significant response to interest rate movements. This development has increased the scope for monetary management; the previous lack of portfolio response to interest rate changes was hardly surprising as the return reflected neither the maturity nor the risk of the instruments.

Both the money and capital markets developed significantly in the 1970s. Two new instruments – NCDs and BAs – were introduced to increase the spectrum of portfolio choice. With the development of the financial markets, the investment portfolio of various financial institutions also increased significantly. Liability management has also increased in importance as borrowing by the respective institutions have become an important source of funds. With the development of the domestic money market there will be less reliance on foreign financial markets; a wider spectrum of instruments in the market will also discourage capital outflows. To encourage development of the market, the Central Bank also provided rediscounting facilities for various instruments. These institutional developments in the financial market have also increased the maturity structure of the portfolios of the financial institutions.

Regulatory controls and the introduction of guidelines by the Central Bank were more extensive during the 1970s; regulatory control was extended not just to encompass the commercial banks but also the finance companies and merchant banks as well as other non-bank financial institutions. This was not only to increase the effectiveness of monetary policy, but to promote a sound financial structure. Guidelines also became more extensive as the direction of monetary policy took on a more allocative thrust. While the Central Bank continues to apply aggregative monetary policy to achieve the goals of economic growth, balance of payments equilibrium and price stability, emphasis has been given to a reallocation of real resources in line with the general national priorities. The Central Bank relied extensively on selective credit policy measures to influence the allocation of funds by the financial sector.

The scarcity of long term funds available for investment is a major concern in the financing of economic development. While importance has been attached to the increased mobilisation of savings for development, particular emphasis is given to increase the proportion of long term funds. While the economy has been responsive to reforms in interest rate policy and to other fiscal and monetary instruments in the mobilisation of saving, the increase in saving has to a large degree been short term. There has been some shift in the maturity structure of deposits towards longer maturities, but events in the domestic monetary markets in 1981 lead to a reversal in the trend as savers took advantage of higher rates at the shorter end during that period.

The demand for longer term funds is likely to increase with the industrialisation of the economy. However, a certain degree of long term financing may continue, based on short term funds; this will depend on the growth and stability of these deposits. Institutions that engage in this type of financing will have an increased need for a developed financial market. The mobilisation of funds of a long term nature by the public sector has generally relied on 'captive' markets; the financing of the public sector with short term instruments will pose certain problems. The demand for Treasury bills by the commercial banks in particular has been largely determined by the availability of excess funds; demand for the instrument may thus not increase with the fiscal need of the government.

The tendency to create new institutions as new needs are identified may also create problems. The efficiency of such institutions depends on their ability to take advantage of economies of scale in their operation. The concern is that the institutions will be too small to be effective and to take advantage of economies of scale. However, where the need for a specialised financial service can be identified as significant, the institution has the prospect of taking advantage of such potential economies of scale.

With the introduction of interest rate reforms, the system has to consider other reforms if the interest rate changes are to be effective; uncertainty in the financial markets will lead portfolio investors to shorten their planning horizon. Policy with respect to interest rates in Malaysia has been to keep interest rates low to stimulate private economic activity. An area of concern now is the interest rate differential between domestic and foreign instruments – with close links between the domestic and international financial markets, any significant differentials could lead to substantial capital outflows.

TRENDS AND PREDICTIONS

The financial system has shown remarkable expansion during the 1970s, and this trend looks likely to continue. There has been a high degree of response from the financial system to the changing intermediation needs of the economy, and in view of the development orientation of Central Bank policy, the financial system is likely to have a more significant role to play in financing future economic development.

While the commercial banks are likely to continue their rapid expansion, the growth of finance companies and merchant banks should cause their relative share of the financial system significantly to increase. The relative share of provident and pension funds is expected to decline; although they currently comprise a significant share of the total financial system, their growth is relatively slow, and largely dependent on growth in the labour force and income levels. These factors need to be considered, as the provident and pension funds are an important source of funds for government development financing.

The domestic participation in ownership in the financial system is likely to increase, both in terms of existing institutions and in the establishment of new ones. Government participation in ownership of financial institutions will depend on government economic policies in the 1980s. In particular, the growth of specialised development finance institutions will be influenced by the development strategies adopted.

Development finance institutions in Malaysia, however, are likely to participate more actively in financing economic development. While to a large degree funding for these institutions will have to come from the government, it is likely that in the future development finance institutions will also have to obtain funding from the domestic capital markets. Their ability to do so will depend to some extent on their performance in generating a loan programme according to the targets that have been set for them. The development finance institutions are also likely to face increased competition from other institutions that provide a wider range of financial services. The development finance institutions thus need to expand to take advantage of economies of scale in order to develop to a minimum optimal size.

In view of the economic objectives of the country, it is crucial that an efficient financial structure be developed, not only to provide an effective means by which savings can be effectively mobilised and channelled to productive investment, but also to provide the mechanism for the implementation of monetary policy. Both the private and public sector are expected to contribute to achieving these ends. While deliberate efforts have been made by the monetary authorities to develop the financial system, there is a need for the system to respond to changing needs and demands in order to make a significant contribution to the development of the country.

NOTES

1. See Fourth Malaysian Plan, Ch. 3, p. 43. For a further discussion, see Kevin Young, William C. F. Bussink and Parvez Hassan (eds), *Growth and Equity in a Multiracial Society: World Bank Country Economic Reports* (Baltimore: Johns Hopkins University Press, 1980).
2. Fourth Malaysian Plan, Ch. 11, p. 198.
3. For a detailed discussion of the Currency Board, see Peter J. Drake, *Financial Development in Malaysia and Singapore* (Canberra: Australian National University Press, 1969) Ch. 3.
4. In 1960, a provision was made whereby the Currency Board would also hold publicly issued dollar securities of (or guaranteed by) the participating governments to a maximum of M$300 million. This provision was never made use of, and in practice the currency issue was backed by sterling by more than 100 per cent: see Peter J. Drake, *Financial Development*, pp. 33–4.
5. Bank Negara Malaysia, *Annual Report 1981*, p. 49.
6. See *Money and Banking in Malaysia* (Kuala Lumpur: Bank Negara Malaysia, 1979) p. 133.
7. For a definition of 'small scale enterprise' and further detail on the requirement, see Bank Negara Malaysia, *Annual Report 1979*, p. 8.
8. Bank Negara Malaysia, *Annual Report 1981*, p. 9.
9. Bank Negara Malaysia, *Annual Report 1981*, p. 48–50.
10. For an empirical analysis of the portfolio behaviour of domestic and foreign banks, see Zeti Akhtar Aziz, 'Commercial Bank Portfolio Behavior in an Open Developing Economy: The Malaysian Case': Ph D thesis (University of Pennsylvania, 1978 (Ann Arbor: University Microfilms International, 1978).
11. Bank Negara Malaysia, *Annual Report 1981*, p. 15.
12. The CGC was established in 1972 to assist small enterprises to have access to funds from the commercial banks. The corporation's CGS guarantees loans provided by the commercial banks to small scale enterprises. A guarantee fee is paid by the commercial banks to the corporation and in return the corporation covers 60 per cent of any defaulting loans.
13. The POSB was established in 1949. For a detailed analysis of the POSB and NSB, see Lee Hock Lock, *Public Policies, Commercial Banks, and Other Deposit Institutions in Malaysia 1957–70* (Kuala Lumpur: University of Malaya Cooperative Bookshop Publications, 1981).
14. Bank Negara Malaysia, *Annual Report 1981*, p. 72.
15. Bank Negara Malaysia, *Annual Report and Statement of Accounts 1978*, p. 72.
16. See Michael T. Skully, *Merchant Banking in the Far East* (Malaysian Ch.) 2nd edn (London: *Financial Times*, 1980).
17. Bank Negara Malaysia, *Annual Report and Statement of Accounts 1977; Money and Banking in Malaysia*, p. 196.
18. Previously, the finance companies operated under the Money Lenders Ordinance 1951; the Companies Act 1965; and the Hire Purchase Act 1967; their activities were under the control of government agencies responsible for the provisions in the respective Acts.
19. Risk assets are defined to include assets other than those which had been

indicated in the Borrowing Companies Act, statutory reserves, and any other assets that had been required by the Central Bank.

20. Eligible liabilities include total deposits net of negotiable certificate of deposits; net borrowing from commercial banks, merchant banks and other finance companies; in addition to NCDs and other instruments discounted (other than repurchase agreements).

21. *Money and Banking in Malaysia*, p. 295.

22. The Minister of Finance in his announcement to the Malaysian Parliament on the new KLSE *inter alia* said: 'I have every reason to believe that the setting up of our own Stock Exchange would not only enable us to act independently in future, even more important, we should be able to plan more effectively in the sense that we should now be in a position to concentrate on our national interests. This should make it easier for us to develop our Stock Exchange into a sound and vigorous institution capable of even more vigorous growth in the future', *Malaysian Parliamentary Debates*, House of Representatives (8 May 1973) col. 1400.

23. New securities issued as a percentage of GNP for four developed countries – USA; Canada; UK; France – for 1971 were respectively 5.7; 4.0; 7.7; and 2.7 per cent: see U. Thin Wai and Hugh J. Patrick, 'Stock and Bond Issues and Capital Markets in Less Developed Countries', *IMF Staff Papers* (July 1973).

24. U. Wai and H. Patrick, 'Stock and Bond Issues' surveys Stock Exchanges in developing countries.

4 Financial Institutions and Markets in the Philippines

ALFREDO E. PASCUAL

INTRODUCTION

(a) The Setting

An archipelago located about 1000 kilometres southeast of continental Asia, the Philippines consists of approximately 7100 islands extending 1800 kilometres north to south between Taiwan and Indonesia. The 11 largest islands constitute 94 per cent of the 30 million hectare land area, of which 42 per cent is classified as forest and mineral land; 48 per cent as plantation and crop land; and the rest as urban and open land. The territorial waters in and around the islands aggregate to 167 million hectares of actual and potential fishing grounds with over 2000 known species of aquatic life. The country has a tropical climate that allows year round cultivation of crops, although seasonal typhoons do bring strong winds and flood waters that sometimes cause destruction, especially in the northern islands.

Growing at an average annual rate of 2.6 per cent since 1972[1] and estimated to be 49.2 million in 1981, the population of the Philippines is basically of Malay stock but considerably mixed with Chinese, Spanish and American strains. Close to 40 per cent of the population is in the labour force, which is relatively young and highly literate.

The Philippines no doubt has the physical and human resources needed for sustained economic development. Since the restoration of independence in 1946 (just after having emerged from the Second World War with a ravaged economy), the Philippines has achieved a satisfactory economic growth rate averaging about 6 per cent a year in real terms. The growth

168

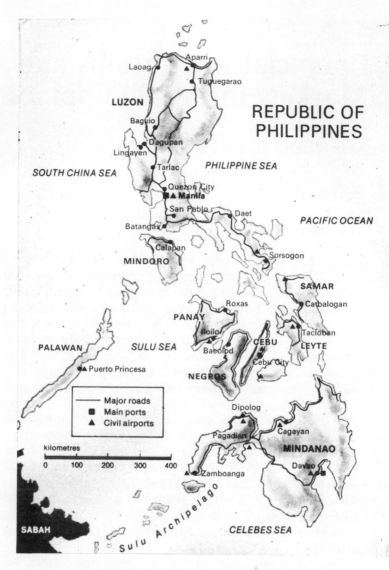

MAP 4.1 Republic of the Philippines

Source: Department of Trade and Resources, *Guide to the Market: Philippines* (Australian Government Publishing Service, 1981).

pattern, of course, has not been without wide fluctuations and serious imbalances, largely brought about by domestic policies and external development.

The import substitution policy adopted in the 1950s favoured the establishment of large scale, capital intensive and city based industries, and resulted in the sluggish agricultural production, constricted employment opportunities and stagnant rural incomes. Yet the burden of financing the machinery and materials imports needed by these urban industries (many merely assembly and repacking plants) fell heavily on the traditional agricultural exports produced by the rural sector.[2] As export earnings from agricultural commodities proved inadequate to support the industrial sector's growing imports, balance of payments difficulties became a drag to development.

Since the early 1970s, the government has been introducing economic reforms in a bid to correct the deficiencies of past development policies, as well as to address the new realities of expensive energy and limited international capital flows. New policies and programmes have been directed to agricultural and rural development; export promotion; energy source diversification; public infrastructure; employment creation; industry rationalisation; and monetary and financial reform. Many of the changes effected coincided with the sweeping political and social reforms instituted during the martial law era[3] (September 1972– January 1981.

Despite the economic difficulties brought about by escalating oil prices, real GNP still grew at an impressive average rate of 6.9 per cent from 1973–9, surpassing the 5 per cent annual average growth rate in the late 1960s and early 1970s. However, faced with double digit inflation rekindled in 1979 and declining prices of traditional exports, the economy slowed down in 1980, posting a GNP growth of barely 4.4 per cent. In 1981, the growth rate further slid to 3.8 per cent; for that year, GNP amounted to $38.7 billion at current prices. Meanwhile, the industrial sector grew faster than the economy as a whole. Its share of GDP at constant 1972 prices increased from 25–36.4 per cent between 1971 and 1981, as against a decline in the GDP share of the sluggish agricultural sector from 33.2–25.6 per cent.

In its external sector, the Philippines has experienced a continuing deterioration of its trade balance since 1974. This situation was the result of several factors: the soaring cost of imported oil; increasing importation of producer goods for the industrialisation programme; and depressed prices of (and demand for) most major export commodities.

In 1981, the trade deficit widened to $2.5 billion, with total imports of US$8.2 billion far exceeding total exports of US$5.7 billion. Traditional exports consisting of mineral products; coconut oil; sugar and forest products; accounted for less than two-thirds of total export receipts. Non-traditional exports[4] contributed over one-third, from a minimal level 10 years ago – semiconductor devices and garments were among the leading non-traditional export products. On the other hand, imports in 1981 consisted mostly of mineral fuels and lubricants (32 per cent) and machineries and other producer goods (64 per cent), with consumer goods comprising only 4 per cent.

The balance of payments deficit resulting from the trade imbalance has been minimised through invisible earnings from non-merchandise trade and transfers. A fairly recent phenomenon, the inward remittance of foreign exchange by the 200000 Filipino contract workers in the Middle East and elsewhere, exceeded US$1.0 billion in 1981. The manpower 'export' programme started in 1975 saw the number of workers destined for overseas growing at an average annual rate of 43 per cent.

To balance the trade account without unduly sacrificing economic growth, the government has focused on energy development, export promotion and industrial expansion. As a complementary measure, it has instituted a series of monetary and financial reforms aimed at making the financial sector more responsive to the demands of the economy. The latest of these reforms involved the adoption of a modified universal banking system in 1980 and the further liberalisation of interest rate policy in 1981. The ultimate objective is to increase the flow of savings intermediated by financial institutions, and to make an increasing proportion of such flows available to industries on longer terms.

(b) An Overview of the Financial Sector

Savings performance in the Philippines has consistently improved since 1967. As shown in Table 4.1, gross domestic savings averaged 25.5 per cent of GDP during the period 1977–8, compared with the respective 23.1 per cent and 19.3 per cent averages during the two previous periods. There were also significant shifts in the composition of savings: the share of government savings appreciably increased, and that of private

TABLE 4.1 Philippine savings ratio

	GNP (%)			Proportion to total		
	1967–71	*72–6*	*77–81*	*1967–71*	*72–6*	*77–81*
Total savings	20.8	25.5	30.0	100	100	100
Domestic savings	*19.3*	*23.1*	*25.5*	*93*	*91*	*85*
1. Government	(2.5)	(5.0)	(6.9)	(12)	(20)	(23)
Net government	(1.8)	(3.6)	(4.5)	(9)	(14)	(15)
Capital consumption allowance	0.7	1.4	2.4	3	6	8
2. Private	(16.8)	(18.1)	(18.6)	(81)	(71)	(62)
Net household	(7.1)	(9.4)	(6.7)	(34)	(37)	(22)
Net corporate	(2.1)	(2.6)	(4.6)	(10)	(10)	(16)
Capital consumption allowance	(7.6)	(6.1)	(7.3)	(37)	(24)	(24)
Foreign savings	*1.5*	*2.4*	*4.5*	*7*	*9*	*15*
Net transfer	.4	.2	...[a]	2	1	...
Net borrowing	1.1	2.2	4.5	5	8	15

[a] Negligible.

Source (basic data): National Economic and Development Authority.

savings correspondingly declined. One important factor in these changes was the major tax reforms undertaken after 1972. Another significant trend in savings performance was the widening resource gap being filled by foreign borrowings, which during 1977–82 financed an average of 15 per cent gross domestic capital formation.

As the prime mobiliser of savings in the economy, the Philippine financial system proved responsive to the growing need for intermediation. The system's total assets grew faster than GNP (at about 20 per cent average yearly), and as a percentage of GNP at current prices rose from 70 per cent in 1966 to 110 per cent in 1981.

A few large government owned institutions, the Central Bank included, presently control about half of the total assets of the financial system, a decline from about 65–70 per cent in the 1960s. However, government control over financial resources extends beyond these institutions. Government banks hold equity investments in a number of rural and private development banks which were organised on the basis of committed government funding, and also in some private domestic commercial banks, which were recently reorganised in accordance with government supported capital build up or rehabilitation programmes.

During the past 10 years, the financial system has undergone a process of rapid evolution.[5] In the early 1970s (from a modest start in the late 1960s) an active organised money market emerged. It was spawned by non-banking intermediaries, led by the then newly formed investment houses, using short term financial instruments with yields way above the low, legally fixed deposit rates offered by the traditional banking system. Unregulated until 1976, the attractive returns from these deposit substitutes provided positive real interest income to investors, and facilitated the flow into financial assets of the liquidity resulting from the economic boom at that time.

In the early 1970s the government also initiated the first major restructuring of the financial system. Under the so called financial reforms of 1972,[6] banking statutes were amended to encourage larger size banking institutions, and to improve the management of domestic liquidity and credit by the monetary authorities. Commercial banks went through a phase of capital expansion to meet increased capitalisation requirements. Some merged or consolidated with other banks; others acquired equity participation from foreign and government banks; the rest undertook capital build up on their own without bringing in institutional partners. The Central Bank assumed authority and responsibility not only over the monetary system but over the entire financial and credit system. Consequently, it began to regulate the quasi-banking[7] functions of banks and non-bank financial intermediaries – 'quasi-banking' meaning the pooling of funds through the issuing of debt instruments known as deposit substitutes, for purposes of relending. With the enactment of the Investment Houses Law in 1973, securities underwriting became the sole domain of the investment houses, although money market operation through quasi-banking remained their major preoccupation.

In 1976, the offshore banking system was established to enhance linkages with overseas financial markets and develop Manila as a major financial centre in the Southeast Asian region. Selected foreign banks were allowed to establish Philippine branches that would operate as offshore banking units. To place the existing banks on a competitive footing with the new entrants, they were given expanded powers over those originally granted in 1970 pertaining to the acceptance of foreign currency deposits and the utilisation of such deposits. The domestic commercial banks, along with the four full banking foreign bank branches, were made to constitute a foreign currency deposit system to parallel the offshore banking system.

The most recent structural changes instituted by the government, embodied in the so called financial reforms of 1980,[8] were aimed at enhancing competition and thus creating greater efficiency among financial institutions, and at increasing the flow of (and access to) longer term funds. To foster competition, the differentiation among categories of banks and quasi-banks (i.e. non-bank financial intermediaries authorised to perform quasi-banking) was reduced, and all functional distinctions among the three types of thrift bank eliminated. Major financial institutions were virtually freed from legislated specialisation: they were granted inherent powers that would enable them to expand the range of their financial services (subject to minimum capitalisation requirements), or otherwise opt for voluntary specialisation based on perceived comparative advantage. To facilitate the generation of long term investment funds, a new type of multipurpose institution was introduced – the expanded commercial bank (the Philippine version of a universal bank) with the combined powers of a commercial bank and an investment house and a legislated size that would permit greater operating economies; wider portfolio diversification; and more aggressive term transformation.

To complement the latest structural reforms, other measures were also implemented in the areas of fiscal, monetary and supervisory policies. The most significant change was the lifting in 1981 of all interest rate ceilings, except for loans with maturity of 1 year or less.[9] The new interest rate policy capped a series of upward revisions made by the Central Bank after it was empowered in 1973 to adjust interest rates in accordance with the demands of the economy. It was thought that by deregulating interest rates, financial institutions would have greater flexibility in their fund intermediation, (especially long term funds) and thus could respond more promptly to domestic and external developments. To facilitate pricing of long term loans on a floating rate basis, the Central Bank started quoting weekly reference rates computed for short term interest periods.[10]

Another change was the revision of reserve requirements. Reserve requirements on short term time deposits and deposit substitutes of commercial banks and quasi-banks were reduced to equal those for rural and thrift banks. This standardisation of reserve requirements was in line with the thrust towards less differentiated financial institutions. At the same time, the reduction was meant to allow lower spreads between funding and lending rates, reserves being an added cost to intermediation.

Also subjected to change was the Central Bank's rediscount policy. In general, the rediscount rates were set at penal levels (i.e. higher than market rates) so as to wean financial institutions from their heavy dependence on cheap Central Bank funds. However, concessional rediscount rates were maintained for a few preferred areas, to encourage lending for such ventures.

Still pursuant to the reduction of functional differentiation among categories of financial institutions and the support of long term lending operations, the Central Bank established a liquidity mechanism for the quasi-banks. To place them on equal footing with the banks in terms of reserve and liquidity management, the quasi-banks were granted overdraft, repurchase and lender of last resort facilities similar to those available to banks.

With regard to fiscal policy, the withholding taxes on interest paid on deposit substitutes and time deposits were made uniform. This change meant a reduction of rate for deposit substitutes, and an increase for time deposits.

FINANCIAL INSTITUTIONS

As shown in Table 4.2, financial institutions in the Philippines are classified into some 15 different categories, excluding the Central Bank and the offshore banking and representative offices of foreign banks. These categories, however, are divided into two broad groupings: the banking institutions and the non-banking financial institutions. Except for the insurance companies, all financial institutions fall directly under the supervisory and regulatory authority of the Central Bank, the nucleus of the Philippine financial system.

Among the major categories of banks and non-banks with quasi-banking functions, the differentiation is not at all absolute. As is evident in Table 4.3, their functions are overlapping, and uniform regulatory requirements are applicable to similar aspects of their respective operations.

TABLE 4.2 Philippine financial institutions[a] by no. of offices and total assets (figures as of end 1981, in ₱ million)

	No. of offices		Total assets	
	Head	Other[b]	Amount	(%)
Banking institutions	*1216*	*2436*	*224659*	*78.7*
Commercial banks	33	1699	164552	57.7
Domestic	(29)	(1694[c])	(145705)	(51.0)
Foreign	(4)	(5)	(18847)	(6.6)
Thrift banks	140	497	11631	4.0
Savings & mortgage banks	(9)	(178)	(6930)	(2.4)
Private development banks	(44)	(138)	(2312)	(0.8)
Stock savings & loan associations	(87)	(181)	(2389)	(0.8)
Rural banks	1040	127	6490	2.3
Specialised government banks	3	113	41986	14.7
Non-bank financial institutions	*1469*	*291*	*60780*	*21.3*
Investment houses	11	37	5865	2.1
Financing companies	369	190	12123	4.2
Securities dealers/brokers	142	—	977	0.3
Investment companies	63	—	5513	1.9
Fund managers	9[d]	—	748	0.3
Lending investors	74	4	35	. . .[e]
Pawnshops	574	60	336	0.1
Government non-bank financial institutions	4	—	23638[f]	8.3
VCCs	8	—	48	. . .
Non-bank thrift institutions	80	—	411	0.1
Building & loan associations	(7)	—	(18)	. . .
Non-stock savings loan associations	(73)	—	(393)	(0.1)
Insurance companies	135	—	11086[g]	3.9
Life	(24)	N/A	(5310)	(1.9)
Non-Life	(111)	N/A	(5776)	(2.0)
Total	2685	2727	285439	100.0

[a] Exclusive of CBP, which had total assets of ₱65447.3 million in 1981.
[b] Includes branches, agencies, extension offices, moneyshops, and representative offices.
[c] Includes 32 overseas offices.
[d] Incomplete.
[e] Negligible.
[f] September 1981.
[g] Preliminary.

Source: CBP; Insurance Commission for data on insurance companies.

TABLE 4.3 Philippine banks and non-bank financial intermediaries performing quasi-banking functions: regulated framework for selected categories (figures in **P**)

	Expanded commercial bank	Commercial bank	Thrift bank	Investment house	Finance Co. with QBF[a]
Minimum paid-in capitalisation	500 m at start	100 m (old) 300 m at start (new)	Based in Metro Manila 10 m (old) 20 m (new) Based outside Metro Manila 5 m (old) 10 m (new)	50 m at start (new) 20 m (old)– to Dec. 1983	As investment house
Inherent powers	Commercial banking[b] Investment house functions Investment in non-allied enterprises	Commercial banking	Full domestic banking[c], including personal and mortgage loans	Investment house functions (underwriting; securities; dealing; equities)	Financing (instalment; financing; receivables; discounting; factoring) Leasing
Additional powers granted	Trust Foreign Currency Deposit Unit (FCDU) Quasi-banking	As expanded commercial bank	Trust Limited FCDU operations Foreign exchange dealership Quasi-banking	Trust Limited foreign exchange operations Quasi-banking	Quasi-banking

Liquidity financing from Central Bank	Available	Available	Available	Available	Available
Equity holdings permitted	30% of commercial banks 100% of financial allied enterprises 100% of non-financial allied enterprises 35% of non-allied enterprises	30% of commercial banks 100% of thrift banks 40% of other financial allied enterprises 100% of non-financial allied enterprises	As commercial bank	40% in non-banks performing quasi-banking No limitation on other non-banks Minority in non-allied enterprises	As investment house
Ownership restrictions	40% or less total foreign ownership 20% or less per family group 30% or less per corporate group	As expanded commercial bank	As expanded commercial bank	At least majority Filipino or less 40% or less per individual, family or corporate group	At least 60% Filipino 40% or less per individual or corporate group

---

a Quasi-bank financing.

b Commercial banking consists of creating and receiving demand deposits; receiving other types of deposits; lending money; accepting drafts; issuing letters of credit; discounting and negotiating promissory notes, drafts, bills of exchange and other evidences of debt; acquiring bonds and other debt securities; and investing in equity of allied undertakings.

c Full domestic banking is defined as commercial banking without international banking operations.

TABLE 4.3 (contd.)

	Expanded commercial bank	Commercial bank	Thrift bank	Investment house	Finance Co. with OBF[a]
Upward conversion possibilities (per Central Bank policy)		To expanded commercial bank	To commercial bank, then to expanded commercial bank	No to commercial bank Directly to expanded commercial bank	No to any type of bank
Net worth: risk asset ratios	10% 8%–500 m–699 m capital 6%–700 m or more capital	10%	10%	10%	10%
Single borrower's limit	15% of net worth	15% of net worth	15% of net worth + additional 15% if for housing of low and middle income borrowers	80% of net worth	80% of net worth

Reserve requirements	As expanded commercial bank			As investment house
	Demand–16%	Demand–16%		
	Savings–16%	Savings–8%		
	NOW^d–16%	NOW–12%		

	Time
	  730 days or less–16%
	  Over 730 days–5%
		Time
		  730 days or less–8%
		  Over 730 days–5%		

	Deposit substitutes
	  730 days or less–16%
	  Over 730 days–5%
		Deposit substitutes
		  730 days or less–16%
		  Over 730 days–5%
			Deposit substitutes 730 days or less–16%
			Over 730 days–5%	

	Interbank^e–1%	Interbank–1%	Interbank–1%	

d NOW refers to a deposit account subject to withdrawal by 'negotiable order withdrawal'. This type of account has not been popular, because many banks offer arrangements for automatic transfer of funds from a savings to a demand deposit account provided certain minimum balances are maintained. Interest rates on savings accounts are generally higher than those on NOW accounts.

e Interbank deposits and borrowings include those between a bank and a non-bank performing quasi-banking functions.

Source: CBP Circulars; Enabling Acts of the respective financial institutions.

(a) The Banking Institutions

Not counting the Central Bank, banking institutions in the Philippines can be broken into four categories: commercial banks; thrift banks; rural banks; and specialised government banks. As distinguished from the non-banks, banking institutions have the exclusive power to obtain funds from the public through the receipt of deposits of the traditional kind i.e., demand, savings and time.

For discussion purposes, the offshore banking units and representative offices of foreign banks are included under this grouping. While they are not considered as part of the domestic financial system, they are nonetheless involved in banking and are likewise regulated by the Central Bank.

(i) *Central Bank of the Philippines (CBP)*

The primary policy objective of the CBP – as redefined in 1972 by an amendment of its charter – is to maintain internal and external monetary stability in the country. Its responsibility for promoting economic growth is shared with the planning agencies of the government.

Founded in 1948 with the passage of Republic Act No. 265, the CBP performs the traditional functions of a Central Bank. It issues the country's currency; administers the monetary, banking and credit system; acts as lender of last resort; discharges banking services for the government and other banks; and manages the country's international reserves. In addition, it implements various laws governing different types of financial institution; undertakes savings promotions programme; manages specialised guarantee and loan funds; and operates a security printing plant; gold refinery and mint.

The policymaking and regulatory powers of the CBP are exercised by the Monetary Board, a five man body composed of the CBP Governor who acts as its Chairman, the Minister of Finance, the Director General of the National Economic and Development Authority, the Chairman of the Board of Investments and a representative from the private sector. The composition of this body reflects the high degree of co-ordination between monetary policy and economic planning.

In fact, monetary policy in the Philippines has been orientated largely towards promoting economic development. Selective credit measures,[11] rather than general or quantitative controls, have been used extensively deliberately to expand or contract specific sectors of the economy. Through the CBP's rediscount window, funds at concessional rates have been directed to favoured activities like agriculture and exports. Rediscount ceilings have often been adjusted upwards to accommodate the credit needs of priority sectors. As a consequence, banks have been encouraged to rely heavily on the CBP as a regular source of loanable funds, not simply as a lender of last resort. With the recent freeing of interest rates, however, the rediscount window has been rationalised to facilitate its influence on the general credit situation, notwithstanding its role in allocating credit to preferred activities.

Until the early 1980s, open market operations were barely used. During 1970–80, the CBP introduced regular issues of its certificates of indebtedness to gather excess liquidity in urban areas for rechannelling to the credit deficient rural sector. Towards the end of the 1970s, these certificates were redesigned to make them market orientated. Sold on an auction basis with tax free features removed, they were then issued only to effect adjustments in liquidity levels. By 1981, an active dealership network in government securities has been established, and more issues of Treasury bills and notes have been made available. Under the present regime of flexible interest rates, open market operations along with other monetary measures are now actively pursued by the CBP in an attempt to stabilise borrowing costs and minimise inflationary pressures.

Since 1976, the CBP has been drawing up an annual financial programme, specifying the domestic credit and money supply levels needed to support a targetted GNP growth rate consistent with a desired balance of payments position and inflation rate. Although invariably revised mid-course to account for unexpected developments, this financial program allows the CBP to co-ordinate the various instruments of monetary and credit policy employed.

At the end of 1981, the CBP had total assets amounting to ₱71571 million, of which 45.7 per cent were in loans and 9.0 per cent in domestic securities. The country's international reserves constituted 28.2 per cent of the total assets.

(ii) *Commercial banks*

The commercial banks dominate the Philippine financial system, controlling almost 60 per cent of its resources (see Table 4.2). There are 33 institutions officially classified as commercial banks: 27 private domestic banks, one government owned bank, one semi-government bank, and the Philippine branches of four foreign banks (see Table 4.4). In addition, two specialised government banks (the Land Bank of the Philippines and the Philippine Amanah Bank) also operate as commercial banks, and are in fact members of the Bankers' Association of the Philippines, the exclusive grouping of commercial banks in the country. Ranked in terms of asset size, the government owned Philippine National Bank is first with 1981 total assets of ₱44866 million (representing 27.3 per cent of the combined resources of the commercial banks), the Philippine branch network of the New York based Citibank a distant second with ₱12637 million, and the local Bank of the Philippine Islands a close third with ₱8489 million.

Although they all have their head offices in Metro Manila, the domestic commercial banks, individually and as a group, have the most extensive nationwide branch network of all the bank categories. Indeed, the rapid branch expansion of the larger institutions has contributed much to the 25 per cent + average yearly asset growth the commercial banks have been achieving since 1972. By the end of 1981, their branches and other offices had reached an average of 58 per bank, ranging from 18–190 (see Table 4.4). Considering the preference of the monetary authorities for branch banking over unit banking, this increase in office numbers should continue.

Among the 27 domestic commercial banks classified as private, two are in reality majority government owned; these are the International Corporate Bank (with the Development Bank of the Philippines as majority owner), and the Philipinas Bank (with the Philippine National Bank as controlling stockholder). A third, the Commercial Bank of Manila, is expected to be taken over by another government institution, the Government Service Insurance System. In addition, three others have minority equity investments from the Development Bank of the Philippines. Two industry orientated private banks – the Republic Planters' Bank and the United Coconut Planters' Bank – are effectively under the control of the government. These two banks, beneficially owned respectively by the sugar and the coconut planters, are similar to the Philippine Veterans' Bank, which is owned by war veterans and officially classified as semi-government commercial bank.

Government involvement in the private banking sector became necessary as part of a string of rescue operations undertaken recently. Banks which encountered difficulty meeting the minimum capitalisation required in the 1970s, as well as financial institutions which suffered immensely from the 1981 financial crisis[12] were assisted. However, most government equity participation is viewed as temporary, and these banks have continued to operate as private institutions.

The capital expansion programme in the 1970s encouraged as many as 10 foreign banks to invest in seven domestic commercial banks. Within a few years, however, half these foreign banks either sold out to, or were bought out by, some local groups. Among the domestic banks with remaining foreign institutional shareholders are the Bank of the Philippine Islands (with Morgan Guaranty Trust Co.), the Far East Bank and Trust Co. (with Chemical Bank of New York), the Rizal Commercial Banking Corporation (with Continental Illinois National Bank and Sanwa Bank Ltd), and the Citytrust Banking Corporation (with Citibank, NA).

A large majority of private domestic banks with neither government nor foreign equity have remained closely related to specific family business groups. Indeed, almost all private domestic banks in the Philippines have their historical roots in the many family owned banks established between 1950 and 1965, when entry was relatively easy and there was no minimum capital requirement. The identity of many of these banks has since been lost due to mergers and consolidations, changes of ownership, or failure and subsequent rehabilitation by new investors; 1974, for example, saw seven bank mergers and consolidations. Between 1975 and 1981, four new commercial banking corporations were organised to take over the assets and liabilities of insolvent banks.

Commercial banking in the Philippines began in 1851 with the establishment of the Banco Español Filipino de Isabel II, now known as the Bank of the Philippine Islands. At the outbreak of the second World War, the country had four domestic and four foreign institutions operating as commercial banks, including the government owned Philippine National Bank which was chartered as early as 1916. Regulation of banking started in 1949, with the establishment of the Central Bank of the Philippines and the implementation of the General Banking Act 1948.

TABLE 4.4 Philippine commercial banks (figures as at end December 1981, in ₱ million)

Bank	Establishment date	No. of offices	Total assets
Private domestic			
Bank of the Philippine Islands[a,b]	1851	129	8489.0
Allied Banking Corpn[a]	1977	76	7430.4
Metropolitan Bank & Trust Co.[a]	1962	131	6940.0
Far East Bank and Trust Co.[a,b]	1960	48	5355.6
Republic Planters' Bank[c]	1953	57	5060.9
Philippine Commercial & Industrial Bank[a]	1960	79	4817.7
United Coconut Planters Bank[a,c]	1963	49	4645.1
Rizal Commercial Banking Corpn[b]	1960	37	4589.2
International Corporate Bank Inc.[d]	1977	22	4552.2
Traders Royal Bank[e]	1963	35	4144.5
The Manila Banking Corpn[a]	1960	57	3650.1
China Banking Corpn	1920	23	3473.4
Pacific Banking Corpn	1955	40	3354.5
Equitable Banking Corpn	1950	35	3209.0
Security Bank & Trust Co. Inc.	1951	40	3129.0
Philippine Bank of Communications[f]	1939	19	3109.9
The Consolidated Bank and Trust Corpn	1963	48	3096.5
Family Bank & Trust Co.	1970	111	3001.2
Insular Bank of Asia & America Inc.	1974	58	2974.6
Prudential Bank[f]	1952	44	2565.2

The Philippine Banking Corpn	1957	43	2324.5
Associated Citizens Bank[e,f]	1962	32	2030.9
Citytrust Banking Corpn[b]	1962	25	1799.6
Producers Bank of the Philippines	1971	30	1771.1
Philippine Trust Co.	1916	19	1119.6
Pilipinas Bank[d]	1975	19	1089.6
Commercial Bank of Manila[e,f]	1981	18	446.9
Government or semi-government			
Philippine National Bank[a]	1916	190	44866.0
Philippine Veterans Bank	1963	28	2726.5
Foreign			
Citibank NA	1902	3	12637.0
Bank of America NT and SA	1947	1	3602.1
The Hongkong and Shanghai Banking Corpn	1875	2	1742.8
The Chartered Bank	1873	3	865.2

[a] Authorised to engage in expanded commercial banking (as of June 1982).
[b] Has foreign institutional shareholders in the minority.
[c] May be considered as a semi-government bank.
[d] Has a government financial institution as majority shareholder.
[e] Has a government financial institution as minority shareholder.
[f] Not licensed to operate a foreign currency deposit unit under CBP Circular 547 as the others, but engages in limited foreign currency deposit operations under CBP Circular 343.

Source: CBP.

Except for the Philippine National Bank and a very few others which have already gone substantially into project finance, commercial banks have generally concentrated on traditional short term commercial lending e.g. working capital and trade finance. This short term orientation was brought about mainly by necessity, as the funds to finance these loans have been likewise available only on a short term basis. The series of interest rate reforms beginning in 1974 have to an extent succeeded in shifting the flow of funds away from short term placements, particularly in the volatile deposit substitutes, and into longer term time deposits. The build up of the latter, however, has not yet been sufficient to allow a greater commitment to long term lending. Recently, commercial banks have also been authorised to issue bonds to help augment their pool of long term funds: Table 4.5 provides more details as to their overall sources and uses of funds.

In addition to the usual commercial banking functions, the domestic commercial banks are authorised to engage in trust operations, to perform quasi-banking functions, and to operate foreign currency deposit units (FCDUs).

Through their respective FCDUs, the commercial banks can accept foreign currency deposits from residents and non-residents, and use the proceeds to acquire foreign currency instruments and to extend foreign currency loans to non-resident as well as resident firms. Governed by the Foreign Currency Deposit Act 1976 and CBP Circular 547, the FCDUs can also engage in FE trading. A local bank is required to have a minimum net worth of ₱150 million in order to qualify for an FCDU licence. Only four commercial banks have not yet qualified; nevertheless, these banks are still allowed to accept foreign currency, subject to certain limitations on the use of the deposited funds, as provided for under CBP Circular 343 1976.

Led by the Philippine National Bank, a number of domestic banks have already gone international. Five of them together account for at least 32 overseas branches and agencies scattered in key cities of the USA, Europe, Southeast Asia and the Middle East. Some 12 of these banks also own subsidiary or affiliate deposit taking companies in Hong Kong, and a few even have full banking subsidiaries in the USA.

In addition to the usual quantitative restrictions imposed on their operations (e.g. risk assets: capital ratio; single borrower's limit; collateral loan value; etc.) commercial banks must observe certain sectoral credit allocations. At least 25 per cent of loanable

TABLE 4.5 Philippine commercial banks' sources and uses of funds (figures as of end December 1981, in ₱ million)

	Amount	% of total
Uses		
Cash	2102	1.3
Claims on financial institutions	12168	7.4
Claims on public sector		
loans	6544	4.0
investments	8583	5.2
Claims on private sector		
loans	83023	50.4
investments	7200	4.4
Unclassified assets	44932	27.3
Total uses	164522	100.0
Sources		
Deposits		
demand	12309	7.5
savings	27017	16.4
time	38406	23.4
others	796	0.5
Due to financial institutions	1222	0.7
Accounts and bills payable[a]	44105	26.8
Unclassified liabilities	26490	16.1
Capital accounts	14207	8.6
Total sources	164552	100.0

[a] Mainly deposit substitutes and advances from the Central Bank.

Source: CBP.

funds should be used for agricultural credit, at least 75 per cent of deposits received in a certain region should also be invested there. However, if compliance is difficult, the banks may as an alternative invest these funds in eligible government securities or institutions.

Under the 1980 financial reforms, domestic commercial banks with a minimum paid-in capitalisation of ₱500 million may be authorised to engage in expanded commercial banking – sometimes referred to as unibanking, short for 'universal banking'. The most significant power of these expanded commercial banks is the authority to function as an investment house – to undertake equity finance of non-allied enterprises, either directly or indirectly through underwriting. Their other privileges include: a reduction in required risk asset : capital ratio upon attainment of a certain capitalisation level; a lowering of gross receipt tax on interest income from long term loans; and access to a special liquidity facility with the Central Bank. The purpose of these additional powers and extra incentives is to place the expanded commercial banks in a good position to satisfy the growing need of industries for long term financing.

The Philippine branches of the four foreign banks in the country operate very much like their domestic counterparts, and are subject to the same banking laws and regulations. However, they are restricted from further branching, and precluded from trust functions. With regard to investments in domestic enterprises (financial or otherwise) they are governed by the same rules applicable to any other foreign investor.

(iii) *Thrift banks*

The thrift banks were a bank category established in 1972 as part of a move to simplify bank classifications. The category encompasses three types of banking institutions – the savings and mortgage banks; the stock savings and loan associations; and the private development banks. Table 4.6 gives a list of the major thrift banks in the country.

The savings and mortgage banks are governed by the General Banking Act 1948. Their primary purpose is to tap small savings and to provide long term credits, housing loans and consumer finance, in addition to investing in bonds and other securities. With one exception, all are based in Metro Manila. Most, however, have branched out to provincial areas. The largest one far surpasses the others in terms of asset size and number of branches.

The savings and loan associations were designed to provide additional savings and credit facilities to the consuming public, industry, commerce and agriculture. Regulated under the Savings and Loan Association Act 1963, they are distributed in key cities and towns throughout the country, with a concentration in Metro Manila and surrounding areas.

The private development banks were established to promote agriculture and industry by providing medium and long term credit at low cost. They have been financially supported by the government through the Development Bank of the Philippines, by way of counterpart capital in the form of preferred stock and rediscounting facilities for long term papers. The Private Development Bank Act 1964 authorised the establish-

TABLE 4.6   Philippine major thrift banks^a (figures as at Dec 1981 in ₱ million)

Bank	Establish-ment date	No. of branches^b	Total assets
Savings & mortgage banks (9)^c			
Banco Filipino Savings & Mortgage Bank^{d, e}	64	76	3016.7
Union Savings & Mortgage Bank^{d, e, f}	68	10	1980.0
Philippine Savings Bank^d	60	25	880.4
Monte de Piedad & Savings Bank^{d, e}	47	15	396.5
Home Savings Bank & Trust Co.^d	68	15	229.2
Banco de Oro Savings & Mortgage Bank	68	18	212.6
First Summa Savings & Mortgage Bank	68	6	149.6
Savings Bank of Manila	62	7	132.9
Private development banks (44)			
Planters' Development Bank^d	61	18	350.2
Urban Development Bank	80	2	310.5
Cavite Development Bank	63	6	117.8
Second Bulacan Development Bank	62	7	111.0
Peoples Development Bank	79	3	102.2
Stock savings & loan associations (87)			
Royal SLA Inc.	71	21	N/A
Homeowners' SLA Inc.	70	14	N/A
Thrift SLA Inc.	68	14	N/A
Davao SLA Inc.	67	10	N/A
Paluwaganng Bayan SLA Inc.	74	10	N/A
First Peso SLA Inc.	68	9	N/A

^a Includes savings and mortgage banks and private development banks with total assets exceeding ₱100 million in December 1981, and stock savings and loan associations with number of branches and other offices exceeding five in December 1980.
^b Includes full branches, agencies, extension offices and moneyshops.
^c Number in the parenthesis indicates the total number of entities under the category as of December 1981.
^d Has limited FCD operations under CBP Circular 343.
^e Authorised to engage in quasi-banking.
^f In 1981, Bancom Development Corporation (an investment house) was merged with this bank in a rehabilitation programme that involved two government financial institutions (the LBP and the SSS) acquiring 70 per cent ownership of the surviving institution.

Source: CBP.

ment of these development institutions in the different provincial areas, although most have gravitated to Luzon.

The 1980 financial reforms eliminated all functional distinctions among the three types of thrift bank. On meeting the minimum capital requirement, any thrift bank may be granted the powers of full domestic banking (i.e. commercial banking without international banking operation). A thrift bank may also acquire separate authority to engage in trust operations; perform quasi-banking functions; undertake limited foreign currency deposit operations; and engage in foreign exchange dealership. It may even lend money against the security of jewellery, precious stones and other similar articles – a function hitherto assigned to pawnshops. With paid-in capital upgraded to at least ₱ 300 million, a thrift bank may qualify to convert into a full fledged commercial bank. A few of the 140 thrift banks have already obtained additional powers under these reforms. One savings and mortgage bank (Family Savings Bank) has even converted to a commercial bank; others, particularly Banco Filipino Savings and Mortgage Bank (the largest) and Union Savings and Mortgage Bank (the second largest, government owned since 1981) are strong candidates for similar conversion.

Because of their expanded powers and the suspension of new bank licensing, thrift banks (especially the generally small savings and loan associations) have become attractive candidates for acquisition by business groups wishing to enter banking; a few have already changed ownership. Recognising the trend, the Central Bank promptly stepped in to regulate such transfers and stem potential concentration of control, by requiring prior approval.

Recently, many thrift banks have gone into origination of home mortgages for the National Home Mortgage Finance Corporation (NHMFC).[13] This operation has proved attractive because the mortgages are immediately purchased outright by the NHMFC and the thrift banks avoid making cash releases from their own resources. The NHMFC pays a commission of 3 per cent of the value of the mortgages purchased.

In 1981, the combined assets of thrift banks amounted to ₱11.6 billion, 65.7 per cent of which was in loans and 11.7 per cent in investments, mostly government securities; aggregate deposits comprised ₱7.2 billion, more than 98 per cent of which were savings and time deposits. The savings and mortgage banks accounted for almost 60 per cent of the thrift bank resources, with the balance about equally divided between the two other types.

(iv) *Rural banks*

The establishment of rural banks, authorised under the Rural Bank Act 1952, was the government's countermeasure to the usurious credit practices prevalent in the countryside, where the bulk of the country's population live and work. Given the primary function of providing adequate credit facilities to small farmers and businessmen, these relatively small institutions operate as unit banks within their specifically defined regions. They accept savings and time deposits, and (with prior authorisation from the Central Bank) even demand deposits.

For the bulk of their funding, the rural banks have relied heavily on government banks. The Development Bank of the Philippines, has invested in preferred stocks of many rural banks as counterpart capital to induce their formation; the Central Bank has provided additional funding through its rediscount window and by way of special time deposits. Since the late 1970s, the rural banking system has served as a conduit for the government's massive financing programmes under supervised credit schemes for the production of rice and other agricultural crops as well as livestock. Many rural banks have been saddled with substantial amounts of unpaid loans under these programmes, particularly on rice production.

Under the 1980 financial reforms, rural banks are no longer restricted to small farmers and merchants in their lending operations. They may also put up branches within their region of operation, provided their capital built up programmes to meet the ₱500 000 minimum requirement are being complied with. Since February 1982, they may be authorised to act as foreign exchange dealers, but basically just to buy foreign currencies from tourists and residents for resale to the Central Bank or the commercial banks.

Since the scope of their activities is still limited, they are being encouraged to establish linkages with commercial banks by accepting equity participation from these larger institutions. From a commercial bank's viewpoint this is a good alternative to the more expensive expansion strategy of establishing new branches. Taking the lead, the Land Bank of the Philippines a specialised government bank also operating as a commercial bank) has developed a programme of equity investment in rural banks.

Another approach to strengthen the competitive posture of rural banks involves integrating rural bank ownership within a particular province, area or region through a holding company. This firm would then either wholly or partially own the member banks, which would retain their individual legal personality. The holding company could integrate the management and operation of the subsidiary banks, thereby broadening their operational capability and stabilising their financial position.

With 1167 offices in 1981, rural banks constituted almost a quarter of all offices, but accounted for only 2.3 per cent of the financial system's total assets; they nevertheless, provided 16 per cent of all institutional agricultural credit. At the end of 1981, rural banks had combined assets of ₱6.49 billion, of which 57.5 per cent were in agricultural loans involving as many as 830000 accounts. However, in 1981, the largest rural bank still had total assets of only ₱55.7 million.

(v) *Specialised government banks*

The specialised government banks include the Development Bank of the Philippines, the Land Bank of the Philippines and the Philippine Amanah Bank. They were organised under different charters to address specific needs.

The Development Bank of the Philippines (DBP) was organised in 1958 under Republic Act No. 2081 to take over the Rehabilitation Finance Corporation, the government's financing arm during the reconstruction period after the Second World War. Since its foundation, the DBP has geared its operation to national development, providing financial assistance to various ventures designed to enhance the country's economy. Its current priorities are for ventures involved in agricultural production; energy generation and conservation; export promotion; and countryside and community development.

The DBP gives large industrial loans to develop national industrial infrastructures essential to economic growth and promote sectoral linkages in the economy, especially the production of inputs to small and medium scale business enterprises. Aside from direct loans in local or foreign currency, the DBP also provides equity investments to complement private initiatives, as well as guarantees to induce domestic or foreign loans granted by other entities to large projects.

At the same time, the DBP lends to smaller industries engaged in generating employment opportunities and promoting production of non-traditional exports; its loans to agriculture support food production for self-sufficiency and raw materials production for the industrial sector. The DBP also provides financing for housing and commercial building construction, and extends technical and financial assistance to private development banks. Its service delivery system – especially to the small borrowers outside Metro Manila – consists of a nationwide branch network of 65 offices. Aside from development banking, the DBP is also engaged in trust operations and quasi-banking.

The risk taking activities of the DBP have not always resulted in viable ventures. With the economic downturn in recent years, it has had an increasing number of problem accounts. It has already taken over some defaulting companies (either by foreclosure of mortgaged assets or by conversion of its loans and advances into equity positions). It has nevertheless been called to rescue non-client firms and inject fresh funds into already ailing enterprises (like some banks affected by the 1981 financial crisis) in support of government sponsored rehabilitation programmes.

At the end of 1981, the DBP had total assets of ₱34707 million, of which 53.4 per cent were in loans and 22.8 per cent in equities and investments, and outstanding guarantees of ₱16180 million, about 60 per cent of which were foreign currency denominated. In terms of asset size, it is second only to the Philippine National Bank.

Major funding sources of the DBP include borrowings from the Central Bank, foreign currency loans (particularly from the World Bank and the Asian Development Bank), foreign currency bonds floated in overseas capital markets, and domestic securities eligible as substitute agricultural lending by banks.

The Land Bank of the Philippines (LBP) was created in 1963 through the enactment of Republic Act No. 3844. Its financing functions originally involved three aspects of the agrarian reform programme: land transfer financing, largely in the form of 25 year bonds issued to land owners for tenanted rice and corn lands transferred to tenant farmers; assistance to farmers by way of technical and financial aid for improved productivity and income; and assistance to former landowners to shift their capital to industrial and other productive business ventures. In 1973, additional powers were granted to the LBP, making it a fully fledged commercial bank. It has also acquired licences to perform trust operations, to engage in quasi-banking functions and to operate an FCDU.

The original resources of the LBP included bonds formerly held by the Central Bank as well as acquired assets and other receivables transferred from the DBP and other government financial institutions. In 1981, the LBP had assets of ₱7073 million, of which 61.2 per cent were in loans and 16.6 per cent in investments. About one-third of the loans represented amortisations receivable from farmers arising from land transfer financing.

The Philippines Amanah Bank was established in 1973 to provide savings and credit facilities to the Muslim population in southern Philippines (Mindanao), where its headquarters are located. It performs the combined functions of a commercial, savings and development bank. It is empowered to make loans and investments; finance allied undertakings; and engage in trust operations. For funding, it can accept demand, savings and time deposits, and issue bonds, debentures and securities. So far, it has relied mainly on government deposits and its own capital in financing its assets.

Compared with the DBP and the LBP, it is quite small, with assets of only ₱211.7 million in 1981. This accounted for just 0.5 per cent of the ₱41986 million total assets of the three banks combined. The DBP's share was 82.7 per cent, and the LBP's 16.8 per cent.

(vi) *Foreign banks*

Although legally permissible, no other foreign banks have been allowed to establish Philippine branches to engage in commercial banking locally, aside from the four with full banking offices existing at the time the Central Bank Act and the General Banking Act 1948 took effect. However, the Central Bank has been licensing foreign bank representative offices since then, and (beginning in 1976) local branches operating as offshore banking units (OBUs). The names and nationalities of these banks as of December, 1981 are listed in Table 4.7.

Governed by Presidential Decree 1034, and its implementing CBP Circulars, the OBUs may engage in virtually all banking transactions with non-residents and with each other, in any currency other than the Philippine peso. They may also perform some limited onshore activities and deal with the FCDUs of the commercial banks in foreign currency deposits and loans as well as foreign exchange trading. With respect to residents other than the FCDUs, the OBUs may extend project related long term foreign currency loans, subject to prior approval by the Central Bank.

Since 1980, OBUs have been granted additional powers in dealing with residents, in recognition of their growing contribution to the economy. In May 1981, for example, they were authorised to handle under special financing arrangements (i.e. open account and document against acceptance) the importation of machinery and equipment by resident borrowers to which they have granted CBP approved long term loans, provided the

TABLE 4.7   Philippine foreign banks[a]

	Nationality
Offshore Banking Units	
Bank of Nova Scotia	Canada
Bank of Credit & Commerce International (Overseas Ltd)	Cayman Islands
Banque de L'Indochine et de Suez	France
Banque National de Paris	France
Credit Lyonnais	France
Société Generale	France
European Asian Bank	Germany
Bank of Tokyo Ltd	Japan
International Bank of Singapore	Singapore
Middle East Bank Ltd[b]	United Arab Emirates
Barclays Bank International Ltd	UK
Lloyds Bank International Ltd	UK
American Express International Banking Corpn	USA
Bank of California NA	USA
Bank of Hawaii[b]	USA
Bankers Trust Co.	USA
Chase Manhattan Bank NA	USA
Chemical Bank of New York	USA
Crocker National Bank	USA
First Interstate Bank of California	USA
First National Bank of Boston[b]	USA
First National Bank of Chicago	USA
Manufacturers' Hanover Trust Co.	USA
Rainier National Bank	USA
Security Pacific National Bank	USA

[a]   Exclusive of the four foreign banks with Philippine branches operating as fully licensed commercial banks (see Table 4.4).
[b]   Not yet operational.

importation involved at least $1 million. At the same time, they were allowed to render financial advisory and related services to local businesses and accordingly collect payment in foreign exchange. In March 1982, the OBUs were permitted to handle foreign exchange remittances of Filipinos working overseas and to open peso deposit accounts with domestic banks to handle such remittances.

Another significant change in OBU regulation occurred in January 1981, when the previous 5 per cent income tax on OBU net offshore income was abolished in a move to improve Manila's standing as a regional financial centre.

Table 4.7   (*contd.*)

	Nationality
Representative offices	
Amford Bank & Trust Co.	Bahamas
Bank of Montreal	Canada
Banque de Paris et des Pays-Bas	France
Credit Lyonnais	France
Paribas	France
Hang Lung Bank Ltd	Hongkong
Wardley Ltd	Hongkong
State Bank of India	India
Export–Import Bank of Japan	Japan
Mitsubishi Bank	Japan
Mitsui Bank Ltd	Japan
Sanwa Bank Ltd	Japan
The National Bank of New Zealand	New Zealand
Banco Español de Credito	Spain
Trade Development Bank	Switzerland
California Overseas Bank	USA
Continental Illinois National Bank & Trust Co. of Chicago	USA
Irving Trust Company	USA
Marine Midland Bank	USA
Mellon Bank NA	USA
Morgan Guaranty Trust Co.	USA
National Bank of Detroit	USA
Pacific National Bank of Washington	USA
Philadelphia National Bank	USA
Republic National Bank of New York	USA
United California Bank	USA
Wells Fargo Bank	USA

Source: Central Bank of the Philippines, 1982.

In 1981, there were 25 licensed OBUs, but only 21 were in actual operation. At the end of 1981, these had total assets of US$4627 million.

As shown in Table 4.7, a number of foreign banks without OBUs maintain representative offices in the Philippines. These offices may deal directly with the public only to promote and give information about the services of their respective banks. They may not conclude or enter into any contracts. The guidelines on the licensing and operation of representative offices were recently spelled out by the Central Bank in a Circular which took effect in March 1982.

(b) The Non-banking Financial Institutions

This grouping refers to financial institutions which employ methods of gathering funds other than traditional deposits from the public for purposes of relending or purchasing of receivables and other obligations. Included in this group are 11 institutional categories: investment houses; financing companies; securities dealers/brokers; investment companies; fund managers; lending investors; pawnshops; government non-bank financial institutions; venture capital companies; non-bank thrift institutions; and insurance companies. The CBP licensed moneybrokers may also be considered as a non-bank financial institution and so constitute a twelfth category. On the other hand, there are other institutions – e.g. credit unions and some specialised government institutions[14] – which may be also regarded as non-banks but are not included in this discussion because they are not officially classified as such.

Apart from this institutional categorisation, the non-banking financial institutions may be divided into two sub-groups: those that are licensed to perform quasi-banking functions (quasi-banks, for short) and those that are not. As shown in Table 4.8, there are 23 quasi-banks, consisting of 10 investment houses, 12 finance companies and one securities dealer. The quasi-banks represent only 1.6 per cent of the total number of private non-banks, but control 32.0 per cent of the total resources of these entities.

(i) *Investment houses*

The investment houses were made to constitute an institutional category in 1974 with the promulgation of Presidential Decree 129, otherwise known as the Investment Houses Law. They were vested with the exclusive power to undertake firm or guaranteed underwriting of securities issued by any private or government entity. In return, they were required to underwrite every year at least the equivalent of 25 per cent of their respective paid-in capital, which in turn should be at least ₱20 million. Despite the mandate, investment houses have mainly concentrated on money market transactions. Even their reported underwriting business has involved mostly non-capital market instruments. Of the ₱3242.4 million securities underwritten in 1981, close to 90 per cent consisted of short term debt securities distributed on a private placement and best efforts basis.

TABLE 4.8 Philippine non-bank financial intermediaries with quasi-banking functions (figures as at end December 1981, in ₱ million)

	Establishment date	Total assets
Investment houses (11)[a]		
Private Development Corpn of the Philippines[c]	1963	1586.3
Ayala Investment and Development Corpn[b]	1936	1203.2
State Investment House Inc.[b]	1972	854.6
The Philippine American Investments Corpn[b]	1973	607.1
AEA Development Corpn[b]	1973	415.5
Merchants' Investment Corpn	1979	407.1
Philippine Pacific Capital Corpn[b]	1974	257.8
First Metro Investment Corpn	1972	244.0
Citicorp Investment Philippines[b]	1974	185.7
Anscor Capital and Investment Corpn	1981	175.6
Financing companies (369)		
Filinvest Credit Corpn[b]	1965	1481.9
FNCB Finance[b, d]	1968	1339.7
BA Finance Corpn[b]	1966	925.5
Paramount Finance Corpn[b]	1955	375.5
Industrial Finance Corpn[b]	1956	298.3
State Financing Center Inc.	1950	212.3
Manphil Investment Corpn	1959	205.8
Commercial Credit Corpn	1957	202.6
Mercantile Financing Corpn	1974	119.2
Asian Consumer & Industrial Finance Corpn	1962	100.0
Bacolod Industrial Finance Corpn	1965	79.8
Cebu International Finance Corpn[b]	1964	71.0
Securities dealers/brokers (142)		
Multinational Investment Bancorporation	1972	273.0

[a] Figures in parenthesis indicates total number of entities under the category.
[b] Has foreign institutional shareholders in the minority.
[c] Operates more as a development finance company.
[d] Officially registered under the name Investors Finance Corporation.

Source: CBP.

Aside from underwriting and quasi-banking functions, investment houses also syndicate foreign and domestic loans; render financial consultancy and investment advisory services; manage investment portfolios for clients; and conduct other activities usually associated with merchant banks. The 1980 financial reforms granted them additional powers; they may now engage in trust functions and undertake limited project related foreign exchange operations. However, they lost the exclusive power to underwrite securities as the expanded universal banks were given investment house functions, specifically underwriting.

Investment house foreign exchange operations are presently confined to servicing the project requirements of certain clientele – foreign exchange earning enterprises such as exporters and service firms with overseas contracts. Specific services allowed include: contracting foreign loans for relending; providing import and export related services such as issuance of letters of credit and discounting of export drafts; holding foreign currency balances with foreign correspondents in connection with the import and export related services; and entering into forward cover contracts with the Central Bank in connection with the foregoing activities.

Of the original 12 investment houses, one was converted to a private development bank in 1981 and two were merged respectively with a commercial and a thrift bank, also in 1981. During the same year, two new institutions were licensed as investment houses, one being the only investment house with no quasi-banking authority. At the end of 1981, there were 11 investment houses with combined assets of ₱5865 million, constituting 15.8 per cent of the total resources of all private non-banks.

The biggest investment house, Private Development Corporation of the Philippines, may be better classified as a development finance institution. It is heavily engaged in project lending, and gets funding from the World Bank and the Asian Development Bank. Six investment houses still have minority equity participation from foreign financial institutions: Citicorp Investment Philippines (with Citibank); Ayala Investment and Development Corporation (with Wells Fargo Bank and Mitsubishi Bank); Philippine Pacific Capital Corporation (with Nomura Securities Ltd, Sanwa Bank and Mitsui Bank); Philippine American Investments Corporation (with Chase Manhattan Bank); AEA Development Corporation (with Deutsche Bank, Bank of Tokyo, Crocker National Bank, Irving Trust Co. and Philadelphia National Bank); and State Investment House Inc. (with Wardley Ltd). With such international linkages, the investment houses expected that the offshore banking system established in 1976 would make them major participants; however, the system was limited to foreign banks.

Even with these additional powers, investment houses may encounter difficulty surviving in the highly competitive environment under the modified universal banking system. Unlike the other non-banks which generally retained their traditional specialised areas of activity, the investment houses may be forced to compete directly with the banks without having the essential banking powers. However, they have certain options. Those affiliated with commercial banks may opt to be absorbed by their parent as part of the latter's move toward expanded commercial banking. Others may acquire banking licences by buying or merging with a thrift bank and eventually converting into a commercial bank. Those belonging to large company groups may of course preserve the *status quo*, and rely on their 'captive' accounts for survival.

(ii) *Financing companies*

Financing companies are corporations or partnerships licensed as such by the Securities and Exchange Commission and organised primarily to extend credit facilities to consumers and to business enterprises through discounting, factoring or leasing. They may be sub-categorised into the quasi-bank and the pure financing companies.

The quasi-bank financing companies are engaged in commercial paper dealership in addition to their traditional functions, and are allowed to borrow from the public. They are much bigger than the pure financing companies that are confined to less than 20 lenders for their fund sources. In 1981, the 12 quasi-bank financing companies listed in Table 4.8 controlled 44.6 per cent of the ₱12123 million combined resources of the 369 financing companies, although they represented only 3.2 per cent of the total number. Six of them have foreign institutional minority shareholders. The more significant include BA Finance Corporation (with Bank of America), Filinvest Credit Corporation (with Chase Manhattan Bank), and FNCB Finance (with Citibank).

A number of the pure financing companies are specialised in terms of clientele, service, or both. Some are 'captive' finance companies of manufacturers. Most notable are Radiowealth Finance Corporation and Ford Credit Philippines Inc. A few (like those established in the mid-1970s as joint ventures between local banks and foreign financial institutions) concentrate on lease financing. Examples are Far East Chemco Leasing and Finance Corporation and Consolidated Orient Leasing and Finance Corporation. The rest specialise in other financing operations, such as factoring of receivables, lending to market vendors, etc.

Between the quasi-banks and the pure financing companies, there is a third sub-category. This consists of those financing companies organised in the late 1970s and early 1980s to participate in the money market as dealers of commercial paper by way of non-recourse sales and as brokers of direct credit transactions between borrowers and investors.

Financing companies emerged in the Philippines in the 1950s, largely to finance the mass distribution of consumer durable goods which Philippine assembly plants were turning out in large numbers. In line with the then government import substitution programme, household appliances and motor cars were assembled in Philippine factories for sale to the domestic market. To create the sales volume, instalment financing plans were devised with the aid of the financing companies.

The passage of the Financing Company Act 1969 placed the regulation and supervision of finance companies under the Securities and Exchange Commission. However, following the 1972 financial reforms, certain aspects of financing company operations (particularly those related to quasi-banking and services pricing) fell under the regulation of the Central Bank.

1980 and 1981 were difficult years for finance companies due to the continuing inflationary pressures affecting the consumer durables market, and to the slump in the automotive industry. As a result, the bigger financing companies shifted to financing real estate and home mortgages. Other firms have gone into commercial and industrial accounts, where both volume and returns are more favourable, mainly due to lower bad debt losses.

In 1981, assets of the financing companies totalled ₱12123 billion, accounting for the biggest share in the total resources of all private non-banks (at 32.6 per cent). Of the total assets of the financing companies, 76 per cent were in loans.

(iii) *Securities dealers/brokers*

Regulated by both the Central Bank and the Securities and Exchange Commission, the securities dealers/brokers buy and sell securities either for their own account (dealership) or for the account of others (brokerage). The majority are active members of either of the two operating Stock Exchanges. The few big ones are involved also in the primary market for securities, undertaking private placement or public distribution of new issues, particularly common stock of mining and oil companies in their exploratory stage. Since firm underwriting of securities was reserved for investment houses, they conduct theirs on a best efforts basis. Sometimes they also participate as members of selling syndicates organised by investment houses for major underwriting commitments. Recently, due to the poor condition of the local stock market, 119 out of the 142 licensed securities dealers/brokers have shifted to the money market, buying commercial paper and selling it on a without recourse basis, or simply arranging direct credit transactions between borrowers and lenders. As a group, they now account for close to 30 per cent of the reported without recourse transactions in the commercial paper market. The biggest, Multinational Investment Bancorporation, is the only securities dealer/broker with a quasi-banking licence, but is not a member of any Stock Exchange.

(iv) *Investment companies*

Officially classified investment companies are corporations with preponderant holdings of financial assets and purporting to engage in investment activities. There are two types, open ended and closed ended. Also known as mutual funds, the open ended investment companies have no fixed amount of paid-in capital; they sell and redeem their shares on a day to day basis and their funds are invested mostly in traded securities. In the 1950s, the pioneering mutual funds in the country met with failure, and this led to the enactment of the Investment Company Act 1960. Since then, the mutual fund industry has not yet fully regained its popularity among investors. Today, there are only four licensed mutual funds: Commercial Mutual Fund Inc.; Malayan Income Fund Inc.; Pacific Fund Inc.; and Trinity Shares Inc.

Of the 59 closed ended investment companies registered with and reporting to the Central Bank, most are in reality closely held companies investing mainly in non-traded equities; they may be better described as holding companies. Only four are listed on the Stock Exchanges – Ayala Fund Inc.; First Philippine Holdings Corporation; House of Investments Inc.; and Monex Investment Co. Inc. Only the first two had trading transactions in 1981.

The investment companies in 1981 had total assets of ₱5513 million, accounting for 14.8 per cent of the resources of the private non-banks combined. Close to 50 per cent of the assets were funded by borrowings.

(v) *Fund managers*

Under a CBP Circular Letter dated 28 March 1974, fund managers are defined as judical or natural persons engaged in the administration of property, or money and its equivalent, for the benefit of the owner or a third person; the definition was meant to be functional rather than institutional. Included in this category are the trust departments of banks; trust departments and investment management departments of investment houses; and various retirement, pension, provident, employee welfare and other similar funds managed by their respective boards of trustees.

The total assets of fund managers reflected in Table 4.2 included only the managed funds of the nine investment houses performing investment management functions, and are thus very much understated. No pertinent figures are readily available, but a good estimate would place the total amount of managed funds in the Philippines at over ₱5 billion.

(vi) *Lending investors*

Lending investors are classified as all persons, partnerships and corporations engaged in the regular business of extending credit utilising mainly their own funds, and which are not categorised elsewhere. They constitute a 'miscellaneous' category of non-banks formally recognised under the 1972 financial reforms and under the direct regulation of the Central Bank. This group includes those non-institutional moneylenders previously operating outside the regulated system. Generally small in size, they normally cater for those unsophisticated borrowers left unserved by the banks and other institutionalised credit outlets. From the time lending investors were required to register with the Central Bank under CBP Circular 394 1973, only 74 have registered: most are sole proprietors.

(vii) *Pawnshops*

Pawnshops are establishments lending short term money on the security of personal property delivered as pledge. They may be organised as sole proprietorships, partnerships or corporations. Although long in existence, they came under the regulation of the Central Bank in 1973 following the promulgation of a Presidential Decree known as the Pawnshop Regulation Act and the implementation of CBP Circular 114. Pawnshops cater mainly for persons with relatively low incomes and immediate and small cash needs. The largest pawnshop in the country has total assets of about ₱12 million; it is located in Metro Manila.

(viii) *Government non-bank financial institutions*

Among the government non-bank financial institutions officially included in this category are the Government Service Insurance System, the Social Security System, the Agricultural Credit Administration and the National Investment and Development Corporation (as mentioned earlier, there are other government owned institutions that may be classified as non-banks aside from these four).

The Government Service Insurance System (GSIS) was established in 1936 to consolidate the various pension programmes for government employees. It has since expanded to include retirement, life and property insurance, as well as salary, policy and real estate loans. Its main sources of funds are member contributions; insurance premiums; interest on loans receivable; and income on investments. Now capitalised at over ₱6 billion, GSIS has been a major provider of long term financing, especially for housing and building construction. In recent years, however, it has started to shift its loan portfolio from real estate to commerce and industry. Aside from loan financing, GSIS also directly invest in stocks and bonds of government corporations and private enterprises.

The Social Security System (SSS) was established in 1954 and began operation in 1958, providing retirement and disability income; death benefits; sickness allowances; and education, housing and salary loans to workers in the private sector. Like GSIS, SSS relies for its funding on member contributions and on income from loans and investments. Its resources are invested in loans; government securities; private securities; and time deposits with government banks.

The Agricultural Credit Association (ACA) was established in 1963, as the credit arm of the government's agrarian reform programme. Its principal objective is to provide agricultural credit to small farmers at subsidised interest rates. ACA assistance consists of production and commodity loans to farmers, and facility and operating capital loans to farmer co-operatives. Other activities include distributing fertilisers and providing technical assistance.

The National Investment and Development Corporation, a subsidiary of the Philippine National Bank, was established in 1963 to promote industrial, agricultural and commercial enterprises through long term lending and equity financing as well as guarantees. It now has majority holdings in 10 subsidiaries, minority equity investments in 20 corporations, and various financial interests in 62 other firms.

In 1981, the four government non-banks combined had total assets of ₱23638 million (mostly accounted for by the GSIS and SSS) and constituting 38.9 per cent of the total non-bank resources.

(ix) *Venture capital companies (VCCs)*

VCCs, the newest category of financial institutions in the Philippines are commercial bank subsidiaries organised under Presidential Decree 1688 issued in April 1980, as implemented by CBP Circular 733. Their main purpose is to provide equity financing to small and medium scale enterprises. Under the Enabling Act, a VCC is initially capitalised at ₱5 million, with the parent bank investing 60 per cent and two government institutions (the Human Settlement Development Corporation and the National Development Company) each contributing 20 per cent. To supplement its equity capital, the VCC may avail itself of low cost, long term loans from the Development Bank of the Philippines. So far, only eight banks have organised VCCs.

An interesting mode of financial assistance developed by the VCCs is transaction financing. Designed to accommodate the entrepreneur's desire to maintain full ownership and control of his enterprise, and at the same time compensate the VCC's risk taking well beyond the low interest rates allowable on short term debt financing, transaction financing involves a joint venture investment made by a VCC on a specific transaction (such as a certain purchase order) for a pre-agreed share of the profits expected from that transaction. Considered as quasi-equity, it does not require the usual collaterals, but releases are made directly to the suppliers of the business.

(x) *Non-bank thrift institutions*

The non-bank thrift institutions in the Philippines are of two types: the mutual building and loan associations (MBLAs), and the non-stock savings and loan associations (NSLAs).

Governed by the General Banking Act, the MBLAs are corporations organised to accumulate savings of stockholders through regular equal periodical payments on stock subscriptions. The accumulated savings and profits are given to the stockholders on surrender of their shares. The MBLAs raise additional funds by borrowing, and they specialise in extending long term mortgage loans to members. Although long established, the MBLAs are fast losing their appeal, as shown by their declining resources they may not survive an increasingly competitive environment.

The membership of a NSLA is confined to a well defined group of persons, for example, employees of affiliated companies. Established under the Savings and Loan Association Act 1963, NSLAs are not allowed to transact business with the general public. They can accept savings and time deposits from, and grant short-term loans to, only members. Unlike the MBLAs, NSLAs are still growing in numbers and in size.

(xi) *Insurance companies*

Supervised and regulated by the Insurance Commission, the insurance companies in the Philippines have not grown as fast as the other major categories of private non-banks. Life insurance cover has been extended to about only 6 per cent of the population; this is because of the relatively high cost of insurance brought about by the widespread availability of low cost policy loans.

The main types of policies offered by insurance companies include life; fire; marine; and health and accident insurance. Their assets are fairly diversified, consisting of policy loans; real estate loans; stocks; bonds; and time deposits. The insurance companies (particularly the life insurers) have continued to be an important source of long term capital.

General insurance business was introduced in the Philippines as early as 1829, through a local representative appointed by Lloyds of London. Life insurance came in 1898, with the establishment of a Sun Life Assurance of Canada office. The first Filipino owned life insurance company was established in 1910. This company (now known as Insular Life Assurance Co. Ltd) also became the first domestic life insurer to mutualise, and so far is the only one to have done so since the late 1970s.

There are now 135 licensed insurance companies: 23 direct writing life insurers (21 domestic, two foreign); 107 direct writing non-life insurers (94 domestic, 13 foreign); and five reinsurers (four domestic, one foreign). Table 4.9 lists the names, total assets and licensing date of the major firms. In 1981, the combined assets of insurance companies amounted to ₱11086 million (representing 29.8 per cent of the private non-banks' total resources).

TABLE 4.9   Major insurance companies[a] in the Philippine (figures as at 31 December 1980, in ₱ million)

	Date licensed[b]	Total assets
Life companies – domestic (21)[c]		
Filipinas Life Assurance Co.	1958	577.5
Great Pacific Life Assurance Corpn	1954	150.4
Insular Life Assurance Co. Ltd	1946	1010.2
Lincoln Philippine Life Insurance Co.[d]	1965	125.4
Philippine American Life Insurance Co.[d]	1947	1967.6
United Coconut Planters' Life Assurance Corpn	1978	399.0
Life companies – foreign (2)		
Manufacturers' Life Insurance Co. Inc.	1945	115.8
Sun Life Assurance Co. of Canada	1945	279.4
Reinsurers – domestic (4)		
Universal Reinsurance Corpn of the Philippines	1949	209.2
Reinsurers – foreign (1)		
Lincoln National Life Insurance Co. Inc.	1976	35.4
Non-life companies – domestic (94)		
Cibeles Insurance Corporation	1965	134.5
FGU Insurance Corporation	1963	299.2
Filriters Guaranty Assurance Corpn.	1961	127.3
Malayan Insurance Co. Inc.	1949	362.1
Mercantile Insurance Co. Inc.	1962	296.9
Philippine American General Insurance Co. Inc.[d]	1946	193.4
Philippines' First Insurance Co. Inc.	1946	116.2
Pioneer Insurance & Surety Corpn	1954	160.7
Non-life companies – foreign (13)		
American Home Assurance Co. (AIU–PI)	1957	152.9

[a] Includes insurance companies with total assets exceeding ₱ 100 million as of 31 December 1980.
[b] Licensed by the Insurance Commission.
[c] Figures in parenthesis indicates total number of companies licensed under the category as of December 1981.
[d] Majority owned by foreign shareholders.

Source: Insurance Commission, 1982.

(xii) *Moneybrokers*

The five moneybrokers licensed by the Central Bank came into being in the late 1970s to service the then newly established OBU and foreign currency deposit systems. In 1981, they handled a combined volume of P347 billion in moneybroking transactions.

FINANCIAL MARKETS

The Philippine financial markets consist of the money market, the capital market and the foreign exchange market. By far the most developed among them is the money market, which is also the most sophisticated in Southeast Asia.

For discussion purposes, the foreign currency transactions of the country's foreign exchange and OBU systems are covered in the section on the foreign exchange market. Strictly speaking, however, these transactions belong to a separate and distinct market which is essentially an international money and capital market like the Asian Dollar Market of Singapore or the Eurodollar market.

(a) The Money Market

The money market in the Philippines has three major sub-markets: the interbank call loan market, the commercial paper market; and the government securities market, all of which are closely interlinked. The government securities market really straddles both the money market and the capital market, as it involves short to long term securities issued by the government and its agencies. For discussion purposes, however, it is included in this section.

Table 4.10 shows the volume of money market transactions in 1981, broken down by types of instrument. Most transactions (over 79 per cent of total volume) involved instruments in the commercial paper market, deposit substitutes of banks and quasi-banks included. Interbank call loans made up 20.3 per cent, and outright transactions in government securities contributed less than 1 per cent. In terms of institutional participation, commercial banks accounted for the bulk of transactions, handling 69.7 per cent of total volume, while investment houses and finance companies took care respectively of 15.0 and 11.9 per cent.

TABLE 4.10 Philippine volume of money market transactions by type of instrument (figures as at end 1981, in ₽ million)

	Amount	% of total
Interbank call loans	66969	20.3
Promissory notes*a*	189532	57.5
Repurchased agreements (over private securities)*a*	20611	6.2
Repurchased agreements (over government securities)*a*	27208	8.2
Certificates of assignment/participation*a*	486	0.2
Commercial paper (of non-financial issuers)*b*	20467	6.2
Commercial paper (of financial institutions)*b*	3459	1.1
Central bank certificates of indebtness	674	0.2
Treasury bills	64	. . .*c*
Other government securities	151	. . .
Total	329621	100.0

a Debt instruments issued by banks and quasi-banks, collectively called deposit substitutes.
b Debt instruments issued by non-financial entities and by financial institutions not licensed to perform quasi-banking functions.
c Negligible.

Source: CBP.

(i) *Interbank call loan market*

In the interbank call loan market, banks and quasi-banks deal directly with each other in overnight borrowing–lending transactions to adjust their daily reserve positions without resorting to the Central Bank. This sub-market had its formal beginnings in 1963, when the Bankers' Association of the Philippines adopted rules to govern call loan transactions among its member banks.[15] At that time, the banks were experiencing severe reserve management problems, due to a continuing balance of payments deficit and a tightening credit policy – (both a result of the *de facto* devaluation of the peso in 1962 when foreign exchange controls were lifted). In 1975, when interbank rates started to fluctuate widely and some astute banks began to trade in the market, further bidding up the rates, the Central Bank decided to impose rate ceilings and prohibit any bank from being both a borrower and a lender in the interbank market in any single day. As a result, the interbank market ceased to be the single most reliable indicator of the liquidity and credit demand–supply situation in the financial system, and the determinant of other money market rates. With the floating of interest rates in 1981, however, the interbank market rates again became free.

(ii) *Commercial paper market*

The commercial paper market developed from the inter company market initiated in 1965. A then newly established investment house brought together 34 different companies with divergent but complementary seasonal cash flows. Using its own borrowing and lending notes, it intermediated between companies with temporary surplus funds and those with seasonal deficits. Banks began to participate in the late 1960s, by floating their own promissory notes. Their objective was to capture funds that could not be attracted by the low yielding traditional bank deposits.

Encouraged by the investment houses, many corporate borrowers came to the market in the early 1970s with their own commercial paper. For them, the high interest rates demanded by money market borrowings were secondary to the ready availability of funds: traditional bank loans, though cheaper, were in short supply. To accommodate placements in small denominations or for short periods, two new instruments were introduced by the market dealers – certificates of participation and repurchase agreements. The resulting flexibility allowed individuals, (even small savers) to become active market participants as investors.

In 1974 alone deposit substitute liabilities of banks grew by 84.8 per cent, faster than their savings and time deposits combined. By 1975, outstanding bank deposit substitutes had grown to an equivalent of over 100 per cent of the total savings and time deposits. To arrest the disintermediation of funds away from traditional bank deposits, various measures were instituted in 1976 and 1977 to moderate the commercial paper market. The deposit substitutes were subjected to interest rate ceilings, minimum trading lots, reserve requirements, and a final withholding tax on interest payments. They were also standardised and limited to three types: promissory notes; repurchase agreements; and certificates of participation/assignment. Lastly, they were required to be registered with the Securities and Exchange Commission along with the commercial paper issues of non-financial entities and non-banks with no quasi-banking licence. The immediate impact of the new regulations was to slow the growth of deposit substitutes. By 1978, their level in the banking system had fallen to an equivalent of 49 per cent of the total time and savings deposits.

Being resilient and innovative, the money market needed only a short time to adjust to the changed regulatory framework. The way around the regulations was to avoid booking deposit substitute liabilities. So the market makers, led by the investment houses, shifted their activity to without recourse transactions, an activity the banks were prohibited from undertaking. Not subjected to yield ceilings and minimum trading lots, commercial paper issues of corporate borrowers were sold outright to investors without recourse to the dealers. To assure investors of prompt repayment however, the dealers simultaneously issued their own post-dated cheques, supposedly in their capacity as paying agents of the corporate issuers. What the 1976–7 regulations thus really accomplished was to drive the market to less regulated activity. As far as the investors were concerned, it did not matter what paper they were buying; the most important consideration was the yield. In fact, the attraction of sustained high returns kept them continually rolling over their placements. This was true not only among individuals, but also among many corporate and institutional investors. By 1980, the outstanding commercial paper sold without recourse had hit P23.2 billion, more than double the level 4 years previously; on the other hand, the outstanding deposit substitutes of banks and quasi-banks amounted to only P19.3 billion, a mere 15.6 per cent increase over the same 4 year period.

The euphoria prevailing in the market between 1978 and 1980 allowed certain unhealthy developments to creep in and weaken the market. Borrowing companies were emboldened to use inherently short term funds for fixed capital investment and other permanent requirements. Undercapitalised non-banks, not authorised to engage in quasi-banking, were able to enter the market as dealers of corporate commercial paper and as brokers of direct credit transactions between borrowers and investors. These same non-banks also succeeded in floating the commercial paper issues of their affiliates. Prepared to pay very high interest rates, these high risk companies eventually eased the prime borrowers out of the market. With the recession, however, many issuers were constrained not only to renew their outstanding obligations, but also to incur new ones to cover operating losses and replace maturing issues. The market's weakness was finally exposed in January 1981, when the sudden departure from the country of a heavily indebted businessman caused investors to withdraw funds placed with or through financial institutions suspected of lending to his various enterprises. Unable to recover their placements, investors then realised that their funds were locked in with some illiquid – if not altogether insolvent – corporate issuers.

Although the government succeeded in mitigating the effects of what later became known as the 'financial crisis of 1981', the commercial paper market underwent yet another period of adjustment and entered a new, more restrictive, regulatory environment.

The most notable of the new regulations was the Securities and Exchange Commission's requirement for a corporation to support its commercial paper issue with committed bank credit lines covering at least 20 per cent of the outstanding amount of the issues. This was intended not so much to provide liquidity back up for the issue as to assure prior credit evaluation of a prospective issuer by qualified institutions like banks. Such being the intention, the credit bureau organised by the Central Bank in April 1982 could eventually perform this evaluation function as part of its responsibility to provide investors with sufficient information on commercial paper issuers. Many issuers have in fact found the credit line requirement too restrictive, and have allowed their commercial paper licences to expire.

Another change was the imposition of a minimum commercial paper denomination of ₱300000, an amount six times the minimum trading lot now imposed on deposit substitutes. This ruling effectively stopped small money market investors from participating in the higher yielding but riskier without recourse to dealer purchases, and confined them to the generally safer deposit substitutes, should they stay in the market. While the Securities and Exchange Commission tightened the registration requirements on commercial paper issues of non-financial corporations and the smaller non-banks with no quasi-banking licence, it loosened up on deposit substitutes by exempting banks and quasi-banks from registration. This stance resulted from the realisation that banks and quasi-banks were already closely supervised and regulated by the Central Bank, and that their registration with another regulatory agency was in practice superfluous.

(iii) *Government securities market*

In the wake of the 1981 financial crisis, the Central Bank moved quickly to reactivate the market for government securities. First, there was need to regain investor confidence in the money market, and it was thought that government securities (being regarded as riskless) could fill the vacuum left by the declining issues of commercial paper. Second, the successful stabilisation of the floating interest rates through open market operations would require an active market for government securities.

To enhance the secondary market, a new network of accredited government securities dealers was established in December 1981. Consisting of eight banks and four non-banks, these dealers were conferred certain privileges such as special inventory financing through a repurchase facility with the Central Bank, and an exclusive right to purchase and sell Central Bank holdings of government securities (but not at auctions, which remained open to the public). In turn, the dealers were obliged to participate on a regular basis in the primary auctions and to trade in the government securities acquired.

The government securities market originated from the Treasury bill programme instituted by the government in 1966, a year after the successful launch of the intercompany market in the private sector. This programme was aimed at financing government expenditure from non-inflationary sources. For 3 years, the government securities market was dominated by Treasury bills which were auctioned weekly. However, the network of accredited dealers organised to support the programme found difficulty in sustaining active trading of the bills in the secondary market.

In the 1970s, the market activity shifted to the Central Bank certificates of indebtedness (CBCIs). Originally intended to mop up excess liquidity in the urban areas for rechannelling to credit deficient rural areas, the CBCIs were later redesigned to make them effective instruments for open market operations. There was also a rush of security issues by different government owned financial and non-financial establishments.

In 1981, over ₱30 billion worth of government securities was outstanding in the market. However, only a small percentage was being actively traded in the secondary market; the bulk was held by banks and other institutions (primarily as legal reserves or agricultural loan substitutes. The generally low yields offered on government securities is the stumbling block to the popular acceptance of these risk free instruments.

(b) The Capital Market

The capital market in the Philippines is very undeveloped compared to the money market. There is a problem in both the demand for, and the supply of, instruments. Potential investors with long term funds find that given high inflation rates, the financial returns of long-term securities are not as attractive as the inflation sensitive investment in real assets, particularly real estate properties. Those prepared to place funds in financial assets, on the other hand, prefer more liquid investments such as short term instruments in the money market; perceived economic uncertainty dissuades them from committing their funds to long term securities. With thin secondary trading in the capital market, investors also worry about being locked in, and being unable to have liquidity when necessary. On the supply side, many otherwise attractive issuers of stocks and other long term securities have chosen to remain closely held enterprises and to rely on bank loans for additional funding. Until recently, they have found no reason to access the capital market directly, as they had been assured by the banks of cheap loans funded by low cost deposits.

The Philippine capital market was organised as early as the mid-1920s when the mining boom and the related heavy outlay required for mining brought a need for an orderly market for stocks. In 1927, the Manila Stock Exchange was established. During its early years, it listed only a few commercial and mining stocks. In 1963, the Makati Stock Exchange was organised in the then emerging business district just outside old Manila; this was followed by the opening of the Cebu Stock Exchange in 1970, and the Metropolitan Stock Exchange in 1974. However, the two new Exchanges were not able to attract enough business; the former closed after 2 years, and the latter is now inactive. At the end of 1981, there were a total of 190 listed companies: 81 on the big and 109 on the small board. Those on the big board included 20 financial institutions; 44 industrial and commercial establishments; and 17 mining companies. On the small board were mostly oil exploration companies and start up mining firms.

In 1975, an automatic common listing of all securities was adopted among the three Exchanges then operating. This was a move to improve the volume of Stock Market transactions by making all listed securities available in all three Exchanges. To include foreign investors into the market, full repatriation of investment was assured, subject to a minimum staying period of 3 months. In 1976, a special 'dollar' board for blue chip stocks was created. Foreign investments made through this board were authorised to be repatriated immediately with no restrictions. Unfortunately, there has never been a meaningful volume of transactions on the dollar board.

As shown in Table 4.11, the Philippine stock market has been in a slump since 1979 and its 1981 performance proved the worst in 9 years. The sad condition of the market could be attributed to a number of factors: the worldwide recession resulted in depressed prices of the export metals produced by the leading listed companies; the deteriorating peso–dollar exchange rate discouraged the entry of foreign investors; a series of financial scandals involved two securities dealers/brokers; and a 10 per cent tax was imposed on capital gains from the sales of listed stocks.

TABLE 4.11   Philippine Stock Market transactions, 1972–81[a] (figures as at end period)

Year	Volume (million shares)	Value in (P million)
1972	23589	608
1973	136365	5933
1974	159704	5145
1975	115096	3146
1976	248581	4506
1977	124870	2505
1978	153033	5470
1979	128881	4925
1980	100518	4602
1981	52011	1349

[a]   Transactions were about equally divided between the two operating Stock Exchanges.

Source: Manila Stock Exchange; Makati Stock Exchange.

To shore up the stock market, the government instituted certain supportive measures. In 1981, the Central Bank initiated a stock financing programme whereby a bank might grant rediscountable loans to investors against pledges of listed high grade shares. There being no takers, the programme was later amended to liberalise the financing and rediscounting terms. In early 1982, the capital gains tax on stock transactions was abolished, and in its place came a transaction tax of 0.25 per cent of the gross selling price of shares sold in the Stock Exchanges. The favourable effects of these measures have yet to be observed.

The government is presently considering the implementation of an old plan to merge the country's operating Stock Exchanges; in view of the current low in market transactions, the need for rationalising the Stock Exchanges to reduce operational costs is strongly felt. There is, however, stiff resistance among the members of the two older Exchanges, the sticking point being the pricing and allocation of seats in the merged Exchange.

In the primary market, the investment houses from 1974–80 had the exclusive power to make firm underwriting agreements. During that period, however, their underwriting activities involved mainly short term debt instruments. Their failure to develop the market for long term securities could be attributed not so much to their preoccupation in the money market but more to the unfavourable economic environment prevailing in the country. At the same time, the investment houses as a group proved unequal to the gigantic task assigned them. With the advent of the expanded commercial banks, following the 1980 financial reforms, the underwriting of stocks and bonds may yet achieve a decent volume.

(c) The Foreign Exchange (FE) Market

FE transactions in the Philippines are closely controlled by the Central Bank. Practically all outward remittances are made through the commercial banking system which provides the necessary FE after a careful review of the required documents. There are several guidelines on the types of transaction eligible for FE approval; no FE may be made available for importing certain items, basically luxury consumer goods. The list of banned items has grown smaller since the round of delisting in early 1982. In the case of interest and amortisation payments on approved foreign obligations, full remittances are permitted without restriction.

FE receipts from exports and from invisibles representing current earnings or income of residents must be surrendered for pesos to the commercial banking system. However, those foreign currency funds not so required may be deposited with local banks authorised to accept foreign currency deposits under either CBP

Circular 343 1972, or CBP Circular 547 1976. As an inducement for doing so, these funds may be withdrawn at any time, and disposed of freely by the depositor.

Foreign borrowings by residents are monitored closely, and require prior approval by the Central Bank. There are guidelines that restrict foreign borrowings to those within the ability of the country to service with its FE earnings. Schedules of minimum maturity periods for various ranges of loan amount, and of maximum interest rates for different maturities, are clearly specified. These schedules are revised as needed to reflect developments in the international financial markets or changes in the country's debt servicing capacity. A ceiling on aggregate foreign borrowings is fixed for each year in accordance with the Foreign Borrowing Act 1970. Under this Act, the debt service burden of the country for any year is limited to a maximum of 20 per cent of the average FE receipts during the past 3 years.

Swap facilities and forward covers are sometimes offered by the Central Bank for loans and other foreign obligations of firms in preferred industries such as exports, but for only limited duration (usually not more than 6 months). Some commercial banks also provide such cover for non-financial clients as part of conventional import or export related services. There are also regulations that limit the pricing of spot and forward contracts, but the bands are wide enough to allow flexibility.

Movements of capital are also closely monitored. Inward foreign investments are required to be registered so that subsequent remittance of profits and repatriation of capital can be assured. Outward foreign investments by residents require prior approval by the Central Bank, and are rarely allowed.

Since the time the peso was unpegged from the US dollar and allowed to float in February 1970, a guiding exchange rate has been determined on a day to day basis and quoted in terms of units per US dollar. The guiding rate for a given day is based on the weighted average of the exchange rates for all interbank sales consummated during the preceding day at the Foreign Exchange Trading Center of the Bankers' Association of the Philippines. This is where commercial banks conduct their daily trading of foreign currencies (basically US dollars) against the peso, mainly to square their respective FE positions. Interbank FE transactions are determined freely between the buyer and seller banks within the range of $2\frac{1}{4}$ per cent below $-2\frac{1}{2}$ per cent above the guiding rate for each trading day. The Central Bank nonetheless closely monitors the trading and occasionally intervenes to prevent abrupt changes and maintain an orderly market. Based on guidelines set by the Bankers' Association for spot transactions, the maximum and minimum buying rates are respectively $\frac{1}{2}$ per cent and 1 per cent below the guiding rate, while the maximum and minimum selling rates are respectively $1\frac{1}{4}$ and $\frac{3}{4}$ per cent above. However, these margins do not apply to transactions involving US$100000 or more.

Despite strict FE control – or perhaps because of it – active parallel markets for FE have been thriving outside the regulation of the Central Bank. The black market for illegally held FE gets its supply from foreign tourists; Filipino workers overseas; and exporters with FE salted abroad. The demand comes from local merchants importing restricted goods, businessmen making authorised investments abroad; and residents transferring their assets overseas. There is also a 'grey' market for FE. In this market, the foreign currency deposits legally held by residents are traded for pesos. It should be noted that these foreign currency deposits are legally allowed to be transferred abroad.

The Central Bank has now taken steps to increase the flow of FE into the official system and out of the black market. In 1981, for example, the Central Bank stopped granting licences to additional FE dealers[16] and decided to utilise the banking system to purchase foreign currencies from tourists and the general public. This decision was made because a number of licensed dealers were discovered to be serving as 'fronts' for black market operations. In February 1982, the banks were authorised to purchase foreign currency notes directly from the public at prices above the guiding rate (the rate paid by banks for such purchases was previously 1 per cent below the guiding rate, much lower than the rate paid in the black market).

With the establishment of the OBU system and the expansion of the FCDU system in 1976, the Philippines has become more closely linked with the international banking community. Indeed, the two systems constitute what may be considered as an international money and capital market, similar to the Asian Dollar Market of Singapore or Hongkong. The market's participants (the OBUs and the FCDUs) are involved primarily in the receipt of foreign currency funds (mostly from external sources in the case of the OBUs) and the transfer of these funds to borrowers from within and outside the country. Onshore lendings, however, must be authorised by the Central Bank. In addition, they are engaged also in foreign exchange trading, except that OBUs may not deal in the local currency.

It seems that the main attraction for the OBUs is the large potential lending business available in the country. As shown in Table 4.12, most funds generated by the OBUs from offshore sources have been channelled to locally based banks and resident non-bank borrowers. Similarly, the FCDUs have served very much as conduits of foreign currency loans to Philippine based establishments.

TABLE 4.12   Philippine Offshore Banking Unit and Foreign Currency Deposit systems: selected data (figures as at end December 1981, in US$ million)

	Offshore Banking Units system		Foreign Currency Deposit system	
	Amount	% of gross resources	Amount	% of gross resources
Gross resources	4627	100.0	5195	100.0
Deposits and borrowings	4479	96.8	4124	79.4
1. Banks	4332	93.6	3085	59.4
Philippine based[a]	(681)	(14.7)	(926)	(17.8)
Foreign based	(3651)	(78.9)	(2159)	(41.6)
2. Non-banks[b]	147	3.2	1039	20.0
Resident	(—)	(0.0)	(838)	(16.1)
Non-resident	(147)	(3.2)	(201)	(3.9)
Placements and lendings	4479	96.8	4874	94.0
1. Banks	2781	60.1	2214	42.6
Philippine based[a]	(1877)	(40.6)	(1157)	(22.3)
Foreign based	(904)	(19.5)	(1057)	(20.3)
2. Non-banks[b]	1698	36.7	2660	51.2
Resident	(1567)	(33.9)	(2660)	(51.2)
Non-resident	(131)	(2.8)	(—)	(0.0)

[a]   Includes FCDUs, OBUs and the Central Bank.
[b]   Includes non-financial and non-bank financial firms.

Source: CBP.

ANALYSIS

The major structural and policy changes introduced recently were meant to correct certain deficiencies in the evolution of the financial system, and to enhance its responsiveness to the intermediation needs of the economy. Although the system continued to mobilise an increasing amount of domestic as well as foreign resources, it failed to provide sufficient medium and long term funds for industrial development. The flow of domestic savings also proved insufficient to reduce the country's dependence on foreign borrowings. Lastly, the cost of financial intermediation tended to be very high.

The significant growth of the financial sector in recent years was achieved with its component institutions growing not only in size but also in number. Because of legislated functional specialisation, a wide variety of banks and non-bank financial intermediaries proliferated, each category performing a limited range of services and catering for a specific segment of the small domestic market. This institutional arrangement induced fragmentation of financial resources, and restricted competition within narrow confines.

With small resource bases individually, a great majority of the private financial establishments were unable to realise a sufficient degree of portfolio diversification and operating economy. The concentration of credit risk exposure resulted in high susceptibility of individual institutions to developments adversely affecting their few clients. On the other hand, the inability to exploit economies of scale led to high transaction costs. These operating characteristics of the financial institutions, coupled with the absence of effective competition among them, invariably brought a high cost of intermediation throughout the system. The old regulatory framework also contributed to the inefficiency of the financial sector. The existence of administrative ceilings (not only on lending rates but also on deposit rates) provided the institutions with legally protected margins; these margins, though already wide, were subjected to further stretching through the widespread use of ingenious techniques that enabled lenders to obtain loan yields beyond the legal maximum.

The failure of the financial sector to provide adequate medium and long term finance could be traced to several factors. Because of smallness, most financial institutions limited their term transformation to avoid exposure to added risk with respect to funding. Even the commercial banks, which always had an overwhelming control of the system's resources, confined their activities to short term lending. While it was true that their deposit holdings had been basically short term, the amount of deposits had not fallen below a certain level which could allow utilisation of a significant portion of their resources for longer term commitments. The commercial banks, however, found no reason to leave the profitable short term market. In the first place, the task of developing the capital market was assigned to the smaller investment houses; with no assured liquidity support from the Central Bank in the meantime, the investment houses avoided long term financing situations where their own funds would be committed. The secondary market for capital instruments could not provide an adequate liquidity mechanism for holders of these instruments.

The repressive interest rate policy in the past also militated against the accumulation of financial savings, especially long term. Unable to offer positive real returns to savers, the financial institutions could not attract long term placements.

The 1980 financial reforms squarely addressed the shortcomings of the system. Functional specialisation among major categories of financial institutions was reduced (and in some cases eliminated altogether) to broaden institutional capabilities, enhance competitive conditions and induce efficient intermediation. Various monetary and fiscal policies were either liberalised or rationalised to attract increased savings to the official system, and encourage lending on a longer term basis. Large, multipurpose institutions – the expanded commercial banks – were introduced to spearhead the development of the long term capital market. Given the clear thrust towards institutional 'bigness', adequate safeguards were instituted to avert undue concentration of economic power and the possible rise of a banking oligopoly.

TRENDS AND PREDICTIONS

The full impact of the recent structural changes in the financial system may be realised only after the economy recovers from the present recessionary situation. For the moment, no real expansion is being carried out in the industrial sector. Competition among institutional lenders remains centered on short term finance as corporate borrowers concentrate on maintaining current operations. Even the few banks which have so far been authorised to engage in expanded commercial banking have not yet pursued aggressive leverage. For the economy to utilise the increased capability of the universal banks, the domestic credit market has first to grow and present opportunities for longer term financial commitments.

Nevertheless, the impact of the liberalised interest rate policy has begun to be felt by the financial sector. Lending – borrowing margins have already narrowed, forcing banks to explore and undertake measures to attain internal operating efficiency. Many banks are turning to computers to streamline operations and reduce manpower costs. The present situation is specially difficult because the interest rate ceilings on short term credits have not been lifted and the assets of the banks are still predominantly short term loans. While the intention is to have a wholly market orientated interest rate structure, the monetary authorities are as yet apprehensive about releasing control on short term rates. This is precisely because bank assets are still concentrated on short term loans, and lifting the remaining ceilings might encourage banks to keep their present positions.

As soon as the credit market becomes active, the regular commercial banks are sure to experience strong competitive pressure, not only from their bigger counterparts (the unibanks), but also from the smaller banks that now have full domestic banking powers. Despite this predicament, however, not all of them are expected to opt for expanded authority; some may wish to avoid the added responsibilities, like securities underwriting, notwithstanding the operational advantages that a unibank may enjoy.

In the long run, the financial sector is likely to evolve an institutional configuration where wholesale multipurpose institutions like unibanks co-exist with smaller retail type establishments. To be competitive, however, the smaller institutions will have to specialise in terms of products or markets. By concentrating on areas where they have comparative advantages, they will be able to exploit certain opportunities too limited for the multipurpose institutions. This is not to say, of course, that there will be no casualties among the country's many small banks and non-banks. Those that fail to make it on their own will be forced to merge with healthier institutions; the ultimate result of these adjustments will be a reduced number of financial entities, with a broadened ownership base.

The future of the financial system is closely interlinked with the performance of the economy: while a responsive system is essential to sustain growth, it is not sufficient by itself to induce economic recovery. This is why the restructuring of the financial system is complementary to a separate effort of the government to restructure the Philippine economy.

On the economic front, the government has focused on energy development and export promotion. The objective is to solve the deteriorating balance of payments problem without unduly sacrificing economic growth. At the same time, the government is laying the foundation for the country's industrialisation thrust. Major industrial projects[17] have been selected for implementation within the 1980s. In due time, the Philippines is expected to develop sufficient internal strength to minimise its susceptibility to adverse external developments.

NOTES

1. The population growth was higher (at 3 per cent a year) during 1970–80. Although not yet conclusive, the decline could be a result of the organised effort of the government to control population, starting in 1969 with the establishment of the Population Commission.
2. Edward K. Hawkins, *The Philippines: Priorities and Prospects for Development. World Bank Country Economic Report* (Washington, DC: World Bank, 1976) provides details of the economic development between 1946–74.
3. On September 21 1972, in response to an increase in domestic unrest, martial law was proclaimed. In accordance with the provisions of the Constitution, the legislative powers of the Congress were suspended and the President assumed legislative power.
4. A 'non-traditional export' product is classified as such by the Board of Investments if its export value does not exceed US$5 million, and its production requires a significant degree of processing.
5. Joselito S. Gallardo, *The Structure of the Financial System of the Philippines, 1950–70* (Manila: Joint IMF–CBP Banking Survey Commission, CBP, 1972) is a research report that provides a description of earlier developments.
6. The financial reforms of 1972 were based on the recommendations of the Joint IMF – CBP Banking Survey Commission constituted in November 1971.
7. 'Quasi-banking' is officially defined as borrowing funds for the borrower's own account from 20 or more lenders at any one time through the issuance, endorsement, or acceptance of debt instruments of any kind (other than deposits) for the purpose of relending or purchasing of receivables or other obligations.
8. The financial reforms of 1980 were based on the recommendations of the Joint IMF–CBP Mission organised in March 1979.
9. For loans and other forms of credit with a maturity of 1 year or less, the interest rate ceilings have been maintained at 16 per cent per annum (for those secured with real estate properties) and 18 per cent per annum (for all

others). These ceilings are being kept to assure that interest rates for long term transactions are established at higher levels, thus in a way encouraging longer term lending. The CBP has recently announced that even these ceilings will be lifted eventually.

10. These reference rates – known as Manila Reference Rates (MRR) – are computed for three interest periods (60, 90 and 180 days) on the basis of the weighted average rates paid on the promissory notes with corresponding maturity periods issued during the preceding week by the 10 commercial banks with the highest level of deposit substitutes. The relevant 10 commercial banks are determined once every 6 months. Prior to May 1982, the MRR was a single rate, computed on the basis of time deposits with a maturity of 2 years or more.

11. Papers by Edita A. Tan, *Credit Measures and Their Impact on the Development of the Financial Structure: IEDR Discussion Paper 74–7* (Quezon City: School of Economics, University of the Philippines, 1974) and *A Note on Central Bank Regulation of the Financial System*: *IEDR Discussion Paper 76–6* (Quezon City: School of Economics, University of the Philippines, 1976) discuss in detail the pattern of financial development in the Philippines, as influenced by the selective credit measures used by the CBP.

12. This commenced on 9 January, when Dewey Dee, a well known businessman, flew out of the country leaving behind ₱635 million in unpaid debt and causing massive withdrawal of funds from financial institutions suspected to have lent money to his various enterprises. Jaime C. Laya, *A Crisis of Confidence and Other Papers* (Manila: CBP, 1982) provides a detailed account of the crisis, including its underlying causes and the corrective measures undertaken.

13. The NHMFC is a government owned institution, established in December 1977 to develop and provide for a secondary market for home mortgages granted by public and private financing institutions. To augment its ₱500 million capital, it is authorised to issue bonds. The NHMFC is also the administrator of the Home Development Mutual Fund (HDMF) a provident type of savings programme among all employees in both the government and the private sector, designed to generate funds for low cost, long term home financing for members. The HDMF is expected to raise at least ₱400 million a year in members' contributions.

14. Among the major government institutions which may be classified as non-banking financial institutions are the NHMFC, the HDMF, and the Philippine Export and Foreign Loan Guarantee Corporation (PEFLGC). The NHMFC and HDMF are described in footnote 13 above. The PEFLGC is primarily involved in providing government supported guarantees to foreign and local creditors of Philippine enterprises, particularly producers of export products and contractors with approved service contracts abroad. Capitalised at ₱2 billion when re-chartered in 1977, the PEFLGC was originally established in 1974.

15. O. V. Espiritu, 'The Interbank Call Loan Market: Crisis and Growth', in Robert J. Manzano *Investment Banking in the Philippines* (Makati, Metro Manila: Media Systems Inc., 1976) pp. 100–3 discusses the birth, development and growth of the interbank call loan market up to mid-1976.

16. Usually licensed as foreign exchange dealers are commercial and service establishments catering for foreign tourists. These dealers are allowed to

buy only foreign currencies, which they are required to sell to the commercial banks within a few days of purchase.

17. To cost about $6 billion at current prices, the 11 major industrial projects include a copper smelter and refinery; a phosphatic fertiliser plant; an integrated steel mill; an aluminum smelter; an integrated pulp and paper mill; a petrochemical complex; diesel engine manufacturing; cement industry expansion; coconut industry rationalisation; heavy engineering industries development; and an alcogas programme.

5 Financial Institutions and Markets in Singapore

LEE SHENG-YI

INTRODUCTION

(a) The Setting

With a land mass of only 225 square miles, Singapore is often said to have no natural resources. The country's geographical position and deep water harbour, however, offer some significant natural advantages. Situated at the tip of the Malayan Peninsula, for example, it is at the crossroads of commerce between East and West; between the Indian and the Pacific Ocean; between the Southern and Northern hemisphere; and in the midst of the archipelago of Southeast Asia. The port has allowed Singapore to develop into the natural trade centre for Southeast Asia, a position which has since been enhanced by the provision of excellent airport facilities and an up to date telecommunication system.

Political stability since the People's Action Party (PAP) came to power in 1959 has been the key factor in economic development in Singapore. Efficient government with an effective civil service, good labour relationships and industrial peace, have been a stimulant to growth. Singapore also inherited from the colonial past a sound infrastructure, particularly with respect to trade, banking, and finance. Entrepôt trade had been well developed in the late nineteenth and early twentieth century. Since the vigorous drive for industrialisation in the 1960s, Singapore has been changed to a trading and manufacturing economy[1] serving as a medium technology workshop in Southeast Asia, and as a trade centre for distributing goods and collecting raw materials in the whole region. The industrialisation drive preceded the develop-

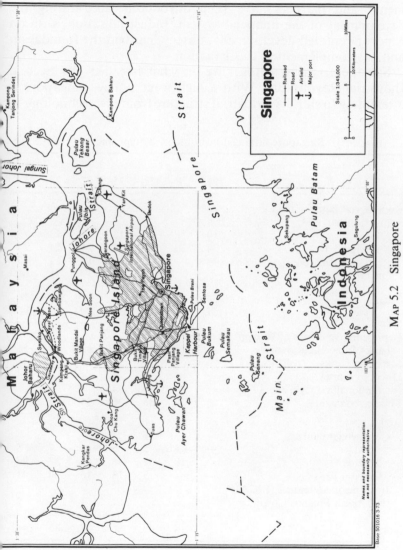

MAP 5.2 Singapore

ment of Singapore as a financial centre in the early 1970s. The Asian Dollar Market was established in 1968 and numerous international banks and financial institutions opened their offices in Singapore (see Table 5.1). New financial institutions, instruments, and markets have been introduced, accelerating the development of the financial system. Industrialisation, with an export orientated development strategy, has laid the foundation and has complemented this situation.

Singapore is now embarking on what is called the 'Second Industrial Revolution'. With a high wage policy, Singapore is attempting to shift its industrial structure from low technology to

TABLE 5.1   Singapore financial institutions, by type and no. 1965–82

	1965	70	73	75	77	78	July 82
Commercial Banks							
Full licence							
local	10	11	11	13	13	13	13
foreign	24	26	24	24	24	24	24
Restricted licence	—	—	12	12	13	13	13
Offshore banks	—	—	7	21	27	31	66
Total	34	37	54	70	77	81	116
	(132)^a	(176)	N.A.^{b}	(243)	(261)	(271)	(347)
Representative offices of foreign							
banks & merchant banks	—	8	31	38	40	44	56
Merchant banks	—	2	17	21	23	27	45
Discount houses	—	—	3	4	4	4	4
International moneybrokers	—	—	3	4	5	6	9
Finance companies	96	36	36	36	34	34	35
ACUs							
Commercial banks							
local	—	4	5	6	7	7	8
foreign	—	10	32	46	53	57	93
Merchant banks	—	—	9	13	16	20	41
Investment companies (PICA							
& Asean Finance Corpn)	—	—	—	1	1	1	2
Total	—	14	46	66	77	85	144

^{a} Figures in parenthesis are no. of bank offices.
^{b} N.A. Not available.

Source: MAS, *Annual Reports 1981–2*; MAS, *Financial Structure of Singapore 1980*, 2nd edn (Singapore: MAS, 1980) p. 16.

medium technology manufacturing. Such a transition requires substantial amounts of investment capital, and will need the full support of Singapore's financial institutions. Singapore's development as a financial sector will thus become even more important in the country's overall performance.

The English language, commonly spoken in Singapore, is the language of both international business and banking; foreign financial institutions have no difficulty in recruiting their executives and support staff from a well educated and well motivated workforce.

Singapore's lack of natural resources and small domestic market may be a disadvantage to some types of development, but its small size is also an advantage, in that it can quickly adapt to new circumstances and impose sufficient social discipline to work toward a common goal. Singapore has made full use of these advantages in response to its role as a natural financial and trading centre for the region.

Industrialisation and financial development are the keynotes of economic development, and complement each other. The financial sector supports the development of the real sector and it in turn provides the financial system with stimulus for further growth. The nature of a country's economy (its economic structure) is the most fundamental basis on which to discuss its financial system and government policy; in Singapore's case, because it has such an open economy, the financial sector that has developed is an internationally competitive one and as a result, since the 1970s there has been a high degree of financial liberalisation and deepening.[2]

(b) An Overview of the Financial Sector

Malaya and Singapore were once one country; Singapore was the international port for the hinterland of Malaya. The monetary and banking frameworks of Malaysia and Singapore were thus very much related and their banks operated in both countries; many banking laws and regulations in Singapore have been the 'follow-up' of a common tradition.

Before the Second World War, there were the Straits Settlements (Singapore, Penang and Malacca), the Federated Malay States (Perak, Pahang, Selangor and Negri Sembilan), and the Unfederated Malay States (Johore, Kelantan, Trengganu, Kedah and Perlis). The Malayan Union was formed in 1945–7, followed by the Federation of Malaya in 1948–63; the Malayan Union and the Federation of Malaya covered the Federated and Unfederated Malay States, Penang and Malacca; Singapore was made a separate colony. Malaysia was formed in September 1963, comprising West Malaysia (the States of Malaya or the former Federation of Malaya), and East Malaysia (Sarawak and Sabah). Singapore joined Malaysia in 1963, but withdrew on 9 August 1965. From 1963–5, Bank Negara Malaysia operated in Singapore.[3] Malaysia and Singapore tried unsuccessfully to maintain a common currency and a common market, but after 12 June 1967 Singapore, Malaysia and Brunei issued their own currencies.[4]

The major financial institutions in Singapore (and their relative importance in terms of aggregate assets, deposits, loans and investments) are shown in Table 5.2 Commercial banks play the leading role in deposits and loans; next comes the Central Provident Fund with respect to members' balances, but with the greatest investment in government securities. The Post Office Savings Bank (POSB) has more deposits and investments than the finance companies, but the latter advance more loans to the general public. Although merchant banks cannot take deposits from the public, they are active in lending to the Southeast Asia region.

The role of financial institutions in the Singapore economy

TABLE 5.2   Singapore financial institutions by total assets, loans and investments (figures as at end 1981, in $ million)

Institution	Total assets	Deposits of non-bank customers	Loans to non-bank customers	Investment (securities & equities)
Commercial banks	44631	20008	25229	2740
Finance companies	42275	2942	3188	115
Merchant banks	19280	—	8917	392
Post Office Savings Bank[c]		2786	1477	894
Central Provident Fund[d]		10219[a]	—	9077
Insurance companies (life & general)		1529[b]	191	658

[a]   Refers to members' balances.
[b]   Refers to Singapore Insurance Fund.
[c]   Figures for the end 1980.
[d]   Figures at the end of March 1981.

Source: MAS, *Annual Report 1980–1*; POSB, *Annual Report 1980* (Singapore: POSB, 1980); CPF, *Annual Report 1980*.

should be analysed in terms of direct and indirect contribution. The four statutory boards – the Monetary Authority of Singapore (MAS); the Currency Board; the Central Provident Fund (CPF); and the POSB – form the public sector; the MAS and Currency Board are the apex of the financial system. Commercial banks; merchant banks; discount houses; finance companies; etc. are the 'modern' sector in financial services. Other financial institutions such as merchant banks; discount houses; finance companies; investment houses; stockbrokers; etc. revolve round the hub of central and commercial banking, providing supplementary and specialised services. Pawnbrokers, money-lenders and moneychangers are the 'old' sector in the financial system, with declining activities. The insurance industry also lags far behind banking, because of the Asian social context, people's attitudes, income tax relief, and other factors unfavourable to life insurance.

These financial and insurance services were in 1974 performed by 1327 establishments, employing 19338 persons, and having gross receipts of $4556 million, value added of $688 million, and remuneration of $223 million.[5]

Employment in the financial sector is estimated at around 2.4 per cent of the employed labour force. The value added of the financial sector is probably about 6 per cent of GDP; this greater share signifies the financial sector's high productivity, rate of remuneration and profit rate.

Financial institutions also play an important role in inducing foreign investment and creating a dynamic multiplier effect. Without vigorous financial development the manufacturing industries could not attain their present state; when funds flow in and out of Singapore in the Asian Dollar Market, more business may be brought to Singapore. This is the 'indirect contribution' of the financial sector.

With the increased 'openness' of the economy, and the trend towards financial liberalisation and deepening, the money and capital markets have rapidly developed. Although Singapore is predominantly a free enterprise economy, with much foreign investment, government action has steadily increased. The Development Bank of Singapore (DBS), for example, takes an active part in development finance as well as in commercial banking and though the DBS is now a public company, the government maintains the controlling share and management. The POSB has also become very active in taking savings deposits and in lending; it plans to expand its lending in industry and commerce and in the Asian Dollar and Asian Bond Markets, and to transact foreign exchange and trade bills. Both the DBS and the POSB have also ventured into merchant banking and discount houses in partnership with international financial institutions. Government direct participation in financial institutions is thus increasing. This is perhaps a strategy to induce competition and efficiency in the financial system by using government or semi-government institutions to take a lead in some measures, such as raising savings deposit rates, computerising branch offices, opening in the evening in some marketplaces, and lending for house building, all of which improve service to customers. The predominant share of the public sector in raising funds in the domestic capital market is another indication of its important role.

Foreign banks and financial institutions enjoy considerable freedom in Singapore, as the government's objective is to develop Singapore as a financial centre. Among the foreign banks in Singapore, 24 have full commercial bank licences and 13 have restricted licences; 63 offshore banks have Asian Currency Units (ACU) licences to operate in the Asian Dollar Market; and 52 representative offices serve as liaison offices between their head offices and Singapore. There are 43 approved merchant banks – many of which are joint ventures between domestic and foreign financial institutions. Some of the local finance companies are also affiliated with foreign banks.

The Asian Dollar Market attracts numerous international financial institutions. Singapore welcomes foreign financial institutions in order to induce more foreign trade and foreign investment, as well as to attract financial expertise, further enhancing the sophistication of the financial system.

FINANCIAL INSTITUTIONS

The rapid development of the financial system is clearly shown in Table 5.2. The growth in terms of new financial institutions was most spectacular from 1970–5 and from 1978–82, with a period of consolidation in between due to the worldwide recession and slow recovery. It is interesting to note that whilst the number of full licence and restricted licence banks has remained constant since 1971–3, offshore banks and representative offices have multiplied. The resolution of the ASEAN Banking Council to exchange desk officers among ASEAN banks in order to enhance trading and investment relations will introduce yet another form of bank representation.

The financial structure of Singapore in July 1982 comprised the MAS; the Singapore Currency Board; 37 full licence commercial banks (13 local, 24 foreign); 13 restricted licence commercial banks; 66 offshore banks (operating only in the Asian Currency Market – ACM); 144 ACUs; 56 representative bank offices; 45 approved merchant banks; 35 finance companies (16 associated with banks, 19 independent); four discount houses; 71 insurance companies; eight international moneybrokers; the Development Bank of Singapore; Post Office Savings Bank; Central Provident Fund; Stock Exchange of Singapore; the Gold Exchange of Singapore; and numerous investment houses and brokers.

(a) The Banking Institutions

(i) *The Monetary Authority of Singapore (MAS)*

The MAS was established under the Monetary Authority of Singapore Act 1970 after the 'currency split' in 1967. It performs all functions of a Central Bank, except currency issue, which is still vested in the Singapore Currency Board. In November 1972 the Act was amended in order that the MAS should act more effectively as the lender of last resort and to strengthen its authorised paid-up capital from $30 million to $100 million.

The MAS aims at monetary stability and at an accelerated growth of the economy and has helped to modernise the financial structure by stimulating the establishment of numerous financial institutions. The balance sheet of the MAS (as shown in Table 5.3) demonstrates its operation as a banker's bank and as a government bank. The MAS uses the deposits of banks, financial institutions, government, and international financial institutions to acquire gold and foreign exchange. These holdings increased by 47 times (from $234 million in 1971 to 10992 million in 1981) whilst deposits increased by 38 times from $227 million to $8624 million. This rapid increase in gold and foreign exchange also reflects Singapore's favourable balance of payments position since 1960, and hence its external monetary stability.

The balance sheet in Table 5.3 does not show clearly the amounts lent to discount houses and banks by way of rediscounting Treasury bills, and other advances. MAS rediscounts Treasury bills (mainly for the discount houses) and trade bills

TABLE 5.3   Monetary Authority of Singapore balance sheet, 1971–81 (figures as at 31 March, in $ million)

	1971	*73*	*77*	*81*
Liabilities				
Authorised capital	30.0	100.0	100.0	100.0
Paid-up capital	30.0	30.0	50.0	100.0
General reserve fund	2.1	25.2	235.0	890.4
	32.1	55.2	285.0	990.4
Balances & deposits of banks & other financial institutions	137.3	599.2	595.8	1123.4
Deposits of government & international financial institutions	89.2	834.1	4626.9	7601.0
Other liabilities including provisions	2.8	3.7	535.5	2019.8
Total	261.4	1492.2	6043.2	11780.8
Assets				
Gold & foreign exchange	233.6	1425.7	5705.1	10992.3
Cash & other assets	27.8	66.5	338.1	599.7
IMF reserve position				128.7
Holdings of SDRs				60.1
Total	261.4	1492.2	6043.2	11780.8

Source: MAS, *Annual Reports 1971 – 80 – 1.*

through the commercial banks. The item 'cash and other assets' includes such loan amounts. The MAS has to enforce the cash reserve ratio and the liquid asset ratio in the banking system. Commercial banks are required to maintain a minimum cash reserve ratio of 6 per cent against their deposit liabilities, and a liquid asset ratio of 20 per cent; the corresponding requirement for finance companies is respectively 6 and 10 per cent. Liquid assets include: cash in hand; balances with the MAS in excess of minimum cash balance; net money at call with the discount houses; Singapore treasury bills and government securities; and trade bills. The idea is to foster local rather than foreign liquidity, as foreign liquid assets are excluded from the statutory liquidity ratio.

It was announced in a Budget Speech that the MAS and Singapore Currency Board would merge to form the Central Bank of Singapore. The MAS underwent a big change in staff in April 1981, but it is not now certain whether a bank will emerge. Although it is only a matter of reorganisation, not of reality, there is a good case for a Central Bank that would centralise the monetary control under one roof and pave the way for flexible currency issue.

A new and unique feature is the Government Investment Corporation, formed in June 1981 to manage the foreign assets of the MAS, the Currency Board and government departments. The idea is to have more long term investment instead of excessive short term liquid assets, a policy more appropriate given. Singapore's large and persistent balance of payments surplus; the investment function is thus to be taken away from the MAS.

(ii) *Singapore Currency Board*

The Singapore Currency Board was established under the Currency Act 1967 and commenced to issue new Singapore dollars on 12 June 1967 to replace the old dollars issued by the Board of Commissioners of Currency of Malaya and British Borneo. In 1967, Singapore declared to the IMF the par value of the Singapore dollar to be 0.290299 grammes of fine gold. The New Singapore dollar continues to be 100 per cent backed by gold and foreign exchange.

It is often argued that under a Currency Board system, the increase or decrease in currency issue is subject to the active or passive balance of payments. But in the present context of Singapore, when there are excess international reserves, the constraint to currency issue is not the international reserves; even if Singapore were to have a passive balance of payments, she could still draw gold and foreign exchange from the holding of other government agents to the Currency Board, and issue new currency accordingly.

(iii) *Commercial banks*

The driving forces of commercial banking in Singapore and Malaysia are foreign trade, foreign investment and economic development.[6] Foreign banks were established primarily for financing and promoting trade between Pan-Malaya and the metropolitan countries and dominions and, consequently, inducing capital from the metropolitan countries to Pan-Malaya. Local Chinese and Indian banks sprang up as an indigenous response to the need of the Chinese and Indian business communities. The banking system thus evolved from the colonial banking system, and the local and foreign banks have been progressing side by side in a sort of 'dual banking system' ever since.[7] At present, the full licensed commercial banks in Singapore (Appendix 5.1) comprise 13 banks incorporated in Singapore, four in Malaysia, and 20 in other foreign countries. In addition, there are 13 restricted licence banks, established in 1971–7, which can have only one business office and cannot accept fixed and savings deposits (except fixed deposits of amounts not less than $250000). They can have ACU licences to operate in the Asian Currency Market.[8] Finally, there is also the offshore side of the local banking industry with 63 offshore licensed banks operating in Asian Currency Market and 53 foreign banks with simply representative offices (see Appendix 5.3).

The historical development of commercial banks can be followed in Appendix A, in which the years of establishment or opening are clearly shown. The 1960s saw the opening of only one local bank – the Development Bank of Singapore (DBS) in 1968. The 1970s saw two – Tat Lee Bank (1974) and International Bank of Singapore (1975); the latter is an equal partnership of the Oversea–Chinese Banking Corporation (OCBC), the United Overseas Bank (UOB), the Overseas Union Bank and DBS for the establishment of branches or representative offices overseas.

In contrast, numerous foreign banks and financial institutions have established offices in Singapore. A glance at the lists of foreign full banks, restricted licence banks, offshore banks, representative offices and merchant banks would suffice to show Singapore's deliberate policy of diversifying its banking connections with different foreign countries.

Among the local banks, there are four major groups – the DBS, the UOB, the OCBC, and the Overseas Union Bank (see Table 5.4).[9] The OCBC merged with the Four Seas Communication Bank in December 1972; the Bank of Singapore has long been a member of this group. The UOB merged with Chung Khiaw Bank in June 1971 and with Lee Wah Bank in December 1972. Other smaller local banks include the Industrial and Commercial Bank, the Asian Commercial Banking Corporation, the Far Eastern Bank and Tat Lee Bank. The DBS should be regarded not only as a commercial bank, but more importantly as a development bank. Among the four Malaysian banks, the Malayan Banking Corporation and the United Malayan Banking Corporation have a large volume of business in Singapore.

TABLE 5.4 Singapore business activity of local banks (figures in S$ million)

Bank	Year of official opening	No. of banking offices in Singapore[a]	Total assets[b]	Deposits[c]	Loans/bills	Investments
Development Bank of Singapore	1968	18	7019.9	2921.1	3054.1	494.1
UOB Group						
United Overseas Bank	1949	31	4987.1	2567.4	1816.8	450.7
Chung Khiaw Bank	1950	16	1927.9	1314.3	1062.3	143.8
Lee Wah Bank	1920	4	569.7	428.8	333.2	53.8
			7484.7	4310.5	3212.3	648.3
OCBC Group						
Oversea-Chinese Banking Corpn	1932	21	4596.3	3196.7	1915.2	530.3
Four Seas Communication Bank	1907	4	436.9	252.1	193.6	46.9
Bank of Singapore	1955	3	92.5	59.2	56.2	8.5
			5125.7	3508.0	2165.0	585.7
Overseas Union Bank	1949	29	4106.4	2360.0	1790.2	267.1
Tat Lee Bank	1974	9	1102.6	559.9	319.5	58.9
Industrial and Commercial Bank	1954	11	840.1	464.5	283.3	58.7
International Bank of Singapore	1975	1	779.6	415.9	260.8	23.4
Asia and Commercial Bank	1959	5	571.8	276.1	171.6	56.7
Far Eastern Bank	1959	5	470.4	263.6	183.9	20.2

[a] As at 31 October 1981.
[b] As at end 1980 (including contra account).
[c] Includes 'deposits and balances of bonds and agents'.

Source: Banks' Annual Reports.

The Chartered Bank, Mercantile Bank and Hongkong and Shanghai Banking Corporation[10] have been important in the banking system, particularly in colonial times, with the Currency Board system and with sterling as the reserve and working currency. The British attitude with respect to lending and management has still some influence on the banking system.

Four American banks operate in Singapore – Citibank (1902), Bank of America (1955), Chase Manhattan Bank (1964), and First National Bank of Chicago (1970). The American influence in the banking system is considerable, particularly with respect to the computerisation process, new forms of finance, money and discount market, and the Asian Dollar Market.

The Japanese banks – Bank of Tokyo (1957) and Mitsui Bank (1963) – are latecomers in Singapore. In addition, there are two Japanese restricted licence banks (Sumitomo Bank (1973) and Mitsubishi Bank (1973)), 11 offshore banks,[11] and seven representative offices. With increasing trade and investment in Singapore, Japanese banks have become very active, particularly in the Asian Dollar Market. It is said that Japanese banks share 30–40 per cent of the business.

As with its economic development strategy, Singapore has adopted the policy of attracting foreign banks from different countries in a diversified manner, so that Singapore has a good access to all important financial markets. There will then be no possibility for banks from any one foreign country to dominate the banking system in Singapore. This inflow of foreign banks is an interesting contrast to the recent establishment of many local banks in Malaysia.

The relative importance of local banks is shown in Table 5.4. The DBS is the largest individual bank but the UOB banking group as a whole dominates the other listings. Generally speaking, local banks are net lenders in the interbank market, whilst foreign banks are net borrowers, because local banks have more branches to collect deposits.

Amongst the 'top 10' commercial banks in Singapore in terms of total assets, (Table 5.5) are four Japanese, three Singapore incorporated two American and one French bank. Bank of Tokyo tops the list, mainly due to its active offshore banking operations; this reflects the strong and growing influence of Japan on the financial system.

In terms of deposits and loans/bills, however, the rankings are

TABLE 5.5 Singapore 'top 10' commercial banks (figures in S$ million)

Bank	Country of incorporation	Total assets	Deposits	Loans bills	Investments
Bank of Tokyo	Japan[a]	8189.0[b]	1765.7	1450.7	22.7
Bank of America	USA[a]	7115.8	5270.6	1088.6	30.6
Development Bank of Singapore	Singapore[c]	7019.9	2921.1	3054.0	622.4
Fuji Bank	Japan[a]	5383.2	2807.7	712.7	35.0
United Overseas Bank	Singapore[c]	4987.1	2567.4	1816.7	518.6
Tokai Bank	Japan[a]	4654.5	4236.3	803.6	71.0
Mitsubishi Bank	Japan[a]	4615.1	2746.5	815.5	69.0
Citibank	USA[c]	4612.7	2523.3	1070.1	45.3
Oversea-Chinese Banking Corpn	Singapore[c]	4596.3	3196.7	1915.2	530.3
Banque Nationale de Paris	France[c]	4498.2	2604.1	1134.9	50.3

[a] As at 31 March 1981.
[b] Figures include operations in both the national and the offshore banking systems (ACU). Figures of foreign banks are not on a global basis, but are based on Singapore operations only.
[c] As at end 1980.

Sources: Banks and Financial Institutions in Singapore Yearbook 1981 (Singapore: Consulton Research Bureau, 1981) pp. 49, 53–4; *A Study of Commercial Banks in Singapore 1980* (Manila; SGV Group, 1980) for investments as at 31 March 1980. The ultimate source of data is the banks' *Annual Reports* and the Registry of Companies, Singapore.

somewhat different. Great care should be taken in the interpretation of Table 5.5. The national banking system and offshore
banking system's assets are somewhat different in significance.
Total assets include 'contra accounts of acceptances, guarantees
and other obligations'; the net assets excluding these would be
useful for indicating the net position. Deposits are important for
indicating the activity of the bank in collecting funds in the
community. It is also interesting to note from Table 5.5 that local
banks have more investments in securities, equities and subsidiary
companies than foreign banks.

The sources and uses of funds of all full licence commercial
banks (local and foreign) can be analysed with respect to their
consolidated balance sheets (Table 5.6). Some interesting points
can be noted:

1. Deposits and loans grew at a fast rate, not only in nominal
   monetary amounts but also in real value, signifying a growing
   economy.
2. Total deposits grew 10.9 times, from $1828 million in 1967 to
   $20008 million in 1981. If we take account of the price change
   (consumer price index), the real value of deposits had still a
   substantial increase of about 5.4 times.
3. There has been a structural change in deposits, as time and
   savings deposits grew faster than demand deposits –
   respectively 12.7 and 7.6 times.
4. Capital and reserves are related to local banks only because
   foreign banks have their capital and reserves on a global
   basis, and it is difficult to specify their capital funds for
   operations in Singapore. The higher growth rate of capital
   funds (27.4 times) than of total deposits signifies the high
   profitability of banks, and also the adequacy of capital funds
   in the banking system.
5. The S$NCD was introduced in 1975 to increase the sophisti-
   cation of the money and discount market, and induce a freer
   flow of funds in the financial system. It is a means of interbank
   lending and borrowing.
6. Bank holdings of Treasury Bills and government securities
   increased rapidly, from $78 million in 1967 to about
   $2600 million in 1981.
7. Domestic investments increased progressively at a fast rate,
   whilst foreign investments tended to decline. This is the result
   of the MAS's deliberate policy of encouraging banks to invest

more in the domestic economy rather than abroad, and to maintain local rather than foreign liquidity; the stability of the Singapore dollar in the foreign exchange market, as compared with the weakness of the pound sterling and the US dollar, may then encourage banks to invest more in the domestic economy.

8. A comparison of accounts due to, and amounts due from, banks abroad shows that Singapore banks have consistently had a net balance due to banks abroad ($3469 million in 1981), implying that Singapore banks draw finance from abroad, and that some foreign banks use head office funds for financing. This inflow of funds also strengthens Singapore as a financial centre.

9. Loans and advances to non-bank customers (excluding bill financing) increased 19.2 times, from $1106 million in 1967 to $21250 million in 1981.

10. The higher growth rate of loans than of deposits implies that banks draw finance from abroad, and that to a small extent they rely upon the increase of their capital funds.

11. The growth rate of loans slowed in the recession period 1974–7 because of the credit stringency and reduced demand for loans.[12] The growth rate of deposits slowed down in the same period, partly because of sluggish business activity and partly because of the inflation effect. There are indications of a cyclical effect on the balance sheets of banks, although the nominal value of all items in the balance sheet has a consistently upward trend.

Overdrafts have been a traditional form of lending. New forms of financing (such as term loans for industrial building and capital equipment, and lease financing for capital equipment) are becoming more and more significant. With the changing economic structure, the composition of bank loans has been undergoing a change (Table 5.7). Loans to general commerce (including imports, exports, wholesale and retail trade) declined from 45 per cent of total loans in 1967 to 30 per cent in 1973, and to 34 per cent in 1981. Loans to manufacturing rose from 21 per cent in 1967 to a height of 34 per cent in 1970, but relapsed to 20 per cent in 1981. Loans to financial institutions had a rising share, to almost 12 per cent in 1981, whilst the share of loans to agriculture, mining and quarrying, professional and private individuals declined. In absolute value, all items went up in step with the increasing tempo

TABLE 5.6 Singapore commercial banks' assets and liabilities, 1967–79 (figures as at end year, in $ million)

	1967	70	73	76	79	81
Liabilities						
Paid-up capital and reserves[a]	138.6	292.3	787.7	1270.9	1861.2	3799.5
Deposits of non-bank customers	1828.2	3194.9	5799.8	8488.5	12178.4	20007.9
Demand	(587.7)	(947.7)	(1786.2)	(2378.2)	(3244.3)	(4441.0)
Fixed	(919.2)	(1818.3)	(3264.8)	(5062.4)	(7473.0)	(13315.4)
Savings	(302.1)	(412.9)	(708.5)	(999.2)	(1394.8)	(2168.1)
Other	(19.2)	(16.0)	(40.3)	(48.7)	(66.3)	(83.4)
Amounts due to banks	583.3	1045.8	3063.0	4432.0	8615.9	15366.0
In Singapore	(291.0)	(599.5)	(964.9)	(1372.2)	(2415.4)	(4241.3)
Outside Singapore[b]	(292.3)	(446.3)	(2098.1)	(3059.8)	(6200.5)	(11124.7)
S$NCDs issued	—	—	—	617.8	515.0	404.5
Other liabilities	233.4	469.0	1068.8	1717.6	3577.3	5052.9
Total assets/liabilities	2783.5	5041.6	10719.3	16526.8	26747.8	44630.8

Assets

Cash	45.1	43.3	70.4	105.3	161.1	222.4
Balance with MAS	95.6	129.0	593.9	511.7	733.7	1195.4
Money at call with discount houses	—	—	354.5	491.4	695.7	1478.0
Treasury bills	278.1	596.0	340.0	328.5	369.9	—
S$NCDs held	—	—	—	380.1	166.2	89.0
Amounts due from banks	557.2	940.8	1746.5	3528.7	5646.6	11824.3
In Singapore	(289.8)	(609.8)	(874.1)	(1370.5)	(1986.6)	(4196.0)
Outside Singapore[c]	(267.4)	(331.0)	(872.4)	(2158.2)	(3660.0)	(7628.3)
Investments						
In Singapore	116.4	232.0	727.0	1365.7	1639.6	2666.9 [d]
Government securities	(77.8)	(90.3)	(333.0)	(762.0)	(908.9)	
Other securities	(38.6)	(142.0)	(394.0)	(603.7)	(730.7)	
Outside Singapore	94.4	93.1	90.0	81.1	51.0	72.7
Loans & advances to non-bank customers	1105.6	2167.7	5146.5	7271.7	12058.7	21249.7
Bills discounted or purchased	331.9	554.4	1124.7	1622.5	3948.3	3979.4
Other assets	159.2	285.0	525.8	840.1	1277.0	1853.0

[a] Refers to local banks only.
[b] Other securities include loans of public authorities, private company stocks, and equity investment.
[c] Amounts due to banks and amounts due from banks outside Singapore include ACUs.
[d] Includes Treasury bills, securities and equities.

Source: MAS, *Annual Reports 1972–80–1; Quarterly Bulletin and Monthly Statistical Bulletin* (various issues 1973–81); information from MAS.

TABLE 5.7 Singapore bank loans to non-bank customers: changing composition, 1967–81 (figures as at end year, in $ million)[a]

	1967		70	
	Amount	(%)	Amount	(%)
General commerce (imports, exports, wholesale & retail trade)	493.5	44.6	678.6	31.3
Manufacturing	236.5	21.4	738.5	34.1
Building, construction & housing	119.9	10.8	178.4	8.2
Mining & quarrying	7.9	0.7	16.2	0.7
Agriculture (mainly rubber, fisheries & forestry)	13.5	1.2	25.1	1.2
Transport, storage & communication	10.9	1.0	33.1	1.5
Financial institutions	33.5	3.0	78.8	3.6
Professional & private individuals	134.5	12.2	285.0	13.1
Others	55.3	5.0	134.0	6.2
Total	1105.6	100	2167.7	100
Index	100		196	

of industrialisation. Loans and advances rose by 22.8 times from 1967 to 1981 (Table 5.7). If we allow for the price change (consumer price index), loans in real value had increased by 11.3 times.

So far, we have discussed the sources and uses of bank funds. In order to analyse the attitude and portfolio management of banks, it is necessary to study some crucial ratios derived from the aggregated balance sheets of banks (see Tables 5.6 and 5.7):

1. The banks are in rather a liquid state as the liquidity ratio (the ratio of liquid assets[13]: deposits of non-bank customers) increased steadily, from 0.41 in 1967 to 0.42 in 1972–3 and to 0.50 in 1979, but relapsed to 0.39 in 1981. This ratio should be considered high by international standards.[14] It denotes 'liquidity' in the true sense, and should be distinguished from the minimum statutory liquid asset ratio (20 per cent), which includes government securities of long maturity. The latter ratio fosters local liquidity, and encourages banks to hold government securities.
2. The cash ratio, relating 'cash' and 'balances with MAS': total deposits, shows more variation–0.054 in 1970, 0.115 in 1973, and 0.711 in 1981. This can be ascribed to variations in the

TABLE 5.7 (*contd.*)

73		76		79		81	
Amount	*(%)*	*Amount*	*(%)*	*Amount*	*(%)*	*Amount*	*(%)*
1549.3	30.1	3335.0	37.5	6643.3	41.5	8516.0	33.8
1418.1	27.6	2378.5	26.7	3741.0	23.4	5048.5	20.0
728.4	14.2	1134.1	12.8	1453.7	9.1	3031.2	12.0
} 33.4	} 0.6	} 72.3	} 0.8	} 79.7	} 0.5	} 144.2	0.6
237.7	4.6	273.4	3.1	722.5	4.5	1795.6	7.1
333.1	6.5	754.2	8.5	1585.8	9.9	3096.1	12.3
596.9	11.6	610.0	6.9	900.8	5.6	2218.8	8.8
249.6	4.8	336.7	3.8	880.2	5.5	1378.7	5.4
5146.5	100	8894.2	100	16007.0	100	25229.1	100
465		804		1448		2282	

a Total loans and advances including bills financing.

Source: MAS, *Monthly Statistical Bulletin* (February 1982) p. 13 (and various issues); MAS, *Annual Report 1980–1*.

required cash reserve ratio, and a desire by banks to hold more (or less) cash over different periods.

3. The loan/deposit ratio, which relates loans and advances (including bill financing): total deposits, complements the liquidity ratio. It showed an increasing trend, from 0.79 in 1967 to 0.85 in 1970, and to 1.26 in 1981. This implies that banks were utilising deposit funds more effectively to finance loans, and some foreign banks had to borrow in the interbank market or from their head offices to finance lending. This ratio is also high by international standards. However, it refers to all banks, (foreign and local); generally, foreign banks have a higher ratio than local banks, because local banks have more branch offices to collect deposits.

4. The percentage of fixed deposits in total deposits had a rising trend, from 50 per cent in 1967 to 67 per cent in 1981, demand deposits declined from 32 per cent to 22 per cent, and savings deposits from 17 per cent to 11 per cent in the same period.

However, in absolute and in real value, all deposits have been increasing.

5. The ratio of domestic investment (including investment in Treasury bills, government securities, other securities and equities in Singapore): foreign investment (securities and equities outside Singapore) had a rising trend, from 4 per cent in 1967 to 37 per cent in 1981.

6. The percentage of loans and investment (or earning assets) in total assets rose from 69 per cent in 1967 to 72 per cent in 1970, but declined to 63 per cent in 1981.

This analysis helps to illustrate the portfolio management of banks and the changes in the structure of their balance sheets in response to government policy and the development of money and capital markets.

(iv) *The Development Bank of Singapore (DBS)*

The DBS was established in 1968 to assume the financial function of the Economic Development Board of Singapore, with the objective of providing long term credit to industry. In 1968, its shareholding was as shown in Table 5.8.

TABLE 5.8 Development Bank of Singapore shareholding, 1968 (figures as at end year, in $ million)

Government of Singapore	48.6
Commercial banks	25.9
Insurance companies and other financial institutions	7.6
Other companies and members of the public	17.9
Total	100.0

Source: DBS Annual Report 1968.

As at the end of 1981, the paid up capital was increased to $228.5 million. The government now holds S$120.2 million (52.7%)[15] and the Chairman, several Directors of the Board[16] and the executive committee are top civil servants appointed by the government. It should be properly called a public sector bank, although its shares are listed in the Stock Exchange.

The DBS's development finance role can be reviewed in Table 5.9. This takes the form of medium and long term loans; equity participation; and guarantees. The DBS provides venture capital

TABLE 5.9 Development Bank of Singapore loans and equity investments industrial distribution, 1977 and 1981 (figures as at end year, in $ million)

	1977			1981			
	Loans	Equity investments	Total	Loans	Equity investments	Total	(%)
General commerce	48.4	1.9	50.3	316.8	12.1	328.9	7.9
Manufacturing	542.8	64.2	607.0	1158.5	63.8	1222.3	29.3
Building & construction	77.7	3.5	81.2	358.8	8.3	367.1	8.8
Agriculture, mining & quarrying	19.4	1.3	20.7	83.3	9.0	92.3	2.2
Transport, storage & communication	102.2	2.0	104.2	1005.2	3.3	1008.5	24.2
Financial institutions	52.9	21.0	73.9	482.2	51.6	533.8	12.8
Others	102.7	5.2	107.9	618.4	8.8	627.2	15.0
Total	946.2	99.1	1045.3	4023.2	148.0	4171.2	100
Index	100	100	100	425.2	149.3	399.0	

Source: DBS, Annual Report 1981, p. 22.

through equity participation in enterprises expected to contribute increased productivity, technical skill and employment in the economy. The DBS usually takes less than a 30 per cent shareholding in the company, and does not seek control.[17]

The increase in loans was greater than in equity investment during 1977–81 (Table 5.9). In 1981, finance to the industrial sector (manufacturing, building and construction) constituted 38 per cent of the total, as compared with 8 per cent for general commerce; 13 per cent for financial institutions; and 24 per cent for transport, storage and communication. In comparing Tables 5.9 and 5.7, note that in 1981 general commerce took up 34 per cent of total loans of commercial banks (Table 5.7); industries 32 per cent; and transport, storage and communication 7 per cent. The emphasis on manufacturing and transport, storage and communication by the DBS signifies its role in industrial finance.

With respect to the uses of funds, loans, equities, bills, accounts receivables and other investments amounted in 1981 to $5030 million, (or 46 per cent of total assets, including contra accounts).

The DBS invested $420 million (4 per cent of total assets) in securities and shares, and maintained $2668 million (24 per cent) in liquid assets in 1981.

The sources of funds included deposits of $4282 million (39 per cent of total liabilities, including contra accounts), borrowing on short and long terms of $2792 million (26 per cent) and capital and reserves of $692.5 million (6 per cent). The DBS borrows from the Singapore government (mainly); the POSB; international institutions (such as the World Bank, Asian Development Bank and Exim Bank (USA)) and issues bonds in the Asian Dollar Market and in other financial centres.

The DBS started its commercial banking in 1969. Commercial banking is apparently more profitable than investment banking because of the quick turnover and good profit in trade bills. In 1980, the DBS introduced the Autosave scheme, whereby funds are automatically transferred from a current account to a savings account of a customer. This is implicitly an indirect way for a depositor to receive interest on his current account, a practice prohibited under the by laws of the Association of Banks in Singapore. The DBS also provides Saturday afternoon banking at some branches. Perhaps the government encourages the DBS to introduce those innovations in order to promote efficiency and healthy competition in the banking system.

The DBS is exempted from the Banking Act 1970, ss. 27–9. S.

27 states that no bank (except the DBS) can acquire share capital of a financial; commercial; agricultural; or industrial undertaking exceeding 40 per cent of the bank's capital funds. S. 28 states that no bank (except the DBS) can acquire any immovable property exceeding 40 per cent of the bank's capital funds. S. 29 states that no bank (except the DBS) can make loans and advances exceeding 30 per cent of the amount of deposits in Singapore (including the deposits and borrowings from any other bank at that bank) on the security of immovable property.[18]

In its unique position to develop the big property projects of the public sector, it is necessary for the DBS to have these exemptions. The DBS has 20 wholly owned subsidiaries, including principally DBS Finance; DBS Land; Singapore Factory Development Ltd; Raffles Centre Ltd; DBS Realty; DBS Trading; General Warehousing; National Engineering Services; DBS Nominees; and DBS Asia (Hong Kong). DBS Finance is very active in providing housing and hire purchase loans. DBS Trading is for gold trading. DBS Land is an investment holding company. In real estate development, big projects undertaken wholly or jointly by the DBS include the Pandan Valley Condominium; the Raffles City Project; Chin Swee Tower; DBS Building; Plaza Singapura; Hillview Industrial Estate; and the Singapore Treasury Building office complex.

In financial institution development, the DBS joined with OUB, Morgan Guaranty International Finance Corporation and others to form the National Discount Company in 1972 (see Appendix 5.6). It also joined with Daiwa Securities of Japan to form the DBS–Daiwa Securities International Ltd in 1972 (see Appendix 5.4) a very active merchant bank in Singapore's Asian bond issues. In conjunction with Sanwa Bank and others, the DBS also formed Singapore Nomura Merchant Banking Ltd in 1972. The DBS has managed many large public issues in its own right, including the Neptune Orient Line, and co-managed 10 of the 22 Asian bond issues.

The DBS thus serves as an instrument of government policy, as a channel through which low interest funds are directed to support the priority sectors. In 1974, the government allocated $100 million credit through the DBS to help finance export bills and pre-export packing loans, and another $4100 million credit through the Economic Development Board (EDB) to finance manufacturing industries for the modernisation of capital equipments at low interest rates. The Small Industries Finance Scheme is funded by the EDB and managed by the DBS, OCBC, and Hong Leong Finance Ltd. There have also recently been the Construction Equipment Financing Scheme, the government's Ship Financing Scheme, and a data resources and computerisation programme.

With its expansion of branches and offices in London, New York, Tokyo, Hong Kong and Seoul, the DBS has made good progress in international banking. Its activity in syndicated loans; ACU operations; Asian bond issues; US$NCDs and SDRNCDs; gold trading; etc. demonstrates the internationalisation of its operations.

The DBS's operations now include those of development banking, commercial banking, and merchant banking. As an institution in the public sector, the DBS may at times tend to be ultra-cautious in financing; there may be an unsatisfied demand for loans, particularly by small local industries who may not be able to pledge adequate collateral and fulfil the loan requirements. There is a case for establishing a private sector development finance bank or corporation which can provide more venture capital and can be more liberal in lending and equity investment. For development finance, there are two important criteria – financial feasibility and economic feasibility. Economic feasibility means that the project financed is expected to contribute to the economy's productivity and employment. Financial feasibility means that project must be able to generate enough profit to return the borrowed fund plus interest payment in time. A financial institution in the public sector may often overemphasise the economic feasibility; a development finance corporation may emphasise financial feasibility, it may be more liberal in long term loans and in equity participation, although it may charge a higher rate of interest. In the Singapore context, there is room for the co-existence of the development banks in both the public and private sectors.

(b) The Non-banking Financial Institutions

(i) *Finance companies*

Finance companies sprang up like mushrooms after the Second World War, particularly during the 1950s and 1960s. The enforcement of maximum deposit rates and minimum lending rates by Bank Negara since 1960[19] caused many banks to organise affiliated finance companies to collect deposits at higher interest rates. Finance companies had been free from regulations until the enforcement of the Company Act (Malaysia) 1965; the Borrowing Companies Act (Malaysia) 1969; the Finance Company Act (Singapore) 1967; and the Hire Purchase Act (Singapore) 1969. As of April 1982, there are 16 bank affiliated finance companies, and 19 non-bank affiliated ones (see Appendix 5.5). There are altogether about 169 members of the Association of Hire Purchase and Finance Companies, including importers and distributors of motor vehicles and consumer durables, which engage in hire purchase business but do not accept fixed deposits.

Finance companies can accept fixed and savings deposits, but not demand deposits. Their deposit rates are usually 1 or 2 per cent higher than those of banks.[20] Their lending rates are consequently higher than banks. They have four main lines of business: housing loans; hire purchase of motor vehicles (principally), television sets, radiograms, air conditioners, refrigerators and other durable consumer goods; lease finance; and investment in real estate, property and stocks and shares.

A study of the consolidated balance sheets of finance companies (Table 5.10) shows some interesting points:

1. Finance companies derived most funds from fixed deposits (64 per cent of total liabilities in 1981); capital and reserves constituted only 16 per cent of total liabilities.
2. Loans and advances (mainly housing loans, hire purchase and lease finance) constituted their major assets (75 per cent of total assets in 1981); securities and equities only 3 per cent; deposits with banks and financial institutions about 17 per cent; and cash and balances with MAS about 4 per cent.
3. The liquidity ratio (the ratio of cash, balances with MAS and deposits with banks and other financial institutions: deposit liabilities) declined from about 30 per cent in 1969–75 to 21 per cent in 1981, implying a decline in liquidity. Finance companies must maintain the minimum cash reserve ratio of 6 per cent and the minimum liquid asset ratio of 10 per cent.[21] The MAS also changed the cash reserve ratio on several occasions, increasing it from $3\frac{1}{2}$ per cent to 5 per cent in August 1972, and to 9 per cent in March 1973 in order to curb inflation, and then lowering it to 6 per cent at the end of 1977.
4. All items in the balance sheet had a continuously rising trend, although hire purchase finance dipped in 1975.

Finance companies had some difficulty in the recession years,

TABLE 5.10 Singapore finance companies' assets and liabilities, 1969–81
(figures as at end year, in $ million)

	1969	73	75	78	81
Liabilities					
Paid-up capital & reserves	73.5	181.2	242.1	308.1	672.1
Deposits	303.3	853.8	1048.4	1510.0	2942.2
Fixed	(263.9)	(779.0)	(965.2)	(1419.2)	(2728.4)
Savings	(9.0)	(25.7)	(36.1)	(55.5)	(75.9)
Others	(30.4)	(49.1)	(47.1)	(35.3)	(137.9)
Borrowings	} 25.5	32.0	26.0	29.2	228.5
Other liabilities		88.6	114.0	170.0	432.6
Total assets/liabilities	402.3	1155.6	1430.4	2017.3	4275.4
Assets					
Cash	1.0	1.5	3.0	2.5	5.0
Balance with MAS	10.5	76.0	62.1	86.6	170.9
Deposits with banks	} 110.8	241.0	300.0	288.8	
Deposits with other financial institutions		34.0	69.0	85.0	707.2
Loans and advances	241.1	724.9	897.0	1397.1	3187.6
Housing loans	(75.5)	(266.6)	(354.6)	(446.4)	
Hire purchase	(67.7)	(221.1)	(191.7)	(354.3)	
Lease finance	(—)	(25.0)	(37.0)	(66.3)	
Others	(97.9)	(212.0)	(313.0)	(530.1)	
Securities & equities	19.9	33.2	38.3	95.2	114.6
Other assets	19.0	45.0	60.0	64.6	90.1

Source: MAS, *Annual Reports 1972–80–1*; MAS, *Yearbook of Statistics* (Singapore: Department of Statistics, 1974–5) p. 145.

particularly in 1975–7, because of keen competition in both deposit taking and lending as the result of Singapore's free banking policy. The government's drastic measures to discourage private motoring reduced the demand for hire purchase credit on motor vehicles significantly; the property market also slumped between 1974 and the first half of 1978. Because of such difficulties, finance companies shifted gradually from consumer credit (hire purchase of consumer durable goods and residential housing loans) to business finance, such as lease financing; bills receivable financing; credit card (for big department stores) financing; discounting facilities for S$NCD; etc. To encourage finance companies to widen their activities, the MAS granted approval under certain conditions to seven finance companies to discount commercial bills of exchange. They have also applied to the MAS for permission to operate in the foreign exchange market; to date (1982) permission has not been granted. This is important, as the finance business in the domestic market is rather limited, whereas finance in the Southeast Asian region – such as foreign trade bill financing, FE operation, participation in the Asian Dollar Market and in syndicated loans – would provide a much wider scope of activities. Finance companies would then complete with banks not only in domestic but also in international finance.

The business activities of finance companies have revived since 1979–80, as shown in their balance sheets (Table 5.10).

The number of finance companies declined from 95 in 1965 to 36 in 1970, since the enforcement of the Finance Company Act (Singapore) 1967 (see Table 5.1). The government desired to eliminate the small, unreliable and speculative financing companies by introducing a minimum capital requirement, public auditing and other regulations. The present number of 35 finance companies is small as compared with about 350 deposit taking companies in Hong Kong, about 250 finance companies in the Philippines, and about 129 authorised finance and securities companies in Thailand.[22] Malaysia's 36 'licensed' finance companies is a figure similar to Singapore, as Singapore and Malaysia had historically similar structures and regulations of banking and finance.

In order to compete in this open economy, some of the finance companies had to merge; the acquisitions started in September 1978 when Hong Leong Finance Co. took over Singapore Finance Ltd. Perhaps there will be more mergers in future. Will some finance companies merge with banks? Or will some smaller ones join to form a bigger institution? Government policy will play a great role, particularly with respect to whether the finance companies are allowed to do foreign exchange business.

Three building societies are registered under the Finance Company Act (Singapore) 1967: the Building Society of Singapore; the Building Society of Malaya (in the OCBC Group); and the Asia Building Society. Unlike the savings and loan associations in the USA and the building societies in the UK, building societies in Singapore do not play a significant role in the financial system.

(ii) *Merchant banks*

With the rising demand for industrial finance and for big consortium loans, and the need for company amalgamations, merchant banks have come to play an important role in the financial system. In the early stage of development, most merchant banks in Singapore (notably Singapore International Merchant Bankers Ltd) were interested in the discount house or short money market business. But after the establishment of four discount houses in 1972 and 1974, the discount business separated from merchant banking.

The Chartered Merchant Banks Ltd (now Arbuthnot Latham Asia Ltd) was the first merchant bank established in Singapore in 1970. The boom years (1971–3) stimulated growth and the recession, (1974–8) retarded it. Since 1980, growth has again accelerated (see Table 5.11). Of the 43 merchant banks in April 1982 (Appendix 5.4), many are joint ventures between local and foreign financial institutions. As merchant banks have worldwide connections and operate in the international financial centres, they provide a forum for local banks to go international, have joint ventures with foreign partners, and absorb financial knowhow.

The merchant banks' main function is to arrange finance, rather than to finance projects directly. As merchant banks are not allowed to accept deposits from the general public (except

TABLE 5.11 Singapore merchant banks' consolidated assets and liabilities, 1974–81 (figures as at end year, in $ million)

	1974	1977	1981
Liabilities			
Capital & reserves	89.7	136.9	909.8
Amounts due to banks	1159.4	1928.0	16295.6
In Singapore	(43.3)	(84.8)	(347.8)
Outside Singapore	(1116.1)	(1843.2)	(15947.8)
Borrowing from non-bank customers	128.7	352.4	1599.1
Other liabilities	44.2	46.7	475.2
Total assets/liabilities	1422.0	2464.0	19279.7
Assets			
Amounts due from banks	436.2	684.1	9440.7
In Singapore	(7.0)	(20.8)	(201.4)
Outside Singapore	(429.9)	(663.3)	(9239.3)
Loans & advances to non-bank customers	922.7	1674.5	8916.5
Securities & equities	27.1	65.6	391.6
Other assets	36.0	39.8	530.9

Source: MAS, *Annual Reports 1976 – 1980–1*.

fixed deposits of not less than $250000 per deposit with a minimum maturity of 1 month, from banks and financial institutions), the funding base is rather limited; they have to borrow in the interbank market, or draw finance from their head offices. Thus in the aggregated balance sheet of merchant banks (Table 5.11) 'amounts due to banks outside Singapore' constitutes the predominant part of liabilities; 'borrowing from non-bank customers' and 'capital and reserves' are next in importance. 'Amounts due from banks outside Singapore', and 'loans and advances to non-bank customers' are the predominant part of assets; 'securities and equities' are next in importance.

Merchant banks tend to specialise in some areas, such as wholesale banking in the Asian Dollar Market (e.g. APCO, Morgan Guaranty, Dresdner); corporate finance (e.g. United Chase and Morgan Guaranty); Asian bond issues and US$NCD (e.g. DBS–Daiwa International and Merrill Lynch); gold dealing (e.g. Rothschild); and hire purchase/lease financing (e.g. Associated Merchant Bank).[23]

As there is no Merchant Bank Act in Singapore, and merchant banks are registered under the Companies Act, they are rather free from various banking regulations. They do not have to maintain a cash reserve ratio or a liquid asset ratio; there is also no specific capital requirement, nor any regulation on their rates of interest on loans and advances.

(iii) *Post Office Savings Bank (POSB)*

The POSB was started in 1876[24] as an institution to collect small savings. But due to low interest rates and various regulations under the Post Office, the POSB could not collect many savings deposits; however, in 1968 the POSB Advisory Committee was appointed to study possible changes and improvements. The Post Office Savings Bank Act (Singapore), No. 13 1971 was then passed, transforming the POSB into a statutory corporation, independent of the Post Office. Many new schemes were introduced, such as a savings competition among schools, a Lucky Draw, a Save-As-You-Earn (SAYE) bonus scheme, a Group Savings Scheme, a Singapore Armed Forces Savings Scheme, a Giro Service and a batch off-line system. The Giro Service 'enables depositors to settle conveniently and without charge bills for [e.g.] electricity; water; gas; telephone; property tax; rental and conservancy charges of public housing; by automatic transfer of the billed amounts from their savings accounts'. The change from the old manual ledger card system to the batch off-line system enabled the computerisation of depositors' accounts; a depositor can now deposit and withdraw money at any POSB office all over Singapore, without the necessity of dealing always with the same office. The conditions of withdrawal have become more liberal, and the former savings limit of $40000 per account has been abolished. The modernisation and computerisation of the POSB is an important factor in enhancing its competitive power in collecting deposits, and in other activities.

In colonial times, the POSB used its deposits to invest in sterling securities. After self government in 1959, and separation from Malaysia in 1965, sterling securities were gradually drawn down to zero in 1969, and the investment is now entirely in Singapore government securities. There was also a statutory requirement that at least 50 per cent of the POSB's assets had be invested in government securities; this stipulation was subsequently amended to include loans to statutory boards, government enterprises and other assets. In March 1981, the main application of deposits included $704 million Singapore government securities (30 per cent of total); $131 million fixed deposits with banks and finance companies including S$NCDs (26 per cent); and $1532 million term loans (65 per cent) → see Table 5.12). In 1982, the POSB embarked on a new phase of lending activities, providing medium and long term finance to the key areas of aviation, shipping and public transport. The POSB has provided big loans to Singapore International Airline; Neptune Orient Lines (Singapore's national shipping line); NTUC Comfort (National Trades Union Congress Workers' Co-operatives Commonwealth for Transport Ltd, for the purchase of taxis and helping drivers own their vehicles); the DBS; the Public Utilities Board; and other government corporations. The Credit POSB, a wholly owned subsidiary, also provides housing loans as long as 20 years to promote house ownership.

The POSB holds the major share of 40 per cent of the Discount Company of Singapore Ltd (See Appendix 5.6); it has also entered the Asian Dollar Market by investing in some Asian dollar unit bonds (such as the Bank of Tokyo and Credit Lyonnais issues), and intends to participate in syndicated loans. In 1976, the POSB co-managed the Keppel Shipyard's third bond issue of S$35 million. With this progress: the number of POSB branches/ offices increased, from 44 in 1971 to 105 in 1980; the number of savings accounts increased, from 555000 in 1971 to 1898000 in 1980; and outstanding savings deposits increased by 30.3 times, from $91 million in 1971 to $2757 million in 1980 (Table 5.12). Many factors contribute to this spectacular expansion of deposits: interest from POSB deposits is tax free and in 1976–8, the interest rate of POSB savings deposits was slightly higher than that of the commercial banks; the modernisation process and various campaigns had success, so much so that commercial

TABLE 5.12 Post Office Savings Bank savings deposits and application of deposit funds, 1966–81 (figures as at end year, in $ million)

	1966	71	73	77	80	March 81
Excess of deposits over withdrawals during year	0.5	15.5	40.1	530.4	69.5	−84.6
Savings deposits outstanding at end year[a]	37.4	91.2	170.9	1589.0	2756.7	2672.1
No. of accounts at end year (000)	252	555	732	1344	1898	—
Main application of deposit funds Government Securities	15.7	86.7	45.9	634.2	727.5	704.4
Fixed deposits with banks & finance companies including S$NCDs	—	—	88.0	363.6	135.2	131.1
Term loans	—	—	30.0	326.9	1460.8	1532.3
Other investments[b]			2.6	156.7		
Advance deposits with MAS during year	—	—	—	229.4		

[a] Including interest credited.
[b] Other investments include shares in quoted and unquoted corporations, bonds and debentures.

Source: POSB, *Annual Reports 1966–80* (Singapore: POSB, 1966–80); MAS, *Annual Reports 1972–1980–1*.

banks and financial institutions became alarmed at the flow of deposits to the POSB. Probably for the sake of appeasing the private sector, the POSB started a two-tier interest rate system in September 1978; it raised the interest rate on savings deposits up to $100000 in one account from 5–5¼ per cent tax free, but reduced the interest rate on deposit accounts in excess of $100000 from 5–3½ per cent, also tax free. The increased interest rate for small accounts (under $100000) was in line with the world market trend, whilst the reduction in interest rate for big accounts (over $100000) was in line with the savings deposit rates of the commercial banks.

One important argument in favour of the POSB is that deposit funds are used mainly to finance public investments (Changi Airport; PSA; PUB; EDB; Housing Development Board; etc.) through the purchase of government securities; the POSB also takes an active role in lending in the economy. Such lending activity needs to be supported by an effective collection of savings deposits, and by providing better services to depositors (such as the modernisation process, longer hours of opening and various other facilities) the POSB really has an edge over other financial institutions with respect to deposit taking.

The POSB is contemplating accepting current accounts from depositors; and in 1983 applied for a commercial bank licence. It can be expected that the POSB will eventually accept all types of deposits; transact foreign exchange business, extend loans and do all business of a commercial bank, as do the savings banks in Germany.

(iv) *Central Provident Fund (CPF)*

The CPF was set up in July 1955 as a statutory board to implement the compulsory scheme to provide workers with benefits at the retirement age of 55, or when they are unfit to work. It is a fund to which both employees and employers contribute; the rates of contribution have been increased progressively from 5 per cent (of the employee's monthly salary) contributed by both employer and employee in 1955 to the total of 38½ per cent in 1980 – the employer contributing 20½ and the employee 18 per cent. In conjunction with the recommendations of the National Wages Council, the total rate has been further increased to 42 per cent (from July 1981) and to 45 per cent (from July 1982). Employee members of the CPF have been permitted to use part of their balance as down payment to purchase flats built by the Housing Development Board, Jurong Town Corporation, and the Housing and Urban Development Company Ltd, and to subscribe to new issues of the Singapore Bus Service (1978), which is under government supervision.

From 1955–1962, interest was credited to members' accounts at 2½ per cent per annum compounded annually. This rate was increased to 5 per cent in 1963, and to 6½ per cent in December 1976. These moderate rate increases only partially alleviated the erosion of money value through the years of inflation.

The progress of the CPF can be summarised in the following figures. The number of members increased progressively, from 465000 in 1967 to 1519000 in 1980; members' outstanding balances increased by 20 times, from $477 million in 1967 to 9551 million in 1980; members' annual contributions increased by 41 times, from $56 million in 1967 to 2296 million in 1980.[25] Savings channelled into the CPF formed 9 per cent of GDP in 1979.

Over 89 per cent of members' balances is used to acquire government securities; the CPF is the greatest holder of government securities (excluding Treasury bills), its share being 70 per cent of the total in 1975–8.[26]

The contribution of the CPF to economic development, and its role in the financial system, are substantial. Compulsory savings of the community are drawn into the CPF, and channelled into government securities which are used to finance public investments for economic development. As the greatest holder of government securities and advance deposits with the MAS, the CPF inevitably has a great influence on the financial system.

(v) *Insurance companies*

In Singapore there are 71 insurance companies, of which six do life insurance only; 48 do general insurance only; eight do both life and general insurance; and nine do reinsurance only. 24 were incorporated in Singapore; four in Malaysia; and the rest in the UK, Hong Kong, the USA, and other foreign countries.

The first reinsurance company, the Singapore Re-insurance Corporation, was established in 1973 to serve as a clearing house for all registered insurers. The Export Credit Insurance Corporation of Singapore was also set up, with participation by the government, insurers and banks, to facilitate and finance exports.

Traditionally, UK and US insurance companies dominated Singapore's insurance business; local insurance companies began to play an active part only in the 1970s. The NTUC Co-operative Insurance Commonwealth Enterprise Ltd (INCOME), set up in 1972, in particular now tries to cover workers' life insurance.

Insurance companies play the important role of averaging the risks for the public, acting as financial intermediaries between savings and investments. They also help finance economic development, by accepting insurance premiums and using the funds to invest in real estate; shares; debentures and Singapore government securities; and to a small extent to advance loans to customers. They do not invest much in Singapore Treasury bills because of the low rate of interest.

The Insurance Act (Singapore) 1966 stipulated that life insurance companies must invest not less than 75 per cent of their statutory funds (assets of insurance funds) in the Second Schedule, inclusive of a minimum 20 per cent in Singapore government securities (the Second Schedule means authorised local assets, comprising primarily Singapore government securities; approved shares and debentures; real estate and land in Singapore; loans secured on real estate; land and insurance policies in Singapore; and cash balance and demand deposits with commercial banks). General insurance companies must invest not less than 55 per cent of their statutory funds in the Second Schedule, inclusive of a minimum 15 per cent in Singapore government securities.

As at the end of 1980, the total assets of Singapore Insurance Funds amounted to $1247 million, including $706 million for life insurance and $541 million for general insurance: by the nature of their work, general insurance companies maintain a more liquid position than life insurance companies. There has been growth in both life and general insurance since 1975; in order to develop Singapore as an insurance and reinsurance centre, the government has implemented several fiscal measures, such as the reduction of stamp duty on marine policy, and the reduction of income tax on reinsurance business and on offshore reinsurance profit from 40 to 10 per cent.

Singapore's regional outlook in the insurance industry is also reflected in its participation in the ASEAN Insurance Commissioners' meetings and the ASEAN Insurance Council. The latter body, formed in 1978 by the various national life and general insurance associations, works to harmonise insurance laws; standardise policies; unify statistical collection; organise regional training courses; and manage the recently established ASEAN Reinsurance Pool.[27]

(vi) *Other financial institutions*

As the financial system of Singapore is well developed, there are numerous financial institutions other than those mentioned above – four discount houses (Appendix 5.6); eight international moneybrokers (Appendix 5.7); 26 gold dealers; 20 leasing companies;[28] one factoring company;[29] and several unit trusts[30] and investment houses.

There is also the unorganised money market in Singapore – pawnshops, moneylenders, and chettiars: the latter finance the domestic trade in rubber and tin. These institutions were important in the nineteenth and early twentieth centuries, but have declined with the modernisation of the Singapore economy.

THE OFFSHORE BANKING SYSTEM

(a) The Asian Dollar Market (ADM)

The ADM and the Euro Dollar Market are in fact two windows of the same offshore banking system. Because funds flow freely between the two markets, the interest rates are very close together. In Singapore, the offshore banking system and the national (or ordinary) banking system progress side by side and are complementary to each other. The ADM is primarily a short term money market (see Table 5.13) whilst the Asian Bond Market is a long term capital market (see Table 5.14).

(i) *Basic principles*

There are two basic principles of establishing a financial centre, and consequently the ADM:

1. free flow of funds
2. minimum taxation.

The free banking policy of Singapore provides the favourable background for the ADM.[31] The full liberalisation of exchange control effective from June 1978 implies the free flow of funds in and out of Singapore for investment and payment purposes. This has helped develop Singapore as a financial centre, and boosted the ADM. When the ADM was established in 1968, the Singapore government had the policy of separating the national banking system from the ADM, but it guaranteed the free movement of funds with respect to the ADM. Singapore residents (including individuals and corporations) were not allowed to deposit Singapore dollars into the ADM unless they had the foreign exchange or control approval. Singapore residents were not permitted to borrow from the ADM to finance trade and investment in Singapore. Gradually, the demarcation between the national banking system and the ADM has been reduced; the flow of funds from the ADM into Singapore contributed to the great credit expansion (and hence inflation) in 1972–4 and also to Singapore's stock market and property market boom in that period. Today, Singapore residents are liberally permitted to deposit and borrow from the ADM.

In order to develop the ADM, taxation was reduced to the minimum. In 1968, prior to the establishment of the ADM, the income tax rate on interest from bank deposits was 40 per cent; this withholding tax was abolished for the sake of launching the ADM, and the income tax on interest from loans (i.e. tax on the lending banks) has been reduced from the normal rate of 40 per cent to 10 per cent. In March 1976, non-residents' holding of Asian dollar bonds and their deposits with Asian Currency Units (ACUs) were exempted from estate duty. Since February 1977, the 10 per cent concessionary tax has been extended to cover all offshore ACU income other than exchange profits and income from transactions in the national banking system. In order to encourage the signing of ACU loans in Singapore, the *ad valorem* stamp duty of 0.5 per cent on ACU offshore loan agreements has been limited to a maximum of S$500 since November 1976. However, international banks and corporations tend to channel their funds to Hong Kong for lending or investment purposes, and hence switch their profit or interest earned to Hong Kong. According to the rules of Hong Kong income tax, income arising outside the territory of Hong Kong would not be subject to tax; in contrast, the income tax of Singapore is on a global basis – income arising anywhere in the world would be subject to tax if it was repatriated back to Singapore.

Prior to 1982, Singapore was primarily a funding centre for taking deposits, whilst Hong Kong was a 'booking' centre for lending. Since Hong Kong has abolished the withholding tax of 15 per cent on interest from foreign currency deposits (in 1982) it will pose a great challenge to Singapore as a funding centre. Traditionally more loan syndications are conducted in Hong Kong than in Singapore.[32]

(ii) *Growth in aggregate assets*

From 1968–73, the ADM's total assets/liabilities were multiplied by two to three times every year; in the subsequent (and more mature) years 1974–81, the average annual growth rate was about 39.5 per cent (Table 5.13), surpassing the growth of the Euro Dollar Market.

The number of ACUs operating in the ADM also increased from a few foreign banks in 1968–69 to 135 in 1982 (Table 5.13). Since 1975, this increase was mainly with respect to the offshore banks and merchant banks (Table 5.1). At the end of 1980, the net size of the ADM (excluding inter-ACU deposits) was about US$44.4 billion. This was about 6 per cent of the narrowly defined Euro Dollar Market, as measured by the Bank of International Settlements (see also Appendix 5.2).[33]

The factors contributing to the rapid growth of the ADM include the increasing number of ACUs, the favourable change in taxation and exchange control regulations in 1976–8, the rapid development of money and capital markets in Singapore, the recycling of the petrodollar, and above all the political and economic stability of Singapore. Freedom from banking regulations and reserve requirements, and the lower income taxation in the offshore banking system, contribute to its greater growth relative to that of the national banking system. More recently, lending in the international capital markets has been more active than in the domestic markets; this worldwide phenomenon may be one of the factors contributing to the growth of the ADM.

(iii) *Sources and uses of funds*

One characteristic feature of the ADM is the predominance of interbank funds, which constitute a much greater proportion of deposits and loans than in the national banking system. With freer banking, greater flexibility and efficiency, funds are channelled through interbank depositing and lending to the most

TABLE 5.13 Singapore Asian Currency Units consolidated assets and liabilities, 1968–82 (figures as at end period, in US$ million)

Year	No. of ACUs[a]	Assets				Liabilities		
		Loans to non-banks	Interbank funds	Other assets	Total assets/ liabilities	Deposits of non-banks	Inter bank funds	Other liabilities
1968	1	1.4	29.0	0.1	30.5	17.8	12.6	0.1
1969	9	0.9	120.5	1.6	123.0 (+303.3)	97.9	23.7	1.4
1970	14	13.9	370.2	5.7	389.8 (+216.9)	243.7	141.0	5.1
1971	19	188.8	850.8	23.2	1062.8 (+172.7)	237.9	811.2	13.7
1972	25	600.9	2331.1	44.1	2976.1 (+180.0)	398.7	2550.1	27.3
1973	46	1214.3	4961.9	101.0	6277.2 (+110.9)	912.8	5249.3	115.1
1974	56	2629.4 (+16.5)[b]	7528.0	199.9	10357.3 (+65.0)	1614.2 (+76.8)	8531.4	211.7
1975	66	3303.4 (+25.6)	9098.5	195.5	12597.4 (+21.6)	2067.7 (+28.1)	10294.3	235.4
1976	69	4048.3 (+22.5)	12951.4	354.4	17354.1 (+37.8)	1960.3 (−5.2)	15067.2	326.6
1977	78	5281.2 (+30.5)	15252.5	484.6	21018.3 (+21.1)	2254.6 (+15.0)	18350.3	413.4
1978	85	6376.8 (+20.7)	19829.7	833.6	27040.1 (+28.7)	3600.0 (+59.7)	21987.2	1452.9
1979	101	8484.0 (+33.0)	28093.7	1585.0	38162.7 (+41.1)	5771.4 (+60.3)	29424.9	2966.4
1980	115	12402.3 (+46.2)	39552.3	2438.0	54392.6 (+42.5)	9322.2 (+61.5)	40879.6	4190.8
1981	132	19452.2 (+56.8)	62173.1	4149.9	85775.2 (+57.7)	13658.9 (+46.5)	66366.3	5749.9
1982[c]	144	23086.3 (+18.7)	64509.3	4793.2	92388.9 (+7.7)	15768.5 (+15.4)	70524.3	6096.1

a ACUs are separate accounting units of banks and financial institutions authorised by MAS to operate in the ADM (see Table 5.1).
b Figures in parenthesis are % annual growth rates (except 1982).
c As at June 1982.

Source: MAS, Monthly Statistical Bulletin (July 1982 and various issues); MAS, Financial Structure of Singapore 1980, 2nd edn (Singapore: MAS, 1980), p. 64.

efficient borrowers; volatile interest rate movements in the ADM contribute to the increased arbitrage operations by banks and other participants, and to the expansion in interbank transactions. At the end of October 1981, loans to non-bank customers constituted only 23 per cent of total assets, interbank funds 72 per cent; 71.6 per cent of the interbank funds are outside Singapore, 25.7 per cent inter-ACU, and 2.7 per cent in Singapore.[34] Deposits of non-bank customers constitute only 17 per cent of total liabilities, interbank funds 76 per cent. 72.2 per cent of the interbank funds are outside Singapore, 24.2 per cent inter-ACU, and 3.5 per cent in Singapore.

Deposits can be categorised into deposits of non-bank customers and interbank deposits (Table 5.13). With respect to non-bank customers Hong Kong; Singapore; Indonesia; and Taiwan are the principal sources of funds (in that order of importance). The ASEAN countries provide about 40 per cent of deposits and Asian countries about 88 per cent. Hong Kong serves to a certain extent as a transmitter of funds from other countries, and Europe contributes about 8 per cent. Surprisingly, the Middle East provides only about 1 per cent, and the USA about 2 per cent.

If interbank funds are considered, the composition of fund sources is somewhat different, as deposits from non-bank customers are less than one-fifth of interbank deposits. London, the centre of the Euro Dollar Market, provides more than one-fifth of the total deposits (including deposits of non-bank customers and interbank deposits), and Singapore more than one-quarter of the total; other countries include Japan; Indonesia; Taiwan; the USA; France; and the Philippines (in that order). The EEC countries are also active in interbank depositing and lending, and funds flow freely between the ADM and Euro Dollar Market. The USA and Canada are less important as a source, as they channel their funds mainly to the Euro Dollar Market. The Middle East started to deposit and borrow at the end of 1972; by June 1979, total deposits (including interbank funds) from the Middle East constituted less than 4 per cent of total deposits. Loans (including interbank lending) to that area were less than 2 per cent of the total. The Middle East is thus not an important source of funds directly; the recycling of petrodollars is mainly channelled through London. However, the importance of the Middle East as a source of funds has been increasing since 1975.

With regard to loans to non-bank customers (uses of funds), it appears superficially that Hong Kong; Indonesia; Singapore; the

Philippines; Malaysia; Thailand; Australia; South Korea; Japan; and Taiwan (in that order) have received the most. The ASEAN countries received about 50 per cent of the total, and the Asian countries about 83 per cent. Europe (mainly the EEC) took up about 3 per cent; Brazil, Panama and other countries took up small percentages. However, many of the loans to Hong Kong are in fact rechannelled to other Southeast and East Asian countries; Indonesia is undoubtedly the biggest borrower.

If interbank lending is considered, Asian countries in 1979 took up more than 75 per cent of total loans, ASEAN slightly less than 40 per cent, and Singapore more than 20 per cent. Hong Kong; Japan; the UK; Indonesia; the Philippines; South Korea; Thailand; Taiwan; and Malaysia (in that order) came next.

Thus in both lending and depositing, the ADM has assumed a regional characteristic, with the predominant percentages being for the Asian and ASEAN countries.

ACU loans are mainly denominated in US dollars. The principal industry groups financed include: non-bank financial institutions; manufacturing; transport; storage and communication; general commerce; building developers; real estate agents and construction; and mining and quarrying (in that order of importance).

Generally, the ACU is not as much used for financing trade in the ADM as in the Euro Dollar Market. The broad industrial group – including manufacturing; mining; quarrying; construction; transport and communication – gains more than half of the ACU funds. Slightly less than one-third of ACU funds is diverted to non-bank financial institutions. This would help the development of a money and capital market in Singapore; moreover, in view of the predominance of interbank funds, the finance to non-bank financial institutions is a logical supplement to the development of the financial system. Small amounts of funds were diverted to agricultural and mining and quarrying work; as the agricultural sector is less dynamic than the manufacturing sector, and cannot afford to pay high interest rates in open competition, it seems inevitable that few funds will be diverted to agriculture. However, in view of the urge for ASEAN economic co-operation, it is hoped that more attention will be paid to the finance of primary production, as Indonesia, Malaysia, the Philippines and Thailand are primary producing countries and require funds for such activities.

(iv) *Interest rate movements*

Deposit rates are reported daily in newspapers and journals and are more uniform than loan rates, which are rather heterogeneous in nature. Bankers usually mark up 1–1½ per cent from the deposit rates to formulate the loan rates. Sometimes multinational corporations have deposits at the ADM and at the same time borrow the same amount from the bank; this is to avoid bringing money back to the USA, inducing income tax liability. In this case, the markup may be as small as 0.25 per cent. Sometimes the head office places deposits at the ADM in order to enable a branch office in the region to have an overdraft facility. An entrepreneur in Indonesia may similarly deposit money in the ACU, so that the bank may lend the equivalent amount to the company operating in Indonesia.

Generally, interest rates in the ADM are very volatile because of the nature of free banking, with keen international competition and without statutory reserve requirement. They follow closely the money and capital markets in New York, London and other financial centres. Indeed, time deposit rates in the ADM and Euro Dollar Market are almost identical. Typically, the 3 month deposit rates peaked in the second half of 1969, declined in 1970 and the first half of 1971, rose to a second peak in August 1971 (after President Nixon's announcements) steadied in 1972, rose to a third peak in March 1973 (after the second US dollar devaluation) rose to a fourth peak in mid-1974, and declined steadily from the end of 1974 to the first half of 1978, due to the recession and slow recovery. In line with the worldwide increase in interest rates and the US dollar depreciation, interest rates in the ACM rose persistently from the second half of 1978 to a height of about 19.5 per cent in March 1980! They dropped sharply to about 8.8 per cent in June 1980, but rose to the all time high of 22 per cent in December 1980; they then came down to around 14.5 per cent in May 1982.

The spread between the deposit and loan rates is the banker's margin which – after allowing for administration costs, the cost of maintaining reserves and default risks – is the profit margin. As competition in the offshore banking system is greater than in national banking, the spread between deposit rate and loan rate is smaller in the former than in the latter.[35]

A comparison of the interest rates in the national and offshore banking systems shows that the average deposit rates in

Singapore are lower than those in the ADM, whilst the average lending rates of the former are at times lower or higher.[36]

(b) The Asian Bond Market (ABM)

The DBS and the government of Singapore pioneered the first three issues in 1971 and 1972, signifying the deliberate government (intention to develop the ABM. The growth was rather sluggish in the early stage (1971–5), particularly during the worldwide recession (1974–5, see Table 5.14). The ABM has

TABLE 5.14   Asian Development Bank issues, 1971–82

Year	No. of issues	Amount (million)	Coupon rate of interest[a] (%)	Maturity (years)
71	1	US$10	8.5	10
72	2	US$20 DM 100	7.75	10–15
73	3	US$100	5.75, 6.5, 8.75	9–15
74	0	–	–	–
75	3	US$47	9, 9.5	5–7
76	9	US$247 DM 50	6.5–9.5 or floating rate[b]	5–15
77	14	US$315 DM 100 A $10	6–8.625, or floating rate[b]	5–15
78	12	US$220 SDR 25 ¥15000 DM 40 A $15	9.5, or floating rate[b]	5–15
79	8	US$315 DM 70	7.0 or floating rate[b]	7–15
80	18	US$659	7.25–12, or floating rate[b]	3–8
81	16	US$725 ¥35000[b]	5–15.5, or floating rate[b]	3–15
82[c]	9	US$323 ¥35000[b]	5.25–15.5, or floating rate[b]	5–15

[a] Coupon rates of interest refer to US$ & bonds only.
[b] Floating rates are usually 0.25% above 6 month LIBOR or SIBOR.
[c] As at Jan.–Sept. 1982.

Source: MAS, *Annual Report 1980–1*, p. 42; information from DBS–Daiwa International Securities Ltd.

become active since 1976, in consonance with the Eurobond market and the world capital market. 1980 saw a high level of activity, with 18 issues amounting to US$659 million. In 1981, there were 16 issues, totalling US$881 million.

Up to the end of 1981, there have been 86 issues amounting to about US$3125 million, but these issues represented only 0.5 per cent of Eurobond issues in 1975; 1.8 per cent in 1976; and 1.7 per cent in 1980.

The issuers and underwriters of Asian Dollar Bonds come from a variety of countries, and include companies; banks; financial institutions; governments; and regional institutions. In particular, Japanese banks and financial institutions play a very active role in this market.

In Table 5.14, the coupon rates of interest refer to US dollar bonds only. Those rates in strong currencies (such as the Deutsche Mark and the Japanese yen) are usually lower. The coupon rates for US dollar bonds were 9–9.5 per cent (averaging 9.33 per cent) in 1975; 6.5–9.5 per cent (averaging 8.44 per cent) in 1976; 6–8.625 per cent (averaging 6.73 per cent) in 1977; and 9.5 per cent or floating rate in 1978. World interest rate rose sharply in 1979–1; since 1976, it has been a common practice to offer floating rates on the basis of LIBOR or SIBOR, as there is less risk to both issuers and subscribers.

It has been commented that these bonds have a poor secondary market. It is important to develop the secondary market, so that bondholders can obtain liquidity if need arises, and the flow of funds in the financial system can be more effectively regulated and utilised. The MAS has conscientiously striven to that end, but although the bonds are listed in the stock exchanges in Singapore; Malaysia; Hong Kong; Tokyo; London; and New York, there are few transactions.

It is a common phenomenon that the primary market for new issues is more active than the secondary market; even in Europe, Eurobonds are not much traded. The more important objective in the capital market is to provide a channel for investors effectively to obtain the finance they require.

(c) Comments on the Offshore Banking System

The ADM has demonstrated its flexibility and ability to prosper under difficult circumstances – oil crises; recession; inflation; international monetary crises; and decline of the US dollar.

Nevertheless, some criticism can be made. It is often alleged that the offshore banking system can transmit inflation easily in the world, because there are few (if any) reserve requirements and no maximum deposit and minimum lending rates. The credit multiplier in the offshore banking system is necessarily greater than that in the national banking system, by virtue of the fact that banks in the offshore banking system maintain their reserves against deposits by their own 'prudential reserve ratios', instead of statutory minimum reserve ratios as in a national banking system. Taxation on the ADM is also less than that in the national banking system.

Free banking with a potentially large credit multiplier, together with international capital mobility, would naturally spread inflation throughout the world if a major country (say, the USA) has inflation. International capital mobility would reduce the influence of monetary policy on domestic interest rates and level of income; the offshore banking system (which facilitates capital movement) would indirectly reduce the effectiveness of monetary policy in restraining a country's inflation.

It is also alleged that the offshore banking system would favour the development of big corporations and big banks. Most borrowers in the ADM and issuers of Asian Dollar Bonds are big corporations, particularly multinational corporations. It would be difficult for small or medium size corporations to borrow or issue bonds in the markets because of their lower credit standing, the complicated legal procedure and the minimum amounts required. Big banks can operate in the offshore banking system more effectively than small ones because of their worldwide connections; financial resources; and efficiency in collecting deposits and lending to big corporations.[37] In the long run, the offshore banking system would inevitably have the effect of favouring big corporations and big banks.

What is the social cost of developing Singapore as a financial centre? What is the effect of these and other financial development on the economy of Singapore? Obviously, Singapore has become more open financially; the national and offshore banking systems are linked by the flow of funds between them. One cost of a financial centre is the fact that small local businessmen and manufacturing industries sometimes find it difficult to borrow in the market because of the high and fluctuating interest rates and the non-availability of credit in times of monetary stringency abroad. To alleviate this problem, the government has provided special funds to encourage exports and manufacturing. Of course, the international capital mobility associated with the ADM may also attract more foreign investment in Singapore's manufacturing industries.

What is the possibility of using the ADM to strengthen ASEAN economic cooperation? At present, the ADM is based on Singapore; the Philippines has tried to develop the offshore banking units (OBUs and FCDUs) at Manila, and is also active in ACU depositing and borrowing in Singapore. Jakarta also hopes to develop an offshore banking system. But the real rivals to Singapore as financial centres – Hong Kong and Tokyo – are outside ASEAN. Bahrain has grown since 1980 even faster than the ADM; a tax haven status and a geographical location between London and Singapore are the major cause of its growth.

To what extent can ASEAN countries make use of the Asian bonds issue or syndicated loans to finance ASEAN development projects? It can be suggested that ASEAN countries should perhaps have preferential access to ACU funds, or facilities for floating ASEAN bonds in the market. At a recent ASEAN meeting, for example, Singapore was entrusted with the task of seeking capital funds for developing ASEAN agriculture and agro based industries.

FINANCIAL MARKETS

(a) The Money Market

When a bank has surplus short term funds (say, overnight or a few days), it has two investment alternatives – the discount market or the interbank market. In the interbank market, brokers match banks having surplus funds with banks having deficits in their day to day operations. As banks must maintain a statutory minimum cash reserve ratio and liquid asset ratio and settle the clearing of cheques, some banks may incur a short term deficit, so they borrow funds in the interbank market.

In the discount market, banks with surplus funds can deposit short term with a discount house, which uses the funds collectively to invest in Treasury bills, government securities, trade bills and S$NCDs, in order to pay interest to the depositors.[38] Unlike the interbank market, banks cannot borrow from the discount houses.

The money and discount market developed rapidly in recent years. Before Singapore separated from Malaysia in 1965, the

Singapore government issued very few Treasury bills; in the 1960s and 1970s, Treasury bills and government securities were issued in large amounts for public finance, as well as for stimulating the money and capital markets.[39] In January 1973, the issue of Treasury bills was changed from a tap to a tender system. In the former, banks desiring to purchase Treasury bills negotiated directly with the Accountant General or the MAS. In the latter, the MAS opened the tender, usually on every Friday, and let the discount houses and banks bid for a specific amount of Treasury bills. The advantage of a tender system over the tap system is that the MAS can control the volume of Treasury bill issue every week, instead of waiting passively for the calls of banks and financial institutions. From a monetary control standpoint, the tender system is a step forward towards in developing the money and capital markets.

Although four types of Treasury bills are issued, namely 91, 182, 273, and 364 day maturities, the biggest volume of issues and transactions is for the 91 day maturity.[40] All bills issued are in nominal values of S$10000 or a multiple of S$10000; they range from S$10000–$1 million denomination.

The first discount house operating in Singapore in 1964–8 was the Short Deposit (Singapore) Ltd.[41] After the currency split, it suspended operations because the Singapore government (prior to the establishment of the MAS in 1971) was reluctant to offer lender of last resort facilities. In 1971, the Singapore International Merchant Bankers Limited (SIMBL), a merchant bank, set up a money market division to function as a discount house. The formal discount market was established in 1972, when three discount houses were established (see Appendix 5.6); a fourth one commenced in 1974. They are all joint ventures of domestic and international financial institutions. Government policy in granting the licences was to encourage domestic banks to join with well known discount houses in England, the USA and Australia. At first, the general managers were all seconded from overseas, but today there is local staffing and management.

There are two important guidelines from the MAS: a gearing ratio or debt/equity ratio; and an asset ratio. The gearing ratio stipulates the maximum amount a discount house can borrow in relation to its capital and reserves; it was 30 in 1972, was changed to 40 in March 1973 as discount activities expanded and reverted to 30 in March 1974, when discount houses increased their capital from S$3 million to S$5 million each. As at the end of 1981, capital and reserves of the four discount houses totalled $42.3 million.[42]

The asset ratio specifies the proportion of assets held. In 1972, discount houses were required to hold at least 85 per cent of their assets in Treasury bills and government securities, and only 15 per cent in commercial papers.

The ratio for commercial bills rose to 20 per cent in May 1973, to 25 per cent in May 1974 and to 30 per cent in May 1975. Out of the 30 per cent limit, not more than 25 per cent may be invested in commercial bills, and not more than 15 per cent in NCDs. The S$NCD was introduced in May 1975; the MAS hopes to activate the discount market by liberalising the proportion of commercial papers.

The MAS provides lender of last resort facilities to the discount houses and lends to them on the collateral of Treasury bills and government securities. The tender of Treasury bills is open to discount houses, banks and financial institutions, but naturally the most active bidders are the discount houses, the specialists in this field.

The 7 day call interest rate in the discount market is lower than that in the interbank market, because banking regulations now define 'liquid assets' to include the net money at call with discount houses, but excluding interbank balances. The lending bank which deposits its surplus fund in the interbank market cannot count that amount as a liquid asset, hence reducing its incentive to supply funds to the market; on the other hand, if it deposits in a discount house, this counts as a liquid asset in the MAS's liquid asset ratio.

The size of the domestic money market has grown rapidly from S$1344 million (100) in 1974 to S$2739 million (204) in 1979. Statistically, this may be measured by the outstanding balances due to banks in Singapore (for the interbank section) and by the average size of assets of discount houses (for the discount market section). The discount market has grown faster than the interbank market; in 1974, for example, the interbank market constituted 71 per cent of the domestic money market, the discount market 29 per cent. In 1979, the respective percentages were 69 and 31 per cent.

The rapid development of the money and discount market has enabled banks and financial institutions to make better use of their short term funds for earning interest, and has therefore enhanced the efficiency and flexibility of Singapore's financial system.

The concept of a money market can be widened to include the foreign exchange market. As Singapore has become more and more a financial centre in the Asia–Pacific region, the volume of foreign exchange transactions has grown rapidly and many international moneybrokers now deal simultaneously in domestic money market, foreign exchange market and ACU operations.

(b) The Stock Exchange of Singapore (SES)

The SES, being a capital market, provides a channel for diverting savings into productive use. It affords investors (holders of shares and bonds) liquidity, and at the same time enables industrial and commercial enterprises to raise equity capital and long term borrowing (debentures) from the general public. In effect, it comprises both the primary market (new issues of capital – see Table 5.15) and the secondary market (turnover of shares in daily operations).

In May 1973, the Malaysian government decided to terminate the interchangeability of currencies between Malaysia and Singapore, and to split the joint Stock Exchange of Malaysia and Singapore.[43] The SES then started as a separate Exchange. It works in close co-operation with the Securities Industry Council (SIC) and the MAS. The SIC was set up in 1973, at the height of the stock market boom, to regulate the conduct of listed companies, particularly with regard to new issues, mergers and acquisitions. A Securities Industry Act was passed in 1973 to control share manipulation and 'insider' trading. Effort has constantly been made to amend the rules and byelaws to make the SES truly a capital market, and not a 'casino' for speculation. The SIC administers the Securities Industry Act 1973, the Singapore code on takeover and mergers and the corporate disclosure policy.[44]

As at 30 June 1981, the SES had 23 member companies comprising 98 stockbroking members, 52 dealers and 430 remisiers.[45] In 1981, there were 270 companies listed in the SES, of which 103 (38 per cent) were incorporated in Singapore; 158 (58.5 per cent) in Malaysia;[46] and only 9 in other foreign countries. From 1973–81, the number of listed foreign companies declined from 45 to 9; the number of listed Malaysian companies increased marginally from 154 to 158; whilst the number of listed Singapore companies increased from 78 to 103.

At the end of 1981, the total paid-up capital of those 270 companies amounted to \$22114 million, and their market capitalisation to \$79302 million.

With respect to share ownership, two surveys were conducted by the Singapore Securities Research Institute in 1975;[47] 63 per cent of the shares were then held by Singapore residents; 22 per cent by Malaysian residents; and 15 per cent by other foreign owners.

Individuals owned 29.4 per cent of listed shares; nominees and trustees (including individuals, corporations, trustee funds, private provident funds, etc.) 22.4 per cent; corporations 38.5 per cent; and institutions 8.4 per cent. Figure 5.1 shows the number and value of shares traded in the SES. The depressed state of the stock market in the second half of 1973 until 1977 reflected clearly the world recession.

A company seeking a listing on the SES must obtain the approval of the SIC and SES. The official listing requirements[48] include:

1. Minimum paid-up capital of S$4 million.
2. A certain proportion of the issued capital in public hands. At least S$1.5 million (or 25 per cent of the issued and paid-up capital, whichever is greater) should be held by not less than 500 shareholders, holding 500–10000 shares each.
3. All allocatees of shares issued by the company must be registered as shareholders, with not more than 10 per cent of such shares registered in the nominees' names. The SES may, however, require disclosure of the beneficial owners of any shares registered in the nominees' names.
4. A prospectus must be approved by the SIC and SES.

A company seeking listing of loan securities (debentures) must meet the following requirements:

1. It has at least S$750000 of issued loan securities of the class to be quoted in not more than two maturities, and at least S$350000 nominal value in each maturity; where there are more than two maturities, it must have at least S$350000 nominal value in each maturity.
2. There are at least 200 holders of such securities.

Apart from these requirements, the company must demonstrate to the authorities that it has satisfactory growth prospects, and that the business (with continuity of good management) should be attractive to the investing public.

Recent developments in the SES include the establishment of a Securities Finance Corporation and margin trading, a Securities Clearing and Computer Services (Pte) Ltd, and a depository receipt system.[49]

The SES has not yet developed to a mature stage (as compared

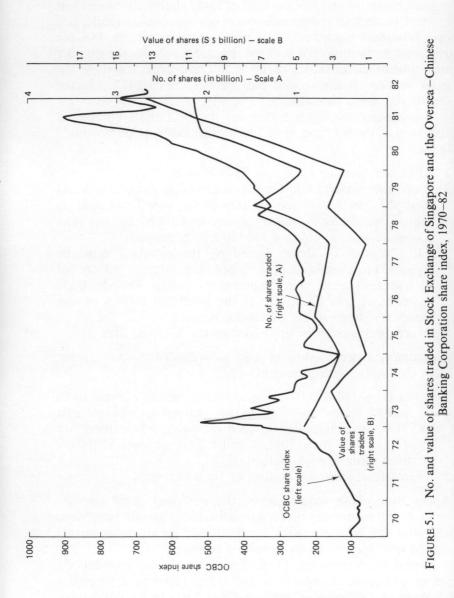

FIGURE 5.1 No. and value of shares traded in Stock Exchange of Singapore and the Oversea–Chinese Banking Corporation share index, 1970–82

with the stock markets in New York, London, and Frankfurt); the number of listed companies (270) and the value of business turnover (see Figure 5.1) are small, and the industrial structure on which the capital market is based is not fully developed. The volume of capital funds originated from the domestic economy is not great, although Singapore (being a financial centre) attracts some inflow of funds. A weakness in the stock market is that there are very few transactions of government securities and fixed interest debentures of the private sector; companies, in fact offer few debentures.

On the other hand, the government has issued many securities in recent years. They are usually purchased and held till maturity by various financial institutions such as the Central Provident Fund; commercial banks; the POSB, insurance companies; etc. to fulfil their statutory requirement: they are seldom sold and bought in the secondary market i.e. the SES. In the primary market shown in Table 5.15, government securities dominate the funds raised in the capital market. The net funds raised by the public sector have risen from $641 million in 1973 to $1743 million in 1980; their share of the total funds raised in the capital market increased from 60 to 98 per cent in 1977, but relapsed to 67 per cent in 1980. The demand for capital funds by the private sector fluctuates in the business cycle, from 40 per cent of the total funds in 1973 (the zenith of the boom) to 2 per cent in 1977 (when the stock market was very dull). By and large, the public sector has a lion's share of the capital funds. However, shares of the private sector are actively traded in the stock market, causing the mistaken illusion that the private sector may tap most funds in the market. In order to stimulate the secondary bond trading, the government has taken several measures,[50] but trading in government securities is still sluggish.

There is no capital gains tax in Singapore, which should be favourable to the SES; consideration could also be given to encouraging private companies to change to public company status by means such as a differential tax system (whereby profits and dividends of public companies are liable to a lower tax rate, as in Indonesia, Thailand and the Philippines). Some people also argue for reducing the stiff regulations of listing. Many companies, wholly or partly owned by the government,[51] could then go public in order to enlarge the number of listed companies and activate the stock market.

TABLE 5.15   Funds raised in the Singapore domestic capital market (figures as at end year, in $ million)

	1973	75	77	80
Public sector				
Gross issue of government securities	750.0	1165.0	1740.0	2300.0
Less redemptions	45.3	138.9	170.6	291.4
Net issue of government securities	704.7	1026.1	1569.4	2008.6
Plus advance deposits	−39.3	18.9	−91.6	−219.1
Less government holdings	24.8	57.8	22.5	64.9
Net funds raised by government	640.6	987.2	1455.3	1724.6
Net issue of statutory boards' securities	—	—	16.0	18.2
Net funds raised by public sector	640.6	987.2	1471.3	1742.8
	(60)[a]	(88)	(98)	(66.9)
Private sector				
Public issue	62.9	18.8	10.2	50.3
Private placement	221.2	91.2	4.0	153.3
Rights issue	111.5	74.9	18.9	201.3
Bonus issue	108.6	6.1	18.5	221.1
Loans stocks, debentures & bonds	—	48.2	—	253.1
Others	70.8	25.4	−68.1	−18.3
Net increase in nominal value of listed equities & securities	574.9	264.6	−16.5	229.4
Net capital raised by private sector	424.8	134.4	33.6	863.5
	(40)	(12)	(2)	(33.1)
New issues	233.6	74.7	33.1	414.7
Premium on new shares	191.2	59.7	0.5	448.8
Total new funds raised[b]	1065.4	1121.6	1504.9	2606.3

[a]   Figures in parenthesis are percentages.
[b]   Net funds raised by public sector & net capital raised by private sector.

Source: MAS, *Annual Reports 1975–1980–1*.

PROBLEMS AND PROSPECTS

Singapore has developed a rather sophisticated financial structure with an international outlook; money and capital markets have progressively improved, and so has the efficiency and flexibility of the financial system. Many new types of financial institution have been established to provide new financial services – leasing companies; export credit insurance companies; a future foreign exchange market and a gold futures market.

The theory of financial liberalisation and deepening[52] has been well applied to Singapore. Since 1975, for example, it has adopted a free banking policy and since June 1978 has completely liberalised its foreign exchange controls. The development of Singapore as an international financial centre; a free banking policy; and a keen desire to promote efficiency, competitiveness and flexibility of the financial system to meet international challenge; necessitated financial liberalisation. Indicators of financial deepening – real cash balance *per capita*; financial asset/GDP ratio; relative share of financial sector in GDP; relative share of financial sector in total labour force; and number of bank offices per 10000 persons – are all favourable to Singapore.[53]

Singapore relies heavily upon market forces in her financial development, although the government takes a central role in stimulating the growth of financial institutions and participates directly in banking activities. There is no regulated interest rate; no arbitrary allocation of credit; and no exchange control.

Foreign or international financial institutions enjoy considerable liberty in Singapore. In other ASEAN countries such as Indonesian, the Philippines (and to a certain extent Thailand) foreign banks are often prohibited from certain financial activities; there are no such regulations in Singapore. The international banks have in fact played a major role in Singapore's development as a financial centre; in inducing foreign industrial enterprises to invest in Singapore; and in introducing management skill to the banking industry. With the challenge of open international competition, the banking system has become more efficient, and achieved dynamic growth.

The question then arises: are the local financial institutions protected? Granting branch office licences to local banks is a small measure of protection, but that is common to practically all countries. The arrangement of restricted licence banks and offshore banks is in fact a measure to avoid overbanking in the national banking system, or excessive competition in deposit taking, which would be detrimental to local banks. However, the demarcation line between restricted licence banks and offshore banks has become very blurred, because as from July 1978 offshore banks have also been allowed to lend money in the national banking system to a limited extent. At present, offshore banks clamour to be 'promoted' to a restricted licence status, whilst, the restricted licence banks wish for full licence standing.

Singapore adopts a policy of an optimum degree of international openness: on the one hand, she desires to welcome international competition in order to boost efficiency and flexibility in the financial system; on the other, she does not want local banks and financial institutions to be 'overshadowed' by the international giants.

The Government has therefore urged local financial institutions to modernise, and small banks to merge with stronger ones, e.g. Chung Khiaw Bank and Lee Wah Bank with United Overseas Bank, and Bank of Singapore and Four Sea Communication Bank with Oversea-Chinese Banking Corporation.[54] Although joint ventures of local and foreign financial institutions are common in merchant banks and discount houses, the government does not favour the takeover of local commercial banks by foreign banks, as evidenced in the case of Chung Khiaw Bank and Slater Walker in 1971.[55]

Historically, monetary and banking relations among ASEAN countries have not been great,[56] Singapore is the only country which has banking representation from all the other ASEAN countries – five Malaysia incorporated banks (four with full licences: Malayan Banking Ltd, United Malayan Banking Corporation, Ban Hin Lee Bank, and Kwong Lee Bank; and are, Bank Bumiputra Malaysia, with an offshore banking license) Bangkok Bank; Bank Negara Indonesia 1946; the Philippines National Bank (an offshore banking licence); three Indonesian bank representative offices (Bank Indonesia, Bank Bumi Daya and Bank Dagang Negara); and two Philippine bank representative offices (Allied Banking Corporation and Metropolitan Bank and Trust). The ASEAN banks now also exchange desk officers. The ASEAN Finance Corporation was established in Singapore in June 1981, to operate as a merchant bank with an ASEAN attitude i.e. to provide venture capital to stimulate joint ventures in the private sector in the ASEAN countries.[57]

There is still a need to increase the depth of Singapore's capital market. Investment houses, unit trusts and other financial institutions should be strengthened so that they can acquire Asian Dollar Bonds or supply funds to the capital market. As it is, whenever the bonds are issued, most funds are subscribed in Tokyo, London and New York. Securities companies complain of the income tax of 40 per cent in Singapore, whereas their counterparts in Japan receives special consideration because they buy and sell on behalf of clients.

Consideration should also be given to establishing a development finance corporation in the private sector, to complement the public sector DBS.

One of the most important problems is that the public sector absorbs too much funds in the market. The Central Provident Fund (CPF), POSB and public authorities held as much as 88 per cent of outstanding government registered stock at the end of 1980; government and government agents' deposits in the banking system are also considerable, and together constitute a contractionary effect on the monetary system, and a heavy net liquidity drain to the government and public authorities. The budgetary operations (including net domestic borrowings) have also been in substantial surplus in the 1960s and 1970s.[58]

Fiscal policy is thus highly contractionary in its monetary effect. To counteract this, the MAS's monetary policy must be consistently expansionary.[59] This bias toward consistent monetary expansion may, however, have unfavourable effects. First, the flexibility of the financial system may be impaired; the excessive mobilisation of funds by the public sector leaves less investible funds for the private sector. This may hinder the development of financial institutions and instruments; the growth of Singapore as a financial centre; and the diversification and development of the money and capital markets. Public borrowings at artificially low interest rates through government securities and the CPF may distort the interest rate structure, the monetary adjustment, and hence the optimum allocation of resources.[60]

The relatively small holding of government securities by the general public (individuals and corporations hold less than 4 per cent), by banks (about 6 per cent), and by insurance companies (2 per cent) has caused open market operation (and so also central bank discount rates) not to be effective in monetary policy. This explains why the MAS has resorted to variation of the minimum cash reserve ratio; bill discounting; direct lending to the banking system; and foreign exchange market intervention as the main instruments of monetary policy and liquidity management. The MAS tends to build up an abnormally large net lender position with the banking system, which may stifle flexibility and growth of the system.

Consideration should be given to reducing the abnormally strong funds absorption by the public sector. The CPF, POSB and other financial institutions, for example, might be allowed to diversify further their investment portfolio by investing part of their fund in first class equities, the ADM and the international capital market. This would help activate the SES and strengthen Singapore's role as a financial centre.

The trend of banking development includes diversification, internationalisation and a free banking policy. Modernisation and computerisation of banking will rapidly spread in Singapore; technological change with respect to computer and electronic services may, in fact precede economic thinking in the monetary and banking field. By bringing banking services into the offices and homes of clients, the technological change will have a great impact on the future financial system.

APPENDICES

Appendix 5.1   Commercial banks in Singapore, May 1982

Name	Place of incorporation	First official opening
Full licence banks		
Oversea–Chinese Banking Corpn[a]	Singapore	1932
Overseas Union Bank[a]	Singapore	1949
Lee Wah Bank[a]	Singapore	1920
United Overseas Bank[a]	Singapore	1935
Four Seas Communications Bank	Singapore	1907
Chung Khiaw Bank	Singapore	1950
The Industrial and Commercial Bank[a]	Singapore	1954
Bank of Singapore	Singapore	1955
Far Eastern Bank	Singapore	1959
Asia Commercial Banking Corpn	Singapore	1959
The Development Bank of Singapore[a]	Singapore	1968
Tat Lee Bank[a]	Singapore	1974
The International Bank of Singapore[a]	Singapore	1975
Malayan Banking Corpn	Kuala Lumpur	1960
United Malayan Banking Corpn	Kuala Lumpur	1961
Ban Hin Lee Bank	Penang	1936
Kwong Lee Bank	Kuching	1926
Chartered Bank[a,b]	UK	1859
Hongkong and Shanghai Banking Corpn[a,c]	Hongkong	1877
Mercantile Bank[b]	UK	1856
Citibank[a]	USA	1902
Bank of America NT & SA[a]	USA	1955
The Chase Manhattan Bank NA[a]	USA	1964
The First National Bank of Chicago[a]	USA	1970
The Bank of Tokyo[a]	Japan	1957
The Mitsui Bank[a]	Japan	1963
Bank of China[a]	China	1936
The Kwangtung Provincial Bank	China	1939

Appendix 5.1   (*contd.*)

Name	Place of incorporation	First official opening
The Bank of Canton[a]	Hongkong	1953
The Bank of East Asia[a]	Hongkong	1953
Algemene Bank Nederland NV[a]	Netherlands	1858
Banque de L'Indochine[a]	France	1905
Indian Overseas Bank	India	1941
Indian Bank	India	1941
Bank of India	India	1951
United Commercial Bank	India	1951
Bank Negara Indonesia (1946)	Indonesia	1955
Bangkok Bank[a]	Thailand	1957
Restricted licence banks		
Moscow-Narodny Bank[a]	London	1971
Banca Commerciale Italiana[a]	Italy	1971
Habib Bank[a]	Pakistan	1971
Banque Nationale de Paris[a]	France	1971
Dresdner Bank AG[a]	W. Germany	1971
Asien–Pazifik Bank AG[a]	W. Germany	1971
American Express International Banking Corpn[a]	USA	1972
European Asian Bank[a]	W. Germany	1972
The Sumitomo Bank[a]	Japan	1973
Credit Suisse[a]	Switzerland	1973
Korea Exchange Bank[a]	S. Korea	1973
Mitsubishi Bank[a]	Japan	1973
First Commercial Bank[a]	Taiwan	1977

[a]   There are 22 full banks and 13 restricted licence banks which are licensed to operate ACUs.
[b]   The Eastern Bank (a UK bank) was merged with the Chartered Bank in July 1971.
[c]   As from July 1973, the Mercantile Bank has been merged into the Hongkong and Shanghai Banking Corpn, and operates under the latter name. So the licence of Mercantile Bank was withdrawn.

Source: MAS, 1982.

Appendix 5.2   Offshore banks[a] by country of origin, May 1982

Offshore banks	Year of commencement in Singapore
USA	
Bankers Trust Co.	1973
Continental Bank	1973
First National Bank in Dallas	1973
Marine Midland Bank	1973

Appendix 5.2   (*contd.*)

Offshore banks	Year of commencement in Singapore
Chemical Bank	1974
Irving Trust Co.	1974
Manufacturers' Hanover Trust	1974
Bank of New York	1975
First Interstate Bank of California	1975
Morgan Guaranty Trust Co. of New York	1975
Republic Bank Dallas	1975
Rainier National Bank	1976
Wells Fargo Bank	1977
First National Bank of Boston	1978
Harris Trust & Savings Bank	1980
Security Pacific National Bank	1980
First National Bank of Houston	1981
Canada	
Toronto Dominion Bank	1973
Bank of Montreal	1974
Bank of Nova Scotia	1974
Royal Bank of Canada	1975
Canadian Imperial Bank of Commerce	1977
UK	
Barclays Bank International	1973
National Westminster Bank	1973
Lloyds Bank International	1974
Nordic Bank	1975
Grindlays Bank	1979
Midland Bank	1980
Japan	
Fuji Bank	1974
Dai–Ichi Kangyo Bank	1976
Sanwa Bank	1977
Industrial Bank of Japan	1978
Tokai Bank	1978
Daiwa Bank	1979
Long-Term Credit Bank of Japan	1981
Mitsui Trust & Banking Co.	1981
Saitama Bank	1981
Sumitomo Trust & Banking Co.	1981
Taiyo Kobe Bank	1981
Australia & New Zealand	
Westpac Banking Corpn	1979

Appendix 5.2 *(contd.)*

Offshore banks	*Year of commencement in Singapore*
Australia & New Zealand Banking Group	1980
National Australia Bank	1981
Bank of New Zealand	1982
ASEAN	
Philippine National Bank	1979
Bank Bumiputra Malaysia	1980
Europe	
Swiss Bank Corporation	1975
Union Bank of Switzerland	1979
Amsterdam−Rotterdam NV	1979
Société Generale	1979
Credit Lyonnais	1979
DG Bank	1980
Banco Urquijo SA	1980
Banque Bruxelles Lambert	1981
Société Generale de Banque	1981
Banque de Paris et des Pays-Bas	1981
Dan Danske Bank	1982
Banque Francaise du Commerce Extérieur	1982
Middle East	
Union de Banque Arabes et Francaises	1981
Gulf International Bank	1982
National Bank of Abu Dhabi	1982
Others	
State Bank of India	1977
Banco do Brazil	1978
Commercial Bank of Korea	1980
Banco do Estado de São Paulo (Brazil)	1982

[a] The total no. of offshore banks is 64.

Source: MAS, 1982.

Appendix 5.3   Foreign banks' representative offices[a] by country of incorporation, May 1982

USA
The Citizens & Southern National Bank
American National Bank & Trust Co. of Chicago
Maryland National Bank

Appendix 5.3　(*contd.*)

State Street Bank & Trust Co.
Centerre Bank
First National Bank of Oregon
Girard Bank
Philadelphia National Bank
Industrial National Bank of Rhode Island
First Interstate Bank of Washington

UK
Scandinavian Bank Ltd
Williams & Glyn's Bank

Japan
The Kyowa Bank Ltd
The Hokkaido Tokushoku Bank Ltd
The Yasuda Trust & Banking Co.
The Nippon Credit Bank
The Toyo Trust & Banking Co.
The Bank of Yokohama
The Mitsubishi Trust & Banking Corpn

Australia & New Zealand
Commonwealth Treading Bank of Australia
The National Bank of New Zealand Ltd

ASEAN
Bank Indonesia
Bank Bumi Daya (Indonesia)
Bank Dagang Negara (Indonesia)
Allied Banking Corpn (Philippines)
Metropolitan Bank & Trust Co. (Philippines)

Europe
Kredietbank NV
Privatbanken A/S
Copenhagen Handelsbank A/S
Kansallis – Osake – Pankki
Banque de Paris et des Pays-Bas
Credit du Nord
Credit Commercial de France
Berliner Handels- and Frankfurter Bank
Banca Nazionale Del Lavoro
Banco Di Roma
Banco Ambrosiano
Monte Dei Paschi Di Siena
Banque Internationale A Luxembourg SA

Appendix 5.3 *(contd.)*

Nederlandsche Middenstands Bank NV
Christiania Bank og Kreditkasse
Den Norske Creditbank
Banco Exterior de Espana
Gotabanken
Svenska Handelsbanken
Credit Suisse
Nordfinanz–Bank Zurich
Swiss Bank Corporation
Swiss Volksbank
Dow Banking Corporation
Ljubljanska Banka

Middle East
National Bank of Kuwait
The National Commercial Bank, Jeddah, Saudi Arabia

Others
Bank of Ceylon
The Korea Development Bank
Bank of Korea
Bank of Seoul & Trust Co.
The Hanil Bank Ltd
Korea First Bank
The Cho–Heung Bank

[a] There are 47 representative offices of commercial banks and 5 representation offices of merchant banks, totalling 52.

Source: MAS, 1982.

Appendix 5.4   Approved merchant banks in Singapore, June 1982

Name	Year of Commencement
Arbuthnot Latham Asia Ltd	1970
Singapore International Merchant Bank Ltd	1970
Asia Pacific Capital Corpn	1972
Citicorp International (Singapore) Ltd	1972
DBS–Daiwa Securities International Ltd	1972
Haw Par Merchant Bankers Ltd	1972
United Chase Merchant Bankers Ltd	1972
Asian–American Merchant Bank Ltd	1973
Associated Merchant Bank Ltd	1973
Dresdner (SEA) Ltd	1973
Guinness Mahon (SEA) Ltd	1973

Appendix 5.4   (*contd.*)

Name	Year of Commencement
Jardine Fleming (Singapore) Pte Ltd	73
Morgan Guaranty Pacific Ltd	73
N. M. Rothschild & Sons (Singapore) Ltd	73
Singapore Nomura Merchant Banking Ltd	73
Temenggong Merchant Bankers Ltd	73
First Chicago Asia Merchant Bank Ltd	74
Morgan Grenfell Asia Ltd	74
Singapore Japan Merchant Bank Ltd	74
Baring Brothers Asia Ltd	75
Wardley Ltd	76
Inter–Alpha Asia Singapore Ltd	77
Credit Suisse First Boston (Asia) Ltd	78
Deutsche Bank Asia Credit Ltd	78
Merrill Lynch International Asia & Co	78
Standard Chartered Merchant Bank Ltd	78
Bank of Montreal Asia Ltd	79
Bank of Nova Scotia Asia Ltd	79
Banque Nationale de Paris (SEA) Ltd	79
Commerzbank (Southeast Asia) Ltd	79
Royal Bank of Canada Asia Ltd	79
Skandinaviska Enskilda Banken (SEA) Ltd	79
Toronto Dominion (SEA) Ltd	79
Armco Pacific Financial Corpn	80
Bankers' Trust International (A) Ltd	80
Canadian Imperial Bank of Commerce (Asia) Ltd	80
Union Bank of Finland (Singapore) Ltd	80
KDB International Singapore Ltd	81
Midland Montagu Asia Ltd	81
Marac Merchant Bank (SEA) Ltd	81
Wells Fargo Asia Ltd	81
Republic National Bank of New York (S) Ltd	82
Banque Internationale A Luxembourg (Asia) Ltd	82

Source: MAS, 1982.

Appendix 5.5   Finance companies in Singapore total assets (figures at end 1980, in $ million)

Company	Amount
Hong Leong Finance Ltd[a]	483.8
Development Bank of Singapore Finance Ltd[b]	255.9
Singapore Finance Ltd	204.3
United Overseas Finance Ltd[b]	196.3

Appendix 5.5 (*contd.*)

Company	Amount
Wayfoong Mortgage & Finance (Singapore) Ltd[b]	156.2
Forward Overseas Credit Ltd[b]	132.5
Credit Corporation (Singapore) Ltd[b]	132.4
Singapore Building Society Ltd[c]	126.5
Tat Lee Finance Ltd[b]	112.1
Overseas Union Trust Ltd[b]	102.9
OCBC Finance (S) Ltd[b]	92.1
Asia Commercial Finance Ltd[b]	89.4
Sim Lim Finance Ltd[d]	85.6
Industrial & Commercial Finance Ltd[b]	73.1
Far East Finance Organisation Ltd	59.7
Overseas Union Finance Ltd[c]	59.5
International Trust & Finance Ltd	59.2
United National Finance (Singapore) Ltd[b,c]	56.7
Sing Investments & Finance Ltd	53.4
The Chartered Finance Company Ltd[b]	46.0
Great Pacific Finance Ltd	43.8
The Malayan Finance Corpn (Singapore) Bhd[b,c]	43.2
Nanyang Finance Ltd[e]	37.6
Golden Castle Finance Corporation Ltd	36.8
Fourseas Finance Ltd[b]	36.4
Building Society of Malaya Ltd[b]	27.8
Kiaw Aik Hang Finance Company Ltd	24.4
Singapore–Malaysia Finance Ltd[b]	18.5
Tong Bee Finance Company Ltd	12.1
Soon Teck Finance (Singapore) Ltd	11.8
Public Finance Company Ltd	8.8
Island Finance Ltd	7.0
Lian Huat Hang Finance Ltd	6.7
Asia Building Society Limited[f]	5.8
Shing Loong Finance Company Ltd[g]	N/A

[a] Hong Leong Finance Ltd took over Singapore Finance Ltd in 1978, but they still operate under separate names.
[b] Bank affiliated: 16 are bank affiliated, and 19 are not bank affiliated.
[c] Figures at 30 June 1981.
[d] Figures at 31 March 1981.
[e] Figures at 30 September 1980.
[f] Figures at 30 March 1980.

Source: Finance Companies' *Annual Reports*; *Banks and Financial Institutions in Singapore Yearbook 1981* (Singapore: Consulton Research Bureau, 1981).

Appendix 5.6 Discount houses in Singapore, May 1982

Company	Year of establishment	Shareholders	% of shares
International Discount Company Ltd	Nov. 72	Oversea–Chinese Banking Corpn	30[a]
		Four Seas Communication Bank	15[a]
		Industrial & Commercial Bank	10
		Clive Discount Corpn	20
		Singapore International Merchant Bankers Ltd	15
		Chase Manhattan Bank	10
Discount Company of Singapore Ltd	Nov. 72	Post Office Savings Bank	40
		United Overseas Bank	25
		Gilbert Investments Ltd (a subsidiary of Gilbert Brothers Discount Co. London)	20
		Chartered Bank	15
National Discount Company Ltd	Nov. 72	Development Bank of Singapore	45
		Overseas Union Bank	15
		Morgan Guaranty International Finance Corpn	35
		Australian United Corpn	5
Commercial Discount Company Ltd	Nov. 74	Tat Lee Bank	25
		Sim Lim Finance Ltd	15
		Singapore Finance Ltd	15
		Hongkong & Shanghai Banking Corpn	20
		Development Finance Corpn	20
		South East Asia Development Corpn	5

[a] As announced in April 1982, the total shares of OCBC and Four Seas Communication Bank have been increased to 51.43 per cent.

Source: MAS, 1982.

Appendix 5.7   International moneybrokers in Singapore, May 1982

Company	Year of Commencement
Herbert Ong Harlow (S) Pte Ltd (joint venture)	1971
Astley and Pearce (Pte) Ltd	1972
Charles Fulton (Singapore) Ltd	1972
Marshalls (Singapore) Pte Ltd	1974
Hung Chue Pedder Martin (Pte) Ltd (joint venture)	1974
Degani & Company	1976
Tan Swee Hee & Co. (Pte) Ltd	1977
Ong Tradition Singapore (Pte) Ltd	1979

Source: MAS, 1982.

NOTES

1. See Lee Sheng-Yi and Y. C. Jao, *Financial Structures and Monetary Policies in Southeast Asia* (Singapore Ch.) (London: Macmillan, 1982) table 8.1, p. 291.
2. Lee Sheng-Yi and Y. C. Jao, *Financial Structures*, pp. 211–15.
3. For a year after the separation of Singapore from Malaysia, and before the currency split, the Singapore government requested Bank Negara Malaysia temporarily to supervise commercial banks in Singapore.
4. For a discussion of the causes and effects, see Lee Sheng-Yi, *The Monetary and Banking Development of Malaysia and Singapore* (Singapore University Press, 1974) pp. 222–42.
5. *Census of Services 1974*, vol. ii (Singapore: Department of Statistics, October 1977) p. 55; Lee Sheng-Yi, 'The Role of Financial Institutions in the Singapore Economy', *AIESEC Yearbook* (Singapore: Nanyang University, 1977–8).
6. Lee Sheng-Yi, *Monetary and Banking Development*, ch. 5; 'Development of Commercial and Merchant Banks', *Monetary and Banking Development of Malaysia and Singapore* (Singapore University Press, 1974) pp. 65–97.
7. For a discussion of the similarities and differences between local and Western banks, see Lee Sheng-Yi, *Monetary and Banking Development*, pp. 83–8.
8. The ACU licence is granted to a banking unit to operate in the ACM. A financial institution (commercial bank; merchant bank; investment company) can apply to the MAS for the licence.
9. See Lee Sheng-Yi and Kenny Wee, 'Liquidity and Growth: The Case of a Local Bank', *South Asian Journal of Social Science* (1975); Lee Sheng-Yi, 'Ownership and Control of Local Banks', *Singapore Yearbook of Banking and Finance 1980–1* (Singapore: Institute of Banking and Finance , 1981) pp. 109–17.
10. The Hongkong and Shanghai Banking Corporation acquired all the share

capital of the Mercantile Bank in 1958, but the two banks operated as two independent organisations under separate Boards of Directors and management until July 1973, when the Mercantile Bank was merged into the Hong-kong and Shanghai Banking Corporation.

11. An offshore banking licence is granted to a foreign bank to operate in the ACM only, but not in the national banking system (such as taking deposits and lending in Singapore).

12. The annual growth rate of loans slowed from 44.4 per cent in 1973 to 10.7 per cent in 1974, and to an average of 11.1 per cent in 1974–7. The growth rate of deposits slowed from 22.4 per cent in 1973 to 12.6 per cent in 1974, and to an average of 11.6 per cent in 1974–7.

13. Liquid assets include cash; balances with the MAS; money at call with discount houses; Treasury bills; trade bills and S$NCDs.

14. Lee Sheng-Yi, *Monetary and Banking Development*, pp. 115–8; table 6.9.

15. Temasek Holdings Pte Ltd (the domestic investment arm of the Ministry of Finance) holds 111.2 million ordinary shares of $1 each fully paid, and the POSB (a statutory board) holds 9.0 million shares: DBS, *Annual Report 1981*, p. 44.

16. About 6 out of 11 Directors of the Board are civil servants: DBS, *Annual Reports*, various years. For an analysis, see Lee Sheng-Yi, 'Ownership and Control of Local Banks', pp. 109–17.

17. The equity investments include shareholdings in Jurong Shipyard; National Iron and Steel; Tata Precision Industries; and Singapore and Fuji Elevator Corporation.

18. There is, however, a provision in s. 29, that 'any bank whose business is principally in such loans or advances may, with the prior written consent of the Commissioner, make such loans or advances in an aggregate amount up to, but not in excess of [60 per cent] of the amount of its deposits in Singapore'.

19. From 1963–5, Bank Negara had jurisdiction over Singapore.

20. From 1960 until 1975, there was a gentlemen's agreement among bank affiliated finance companies not to pay deposit rates higher than the bank's by more than 1 per cent.

21. Under s. 25(4), Finance Company Act 1967, liquid assets are defined as:
    (a) Singapore notes and coin
    (b) net balances with banks in Singapore
    (c) net money at call in Singapore
    (d) Singapore Treasury bills
    (e) other assets that the MAS may prescribe.

22. Lee Sheng-Yi and Y. C. Jao, *Financial Structures*, chs 2; 6.

23. Michael T. Skully, *Merchant Banking in the Far East*, 2nd edn (Singapore ch.) (London: *Financial Times*, 1980); Anthony Teo and Eric K. Sim, 'Prospects of Merchant Banking in Singapore ', *Singapore Banking and Finance 1977* (Singapore: Institute of Banking and Finance, 1977).

24. Savings Bank Ordinance, No. VI 1876 (Straits Settlement); *The Post Office Savings Bank of Singapore: 100 Years* (Singapore: POSB, July 1977) pp. 20–1; 23–4; 26; 29–31.

25. CPF, *Annual Reports 1967–80*; MAS, *Annual Report 1980–1*.

26. MAS, *Financial Structure of Singapore 1980* (Singapore: MAS, 1980) pp. 45–8; MAS, *Annual Report 1980–1*; Lee Sheng-Yi, *Public Finance and*

Singapore 293

Public Investment in Singapore (Singapore: Institute of Banking and Finance, 1978) p. 158.
27. Michael T. Skully, *ASEAN Regional Financial Cooperation: Developments in Banking and Finance* (Singapore: Institute of Southeast Asian Studies, 1979) pp. 10–11; 27–31.
28. They include notably GATX Leasing (Pacific) Ltd; Orient Leasing Singapore Ltd; Orion Leasing Singapore Pte Ltd; Singapore Leasing International Pte Ltd; and Singapore Industrial Equipment Pte Ltd. Some merchant banks and finance companies also do leasing business (such as Associated Merchant Bank Pte Ltd, and Credit Corporation Singapore Ltd).
29. The only factoring company in Singapore is Heller Factoring (Singapore) Ltd – a joint venture of the DBS (25 per cent); OCBC (25 per cent); Walter E. Heller Overseas Corpn, USA (40 per cent); and Heller Factoring (Hong Kong) Ltd (10 per cent). Credit Factoring International (Singapore) Ltd was in fact the first factoring company established in 1974, but was short lived.
30. They include Singapore Unit Trust Ltd; Asia Unit Trust Ltd; and Chartered Unit Trust Ltd.
31. Since July 1975, banks have been free to set their own lending and deposit rates. Furthermore, since September 1981, this freedom has been extended to cover large domestic transactions ($40000 or over), such as letters of credit; loans and overdraft; securities transactions; and mail and telegraphic transfer – a partial removal of the regulated charges of the Association of Banks in Singapore.
32. The advantage of Hong Kong over Singapore in loan syndications has been subject to debate. It has been argued that Hong Kong has more international lawyers and accountants with specialised experience in the negotiation and formulation of loan agreements, and also a sophisticated printing industry which can print a prospectus, loan agreement and other documents speedily. In fact, Singapore is catching up in those aspects. A long history as a financial centre; a greater number of international banks and financial institutions; a relatively more advanced financial structure; relatively freer markets; and the lower business income tax probably contribute to the competitive edge of Hong Kong over Singapore.
33. MAS, *Annual Report 1980–1*, p. 43.
34. MAS, *Monthly Statistical Bulletin* (November 1981) p. 29.
35. See Lee Sheng-Yi, 'Recent development in Asian Currency Market and Asian Bond Market': *Occasional Paper no. 32*, Institute of Economics and Business Studies, Nanyang University (April 1979) pp. 17–18, particularly table 3.
36. Lee Sheng-Yi and Y. C. Jao, *Financial Structures*, Ch. 3; graph 3.1.
37. In the recession (1974–6), small banks in the EDM could not collect many deposits; the recycling of petrodollars was mainly in the hands of the bigger banks.
38. An individual bank with the surplus funds for overnight or for a few days cannot invest it in Treasury bills, because the stamp duties and other transaction costs may be greater than the interest rate earned. Under the management of a discount house, those odd short term funds can collectively be fully utilised for investment.

39. See Lee Sheng-Yi, *Public Finance and Public Investment*, pp. 153–5.
40. The Ministry of Finance, in conjunction with the MAS, started to issue 182 day bills in February 1974 and 273 day and 364 day bills in 1975. But they are not very popular, and the volumes of issues are not big, relatively speaking. The 91 day bills are issued regularly every week, and the 182 day bills every month. The 273 day and 364 day bills are issued only on an intermittent basis, depending upon market conditions.
41. The Short Deposit (Malaysia) Ltd (an Australia concern) was established in 1964 with encouragement from Bank Negara Malaysia.
42. For the assets and liabilities of discount houses, see MAS, *Annual Report 1980–1*, p. 28; *Monthly Statistical Bulletin* (February 1982) p. 18. See also Tan Chwee Huat, *Financial Institutions in Singapore*, 2nd edn (Singapore University Press, 1981) pp. 163–5.
43. For a brief history of the Stock Market in Singapore, see Tan Pheng Theng, 'The development of the securities industry', *Securities Industry Review*, vol. 4, no. 1 (April 1978) p. 6; Saw Swee-Hock, *The Securities Market in Singapore* (Singapore: Singapore Securities Research Institute, 1980) pp. 1–6.
44. A Corporate Disclosure Policy Manual has been devised by the SES for listed companies on the kind of corporate information required, and the manner in which to disclose it to the investing public.
45. A remisier is a dealer of shares and bonds on behalf of customers, who receives commission (but not salary) from a broking firm.
46. All these Malaysian incorporated companies are also listed on the Kuala Lumpur Stock Exchange, and are some Singapore incorporated companies.
47. For a detailed analysis of the findings, see Grace Ooi, *Report on the Share Ownership Survey, 1975* (Singapore: Securities Research Institute, 1975). The results of the surveys have also appeared in the March, April, May, July, November and December 1976 issues of the Singapore *Stock Exchange Journal*, and the September 1977 issue of the *Securities Industry Review*.
48. SES, Listing Manual and Corporate Disclosure Policy.
49. The SFC extends loans to clients against share collaterals, so investors can trade on a deposit margin. But since the government discourages speculation, the SFC has not made much progress. The Securities Clearing and Computer Services Ltd commenced operations in January 1979 to provide fast clearing facilities. The Depository Receipt System, (introduced in July 1979) enables local investors to invest in shares listed on foreign Stock Exchanges; for the mechanism, see Margaret Koh, 'The Depository Receipt: An Investment to Simplify International Transaction in Securities', *Stock Exchange of Singapore Journal* (July 1976).
50. These include the MAS and the CPF taking part in buying and selling government securities in the SES; reduction of the brokerage rate for trading in government securities; and reduction of the standard lot of trading in government securities from $1 million to $250000, to stimulate the interest of the smaller and individual investors.
51. Lee Sheng-Yi 'Public Enterprise and Economic Development in Singapore', *Malayan Economic Review* (October 1976) pp. 49–73.
52. See E. S. Shaw, *Financial Deepening in Economic Development* (New York: Oxford University Press, 1973). R. I. McKinnon, *Money and Capital in*

Economic Development (Washington: Brookings Institution, 1973); R. I. McKinnon (ed.), *Money and Finance in Economic Growth and Development* (New York: Marcel Dekker, 1976); and Symposium on Finance in Developing Countries, *Journal of Development Studies* (January 1977) pp. 1–143.

53. Lee Sheng-Yi and Y. C. Jao, *Financial Structures*, pp. 211–15; 294.
54. Currently, there is a rumour that Asia Commercial Banking Corporation (ACBC) may be merged with OUB, as the managing director of OUB (Mr Lee Hee Seng) has recently been appointed as Chairman of ACBC.
55. In contrast, in Hong Kong's banking crisis in 1965, 14 local licensed banks were merged with foreign banks and financial institutions. As in 1982, of the 34 local licensed banks, only 15 are independent of foreign participation and control: see Lee Sheng-Yi and Y. C. Jao, *Financial Structures*, pp. 14; 236; table 2.4.
56. Lee Sheng-Yi and Y. C. Jao, *Financial Structures*, pp. 216–18.
57. See Lee Sheng-Yi, 'ASEAN Finance Corporation', Singapore–Chinese commemoration of 75th Anniversary (1981); Michael T. Skully, *Merchant Banking in ASEAN: A Regional Examination of its Development and Operations* (Kuala Lumpur: Oxford University Press, 1982).
58. Lee Sheng-Yi, *Monetary and Banking Development*, pp. 163–5, particularly table 9.4.
59. John R. Hewson, 'Monetary Policy and the Asian Dollar Market', MAS, *Papers on Monetary Economics* (Singapore University Press, 1981) pp. 171–4.
60. The arguments in favour of permitting free market rates of interest for government securities are represented in Lee Sheng-Yi, *Monetary and Banking Development*, pp. 160–1.

6 Financial Institutions and Markets in Thailand

MICHAEL T. SKULLY

INTRODUCTION

(a) The Setting

The Kingdom of Thailand consists of territory of some 514000 square kilometres and borders Burma to the north and west, Laos to the north and east, and Kampuchea and Malaysia respectively to the southeast and southwest. Though strategically located in terms of South East Asia, it is positioned near a number of insurgent actions (along the Burma, Malaysian, and Lao borders, and of course the Kampuchea conflict). In addition to the uncertainty and damage these events cause within Thailand, they have also produced a substantial resettlement problem with Kampuchean and Lao refugee camps located in the eastern half of the country.

Thailand is only indirectly involved in these conflicts, but its government has long been aware of the potential problems they may cause, particularly in respect to the country's own insurgency problems. As a result, a series of government programmes have been implemented to improve the lot of Thai farmers, diversify the economy away from its dependence on agriculture and reduce the income disparity between the country's rich and poor. There is little question that these measures have helped ensure a strong economic performance in terms of growth of GDP (7 per cent average increase over the last 12 years); whether the objectives have been accomplished is another matter. Rather than reducing the income disparities, the position has in fact become worse – particularly in rural areas.[1] As one study found, 'about 25 per cent of the population lives in extreme poverty [and]

MAP 6.1   Thailand

Source: Australian Department of Trade and Resources, 1982.

the gap between the relatively wealthy urban Thai and his country cousin in the north, northeast and south is becoming a major concern'.[2] As shown in Table 6.1, while the manufacturing sector is now the second largest component of the economy, many industries that have developed are based primarily on import substitution and are not necessarily the best suited for the Thai economy. As one writer explained, they are 'insufficiently export orientated; heavily dependent on imported raw materials, intermediate goods and machinery; use an excessive proportion of imported energy; remain concentrated in Bangkok; have insufficient linkage with agriculture; and are insufficiently labour intensive'.[3]

These industries were nevertheless quite successful until the mid-1970s, when energy costs and world trade began to affect their competitiveness and Thailand's overall economic position. In 1980, with the assistance of World Bank consultants, a massive structural adjustment programme was developed for the Thai economy. Its emphasis was to reduce the country's dependence on heavily protected, import substitution business and concentrate on export orientated industries instead. These (together with the government's own Five Year Plan) are intended to encourage future investment in, and restructuring of, 10 key industries with export potential. These include vehicle assembly; electronics and

TABLE 6.1 Thailand Gross Domestic Product by industry origin, 1981

	% of GDP
Agriculture, fishery, forestry	24.2
Mining & quarrying	1.6
Manufacturing	20.8
Construction	5.5
Electricity & water supply	1.9
Transportation & communication	6.4
Wholesale & retail trade	16.6
Banking, insurance & real estate	6.3
Ownership of dwellings	1.5
Public administration & defence	4.3
Services	10.7
Total	100.0

Source: Bank of America, *Thailand: Economic Update* (October 1982) Appendix 2.

electric appliances (1982); chemical and plastic products (1983); iron and steel (1984); textiles (1985); and wood, rubber, leather products and food processing (1986).

It is hoped that this new direction in industrial policy will be reflected in a much improved economic position, but any such benefits will come only in the longer term. At present, the new industries will require substantial investment in new plant and equipment and will very much work against – not help – the country's already troubled balance of payments. To cover these potential problems, Thailand has arranged some massive borrowings from the IMF/World Bank group as well as other international public and private sources. These monies, however, will provide only part of the funds required, and Thailand's own financial sector will be called upon to provide the rest.

(b) An Overview of the Financial Sector

Unlike the other ASEAN countries, Thailand retained its full independence during the European powers' colonisation of Asia, and as such might be expected to have had a somewhat different financial structure to its neighbours. In practice, however, many of the same foreign banks – such as the Hongkong and Shanghai Banking Corporation and the Chartered Bank – were the first to establish the local banking industry as in the other countries, and (at least on the surface) the sector itself has been similarly structured in its development.

The commercial banks (initially foreign and, much later, domestic ones) soon replaced the private moneylenders as the major force in the local financial sector. These were later supplemented by some specialist rural lending institutions and government bodies. More recently, other specialist institutions – particularly non-banking ones – developed, as did the money market and stock exchanges. The major types of financial institution in Thailand, together with their respective total assets, are shown in Table 6.2.

As shown in Table 6.2, the commercial banks are by far the most important, accounting for some 67.4 per cent of the financial sector's total assets. The finance companies are the second largest, but with only a 14.6 per cent share spread over some 112 companies (compared to only 30 banks), their relative significance within the market is very much smaller. The other institutions are primarily government owned or controlled insti-

TABLE 6.2 Thailand financial institutions by total assets, 1981 (figures as at end 1981, in million baht)

% of total	Institution	Total assets
67.0	Commercial banks (30)[a]	353172.4
14.6	Finance and securities companies (112)	76896.7
1.5	Life insurance companies (12)	8085.0[b]
1.3	Agricultural co-operatives (906)	6751.8[b]
1.1	Savings co-operatives (336)	5566.3[b]
0.6	Pawnshops (321)	3326.1[b]
1.0	Credit foncier companies (33)	5124.9
5.9	Government savings bank (1)	31173.2
3.7	Bank for Agriculture and Agricultural Cooperatives (1)	19336.3
1.1	Industrial Finance Corporation of Thailand (1)	5532.1
2.2	Government Housing Bank (1)	11742.0
—	Small Industrial Finance Office (1)	55.2
100.0	Total	526762.0

[a] Figures in parenthesis show no. of companies of each type.
[b] Estimated.

Source: Bank of Thailand, 1982.

tutions of which the Bank of Thailand (unfortunately excluded in Table 6.2) is the most important. Also unreflected in these statistics are the substantial number of unlicensed moneylenders, who comprise a major portion of Thailand's so called 'unorganised' money market.[4]

FINANCIAL INSTITUTIONS

The Thai financial sector comprises a wide range of financial institutions, most of which are dealt with during this discussion. These include the Bank of Thailand; the commercial banks; the Government Savings Bank (GSB); the Government Housing Bank (GHB); the Bank for Agriculture and Agricultural Co-operatives (BAAC); the Small Industries Finance Office (SIFO); the Industrial Finance Corporation of Thailand (IFCT); the finance and securities companies; general insurance companies; reinsurance companies; life insurance companies; credit foncier companies; agricultural co-operatives; pawnshops; mutual funds;

provident funds; and (although not established) the discount houses.

(a) The Bank of Thailand

The Bank of Thailand was established on 10 December 1942 under the Bank of Thailand Act BE 2485 (1942) as the country's Central Bank. It developed from the work of the Thai National Bank Bureau which had been formed in 1939 to perform certain central bank activities and to organise the formation of a full central banking institution. The Bank of Thailand subsequently assumed the duties and the net assets of the Bureau.[5] It also assumed the note issuing functions previously conducted by the Ministry of Finance's Currency Division.[6]

The Bank is currently managed by an 11 member Court (rather than a Board) of Directors chaired by the Bank's Governor. Both the Governor and Deputy Governor (who is also the Vice-chairman) are appointed by the King on the Cabinet's recommendation, and serve until they either resign or are replaced by the government. The other members are appointed by the Cabinet on the advice of the Minister of Finance and similarly serve at the pleasure of the government of the day.

As a Central Bank, the Bank of Thailand's major functions are to act as the national note issuing authority within the country; serve as the fiscal agent of the government; provide specific banking services to the commercial banks and other financial institutions; and advise on and carry out the government's monetary and credit management policies. In addition, the Bank is authorised by the Ministry of Finance to supervise Thailand's commercial banks and finance, securities and credit foncier companies; manage the government's debt and international reserves; administer the exchange control system; and represent and advise the government in its relations with international financial organisations.

(i) *Note issuing activities*

The Bank of Thailand has the sole right to issue bank notes within Thailand. Their issue is controlled under the Currency Act BE 2501 (1958), which requires that all currency be fully backed by assets and that 60 per cent of these be in the form of gold, foreign currency and foreign assets with a maturity of one year or less. As

TABLE 6.3   Bank of Thailand assets and liabilities (figures as at
end June 1982, in million baht)

Assets

Foreign assets	58706.7
Gold	(22871.4)
Foreign Exchange	(33973.4)
Holdings of SDRs	(359.4)
Contribution to IMF	
Gold	(896.8)
Foreign Exchange	—
SDRs	(605.7)
Baht contribution to IMF	6456.0
Claims on central government	80285.2
Balance at provincial treasuries	(21967.4)
Treasury bills	(5403.2)
Government bonds[a]	(48781.5)
IFCT debentures	—
Loans and rediscounts for IFCT	(652.2)
Loans and rediscounts for BAAC	(3500.0)
Coins in Issue Department	(7.9)
Claims on commercial banks	
and financial institutions	22154.3
Loans	(5383.2)
Rediscounts	(16771.1)
Other assets	181.8
Total assets	167784.0

Liabilities

Notes in circulation	52494.6
Deposits	18208.7
Central government	(11564.3)
Counterpart funds	—
Private sector	(319.9)
Commercial banks	(5990.6)
Government Savings Bank	(6.3)
Other financial institutions	(327.6)
Allocations of SDRs	2266.2
IMF holding of baht[b]	22580.9
Loans from trust fund[b]	3505.7
Other foreign liabilities[c]	1151.1
Capital accounts	67565.2
Other liabilites	11.6
Total liabilities	167784.0

[a] Including IBRD participation certificate and Tin Buffer Stock
certificate.
[b] Formerly published as liabilities to IMF.
[c] Including liabilities to non-residents in baht.

Source: Bank of Thailand, *Quarterly Bulletin* (June 1982), pp. 6–7.

shown in Table 6.3, as of June 1982 the Bank of Thailand had 52494.6 million baht of notes outstanding (31.3 per cent of the Bank's total liabilities and capital). Its foreign assets holding of 58706.7 million substantially exceeded the Act's requirements.

(ii) *Fiscal agent to the government*

As the fiscal agent of the Thai government, the Bank of Thailand fulfills a paying and receiving role for government's revenue and expenditure and for government enterprises. It also provides normal bank services for these clients – current accounts; credit facilities; and foreign exchange transactions. In terms of credit, the Bank's maximum unsecured short term loans and advances to the government are limited under the Bank of Thailand Act to an amount equal to 25 per cent of the Government's annual budget. The Bank lends to the government mainly by purchasing Treasury bills and government bonds. As was shown in Table 6.3, the Bank's holdings of these securities as of June 1982 were respectively 5403.2 and 48781.5 million. Together they comprised 32.3 per cent of the Bank's total assets. The Bank of Thailand also makes longer term loans in support of certain government development programmes.

(iii) *Banker to the commercial banks*

In its role as banker to the commercial banks and certain other financial institutions, the Bank of Thailand serves as the depository for their legal reserve requirements and provides certain lender of last resort facilities to the commercial banks. These loans may be made on a discretionary basis against government and government guaranteed bonds or through the purchase of certain promissory notes through the Bank's rediscount window. As was shown in Table 6.3, such claims on financial institutions comprised 22154.3 million (or 13.2 per cent of the Bank of Thailand's total assets), and of these rediscounts were more significant. The discretionary loans are intended as a true lender of last resort facility, with the interest rate varied in line with market conditions. The amount available and the rate charged varies with a bank's total deposits. The banks have made extensive use of this borrowing facility, but with the Bank of Thailand's establishment of a government securities repurchase market such borrowings are expected to decline in importance.

The promissory note rediscounting facility, while also providing liquidity support, is designed to encourage bank lending to certain sectors such as exports, agriculture, and certain industries by discounting their bills or promissory notes at concessional rates of interest. The IFCT and the BAAC also have access to this 'window', as have at times the finance and securities companies. These advances have increased steadily over recent years, but the total volume remains relatively small due to the administrative costs and loan rate ceiling such rediscounting entails.

As an additional banking service, the Bank also handles the daily clearing of cheques within the Bangkok metropolitan area, helps organise similar centres at the provincial level, and arranges the transfer of funds between the provincial and Bangkok clearing facilities. Its three provincial branches at Hat Yai (Southern Region); Khonkaen (Northern Region); and Lampang (also Northern Region) assist in this process.

(iv) *Monetary policy*

Perhaps the Bank's most important role is the maintenance and control of Thailand's money supply and monetary policy. Its goal is to obtain monetary stability while maintaining sound economic growth within the country. In this, price stability has recently been a particular problem, with external factors such as the energy crisis adversely affecting the domestic economy.

The Bank implements its monetary policies by a number of means. Potentially the most important is the direct controls it can exercise over the financial sector through its administration of a variety of statutes. These (which include the Bank of Thailand Act; the Currency Act; the Exchange Control Act BE 2485 (1942); the Commercial Banking Act BE 2505 (1962); and the Finance, Securities and Credit Foncier Business Act BE 2502 (1979) allow the Bank to set the legal reserve asset ratios, risk assets : capital ratios; the maximum interest rates on loans and deposits; and the amount of credit allocated to certain types of customers. Besides these statutory measures, the Bank can also implement a number of policy instruments in line with economic conditions (the use of rediscounting facilities is probably the most important). The Bank of Thailand's Governor may use his own position to influence financial institution policy by way of moral suasion. In recent years the Bank has tried to make more use of the second category and implement monetary policy by way of more general market orientated policies; it has also been more active as a stabilising force within the financial sector and in developing new institutions and instruments.

(b) The Commercial Banks

The commercial banks are one of the oldest (as well as the largest) of Thailand's financial institutions. As was shown in Table 6.2, they comprise some 67 per cent of the financial sector's total assets, and play a major role in both the mobilisation and allocation of the country's capital resources. At the end of 1981, for example, commercial banks accounted respectively for 70.2 and 68.8 per cent of Thai household saving at (and the credit extended by) financial institutions. This section examines the development of commercial banking in Thailand; the industry's market structure; its legislative controls; lending, deposits and its possible offshore role.

(i) *Development*

Thai's banking (in a modern sense) can trace its birth to 2 December 1888, when the Hongkong and Shanghai Banking Corporation opened its first branch in Bangkok. It was followed 6 years later by the Chartered Bank and, as shown in Table 6.4, a total of 12 banks were formed prior to the Second World War; five of these were incorporated in Thailand. The oldest of these Thai banks, The Siam Commercial Bank, was established on 30 January 1906, and developed from the Thai 'Book Club'[7] which had been founded 4 October 1904. The Second World War and the Japanese presence in Thiland later forced the foreign banks to suspend operations, and during 1942–5 another five Thai banks opened to replace them. Additional local and foreign banks were established or re-established after the war, up until 1955 (when the Thai Cabinet passed a resolution to restrict the approval of new banks).[8] Since then, it has been more difficult to obtain licences and new foreign entry is permitted only where a bank of that country is not already represented, or for reasons of reciprocity. The last foreign bank to establish operations – the German based European Asian Bank – was successful due to both the lack of previous German representation and a desire by the Thai Farmers' Bank to open a branch in Germany.

TABLE 6.4 Thailand commercial banks by local establishment date and nationality[a]

Bank	Nationality	Year of opening
The Hong Kong and Shanghai Bank Ltd	Hong Kong	1888
The Chartered Bank	UK	1894
Banque de L'Indochine Ltd	French	1897
Siam Commercial Bank Ltd	Thai	1906
Four Seas Communication Bank Ltd	Chinese	1909
The Bank of Canton Ltd	Chinese	1919
Mercantile Bank Ltd	British	1923
Wang Lee Bank Ltd	Thai	1933
Tan Peng Chun Bank Ltd	Thai	1934
Yokohama Specie Bank Ltd	Japanese	1936
The Bank of Asia Ltd	Thai	1939
The Siam City Bank	Thai	1941
The Provincial Bank Ltd	Thai	1942
The Bangkok Bank of Commerce Ltd	Thai	1944
Bankgkok Bank Ltd	Thai	1944
Bank of Ayudhya Ltd	Thai	1945
The Thai Farmers' Bank Ltd	Thai	1945
Bank of China Ltd	Chinese	1947
Indian Oversea Bank Ltd	Indian	1947
The Laem Thong Bank Ltd	Thai	1948
The Union Bank of Bangkok Ltd	Thai	1949
The Thai Danu Bank Ltd	Thai	1949
The Nationale Hansdales Bank NV	Dutch	1949
Bank of America NT & SA	American	1949
Agricultural Bank Ltd	Thai	1950
Bangkok Metropolitan Bank Ltd	Thai	1950
The Mitsui Bank Ltd	Japanese	1952
The Thai Military Bank Ltd	Thai	1957
First Bangkok City Bank Ltd	Thai	1960
The Bank of Tokyo	Japanese	1962
The Chase Manhattan Bank NA	American	1964
United Malayan Banking Corpn Ltd	Malaysian	1964
The Asia Trust Bank Ltd	Thai	1965
The Krung Thai Bank Ltd[a]	Thai	1966
The European Asian Bank NV	German	1978

[a] This Table reflects historical establishment details only. Yokoham Species Bank, for example, did not survive the Second World War, the Bank of China is now the International Commercial Bank of China, and the Four Seas Communications Bank is Singapore based.

[b] Formed in March 1966 as a result of a merger between the Bank of Agriculture and The Provincial Bank.

Source: Bank of Thailand, 1982.

(ii) *Market structure*

The Thai banking industry is dominated by the Bangkok Bank which is the largest domestic bank within Thailand and the second largest in ASEAN.[9] As shown in Table 6.5, it accounts for 36.8 per cent of the domestic banks' total asset and 34.8 per cent of the overall banking sector within Thailand. Besides the Bangkok Bank, the Krung Thai Bank and the Thai Farmers' Bank are also large institutions, in respect both of the local banking industry and of the region. This position means that the top three banks in Thailand together control 60.2 per cent of the industry.

Due to their operating and branching restrictions, the foreign banks have continued to lose ground in terms of asset growth, and in 1981 together held only a 5.3 per cent share of the sector's assets (compared to 10.8 per cent in 1971). Individually, the foreign banks appear even less important in terms of assets. In 1981, for example, the largest locally (the Chase Manhattan Bank) ranks 14th among Thailand's 30 banks, and is smaller than all but two of the domestic institutions.

This evaluation by size, however, understates the importance of the foreign banks, for within the market these institutions often concentrate only on certain areas of wholesale banking. Much of the foreign bank business is done offshore, and is not reflected in local asset holdings.

In terms of the domestic market, the relative asset holdings of the Bangkok Bank, Krung Thai Bank and Thai Farmers' Bank only partially reflect the degree of concentration within Thai banking. Of equal importance are the banks' equity links with the major Thai–Chinese business families. Most domestic banks were established by Thai–Chinese trading house interests to help finance their own operations. Most have retained these early connections, and to this day such major institutions as the Bangkok Bank (Sophonpanich family), Thai Farmers' Bank (Lamsam family), Bank of Ayudhya (Ratanarak family), the Bangkok Metropolitan Bank (Telapaibul family), and the Bank of Asia (Euachukiates family) are all effectively family controlled institutions.[10] The government is also an important factor in Thai bank ownership. Besides its more than 90 per cent shareholding in the Krung Thai Bank and the BAAC, the government is also a minority shareholder in the Siam Commercial Bank, the Bangkok Bank, the First Bangkok City Bank, the Bank of

TABLE 6.5   Thailand commercial banks by total assets (figures at end year, in million baht)

Bank	1971 Assets	1971 Market share (%)	1981 Assets	1981 Market share (%)
Domestic banks				
Bangkok Bank Ltd	15559	31.6	146557	36.8
Krung Thai Bank Ltd	8486	17.2	51906	13.0
Thai Farmers' Bank Ltd	3534	7.2	54685	13.7
Siam Commercial Bank Ltd	2662	5.4	22533	5.7
Bank of Ayudhya Ltd	3426	6.9	18387	4.6
Bangkok Metropolitan Bank Ltd	2443	5.0	18332	4.6
Bangkok Bank of Commerce Ltd	2063	4.2	17625	4.4
First Bangkok City Bank Ltd	1680	3.4	14270	3.6
Siam City Bank Ltd	2177	4.4	11953	3.0
Thai Military Bank Ltd	1865	3.8	11433	2.9
Asia Trust Bank Ltd	1088	2.2	8036	2.0
Bank of Asia Ltd	1289	2.6	8022	2.0
Union Bank of Bangkok Ltd	1722	3.5	6358	1.6
Thai Danu Bank Ltd	760	1.5	3859	1.0
Laem Thong Bank Ltd	492	1.0	2449	0.6
Wang Lee Bank Ltd	17	0.1	2151	0.5
Total domestic banks	49263	100.0	398556	100.00
Banks incorporated abroad				
Mitsui Bank Ltd	831	13.9	3257	14.7
Chase Manhattan Bank NA	561	9.4	3544	16.0
Bank of Tokyo Ltd	959	16.0	3536	15.9
Bank of America NT & SA	765	12.8	2645	11.9
United Malayan Banking Corpn Ltd	516	8.6	2613	11.8
Chartered Bank	695	11.6	1296	5.8
Indosuez Bank	271	4.5	1469	6.6
Hongkong & Shanghai Banking Corpn Ltd	604	10.1	1110	5.0
European Asian Bank	—	—	905	4.0
International Commercial Bank of China	276	4.6	1517	2.3
Bharat Overseas Bank	76	1.3	523	2.4
Mercantile Bank	175	2.9	311	1.4
Far Seas Communications Bank	157	2.6	262	1.2
Bank of Canton Ltd	102	1.7	226	1.0
Foreign bank	5988	100.0	22214	100.0
TOTAL BANKS IN THAILAND	55251	n.a.	420770	n.a.

Sources: *Bangkok Bank Monthly Review*, August 1981, p. 293; and the Bank of Thailand, 1982.

Ayudhya, the Thai Military Bank, and the Union Bank of Bangkok. The Crown Property Bureau is also a major shareholder in the Siam Commercial Bank.

These various corporate and government connections suggest that there is a great potential for many Thai bank loans to be made on other than an independent basis, and much of the lending is concentrated on family business. One banker in fact suggested that about 70 per cent of total outstanding credits extended by the banking system at present are granted to bank customers numbering less than 20000 who borrow more than 1 million baht each'.[11] These wealthy family connections also mean that bank loans could be directed for political purposes as well. As one study concluded, the 'political influence on banking is strong. Some banks have generals and prominent politicians as chairmen or directors'.[12]

These connections have also helped to make Thai bankers somewhat more political than in other countries, with many former bankers assuming high government office. The presence of former Bangkok Bank executives within the Thai government is such that they are sometimes referred to collectively as the 'Bangkok Bank Mafia'.[13] The senior management of the banks themselves are often heavily involved in their own business operations, and (as the Governor of the Bank of Thailand complained) many 'leave too little time for the daily management of their banks'.[14]

Besides concentration in terms of assets and corporate connections, Thai banking is also heavily concentrated in terms of branch locations, with approximately a third of its 1500 branches located within Bangkok. This concentration would be even stronger were it not for substantial restrictions in new metropolitan (as opposed to rural branch) openings. Since 1978, however, even rural branches have become less attractive, since new branches are expected to relend approximately 60 per cent of the deposits they collect within that region, and that a third of these must be for agricultural related purposes. These measures have to some extent helped redress the problem of rural deposits being used to finance Bangkok based lending, and in May 1982 provincial loans comprised 25.9 per cent of total bank advances.

As of May 1982, Thailand's 16 domestic banks had 1579 branches within Thailand, and the 14 foreign banks 20 branches. In addition to their domestic branches, the Thai banks since 1955 have established representation overseas and at the end of

September 1982 had 19 branches in such countries as Hong Kong; Japan; Singapore; England; Malaysia; Taiwan; the USA; Indonesia; Germany; and Macau.

(iii) *Regulation*

The banking sector is regulated by the Bank of Thailand and the Ministry of Finance under the Commercial Banking Act 1962 (revised in 1979). These provide for a number of fairly standard ratios, as well as some interesting ownership requirements introduced in the 1979 amendments. The Bank of Thailand Act and the Currency Act are also of importance, and are discussed elsewhere.

The basic ratios include a capital : risk asset gearing limit 1 : 8.5 in 1982); a reserve requirement ratio (a total at 7 per cent : 2 per cent on deposit with the Bank of Thailand, not more than 2.5 per cent in government securities, not more than 2.5 per cent in cash on hand); and a maximum loan limit to any one person equal to 25 per cent of the bank's capital. There are also provisions for selective credit controls and more specific capital : asset ratios, but these have not been formally applied. Other powers include maximum interest rate ceilings; conditions for opening new branches; and foreign exchange controls.

The 1979 amendments seek to reduce the concentration of ownership and control that characterises Thai banking. The banks' shareholdings in other companies are now limited individually to no more than 10 per cent of that company's share outstanding, and in aggregate to no more than 20 per cent of the banks' shareholders' funds. It also limits an individual shareholding in a commercial bank to no more than 5 per cent of the shares outstanding. These requirements effectively apply only to new holdings, however, and are generally not retrospective.

Perhaps the most important aspect of the 1979 amendments was the time schedule under which Thailand's largely family controlled banks were to be transformed into investor owned institutions. They required that commercial banks should have at least 250 natural persons, with no more than 0.5 per cent each, holding more than 50 per cent of the banks' shares: three-quarters of these had to be held by Thai citizens. The act provided a 3 year timetable over which this was to be accomplished. In the first year, for example, at least 100 natural persons had to hold 20 per cent of the shares; in the second year, 200 had to hold at least 40 per cent;

at the end of the third year, the end goal of 250 holding at least 50 per cent had to be achieved. The banks can request 6 month extensions at any stage, but the end goal must be reached within 5 years. Most banks reached the first level without much difficulty, but few were able to comply with the second (8 March 1981) deadline of a 40 per cent holding and only three, small and medium size banks were able to meet the third.[15] With the recent optimism in the world securities market, it seems possible that banks could fulfil their quota of shareholders by 8 March 1984, but many bankers remain doubtful. There is a fine for non-compliance, but what is more worrying is the suggestion that a government sponsored mutual fund – the Financial Institution Development Fund – might be used to purchase the necessary holdings.

(iv) *Uses of funds*

As shown in Table 6.6, the commercial banks devote approximately three-quarters of their assets to bills, loans and overdrafts. Their other assets are held primarily in the form of cash or easily marketable securities, both to fulfil Bank of Thailand regulations and to ensure adequate liquidity.

In terms of bank lending, Thailand's banking system developed primarily to finance foreign and domestic trade, and today trade financing still accounts for a major portion of bank advances. As shown in Table 6.7, for example, the banks' import, export and domestic trade together comprised some 42.6 per cent of all bank advances. Manufacturing is the next major group. Loans for agricultural purposes, despite the Bank of Thailand's efforts, are relatively low in comparison. Nevertheless, 1981's 6.2 per cent shows improvement over 1980's 5.6, and a marked increase from 1976 when agriculture's share was only 2.1 per cent. Since 1979, each bank has been required to direct an amount equal to 13 per cent of its deposits to the agricultural sector: 2 per cent of this can be to agro-based industry, but the other 11 per cent must be either lent to farmers or deposited with the BAAC.

The banks are not against rural lending as such. The problem is that these loans are both risky and expensive to administer; many banks when lending for agricultural purposes often prefer to advance the fund collectively to a group of farmers, rather than lend to each farmer on an individual basis.)

Most bank loan interest rates are set on a floating rate basis,

TABLE 6.6   Thailand commercial banks by asset type (figures as
at end May 1982, in million baht)

Cash and balances at banks	*33276.6*
Cash on hand	5671.8
Foreign currency on hand	274.5
Balances at banks:	
Bank of Thailand	6824.2
Other banks in Thailand	9814.1
Banks abroad	10692.0
Cash items in process of collection	*1684.8*
Investments	*44976.2*
Central government securities	
Treasury bills	916.0
Bonds	38700.9
Domestic securities	
IFCT shares & debentures	280.5
Private	4822.0
Foreign securities	256.8
Bills, loans and overdrafts	*279437.8*
Bills:	
Domestic	51962.9
Import	6103.0
Export	10322.2
Trust receipts	13296.6
Loans & overdrafts:	
Private residents	197644.0
Banks in Thailand	14.0
Non-residents	95.1
Fixed & other assets	*19847.7*
Total assets	*379223.1*

Source: Bank of Thailand, *Quarterly Bulletin* (June 1982) pp. 8–9.

subject to a government regulated interest ceiling. Until 1980, the
maximum bank lending rate by law was 15 per cent; it now stands
at 19 per cent. The rates actually charged are subject to
negotiation, but are commonly set against a 'prime rate' base
point. The prime rate used is usually set by the big five of Thai
commercial banking (the Bangkok Bank; Krung Thai Bank; Thai
Farmers' Bank; Bank of Ayudhya; and the Siam Commercial
Bank). In theory, these banks and the rest of the industry charge
this rate, as the name implies, to their best customers; the others
pay something greater. In practice, many customers pay much
less, and the rate chosen often varies not only from bank to bank
but also from branch to branch.[16]

TABLE 6.7 Thailand commercial banks bills, loans and overdrafts by industry type (figures as at end December 1981, in million baht)

% of total	Industry	Amount
6.2	Agriculture	16042.1
0.7	Mining	1806.7
22.6	Manufacturing	58329.3
5.1	Construction	13033.5
2.7	Real estate business	6972.7
9.7	Imports	25110.1
10.1	Exports	26077.0
22.8	Wholesale & retail trade	58816.9
2.3	Public utilities	5963.5
4.9	Banking & other financial business	12748.4
4.7	Services	12032.3
8.2	Personal consumption	21184.9
100.0	Total	258117.4

Source: Bank of Thailand, *Quarterly Bulletin* (June 1982) pp. 16–17.

Most bank advances are made in the form of an overdraft, and in theory are of a short term, temporary nature. In practice, most overdrafts are easily renewed and sometimes used for medium as well as short term lending. The banks also grant some direct short and medium term advances, and provide bill discount facilities, particularly in respect of trade and agriculture. While the rates are effectively much the same for each type of lending, the rediscount rates on certain types of bill facilities are subsidised by the Bank of Thailand to encourage specific activities; these categories include some bills for exports; agriculture; and industrial undertakings.

TABLE 6.8 Thailand bank credit card plans

VISA	Thai Farmers' Bank
	Siam Commercial Bank
	Bank of America
Master Card	Thai Farmers' Bank
	Hongkong and Shanghai Bank
	Siam Commercial Bank
Thai Farmers' Card	Thai Farmers' Bank
Multi Purpose Card	Bangkok Metropolitan Bank

Source: 'Baht Credit Cards: American Express Comes In', Bangkok Bank, *Monthly Review* (October 1981) p. 403.

As an adjunct to their consumer lending activities, some banks also offer credit cards to their customers. As shown in Table 6.8, there were four bank credit card schemes in operation in 1981. In addition, American Express (Thailand) – a venture owned 22.5 per cent by American Express, 55 per cent by the Bangkok Bank and 22.5 per cent by SEA Tours – and Diners' Club (Thailand) both issue their respective credit cards locally.

(v) *Sources of funds*

As shown in Table 6.9, the Thai banking industry obtains most of its funds by way of deposits – some 74 per cent in 1982. Borrowings from other banks are also important, and accounted for additional 12.6 per cent of the banking sector's assets and liabilities. The bank's own funds provided another 6.1 per cent.

TABLE 6.9   Thailand commercial banks' capital and liabilities by type (figures as at end May 1982, in million baht)

	Amount
Demand deposits	*29797.1*
Banks in Thailand	5096.1
Central government	3793.8
Private residents	20094.5
Non-residents	812.7
Savings deposits	*43193.2*
Banks in Thailand	3.0
Central government	1191.6
Private residents	41741.6
Non-residents	257.0
Time deposits	*204558.1*
Banks in Thailand	26.4
Central government	6364.9
Private residents	197366.0
Non-residents	800.8
Other demand liabilities	*4423.7*
Marginal deposits	*281.9*
Borrowings	*47863.7*
Bank of Thailand	22806.5
Other banks in Thailand	3100.6
Banks abroad	21956.6
Capital accounts	*23281.8*
Other liabilities	*25823.6*
Total liabilities	*379223.1*

Source: Bank of Thailand, *Quarterly Bulletin* (June 1982) pp. 8–9.

The remaining percentage was composed of a variety of miscellaneous categories.

As shown in Table 6.9 also, commercial bank deposits come in three basic varieties: demand, savings and time. Of these, time deposits are the most important and in 1982 accounted for some 72.5 per cent of total bank deposits. The interest paid on time deposits varies with the term of the deposit itself, and in mid 1982, 3–6 month deposits earned 10 per cent; 6–12 month 11 per cent; 1–2 years 13 per cent; and over 2 years 14 per cent. Neither current accounts (demand deposits) nor fixed deposits withdrawn within less than 3 months earn interest; savings deposits earn interest at 9 per cent per annum, and may be withdrawn at any time.

The Bank of Thailand has the power to set bank deposit rates, and traditionally the maximum rate allowable is also that offered by the banks. In September 1982, however, the Bank of Thailand encouraged the banking sector to drop their deposit and lending rates on their own initiative as a step towards a more market orientated interest rate policy.

Bank deposits are a particularly attractive means of investment, as the interest paid is subject only to a 12.5 per cent withholding tax (until 1981 10 per cent): no additional tax is payable. This is particularly attractive to more wealthy investors, and perhaps explains why the Bangkok metropolitan area provides a major proportion of time deposts whereas the rural areas account for the greater share of savings account funds: a breakdown of the specific amounts is shown in Table 6.10.

This withholding tax system on bank deposit interest is to continue until 1986, but in 1987 a new withholding tax reflecting the depositors' personal income tax rates is to be used instead. If adopted as planned, it should have a major impact on the banks' present deposit structure.

In addition to the normal types of deposit, the banks may also accept foreign currency deposits, and in February 1980 the Thai Farmers' Bank became the first Thai bank to raise funds by way of a floating rate certificate of deposit (CD) issue in the Euro Dollar Market. Though the banks would very much like to issue CDs within Thailand as well, since 1979 this matter has been under discussion with the various regulatory bodies; apparently CDs are not presently covered under the Thai commercial code, and some amendment will be required to produce the correct legal environment.

TABLE 6.10   Thailand commercial banks deposit type by source
(figures as at end February 1981, in million baht)

Deposit	Bangkok metropolis	Other provinces	Total
Demand	21833.5	6654.9	28488.4
Savings	13833.2	14979.1	28812.3
Time	99308.6	63183.5	162492.1

Source: Bank of Thailand, *Quarterly Bulletin* (March 1981) p. 12.

(vi) *Foreign bank representative offices and offshore banking.*

As of December 1982, there were 25 foreign banks with representative offices in Thailand – 13 North American; three French, eight Japanese; and one Korean: their names and establishment dates are shown in Table 6.11. These numbers have increased sharply in recent years due to Thailand's foreign borrowing requirements and, to a lesser extent, the possibility of an offshore banking centre being established in Bangkok.

The Bank of Thailand has apparently already conducted a feasibility study on offshore banking, and determined a number of preconditions before such a project may proceed. The Thai commercial codes, for example, require amendment to allow any Offshore Banking Units (OBUs) a special concessionary tax rate of 10 per cent (rather than the normal 40 per cent). The Commercial Banking Act would also require amendment, as would the foreign exchange control system. Bangkok's telecommunication system would also need substantial improvement.

The specifics of any OBU operations are yet to be determined, but basically the government is aware that to attract new business (and thus more taxation revenues and employment) it will need to allow the OBUs some access to the local market. Some suggest a 30 per cent local : 70 per cent offshore business ratio, while others recommend a set dollar limit for an OBU's domestic advances.[17] Probably a very restricted local wholesale licence – with its domestic business subject to normal Thai banking laws and its offshore business conducted through a separate regulated OBU – would be the best compromise.

The relationship established between those banks with a local representative office and those obtaining an OBU licence remains to be seen. One publication, however, reported that in considering

TABLE 6.11   Thailand foreign representative offices by establishment date and nationality

Bank	Nationality	Establishment date in Thailand
The Export–Import Bank of Japan	Japanese	15 Aug. 1957
Manufacturers' Hanover Trust Company	American	Jul. 1968
Korea Exchange Bank	Korean	10 Feb. 1970
Banque Francaise du Commerce Extérieur	French	Jun. 1970
Continental Illinois National Bank and Trust Company of Chicago	American	16 Jun. 1971
Société Generale	French	1 Mar. 1976
Bankers' Trust Company	American	17 Nov. 1976
Banque Nationale de Paris	French	1 Nov. 1977
The Bank of California NA	American	30 Aug. 1979
Chemical Bank	American	7 Sept. 1979
Crocker National Bank	American	5 Oct. 1979
Citibank NA	American	1 Feb. 1980
First Interstate Bank of California	American	17 Jun. 1980
The Bank of Nova Scotia	Canadian	15 Oct. 1980
Wells Fargo Bank	American	17 Nov. 1980
The Royal Bank of Canada	Canadian	1 Jun. 1981
Security Pacific National Bank	American	9 Jul. 1981
Banque de Paris et des Pays-Bas	French	1 Jan. 1982
The Sumitomo Bank Ltd	Japanese	18 Jan. 1982
The Sanwa Bank Ltd	Japanese	16 Feb. 1982
The Tokai Bank Ltd	Japanese	17 Feb. 1982
The Dai-Ichi Kangyo Bank Ltd	Japanese	1 Mar. 1982
The Long Term Credit Bank of Japan Ltd	Japanese	5 Mar. 1982
The Fuji Bank Ltd	Japanese	25 Mar. 1982
The Mitsubishi Bank Ltd	Japanese	21 Dec. 1982
The Taiyo Kobe Bank Ltd	Japanese	Expected 1983
The First National Bank of Boston	American	Expected 1983
The Philadelphia National Bank	American	Expected 1983

Source: Bank of Thailand, 1982.

applicants the Bank of Thailand might 'prefer to upgrade existing representative offices rather than grant new licences to banks hitherto having no presence in Thailand'.[18] As there are no significant restrictions on establishing representative offices in Thailand and the fifth 5 Year National Development Plan will require substantial borrowings, many other banks may also consider a Thai representative office worthwhile.

(c) The Government Savings Bank (GSB)

The GSB is the largest government owned financial institution after the Bank of Thailand; in 1981, its assets of 31173.2 million baht comprised 5.9 per cent of the financial sector's total assets.

The GSB commenced operations on 1 April 1913 as the Royal Treasury's Savings Office with a 100000 baht grant from the then King of Thailand. The office was later transferred in 1929 to the Post and Telegraph Department where it operated under the Postal Savings Office. In 1947 it was reconstituted under the Savings Bank Act BE 2489 (1946), and expanded to provide a full banking operation, the role it still fulfils today.

The GSB invests most of its funds in government securities – in

TABLE 6.12   Government Savings Bank assets and liabilities (figures as at end May 1982, in million baht)

Assets	
Cash and balances at bank	1809.7
Notes & coin	197.5
Balances at banks	
Bank of Thailand	21.8
Commercial banks	1590.4
BAAC	—
Cash items in process of collection	13.8
Loans & overdrafts	2143.5
Private sector	(590.3)
Government enterprises	(1553.2)
Claims on central government	27699.9
Government securities	(27699.8)
Balances at provincial treasuries	(0.1)
Claims on IFCT	8.0
Other assets	1351.8
Total assets	33026.7
Liabilities	
Private sector deposits	26582.3
Demand deposits	(197.2)
Time & savings deposits	(26385.1)
Government enterprise deposits	198.4
Commercial bank demand deposits	6.6
Savings bonds & premium savings bonds	1970.2
Insurance	124.6
Capital accounts	2322.8
Other liabilities	1821.8
Total liabilities	33026.7

Source: Bank of Thailand, *Quarterly Bulletin* (June 1982) pp. 20–1.

May 1982 these accounted for 83.9 per cent of the Bank's assets. Through its Banking Department, it also makes overdrafts and other advances to individuals and business enterprises. As shown in Table 6.12, loans to public sector enterprises are the most important; in May 1982, these accounted for 4.7 per cent of the GSB's assets compared to 1.8 per cent for the private sector.

In terms of funding, the GSB obtains most of its money through deposits. In May 1982, they accounted for 26787.3 million baht (80.5 per cent of the GSB's total liabilities and capital). They are accepted in the form of demand, savings and fixed deposits; the latter is the most important with a 12 month period being the most popular. Plans for a new type of savings account offering above average interest rates (annouced in mid-1982) may cause savings deposits to become more significant. In addition to deposits, the GSB also raises funds through Giro transfers; savings annuities; deposits for housing; travellers' and gift cheques; premium savings certificates and savings bonds and life endowment policies and education annuities. Of these, only the premium savings certificates and savings bonds are significant; in May 1982 they together accounted for 1970.2 million baht (6 per cent of the GSB's funds).

The GSB has the most extensive branch network of the banks in Thailand, with 416 offices at the end of 1981. In addition, it also operates a number of mobile (and even some floating) bank offices to serve the smaller and more remote areas.

(d) The Government Housing Bank (GHB)

The GHB is the fourth largest of Thailand's primarily government owned financial institutions; in 1981, its assets of 11742 million baht comprised 2.2 per cent of the financial sector's total assets.

The GHB was established under the Government Housing Bank Act BE 2496 (1953), to assist middle income families to purchase their own homes; it is wholly owned by the Thai Government and supervised by the Ministry of Finance.

As shown in Table 6.13, the bulk of the GHB funds (some 80 per cent in 1981) are used for loans and advances – primarily for housing related purposes. Of its 1 477 million baht worth of advances in 1981, for example, some 412 million (27.89 per cent) were in the form of mortgage loans to 6645 individual borrowers. The remaining 1065 million was devoted to 446 housing project developments, and included both overdrafts and long term advances. At one time the GHB also bought and developed land for home construction purposes and resold this to customers on instalment basis; in conjunction with the GSB, it sometimes built homes as well. In 1973, however, these development functions were assumed by the National Housing Authority.

Prior to 1973, the GHB's ability to raise funds was limited as it could not accept deposits of less than 2 years. It therefore depended primarily on its own capital and borrowings from the government and the GSB. In 1973, however, it was freed of its maturity restraint and deposits now comprise a major portion of its funding. In 1981, for example, they amounted to 5890.2 million (50.2 per cent) of the GHB's total funds. The Bank now

TABLE 6.13   Government Housing Bank sources and uses of funds (figures as at 31 December 1981, in million baht)

Sources of funds	
Capital accounts	639.1
Deposits	
Demand	4348.0
Savings	35.1
Time	1494.2
Fixed on housing deposits	12.9
Borrowings	
Domestic	3182.0
Foreign	1809.1
Other liabilities	221.1
Total	11742.0
Uses of funds	
Cash in hand and balances at banks	1939.5
Balances at Bank of Thailand	57.6
Advances	9410.9,
Overdrafts	2813.8
Individual loans	2850.7
Project loans	3706.4
Bills discounted	—
Short term loans	
(*less* reserve for bad debts)	(49.5)
Investment	0.1
Fixed and other assets	383.4
Total	11742.0

Source: *Financial Institutions in Thailand* (Bangkok: Bank of Thailand 1982) Appendix 12.

accepts four types of deposits: demand; savings; time; and fixed housing. Of these, demand deposits are the most important, and accounted for 73.8 per cent of the total in 1981.

In addition to deposits, the Bank still obtains substantial monies from borrowings; in 1981, these accounted 42.5 per cent of its total funds. Of these borrowings, 36.2 per cent were from foreign sources. The GHB is also permitted to issue bonds and debentures under the government's guarantee.

(e) The Bank for Agriculture and Agricultural Co-operatives (BAAC)

The BAAC is a primarily government owned financial institution, which was established on 1 November 1966 to assume the functions of the Bank of Co-operatives. It operates under the Bank for Agriculture and Agricultural Co-operatives Act BE 2509 (1966), and is under the direct supervision of the Ministry of Finance. The Bank's main function is to provide credit to the agricultural sector – both directly and through agricultural co-operatives and farmers' associations: of its 13453 million baht in loans outstanding at the end of fiscal 1981 66.8 per cent were to client farmers; 30.5 per cent to agricultural co-operatives; and 2.7 per cent to farmers' associations.

Its loan facilities for client farmers may be of a short, medium, and long term nature, with short term lending comprising approximately half of these advances (54.8 per cent in the fiscal year 1981). The short term loans primarily relate to main crop production (rice or maize) or other agricultural production purposes (such as vegetable gardening) and are of a seasonal, working capital nature. The BAAC's medium term lending is to finance the purchase of farm machinery or draught animals, and is normally made over a 3 year period. The longer term loans are normally made in the form of an instalment loan over 15 years, and are designed to help farmers purchase or develop land or fixed assets for agricultural usage. A small number of long term advances are also made in certain cases over a 10 year period, to help farmers regain land lost under a mortgage default.

The BAAC supports the operations of agricultural co-operatives through four types of advances: to fund onlending to members; to purchase agricultural material and equipment for resale to members; to purchase and market members' agricultural production; and for the co-operatives to improve their own production related facilities. Of these, onlending finance is the most important and in the fiscal year 1981 comprised some 88.5 per cent of the BAAC's advances loans to the agricultural co-operatives and 99 per cent of its advances to farmers' associations.

As shown in table 6.14, deposits comprise approximately half of BAAC's funding. It obtains some 28.5 per cent of these from the general public through a normal savings and time deposit accounts programme, and the remainder from the commercial banks under a special Bank of Thailand directive. Those commercial banks unable to meet their agricultural lending target (in 1982 an amount equal to 11 per cent of their deposits at the end of the previous year) must deposit their shortfall with the BAAC; as few banks are able to fulfil their lending targets, they together provide a major portion of the BAAC's funding.

Next to deposits, notes payable are the largest form of BAAC funding; in 1981 they comprised some 17.3 per cent of the Bank's

TABLE 6.14   Bank for Agriculture and Agriculture Co-operatives, assets and liabilities, 1981–2 (figures as at 31 March 1982, in million baht)

Cash on hand and on deposit with other banks	6352920321.30
Government bonds	59000000.00
Other current assets	136170055.00
Loans to farmers' institutions	3968317698.58
Loans to client farmers	9155302942.46
Fixed assets	310284959.05
Reserves for exchange rate fluctuations	200299478.30
	20182295455.65
Deposits	11401904096.16
Notes payable	3500000000.00
Loans payable	11042333.75
Other current liabilities	544016414.05
Long term foreign borrowings–USAID	104786929.40
Long term foreign borrowings–OECF	1847183528.49
Long term foreign borrowings–World Bank	146151823.22
Long term domestic borrowings	312777889.59
Paid-up capital	1604999800.00
Donated assets reserves	348802.91
Other reserves	57033000.00
Accumulated profits	520125992.48
Unappropriated profit	131924845.60
	20182295455.65

Source: BAAC, *Annual Report 1981*, p. 100.

total capital and liabilities. This is a particularly important source of funding for, unlike the deposits (which involve normal interest charges) these notes are discounted to the Bank of Thailand at a concessional rate. Traditionally this was set at 5 per cent, but in 1981 the interest rate was effectively only 1 per cent over the first half of the year, and 3.5 per cent for the remainder.

In terms of overseas funding, the Japanese government's Overseas Economic Co-operation Fund is the BAAC's largest lender, and in 1981 provided some 9 per cent of the Bank's total capital and liabilities. The US government's USAID and the World Bank group are also important sources of long term borrowings.

Though the BAAC accounted for only 3.7 per cent of the financial sector's assets in 1981, this understates its importance within the Thai economy. In the fiscal year 1981, for example, the BAAC provided direct financial support to 1038103 Thai farm families and indirectly, (through agricultural co-operatives and farmers' associations) an additional 1022211 families: some 2060314 (40.7 per cent of Thailand's 5.5 million farm families) received BAAC support over the year.

In addition to its lending role, the BAAC also (through its branch network) helps to mobilise savings from the rural sector. At the end of the fiscal year 1981, for example, the BAAC had 62 provincial branches and 513 field offices (involving a staff of 3941) as well as a head office of 929. This rural branch network also fulfils an important advisory function for the small farmer; the head office similarly advises the co-operative movement, and has played a major role in government's Restructuring of Agricultural Co-operatives in Poor Financial Condition Project.

(f) The Small Industries Finance Office (SIFO)

SIFO was established in March 1964 as the Loan Office for Small Industries Development, and assumed its present name in 1970. It is managed by the Loan Board (whose nine members are appointed by the Thai Cabinet) and operates under the supervision of the Department of Industrial Promotion of the Ministry of Industry. SIFO's main purpose is to provide concessional small, medium and long term loans, and technical advice to small industry. As it has only one office, however, it relies on the government owned Krung Thai Bank's branch network for much of its business. To be eligible for SIFO finance, a business may not have capital or fixed assets of more than 5 million baht, nor be in an industry eligible for assistance from the IFCT. In 1982, the four main categories of SIFO lending were to the manufacturing; handicraft; cottage or home; and service industries (excluding tourism and transport): manufacturing traditionally absorbs around 85 per cent of SIFO advances.

Most SIFO advances are to finance the purchase of plant and machinery, equipment, or to erect new buildings or construct plant. It also loans some funds for working capital and land acquisition purposes. The loans themselves can be made up to 1 million baht, and are usually for terms of 3–7 years up to a maximum of 10 years, repayable by instalments – often with a 1 or 2 year grace period.

SIFO evaluates and recommends the loan; the Krung Thai Bank assesses the security, advances the funds, and assumes all credit risks.

The funds are advanced from SIFO's special account with the Krung Thai Bank, which is in turn funded partly by the government and partly by the Bank itself. SIFO receives an allocation of funds as part of the Industrial Promotion Department's annual budget; these funds are then deposited by SIFO in the special account and matched by the Krung Thai Bank on a 3 for 1 basis. SIFO then receives interest on its part of the account – in 1981 at 6 per cent per annum – and the Krung Thai Bank receives the full 16 per cent interest income from the loans.

Between 1960 and the fiscal year 1980, the government allocated some 53650000 baht to SIFO. As shown in Table 6.15, at the end of 1981 50.5 million was invested in the special account with the Krung Thai Bank; the bank's matching allocations of 151.5 million baht gave the account 202 million in loanable funds.

(g) The Industrial Finance Corporation of Thailand (IFCT)

The IFCT commenced operations in November 1959 (under the Industrial Finance Corporation of Thailand Act BE 2502) 'to promote industrial development and to assist in the development of the capital market of Thailand'.[19] It was established with the assistance of the World Bank's IFC to replace the financially troubled Industrial Bank of Thailand as the country's major private sector development finance institution.

While the company was established by statute, it is nevertheless privately owned, and up to 1982 had no direct Thai government

TABLE 6.15   Small Industries Finance Office sources and uses of funds, 1981
(figures as at 31 Dec 1981, in thousand baht)

Sources of funds	
Capital accounts	53650
Current liabilities	69
Profit & loss accounts	1500
Total	**55219**

Uses of funds	
Cash in hand	6
Cash at Ministry of Finance	1222
Cash at banks	
Bank of Thailand	11
Krung Thai Bank	50500
Government Savings Bank	862
Accrued income	1171
Fixed assets	218
Other assets	1229
Total	**55219**

Source: Financial Institutions in Thailand (Bangkok: Bank of Thailand, 1982) Appendix 16.

participation. It is listed on the Securities Exchange of Thailand and in June 1981 had 1183 individual and corporate shareholders. Of these 1142 shareholders (holding 69 per cent of the shares) were Thai, and the remaining 41 shareholders (with 31 per cent of the shares) were foreign.

Within both categories, the institutional ownership was quite high, with banks in aggregate owning 55.7 per cent shares outstanding; finance and securities companies 21.1 per cent; and insurance companies 5 per cent. Individuals and private companies (some 1052) owned the remaining 18.2 per cent. In terms of the shareholders themselves, the Krung Thai Bank (a primarily government owned institution) had the largest holding with a 20.9 per cent interest. The Mitsui Bank and the Deutsche Gesellschaft für Wirtschaftliche Zusammenarbeit were the second and third largest, with respectively 6.8 and 6.3 per cent. 12 of Thailand's domestic banks and 11 of the foreign banks operating branches within Thailand were also shareholders.

As shown in Table 6.16, medium and long term loans comprise the major portion of the IFCT's assets (78.6 per cent in mid-1982). Most of its other funds are in liquids, or held in support of its own

T_ABLE_ 6.16   Industrial Finance Corporation of Thailand assets and liabilities
(figures as at 30 June 1982, in million baht)

Assets	
Cash in hand & cash at banks	1.15
Time deposits & short term bills	793.54
Thai government securities	1.60
Loans to private sector	4490.31
Equity investment	202.58
Fixed assets	50.65
Other assets	304.83
Total assets	5844.66
Liabilities	
Long term borrowings	
Domestic	
Commercial banks	—
Bank of Thailand	191.61
Government	169.27
AID	8.00
Bonds & debentures	100.00
Foreign	
KfW	318.68
IBRD	986.98
ADB	797.12
Danish government	13.22
Exim Bank	824.36
Syndicated yen loan	328.77
Long term Credit Bank	353.14
Syndicated Singapore Loan	285.11
Commonwealth Development Corporation	245.34
Capital account	832.46
Other liabilities	390.60
Total liabilities	5844.66

Source: Bank of Thailand, *Quarterly Bulletin* (June 1982) pp. 22–3.

operations. It is also allowed to make equity investments in client companies, but as yet this has not been an important part of its operations: up to the end of 1981, for example, the IFCT had approved a total 314 million baht of equity participation in 25 companies.

Loans are made available for economic and technically viable development projects within certain industries, and usually for amounts not less than 1 million baht. The maximum size for any one project, however, is limited to 25 per cent of the IFCT's total equity. While these loans may have a maturity of up to 15 years (an average of 7–8 years), the interest charged is usually adjusted on a 6 month basis. The actual rate is a function of the IFCT's cost of funds, plus an appropriate margin to cover administration. The charge on foreign currency loans include forward cover via a special agreement with the Ministry of Finance. As of mid-June 1982, the standard rate for both domestic and foreign currency loans was set at 16 per cent. Concessional rates of 15 and 15.5 per cent are available for agricultural and decentralising or energy saving projects. As with the banks, special rates are also provided for government sponsored projects, and are made possible through a concessional refinancing facility provided by the Bank of Thailand.

In terms of its advances, agricultural related enterprises have received the largest amount of IFCT funds. The rest was distributed, as shown in Table 6.17, among a wide range of

TABLE 6.17 Industrial Finance Corporation of Thailand outstanding loans by industry type (figures as at 31 December 1981, in thousands baht)

Industry	No. of clients	Outstanding loans Amount	% of total
Agro-industries, agri-business & food processing	74	631563	14
Mining & quarrying	2	13308	—
Tobacco curing & redrying	3	13391	—
Textiles & textile products	14	120305	3
Wood products	9	142247	3
Pulp, paper & paper products	5	118929	3
Chemicals & plastic products	17	204313	5
Petroleum, coal	5	151378	3
Rubber	5	37648	1
Cement	2	489807	11
Ceramics & tiles	8	394149	9
Glass	1	155536	3
Other non-metallic mineral products	11	215062	5
Basic metal & metal products	18	467143	11
Machinery & equipment	19	385301	9
Construction	1	50000	1
Transport & storage facilities	23	352982	8
Service industries	13	426494	10
Other industries	4	56942	1
Total	234	4426498	100

Source: FCT, *Annual Report 1981*, p. 70.

manufacturing and service industry activities.

Besides advancing monies directly, the IFCT may also guarantee client borrowings from other institutions, or assist in underwriting debt or equity issues. It also will act in an advisory capacity on a variety of technical matters.

The IFCT raises the bulk of its funds through borrowings: it cannot accept deposits. As was shown in Table 6.16, a large portion of these were from foreign sources (71.1 per cent in 1981) and generally from government or international agencies (60.5 per cent): the World Bank has traditionally been the IFCT's largest lender, with the Asian Development Bank and various Japanese government agencies also of major importance. These foreign loans are generally guaranteed by the Thai government and are normally at better rates and terms than those available from commercial sources – particularly in respect to their maturities. The IFCT would like permission to accept term deposits as well, and has attempted to expand its local fund raising through the issue of bonds and debentures. The Bank of Thailand and the Thai government, however, remain its most important domestic long term funding source, with respectively 3.3 and 2.9 per cent of total funds. Shareholders' equity should become a more important source of funds in 1983 when the IFCT's paid-up capital is increased from 400 million to 700 million baht; its present shareholders' equity comprises 14.2 per cent of the firm's funds.

In addition to its direct activities, the IFCT has a number of subsidiary or affiliated companies providing more specialised services; these include the Thai Factory Development Co. Ltd (factory development and construction); Industrial Management Co. Ltd (industrial consultancy); Thai Orient Leasing Co. Ltd (equipment leasing); and, in conjunction with the Ministry of Finance and the IFC, Thailand's first mutual fund, the Mutual Fund Company. The IFCT also helps administer the government's Industrial Development Fund and the Capital Market Development Fund.

(h) Finance and Securities Companies

The finance and securities companies[20] are second in importance only to the commercial banks and, as was shown in Table 6.2, the industry's 76896.7 million baht in assets in 1981 comprised 14.6 per cent of the financial sector's total assets.

These firms are perhaps the most difficult of the Thai financial institutions to examine, since the overall category includes three quite separate operations. First there are those companies licensed solely for the finance company business; these firms generally specialise in consumer instalment lending and other types of corporate advances normally associated with finance companies overseas. The second group are firms licensed only for the securities business; these largely equate to stockbrokers. The third group are companies licensed for both the finance and securities business: the leading firms in this category operate not unlike the overseas merchant/investment banks. Of the 112 finance and securities companies authorised at the end of June 1982, 84 were licensed for both finance and securities business.

(i) *Development*

The finance and securities companies in a modern sense can trace their development as finance companies from December 1961, when the first firm (the Bangkok Investment Company) was established. This was in fact an expansion of what was previously the finance arm of a local Fiat car dealer[21]; other firms soon followed but initially at least vehicle purchase finance dominated the industry. Consumer durable financing (for refrigerator and television set purchase), was also important, as was the sale of insurance policies for these items. These finance companies later diversified into certain types of corporate lending as well.

The more 'merchant banking' style of finance and securities company developed somewhat later. The first of these, (the Thai Investment and Securities Company, or TISCO), commenced operations on 31 March 1969, and others soon followed; by the end of 1969, there were some 26 companies in operation. Their numbers grew rapidly: by 1973 there were 51 companies; by 1974 99; by 1975 114; and by 1977 128.

This rapid growth resulted partially from a moratorium on new bank licences, and a desire by foreign banks to establish local operations. Overseas banks found these companies gave them direct access to an otherwise closed domestic market, and soon over 50 foreign financial institutions had local interests. Thai banks also registered these firms in great numbers, often more than one per parent company, and at one time seven banks were said to control 21 of the SET's 30 member firms. Ironically, suggestions of controlling the industry's growth resulted in a further influx of new companies and during 1970–7 it grew at an average of 90.3 per cent.

This rapid increase in numbers and asset size concerned the government; on 26 July 1972, National Executive Council Announcement No. 58 was made to control further entry. Since 1977, no additional full licences have been permitted.

Announcement No. 58 nevertheless left the finance and securities companies quite free in their operations compared to the commercial banks and gradually the government was forced to impose further controls over their operations. On 11 May 1979 the Finance, Securities, and Credit Foncier Business Act BE 2502 finally formalised these arrangements.

(ii) *Market structure*

There are 112 finance and securities companies in Thailand: the names and relative importance of each at the end of 1980 is shown in Table 6.18. Despite the large number, the industry is highly concentrated in (and the business controlled by) a relatively small number of firms. On an asset basis, for example, the top 10 companies in 1981 controlled 29.7 per cent of the total: a list of these firms' major shareholders, and their 1981 assets, are shown in Table 6.19. This percentage, however, understates the importance of the major firms, as much of the industry's business is fee rather than fund based, and hence not directly reflected in balance sheet size. Also unreflected is the close affiliation between the commercial banks and the major companies. The largest, for example (Asia Credit) is affiliated with the Bangkok Bank. Dissolving these relationships is one of the precise objectives of the 1979 Act's shareholding requirements.

TABLE 6.18   Thailand finance and securities companies by total assets (figures as at 31 December 1980, in million baht)

Company	Total assets
Asia Credit Co. Ltd	3853
The Thai Investment and Securities Co. Ltd	2587
Phatra Thanakit Co. Ltd	2247
Wardley Thailand Ltd	2176
Union Finance Co. Ltd	1784
Ayudhaya Investment and Trust Co. Ltd	1574
The Book Club Finance and Securities Co. Ltd	1500

331

TABLE 6.18 (*contd.*)

Company	Total assets
The Siam Industrial Credit Co. Ltd	1367
Thai–Oversea Trust Co. Ltd	1287
Bangkok First Investment and Trust Co. Ltd	1284
Equity Development Finance and Securities Co. Ltd	1267
International Trust and Finance Co. Ltd	1232
Bangkok Investment Co. Ltd	1888
Poonpipat Finance and Securities Co. Ltd	1169
First Bangkok City Finance Co. Ltd	1129
Cathay Trust Co. Ltd	1078
Siam Commercial Trust Co. Ltd	1030
Bangkok Nomura International Securities Co. Ltd	1028
Citycorp Finance and Securities (Thailand) Ltd	1018
Erawan Trust Co. Ltd	1000
Thai Financial Syndicate Ltd	997
General Finance and Securities Ltd	969
Dhana Siam Finance and Securities Co. Ltd	963
First Trust Co. Ltd	945
Nava Finance and Securities Co. Ltd	919
Continental Illinois Thailand Ltd	904
International Finance and Consultants Co. Ltd	818
Metropolis Trust and Securities Co. Ltd	779
CMIC Finance and Securities Co. Ltd	751
The South East Finance and Securities Co. Ltd	737
Siam Finance Corporation Ltd	711
Mithai Europartners Finance and Securities Co. Ltd	701
Panich Finance Co. Ltd	695
Multi-Credit Corporation of Thailand Ltd	688
Yawaraj Finance Co. Ltd	649
Thai Rung Ruang Trust Co. Ltd	611
Bangkok Tokyo Finance and Securities Co. Ltd	601
Bangkok Metropolitan Trust Co. Ltd	595
The Ocean Securities and Finance Co. Ltd	581
Thai Financial Trust Co. Ltd	555
Commercial Trust Co. Ltd	532
Thai Financial Development Corpn Ltd	523
Thai–Mitsubishi Investment Corpn Ltd	516
Sakol Real Estate & Finance Co. Ltd	506
The Asia Financing and Trust Co. Ltd	502
B.A. Finance and Securities (Thailand) Ltd	485
Siam Investment and Trust Co. Ltd	475
CCC Finance Co. Ltd	469
Orient Trust Co. Ltd	460
Grand Trust and Securities Co. Ltd	440
Krung Thai Finance and Securities Co. Ltd	439
Inter Credit and Trust Co. Ltd	438

TABLE 6.18   (contd.)

Company	Total assets
Midland Merchant Finance Ltd	429
Bangkok Finance Co. Ltd	423
Nateethong Finance and Securities Co. Ltd	411
Kamol Sukosol Investment and Trust Co. Ltd	403
Kiatnakin Finance and Securities Co. Ltd	399
Sincere Trust Co. Ltd	395
Thai Fuji Finance and Securities Co. Ltd	385
Chatiphaibul Finance Corpn Ltd	382
Cathay Finance and Securities Co. Ltd	380
Sahaviriya Trust Co. Ltd	377
First City Investment Co. Ltd	374
Bara Investment and Securities Corporation Ltd	362
United Finance Corpn Ltd	348
Asia Financial Syndicate Co. Ltd	345
Thai Finance Co. Ltd	337
Universal Trust Co. Ltd	331
Thai Tanakorn Trust Co. Ltd	322
Lamthong Finance Co. Ltd	304
Metropolitan Investment and Trust Ltd	282
Chartered Finance and Securities (Thailand) Co. Ltd.	275
Dynamic Eastern Finance Co. Ltd	270
Thai Rutta Finance and Securities Co. Ltd	258
First Siam Financial Corpn Ltd	244
Phornprapha Trust Co. Ltd	232
Progressive Finance Co. Ltd	224
People Trust Co. Ltd	219
National Finance and Securities Co. Ltd	216
Charoenkrung Finance and Securities Co. Ltd	210
Bangkok Credit Ltd	206
Lila Finance and Securities Co. Ltd	203
Teerachai Trust Corpn Ltd	202
Subthavee Trust Co. Ltd	194
Ruam Thai Development Trust Co. Ltd	192
Thai United Trust Co. Ltd	189
Sino–Thai Trust Investment and Securities Co. Ltd	185
Yipintsoi Finance Co. Ltd	174
Chao Phya Finance and Securities Co. Ltd	171
Cheing Mai Trust Co. Ltd	168
Thaksin Finance Co. Ltd	151
Krung Thong Trust & Finance Co. Ltd	150
The Thai Saving Trust Finance Co. Ltd	147
Eastern Commercial Trust Co. Ltd	144
National Finance Co. Ltd	142
Thai Central Finance Co. Ltd	140
Thong Thana Trust Co. Ltd	139

Table 6.18   (*contd.*)

Company	Total assets
Commercial Financing Co. Ltd	126
Nam Tong Trust Co. Ltd	119
The Productive Trust Co. Ltd	117
United Malayan Trust Co. Ltd	115
Muang Thong Trust Co. Ltd	112
Financial Trust Co. Ltd	111
Bangkok Finance and Trust Corpn Ltd	89
United Finance Co. Ltd	88
Sakul Thai Trust Co. Ltd	86
Metropolitan Finance and Securities Co. Ltd	83
Pacific Finance and Securities Ltd	83
Thai Finance and Securities Co. Ltd	81
Eastern Trust Co. Ltd	63
Athon Trust and Securities Co. Ltd	45
Trust Bangkok Co. Ltd	42
Total	65146

Source: *Financial Institutions in Thailand* (Bangkok: Bangkok Bank Ltd, 1981) pp. 28–30.

(iii) *Uses of funds*

Most finance and securities companies funds are used as loans and receivables. In 1981, for example, as shown in Table 6.20, these categories accounted for 65389.6 million baht (85 per cent of the industry's funds). Instalment credit was the industry's initial area of lending specialisation, but short term commercial lending – often by purchasing customer promissory notes–has since become its most important activity. Some firms also extend real estate and development finance.

Finance and securities company advances are subject to certain Bank of Thailand restrictions. The maximum loan to one borrower can be no more than an amount equal to 35 per cent of the lender's capital (30 per cent as of 1 May 1983). The maximum interest rate allowable on their advances is also subject to a Bank of Thailand ceiling – 21 per cent in June 1982. The amount or growth of any category of loans outstanding may also be subject to control; in 1982, for example, the growth in the amount of car hire purchase loans outstanding was limited to an increase of 5

TABLE 6.19 Thailand 'top 10' finance and securities companies by major shareholders and total assets (figures as at end 1981, in million baht)

Total assets	Company	Major shareholders	(%)
4275	Asia Credit Co. Ltd	Asia Credit Co. Ltd	21.37
		Asia Investment Co. Ltd	10.04
		Krung Thai Bank Ltd	8.80
		Others	59.79
3268	The Thai Investment & Securities Co. Ltd	BT Foreign Investment Corpn (USA)	67.50
		Thai Farmers' Bank	20.00
		Dai–Ichi Kanyo Bank (Japan)	10.00
		Others	2.50
2705	Union Finance Co. Ltd	Universal Commercial Co. Ltd	11.31
		Thongdee Pakornsiriwongs	10.50
		Others	78.19
2392	Phatra Thanakit Co. Ltd	Lamsam Estate Co. Ltd	21.11
		Thai Farmers' Bank	12.78
		Loxley (Bangkok) Co. Ltd	17.78
		Others	48.33
2237	Wardley Thailand Ltd	WTL Ltd (Hong Kong)	100.00
1821	Ayudha Investment & Trust Co. Ltd	Ayudha Bank	20.00
		Others	80.00

TABLE 6.19 (*contd.*)

Total assets	Company	Major shareholders	(%)
1621	Bangkok First Investment & Trust Co. Ltd	Bangkok Bank Ltd	20.00
		Citibank Oversea Investment Corpn	10.00
		Others	70.00
1562	The Book Club Finance & Securities Co. Ltd	Crown Property Bureau	25.00
		The Siam Commercial Bank Ltd	20.00
		The Long Term Credit Bank of Japan Ltd	46.50
		Others	8.50
1509	The Siam Industrial Credit Co. Ltd	The Sanwa Bank Ltd	33.96
		The Crown Property Bureau	20.00
		Sanwa International Finance	15.00
		The Siam Cement Co. Ltd	10.56
		The Siam Commercial Bank Ltd	10.14
		Sripaoidh Co. Ltd	10.00
		Others	0.34
1428	International Trust and Finance Co. Ltd	Investment Holding Ltd	27.82
		Associated Investment Co. Ltd	23.49
		Windmill Investment & Finance Co. Ltd	9.98
		Others	38.71

TABLE 6.20 Thailand finance and securities companies' sources and uses of funds (figures as at 31 December 1981, in million baht)

Sources of funds	
Capital accounts	7333.3
Borrowings	67572.4
Commercial banks	(6720.8)
Local promissory notes payable	(59561.0)
Other borrowing	(1290.6)
Other liabilities	1991.0
Total	76896.7
Uses of funds	
Cash and balances at banks	3247.3
Investment in securities	5882.1
Thai government securities	(3762.4)
Listed and authorised securities	(1216.0)
Other securities	(903.7)
Loans and receivables	65389.6
Assets for resale	416.2
Other assets	1961.5
Total	76896.7

Source: *Financial Institutions in Thailand* (Bangkok: Bank of Thailand, 1982) Appendix 9.

per cent per annum. The total amount of a company's loans outstanding (regardless of type) is also subject to a capital : risk asset limit of 6 per cent (a 16.7 : 1 risk assets : capital ratio).

In terms of finance company lending, loans to manufacturing industry are the most important, and in mid-1981 accounted for 14305 million (25.3 per cent) of the industry's advances. The other major categories, and their relative importance, are shown in Table 6.21.

The industry's other major use of funds is in cash or bank deposits and in securities investments. The former is done in part to meet the Bank of Thailand's liquidity ratio requirement that an amount equal to 7 per cent of a finance and securities company's total borrowings be held in specified liquid assets. Within the 7 per cent holding, an amount equal to no more than 1 per cent can be deposited or placed at call with domestic banks, but at least 0.5 per cent must be deposited with the Bank of Thailand and at least 5.5 per cent held in government securities. As of the end of 1981,

TABLE 6.21   Thailand finance and securities companies' loans by industry (figures as at 30 June 1981, in million baht)

Industry	Amount	% of total
Manufacturing	14305	25.3
Personal consumption	9560	16.9
Wholesale & retail trade	8725	15.4
Construction & real estate business	7623	13.5
Banking & other financial business	6644	11.8
Public utilities & services	4735	8.4
Imports	2571	4.5
Exports	1037	1.8
Agriculture, fisheries & forestry	777	1.4
Mining	563	1.0
Total	56540	100.0

Source: Bank of Thailand, cited in *Financial Institutions in Thailand* (Bangkok: Bank Ltd, 1982) p. 37.

cash and bank deposits (including deposits with the Bank of Thailand) were equal to 4.8 per cent of finance company borrowings. Investment in government securities amounted to an additional 5.6 per cent.

Besides government securities, the industry held some 1216 million baht (1.6 per cent of its assets) in registered, listed and authorised (SET) securities. These are held for investment purposes, and in some cases may result from private placement or underwriting activities. For the most part, however, these and the other basic securities industry (merchant banking) functions – such as securities underwriting; private placements; brokerage; and financial advice – are of an agency nature, and hence not usually reflected in the balance sheet.

(iv) *Sources of funds*

The finance and securities companies obtain most funds through borrowings (87.9 per cent in 1981). These are raised primarily from commercial banks and promissory note issues. The latter is the most important, and in 1981 accounted for 77.5 per cent of the industry's total funds. The notes are not deposits but are nevertheless considered as such by most purchasers. Their rates on issue are controlled by the Bank of Thailand; in July 1981, a two-rate ceiling was introduced, placing a maximum of 15 per cent on at call notes and 16 per cent on those with a maturity of 30 days or more. The maximum rate as of June 1982 was still 16 per cent, but in times of tight liquidity some finance companies apparently often pay clients more by giving 'free' gifts to large note purchasers. The minimum size of the notes is also controlled, and set at 10000 baht for the Bangkok metropolitan area and Prakarn and Nonthaburi provinces. The minimum is 5000 baht for notes sold in other provinces. Individuals are the major purchasers of these securities, and in June 1981 they owned 33070 million (58.2 per cent) of the industry's promissory notes outstanding. A listing of the other categories, and their relative importance, is shown in Table 6.22.

Shareholders' equity has not been a major source of funding (9.5 per cent in 1981), but should increase in importance as the finance companies conduct new share offerings in an attempt to comply with government public ownership plans. As with the commercial banks, the government wished to break the rich families' (and foreign companies') control of the industry, and its 1979 Act included a provision for each licensed company to have at least 100 ordinary persons as shareholders, each holding 0.6 per cent or less of the shares outstanding, in aggregate controlling 50 per cent of the company. This goal was to be complied with under the following schedule: at least 50 individual shareholders holding not less than 25 per cent of the shares outstanding within 3 years (10 May 1982); 75 shareholders holding 40 per cent within 5 years

TABLE 6.22 Thailand finance and securities companies' deposits by source (figures as at 30 June 1981, in million baht)

Source	Amount[a]	% of Total
Individuals	33070	58.2
Limited company & partnership	8998	15.9
Commercial banks	6686	11.8
Finance companies	3427	6.0
Other financial institutions	2362	4.2
Other juristic persons	2238	3.9
Total	56781	100.00

[a] Including bank overdraft, accounts payable and notes payable.

Source: Financial Institutions in Thailand (Bangkok: Bangkok Bank Ltd, 1981) p. 34.

(10 May 1984); 100 shareholders holding 50 per cent within 7 years (10 May 1986). No new shareholders should hold more than 10 per cent of the shares outstanding, and those holding more than the maximum prior to 1979 must reduce their holdings down to this level by the 10 May 1986 deadline. The collapse of Raja Finance, and the poor performance of the Thai stock market, has made it difficult for the finance and securities companies to sell their shares at reasonable prices, and by the 1982 deadline only 25 of the 112 companies had complied. The Ministry of Finance has apparently agreed that the industry's overall failure was beyond its control for in November 1982 the deadlines for the divestiture programme were extended by 18 months. Nevertheless, these requirements will mean substantial changes in finance company shareholdings, and possibly many mergers in the future. A further requirement that these companies be 60 per cent (75 per cent for new firms) Thai owned has already caused some foreign banks (such as Chase Manhattan and Continental Illinois) to sell their entire shareholdings.

(i) General Insurance

The general insurance industry's origins in Thailand are difficult to determine. It was probably started by foreign interests in the late 1800s, and was of sufficient size by 1929 to require specific regulatory control. The oldest foreign company still operating in Thailand today, (the New Zealand Insurance Company) commenced local operations on 3 July 1930. The oldest local firm (Patara Insurance) was established some two years later, on 28 February 1932. There have been many companies in operation both before and since; those that have survived, along with their local establishment dates, are shown in Table 6.23. Prior to the Second World War, foreign firms dominated the industry, but with the Japanese occupation of Thailand most were forced to suspend operations. A number of Thai firms developed to replace them, and prior to the Insurance Act BE 2510 (1967) there were some 70 firms in operation.[22] Since that time, the numbers have declined slightly and there are now 59 licensed firms: 52 locally incorporated, and seven foreign. The number of companies would be smaller but for three specialist health insurance companies, which entered the industry in the late 1970s.

Non-life insurance companies in Thailand are regulated by the Insurance Commissioner and Minister of Commerce under the

Insurance Against Loss Act BE 2510 (1967), and a series of regulations issued under that Act. To be licensed, a firm must first make certain security deposits and fulfil certain minimum capital requirements depending on its type of business. The Act also requires the premiums charged be approved by the Minister. At present, the Insurance Commissioner sets the minimum premium rates or tariffs for fire; motor vehicle; all risks; and personal accident insurance business within Thailand. Special (i.e. lower) rates can be charged, but must be approved in each instance by the Commissioner: as a rule, the companies follow the set tariff fairly closely. The Act also limits the risk exposure within the industry, by allowing no risk undertaken without reinsurance to exceed more than 10 per cent of the firm's capital funds. It prescribes certain reporting and operational requirements in respect of the firm's selling and policy arrangements and (through later regulation) provides similar investment guidelines to those for the life companies.

The security deposit required depends on the types of business the firm conducts. Licensing for the marine and transport insurance business alone requires a deposit of 1 million baht, while other businesses involve up to $1\frac{1}{2}$ million. As with the life companies, these deposits may be made in cash, Thai government bonds or other assets approved by the Minister; government bonds are the most common. The firm's capital requirements are similarly graduated, raising from $2\frac{1}{2}$ million baht for marine and transport up to $3\frac{1}{2}$ million.

In terms of relative asset size, the non-life insurance business is not as concentrated as either the banking or life insurance industry. The largest firm (Bangkok Insurance), for example, accounts for only 15.8 per cent of the industry's assets. The second and third largest, (South East Insurance and Ocean Insurance) hold respectively only 10.4 and 3.9 per cent. The relative asset holdings of both local and foreign firms are shown in Table 6.24. Though individual premium volumes are not available, it is believed that the 10 largest firms earn more than half the business available.

Of the three major categories of non-life business in Thailand, fire insurance is the most important. In 1981 it comprised 45.4 per cent of the 3797323 million baht worth of direct business written. Automobile business was second (with 26.6 per cent) and marine and transport third with (14.0 per cent). Other more specialist lines accounted for the rest. Foreign firms were most significant in

TABLE 6.23   Thailand non-life insurance companies by establishment date

Company	Commencement date
The New Zealand Insurance[a,b]	3 Jul. 1930
Patara Insurance	28 Feb. 1932
Luang Lee Insurance	1935
Thai Insurance	1938
American International Assurance	1 Oct. 1938
Thai Commercial Insurance	1940
General Insurance	1941
Safety Insurance	12 Sept. 1941
Thai Sreshtakich Insurance	2 Feb. 1942
Bangkok Thonburi Insurance	12 Oct. 1944
Union Insurance	10 Apr. 1945
Sri Muang Insurance	6 Jun. 1946
South East Insurance	22 Jul. 1946
Deves Insurance	1 Jan. 1947
Thai Prasit Insurance	3 Feb. 1947
Thai United Insurance	24 Feb. 1947
Bangkok Insurance	15 Apr. 1947
Samaggi Insurance	28 Jul. 1947
Nam Seng Insurance	1948
Menam Warehouse Insurance	11 Feb. 1948
China Insurance (Thai)	16 Sept. 1948
Ocean Insurance	11 Jan. 1949
Inter Life Insurance[c]	28 Jan. 1949
New Hampshire Insurance[a,d]	16 Mar. 1949
Nam Hua Insurance	27 Jun. 1949
Soon Heng Lee Insurance	10 Nov. 1949
Ayudhaya Insurance	1950
First Insurance	2 Jan. 1950
Chalerm Nakorn Insurance	29 Feb. 1950
Asia Trust Insurance	15 Dec. 1950

marine and transport, where they wrote 22.3 per cent of the business.

In terms of investment, non-life companies, as shown in Table 6.25, structure their assets differently to their life insurance counterparts. Private sector securities were the most important investment (31.3 per cent of the industry's assets), and cash and bank deposits were second (20.4 per cent). Both categories are generally highly liquid, and reflect the annual nature of the industry's policy cover as opposed to the much longer term characteristics of life policies.

TABLE 6.23   *(contd.)*

Company	Commencement date
Union Prospers Insurance	1951
Wilson Insurance	4 Jan. 1951
Synmunkong Insurance	24 Jan. 1951
Muang Thai Insurance	1 Feb. 1951
New India Assurance[a]	2 May 1951
Sahawattana Insurance	4 Sept. 1951
Pacific Insurance	8 Oct. 1951
Dhiypya Insurance	9 Nov. 1951
International Assurance	8 Apr. 1952
Universal Insurance	14 Jun. 1952
Shiang Ann Insurance	28 Dec. 1952
ETB Insurance	1953
Thai Asia Insurance	1953
Thai Metropol Insurance	21 Jan. 1953
Home Insurance[a]	16 May 1955
Bangkok Union Insurance	5 Feb. 1962
Taisho Marine & Fire Insurance	20 Aug. 1964
British Traders Insurance[a]	1 Oct. 1967
Commercial Union Assurance[a]	1 Oct. 1967
Guardian Assurance[a]	3 Oct. 1967
Reng Phatana Insurance	29 Mar. 1971
Kamol Sukosol	29 Oct. 1973
Viriyapanit Insurance	3 Feb. 1974
Pipat Insurance	15 Aug. 1975
Narai International Insurance	27 Nov. 1976
Thai Reinsurance	4 Aug. 1978
Thailand Medical and Health Centre	22 Aug. 1979
Thai Health Insurance	29 Sept. 1979
Siam Insurance	29 Sept. 1979
Krung Thai Health Insurance	8 May 1980
Guardian Assurance (Thailand)	9 Oct. 1980
American Family Life Assurance (Thailand)	2 Jan. 1981
Assets Insurance Co. Ltd	Nov. 1982
Rattanakosin Insurance Co. Ltd	Nov. 1982

[a]   Foreign incorporated insurers.
[b]   Converted to a Thai Subsidiary, New Zealand Insurance (Thailand) Co. Ltd in 1982.
[c]   Formerly Thong Hua Heng Insurance.
[d]   Formerly Hanover Insurance.

Source: cited in *Financial Institutions in Thailand* (Bangkok: Bangkok Bank Ltd, 1980) pp. 68–70.

(j) Reinsurance Companies

The Insurance Act 1967 forced firms to seek reinsurance coverage for any single risk worth more than 10 per cent of their capital.

TABLE 6.24   Thailand non-life insurance companies by total assets (figures as at
31 December 1981, in thousand baht)

Locally incorporated firms	
Bangkok Insurance	674288
South East Insurance	442669
The Ocean Insurance	166558
ETB Insurance	158232
Sri Muang Insurance	122960
Patara Insurance	120451
Dhipya Insurance	110120
Thai Reinsurance	103789
Pacific Insurance	101386
Ayudhaya Insurance	86453
Shiang Ann Insurance	81635
Synmunkong Insurance	77664
Guardian Assurance (Thailand)	73833
Deves Insurance	72711
Safety Insurance	69904
Asia Trust Insurance	68487
Pipat Insurance	67568
Nam Seng Insurance	67077
Universal Insurance	63735
Thai Prasit Insurance	61502
Thai Metropole Insurance	56675
Narai International Insurance	53553
Luang Lee Insurance	52690
Muang Thai Insurance	50329
Bangkok Union Insurance	47033
Kamol Sukosol	42550
Thai Insurance	41820
Thai Asia Insurance	41783
Soon Heng Lee Insurance	40637
Chalerm Nakom Insurance	38922
Union Insurance	35954
Reng Patana Insurance	33766
China Insurance (Thai)	33068
First Insurance	30460
General Insurance	28909
International Assurance	28755

This requirement meant that a substantial amount of Thai premium income was therefore being ceded overseas; in 1977, for example, 17 per cent of the direct general insurance business written by companies in Thailand was ceded to other companies within the country, and some 48 per cent went overseas.

To reduce this outflow, the Thai Reinsurance Corporation was established on 4 August 1978. It is owned by all the local insurance companies (whose shareholdings range between 1–2.6

TABLE 6.24 (*contd.*)

Thai Sreshtakich Insurance	26901
Wilson Insurance	26792
Thai United Insurance	26510
Viriya Panit Insurance	24096
Thai Commercial Insurance	21194
Bangkok Thonouri Insurance	20951
Inter Life Insurance	19712
Sahawattana Insurance	19207
Menam Warehouse Insurance	18710
Union Prospers Insurance	17428
Nam Hua Insurance	14289
Samaggi Insurance	13104
American Family Life Assurance (Thailand)	10789
Siam Insurance	10003
Krung Thai Health Insurance	9913
Thai Health Insurance	9829
Thai Medical Care	7109
Thailand Medical and Health Centre	5078
Total assets of locally incorporated firms	3749541
Foreign firms	
New Hampshire Insurance[a]	163556
Commercial Union Assurance	117876
Taisho Marine & Fire Insurance	79493
Home Insurance	53165
New Zealand Insurance	31568
American International Assurance	29697
Hanover Insurance[a]	29557
New India Assurance	19415
Total assets of foreign firms	524327
Total non-life company assets	4273868

[a] These firms have merged, and Hanover has ceased operation. Legally, however, the transfer of assets has not been completed and so the two are reported separately.

Source: Technical Division, Office of Insurance, Ministry of Commerce cited in *Financial Institutions in Thailand* (Bangkok: Bangkok Bank Ltd, 1982) pp. 68–74.

per cent) and is intended to increase the industry's overall retention capability. Besides being better placed to gain overseas reinsurance business in return, Thai Re—by dealing on a national basis—is well placed to advise the industry on a variety of technical matters.[23]

Other firms have since been encouraged to enter the business,

TABLE 6.25 Thailand domestic non-life insurance companies' assets and liabilities by amount and % (figures as at 31 December 1981, in thousand baht)

% of Total		Amount
	Assets	
20.4	Cash & bank deposits	764130
—	Deposits with Registrar	1250
4.8	Government & public enterprise securities	180446
31.3	Private sector securities	1173581
5.2	Loans	196042
2.2	Operating assets	81955
5.9	Immovable assets	220784
10.9	Premiums due & uncollected	406725
2.2	Amounts due under reinsurance treaties	82921
13.2	Amounts due from other reinsurers	494459
1.7	Investment income accrued	64657
2.1	Other assets	79991
0.1	Other investments	2600
100.0	Total assets	3749541
	Liabilities	
20.2	Unearned premium reserves	756761
16.4	Loss reserves & unpaid losses	615170
15.5	Amounts withheld under reinsurance treaties	580749
11.0	Amounts due to other reinsurers	414108
1.2	Bank overdrafts & loans	44858
1.0	Accrued expenses	37638
10.2	Other liabilities	384793
18.9	Paid-up capital	709276
6.8	Surplus reserves	254309
(1.4)	Retained earnings (losses)	(54601)
0.2	Appreciated value of shares	6480
100.0	Total liabilities & capital	3749541

Source: Technical Division, Office of Insurance, Ministry of Commerce, cited in *Financial Institutions in Thailand* (Bangkok: Bangkok Bank Ltd, 1982) pp. 73–9.

and on 8 May 1980 the Minister of Commerce established the specific conditions under which new firms would be permitted. Such firms must have a registered capital of 50 million baht, with not less than 25 million fully paid; Thai nationals holding at least 75 per cent of the shares outstanding; no single shareholder holding more than 5 per cent of the registered capital; and a 9 man Board of Directors of which at least three-quarters must be

Thai. The two new firms entering the industry in November 1982 had registered and paid-up capital respectively of 60 million and 30 million baht, suggesting that a new minimum had been established.

An examination of 1981's direct general business: foreign reinsurance ratio might suggest that foreign treaties have become more rather than less important (with 55 instead of 1977's 48 per cent); this disguises two factors. First, the business ceded to other local companies now stands at 24 per cent of the business written. Second (and more important), the amount of reinsurance assumed from overseas has grown from 18.1 to 25.5 per cent of the business written. There is considerable potential in further growth in these percentages, for the reinsurance paid out still exceeds the reinsurance paid in by a ratio of two : one.

Though not directly related to the Thai reinsurance industry (as it does not operate directly in Thailand) the Asian Reinsurance Corporation (of which Thailand is a member) is headquartered in Bangkok.

(k) Life Insurance

The life insurance industry, like the general insurance business, has no easily determinable starting date, but some sources suggest that at least some business was conducted 'long before the reign of King Chulalungkorn'.[24] In any event, the industry was of sufficient size, by 1929 to require regulation; the first insurance Act was passed, and the Ministry of commerce opened a special office for its supervision. Initially most companies were simply branches of foreign insurers but by 1941 around half a dozen local firms had been established.[25] Others were formed during the Second World War when the Japanese presence in Thailand forced most foreign companies to cease operation. These, however, appear not to have survived through the 1940s. Many companies established in the 1950s and early 1960s also ceased operation when the first specific life insurance legislation was passed in 1967 (the Life Insurance Act BE 2510).

The oldest life company in operation (American Interntional) dates to 10 October 1938, while the oldest local company (Thai Sreshtakich Insurance) was founded in 1942. The specific dates for the other firms are shown in Table 6.26. Of these 13 companies, 11 are locally incorporated and two are foreign. Six of these firms are also engaged in the general insurance business.

TABLE 6.26   Thailand licensed life insurance companies by local commencement date

Company	Business Commencement date
American International Assurance[a]	1 Oct. 38
Thai Sreshtakich Insurance	2 Feb. 42
Thai Life Insurance	19 Mar. 42
South East Insurance	22 Jul. 46
Thai Phasit Insurance	26 Mar. 48
Inter Life	2 Mar. 51
Muang Thai Life Assurance	7 Mar. 51
The Ocean Insurance	21 Mar. 51
Ayudhaya Life Assurance	20 Apr. 51
Bangkok Assurance[b]	24 Apr. 51
China Underwriters Life & General Insurance[a]	4 May 61
Thai Reinsurance	4 Aug. 78
Maha Nakorn Life Insurance	22 Feb. 79

[a]   Foreign firms.
[b]   Formerly Siam Life Insurance.

Source: Technical Division, Office of Insurance, Ministry of Commerce, cited in *Financial Institutions in Thailand* (Bangkok: Bangkok Bank, 1981).

In terms of total assets, the industry is dominated by two firms (Ocean Insurance and American International Assurance) which respectively hold 35.3 and 25.8 per cent of the total life company assets. In terms of business in force, however, the rankings differ slightly. American International occupies first place and Ocean Insurance second with respectively 29.5 and 26.6 per cent. What is significant is the much greater market share held by Thai Life Insurance (19.7 per cent) against only 16 per cent of total assets. The difference is due to the importance that the so called industrial policies (policies sold and collected door to door) play in the local market (34.3 per cent of the total business in force in 1982) and approximately half of the business held by local companies). An indication of the relative importance of the type of business to each firm is shown in Table 6.27. While not reflected separately in these figures, endowment policies (sold as life or industrial business) are the most popular in Thailand, and account for some 80 per cent of all policies.[26]

Life companies in Thailand operate under the Life Assurance

TABLE 6.27 Thailand life companies by total assets and business in force (figures as at 31 December 1981, in thousand baht)

Total assets	Company	Ordinary life insurance				Industrial		Group insurance		Total	
		Whole life & endowment		Term & other							
		No.	Amount	No.	Amount	No.	Amount	No.	Amount	No.	Amount
	Locally incorporated firms										
2851776	The Ocean Insurance	3171	211256	5	1427	748527	13295907	39	593860	751742	14102450
1292338	Thai Life Insurance	110715	5839485	1616	67530	335113	4473606	15	45654	447459	10426275
672570	Muang Thai Life Assurance	26251	3379086	316	82580	—	—	78	554369	26645	4016035
472878	South East Insurance	33069	3224079	4614	470302	797	14157	40	213486	38520	3922024
243089	Inter Life Insurance	1336	440339	13164	784192	21010	226074	25	115250	35535	1565855
172483	Thai Prasit Insurance	15852	977763	36	25400	8240	128200	11	34500	24139	1165863
163005	Ayudhaya Life Assurance	11121	793528	—	—	1629	14369	—	—	12750	807897
78806	Bangkok Assurance	2668	266541	15	2250	—	—	—	—	2683	268791
32932	Maha Nakom Life Insurance	244	50690	—	—	—	—	—	—	244	50690
5045	Thai Sreshtakich Insurance	174	15337	—	—	205	3477	—	—	379	18814
3218	Thai Re-insurance	1	50	—	—	—	—	—	—	1	50
5988140	Total	204602	15198154	19766	1433681	1115521	18155790	208	1557119	1340097	36344744

TABLE 6.27 (contd.)

Total assets	Company	Ordinary life insurance				Industrial		Group insurance		Total	
		Whole life & endowment		Term & other							
		No.	Amount	No.	Amount	No.	Amount	No.	Amount	No.	Amount
	Foreign firms										
2008974	American International Assurance	74673	12581891	2644	477231	—	—	660	2576182	77977	15635304
75010	China Underwriters Life & General Insurance	3203	395004	25	8660	—	—	122	595974	3350	999638
2083984	Total	77876	12976895	2669	485891	—	—	782	3172156	81327	16634942
8072124	Grand total	282478	28175049	22435	1919572	1115521	18155790	990	4729275	1421424	52979686

Source: Technical Division, Office of Insurance, Ministry of Commerce, cited in *Financial Institutions in Thailand* (Bangkok: Bangkok Bank Ltd, 1982) pp. 54; 60.

Act BE 2510 1967, and a series of ministerial regulations issued under that Act. The Act provides for a variety of reporting and operational requirements most of which relate to investment and selling arrangements. It also requires that a company must place a security deposit of 2 million baht with the Registrar of Insurance Companies, and have a capital of at least 5 million baht. The Act also allows the Minister of Commerce to make companies deposit a portion of their insurance reserves with the Registrar (generally not utilised) and to approve the premium rates charged.

The Life Insurance Act restricts the firms' investment primarily to Thai government and government guaranteed bonds and bonds of the World Bank; securities of the IFCT; shares and debentures of certain non-casualty insurance related Thai registered limited companies; foreign life companies not having branches in Thailand; bank bills of exchange; promissory notes guaranteed by a domestic bank; certain finance company bills of exchange and promissory notes; mortgages guaranteed by a domestic bank; loans to the NHA; loans to agricultural co-operatives; loans to farmers for agricultural purposes; and deposits with domestic banks. As of 1981, as shown in Table 6.28, loans accounted for the largest portion of life company investment (some 41.6 per cent of the industry's assets). Private securities holdings were second (29.3 per cent) and cash and bank deposits third (8.7 per cent).

(l) Credit Foncier Companies

The credit foncier companies are one of the smaller groupings of financial institutions, and despite some 33 separate companies their assets still accounted for only 5124.9 million baht in 1981 (just under 1.0 per cent of the financial sector's total assets).

The oldest credit foncier company in Thailand dates to 1958, but most were established in the early 1970s. Their development closely followed that of the finance and securities companies and they are regulated under the same legislation – the Finance, Securities and Credit Foncier Business Act BE 2522. They specialise in long term savings and the real estate mortgage finance and fulfil a quasi-savings and loan association or building society role within Thailand.

The credit foncier companies as an industry are characterised by a high degree of market concentration, with the five largest firms in 1980 accounting for 53.2 per cent of the industry's assets.

TABLE 6.28   Thailand life insurance companies' assets and liabilities (figures as at 31 December 1981, in thousand baht)

% of total		Amount
	Assets	
8.7	Cash & bank deposits	703544
2.3	Accrued income	183874
—	Other investments	61
5.5	Government & public enterprise securities	441476
29.3	Private securities	2362174
41.6	Loans	3361959
8.1	Immovable assets	655845
1.5	Operating assets	124207
3.0	Other assets	238484
100.0	Total assets	8072124
	Liabilities & capital	
—	Bank overdrafts & loans	3118
0.5	Unpaid losses	42102
0.2	Amounts due to other reinsurers	14720
0.4	Accrued expenses	30432
—	Amounts withheld on reinsurance treaties	342
2.2	Other policy liabilities	173403
3.7	Other liabilities	299751
0.2	Head office account	17256
85.8	Life insurance policy reserves	6924780
7.0	Capital funds	566211
100.0	Total liabilities & capital	8072124

Source: Financial Institutions in Thailand (Bangkok: Bangkok Bank, 1982) pp. 54–7.

As of July 1982, there were 33 licensed companies: their names, establishment dates, and relative importance are shown in Table 6.29.

Loans and receivables comprise their major use of funds, as shown in Table 6.30, 2931.2 million baht (57.2 per cent) in 1981. The companies must also maintain a portion of their funds in the form of liquid assets. At present, this Bank of Thailand liquidity ratio stands at 5 per cent of their total borrowing. The funds must be held in the following proportion of total borrowings: deposits or call loans to domestic banks, not to exceed 1 per cent; unobligated government securities, not less than 3.5 per cent; on deposit with the Bank of Thailand, at least 0.5 per cent.

Credit foncier companies usually lend on the basis of fixed asset

TABLE 6.29   Thailand credit foncier companies by total assets and establishment date (figures as at 31 December 1981, in thousand baht)

Company	Establishment date	Amount
Asian Credit Foncier Co. Ltd	1972	293545
Bangkok Home Ltd	1969	441737
Chalermlok Credit Foncier Co. Ltd	1974	45234
Credit Foncier International Cities Co.	1974	13618
Credit Foncier Muang Thai Co. Ltd	1974	20687
Credit Foncier Paiboon Co. Ltd	1974	27014
Credit Foncier Sakol Siam Co. Ltd	1971	137980
Credit Foncier Serisakol Thanakij Co.	1969	518145
Credit Foncier Sin Thai Co. Ltd	1978	25959
Credit Foncier Southeast Co. Ltd	N/A	95086
Credit Foncier Srinakorn Pattana Co.	1973	124503
Credit Foncier Tarakorn Co. Ltd	1972	132825
Credit Foncier Unico Housing Finance Co.	1977	104351
First Bangkok City Credit Foncier Co.	1974	16494
General Credit Foncier Co. Ltd	1973	70070
Kamol Sukosol Credit Foncier Co. Ltd	1978	12161
Land & Houses Credit Foncier Co. Ltd	1967	33955
Maco Credit Foncier Ltd	1969	43287
Nakorn Thai Investment Co. Ltd	1968	42195
Premruetai Land & Housing Co. Ltd	1967	236910
Sahaviriya Credit Foncier Co. Ltd	1964	51177
Shiang Ann Credit Foncier Ltd	1970	40118
Siam Investment Funds Ltd	1971	20861
Sinkahakan Credit Foncier Co. Ltd	1978	545671
Thai Credit Foncier Co. Ltd	1958	41330
Thai Credit Promotion Credit Foncier	1972	72376
Siri Thanporn Credit Foncier Co. Ltd	1968	12594
Social Development Credit Foncier Co.	1967	7686
Thai-Land & Housing Credit Foncier	1972	387274
Thanakij Credit Foncier Co. Ltd	1974	155846
Thaninthorn Credit Foncier Co. Ltd	1971	37673
United Credit Foncier Co. Ltd	1978	44213
Yawaraj Credit Foncier Co. Ltd	1973	250909

Source: Bank of Thailand, 1981.

security. This may be done under either a mortgage loan or instalment credit/hire purchase contract. Mortgages are the most common, and as of the end of 1981 comprised 40.9 per cent of the industry's assets. As of July 1982, the maximum rate charged by credit fonciers was subject to a 21 per cent per annum ceiling. Since 16 March 1982, they have also been able to make unsecured

TABLE 6.30   Thailand credit foncier companies by sources and uses of funds
(figures as at 31 December 1981, in million baht)

Sources of funds	
Capital funds	721.0
Borrowing	3977.2
Bank overdraft & loans from bank	(653.7)
Notes payable	(2808.0)
Other borrowings	(495.5)
Debentures	(20.0)
Other creditors	91.1
Other liabilities	335.6
Total	5124.9
Uses of funds	
Cash & balances at bank	397.3
Investments	171.3
Government securities	(96.0)
Listed & authorised securities	(4.4)
Other securities	(70.9)
Receivables & loans	2931.2
Mortgage loans	(2096.6)
Instalment & hire purchase receivables	(485.4)
Short term loans	—
Allowance for doubtful accounts	(8.8)
Net receivables	(292.8)
Properties foreclosed	(65.2)
Other debtors	93.8
Other properties	728.2
Other assets	803.1
Total	5124.9

Source: Financial Institutions in Thailand (Bangkok: Bank of Thailand, 1982) Appendix 10.

call loans to commercial banks; the Government Housing Bank; finance companies; and other credit foncier companies, provided that the loans did not exceed 20 per cent of the borrower's paid up capital and that the total call loans together did not exceed an amount equal to 100 per cent of the credit foncier company's own capital. Normal secured advances to one borrower are also limited in respect to the credit foncier capital – in 1982 50 per cent.

The total loans outstanding are also dependent on the credit foncier's total capital as they are subject to the Bank of Thailand's risk asset : capital ratio requirement. As of July 1982, a company's total shareholder funds must equal at least 6 per cent of its risk assets (a 16.7 : 1 risk assets : to capital ratio).

On 25 March 1982, amendments to the Finance, Securities and Credit Foncier Business Act allowed credit foncier companies to expand their business in a number of other areas. They may now, for example, lend to customers who use the company's promissory notes as collateral security. The actual amount depends on the maturity of these securities: 60 per cent of the value if the securities' remaining life is over 2 years; 75 per cent if it is between 1–2 years; and 90 per cent if under 1 year. The maturity of the loan, however, may not exceed that of the promissory notes used as collateral, nor may these notes be used for any other purpose.

The credit fonciers' funding is by way of promissory note sales to the public, and in 1981, as shown in Table 6.30, these comprised 54.8 per cent of the industry's total funding. The notes themselves must be issued with an initial maturity of at least 3 years, and for at least 1000 baht. As of June 1982, the maximum interest rate allowable on these notes was 16 per cent per annum. In addition to their own capital, credit foncier companies also borrow from banks and other sources (including other credit foncier companies); at the end of 1981, such borrowings accounted respectively for 12.8 and 9.7 per cent of their total borrowing.

(m) Agricultural Co-operatives

The agricultural co-operatives in Thailand were first established in 1916 in the form of village credit co-operatives, but by 1982 there were some six different types including agricultural; fishery; land settlement, thrift and credit; consumer and service co-operatives). The small village agricultural credit co-operatives for the most part were merged with larger co-operatives in the mid-1970s to ensure their viability, and allow them to provide a wider range of services. As shown in Table 6.31, of the 1982 co-operatives registered under the Co-operative Act BE 2511 at the end of 1981, agricultural co-operatives were the most important category, with 961, (51 per cent) of the total numbers and 801935 (or 40 per cent) of total membership). In addition to these financial orientated institutions, there were also 3822 farmers' associations which indirectly provided some financial services to the rural sector.

The agricultural co-operatives were established to assit farmers in all aspects of farming; credit plays a very important role. These institutions, however, often suffer financial problems due to their

355

TABLE 6.31 Thailand co-operative societies: nos. and members by type, 1978–81

	1978		79		80		81	
	No.	Membership[a]	No.	Membership[a]	No.	Membership[a]	No.	Membership[a]
Agricultural	815	650236	841	711117	857	743105	961	801935
Fishery	10	1769	10	2390	15	3323	20	4269
Land settlement	86	56579	111	66523	111	66523	83	62040
Thrift & credit	258	448589	310	501777	327	514695	392	647523
Consumer	172	275964	188	298093	198	303538	243	436307
Service	123	29812	136	35356	171	41510	183	56069
Total	1464	1462949	1596	1615256	1679	1672694	1882	2008143

[a] Households.

Source: Thai Ministry of Agriculture and Co-operatives, 1982.

small size and a general lack of managerial experience. To improve this position, the government in 1980 introduced a 'Restructure of Agricultural Co-operatives in Poor Financial Condition Project' as a form of rescue operation for those institutions in particular difficulty. Under this programme, a number of co-operatives are selected each year for special assistance by the government and the BAAC. The Co-operative League of Thailand has also been helpful in this improvement process.

The societies place their funds in the form of liquid assets and in loans to members. The latter are usually the most important, and are made in the form of short, medium and long term advances. The short term loans are primarily to cover seasonal crop financing requirements, the medium ones for purchasing farm animals and equipment, and the longer ones to refinance existing mortgages. The attraction of these co-operative loans is that the maximum rate allowable is set by the government at 12 per cent per annum.

The agricultural co-operatives can raise funds on deposits. These interest rates are also controlled, and in mid-1982 stood at 9 per cent per annum for savings account deposits; 10 per cent for 3 month fixed deposits; 11 per cent for 6 month fixed deposits; and 13 per cent for 12 month – 2 year money. In practice, deposits provide only a very small portion of the co-operatives' funding; they rely instead on monies borrowed from BAAC and from their members' capital subscriptions.

(n) Savings Co-operatives

Thailand's savings co-operatives are said to date from 1946, but in practice it was not until the mid-1950s that they became particularly popular among Thai savers.[27] These organisations fulfil the role of a credit union within the country, and in many cases the industry is referred to by that name. As with other co-operatives, credit unions are regulated under the Co-operative Act BE 2511 (1968), and supervised by the Department of Co-operative Promotion and Co-operative Auditing within the Ministry of Agriculture and Co-operatives. The number of savings co-operatives grew from 108 in 1970 to 239 in 1979; at the end of 1981, there were 336 savings co-operatives registered under the Act. Most were on an occupational basis with teachers, the police, and other public servant groups being the most active.

Savings co-operatives devote the bulk of their funds in loans to members. Most are small medium term unsecured loans to finance consumer durables purchases, and are repaid by regular salary deductions through the employer. The credit unions also provide some shorter term emergency loans, and in some cases long term housing finance. The maximum loan size to one borrower, however, may not exceed 10 per cent of the co-operative's assets. As a rule, the interest rates on savings co-operatives' advances are highly competitive, and often much lower than other private sector alternatives.

Unlike the agricultural co-operatives, the savings co-operatives have had little access to borrowing, and instead rely primarily on their members' contributions. While the credit unions can accept both fixed and savings deposits, most funds from members come in the form of paid-up shares in the co-operative; these are generally made through regular payroll deductions. Unlike most overseas credit unions, members are generally required to make a minimum monthly subscription as a condition of joining.

(o) Pawnshops

The pawnshops are the oldest institutions within Thailand's formal financial sector: the first was established in 1866. As in other countries, they lend against the security of a variety of portable assets – commonly jewellery, electronic goods and household wares. There are three types of pawnshops in operation under the Pawnshop Act BE 2505 (1962) and the Pawnshop Act BE 2517 (1974): private, Federal government, and municipal government pawnshops. The Ministry of the Interior is responsible for administering the Act, and at the end of 1981 there were 321 licensed pawnshops within the country.

The Federal government pawnshops are run as business enterprises. They are supervised by the Public Welfare Department of the Ministry of the Interior, and operate only within the Bangkok metropolitan area. The Federal pawnshops lend in small amounts (primarily for consumer finance purposes) and in mid-1982 were subject to the following rate schedule; loans of 1–500 baht 1.25 per cent per month; of 50–1999 baht 1.50 per cent; of 2000 baht 2 per cent; of over 2000 baht 1.25 per cent. The amount lent depends on the assets presented; on gold and jewellery, pawnshops normally lend up to 80–90 per cent of the item's appraised value. Diamonds receive up to 60–80 per cent, electrical goods around 50 per cent.[28] Besides their own capital resources, the government pawnshops also receive occasional allocations of funds through the Federal budget and by borrowing from the GSB and other institutions. In 1981, the 14 government owned pawnshops in operation served a total of 272678 customers.[28]

The private pawnshops are run for profit by private sector interests, and like the Federal government's institutions operate primarily within the Bangkok metropolitan area. They are regulated by the Police Department of the Ministry of the Interior, and must have their licence renewed annually. These pawnshops rely primarily on their own resources to finance their operations, but also borrow from the banks and private persons: they are predominantly owned by Thai Chinese families. Private pawnshop lending is also subject to control, and the rate schedule as of mid-1982 is as follows: loans of 1–2000 baht 2 per cent per month; of 2001–10000 baht 1.25 per cent. Unlike their government and municipal counterparts, the private pawnshops often lend for small business as well as consumer purposes.

The municipal pawnshops are established by local municipal governments, and may operate only within their respective jurisdictions. They are still, however, subject to the Pawnshop Acts and the Ministry of the Interior's overall supervision. Unlike the government owned operations, the municipal pawnshops are generally staffed by municipal employees and operated more along government than business enterprise lines. Their lending operations are subject to the same interest rate restraints as the government pawnshops, and are funded primarily from their own capital and local goverment budget allocation.

(p) Mutual Funds

Thailand's first openend mutual fund, The Thai Investment Fund, commenced operations in February 1963, and was managed by IBEC Thailand Ltd – an affiliate of the Rockerfeller controlled International Basic Economy Corporation.

Two other mutual fund companies (in name at least), the Bangkok Mutual Fund and the National Mutual Fund, were established in 1964. None of these ventures proved successful.[29]

It was not until more than 10 years later, in 1975, that another firm (the Mutual Fund Company) entered the industry. It was sponsored in part by the IFCT, and the IFCT is still a major shareholder.

In 1982, it was the only major operator of unit trusts or mutual funds within Thailand, and managed three such funds: Sinpinyo Fund (or, as it is translated, the 'Evergreen' Fund) One, Two and Three: all are listed on the SET. The company planned to introduce an additional fund in 1982, but the share market's poor performance in the first half of the year forced its postponement.

(q) Provident Funds

Most larger companies in Thailand operate provident funds for their more senior staff, but as yet they are not a major source of investment funds within the country. A Provident Fund Act has long been under consideration; in late 1982 it had cleared Cabinet but had not been formally introduced into the legislative process.

(r) Discount Houses

When the Bank of Thailand established its government re-purchase market in 1979, it was expected that a number of discount house type securities dealers would be established to help promote it into a true government securities market. They were also envisaged as playing a major role in developing a market for bank CDs, and both were recommended in the fifth National Social and Economic Development Plan. By 1981, three private groups had submitted application proposals and a minimum capital requirement of 20 million baht was mentioned in the regional press.[30] As of mid-1982, however, no discount houses had yet been licensed.

FINANCIAL MARKETS

There are three major financial markets within Thailand: the money market; the stock market (in the form of the SET); and the foreign exchange market. The 'unorganised' or informal money market might also be considered a separate market in its own right, but is discussed within the money market section.

(a) The Money Market

The Thai money market consists of an interbank call market; a government securities market; and a more general commercial paper market (including post-dated cheques). There is also a substantial 'unorganised' or informal money market.

(i) *Interbank call market*

The interbank call market is the oldest of the formal money markets, and dates to before the Second World War. The market is fairly well developed, with a substantial volume of at call and overnight transactions. The larger domestic banks are the traditional lenders within the market, and the foreign banks, finance companies and smaller local banks are generally borrowers. The actual position of any one borrower, however, varies with daily cash flows and reserves and there is substantial intra lending within each group. Longer borrowings or more risky advances are normally made by way of repurchase agreements, rather than direct advances.

(ii) *Government securities market*

The government securities market is a growing component of the Thai money market and many more transactions are conducted by the Bank of Thailand, the banks and finance companies directly than on the SET. Higher interest rates and reserve requirements (coupled with greater government funding needs) have substantially increased the amount of these securities outstanding. The Bank of Thailand's introduction of the government bond repurchase market on 9 April 1979 was part of the Bank's Money Market Development Project effort to promote more secondary trading in these securities, and hence allow the government to implement its monetary policy through open market operations. Even so, most buyers still hold their securities to maturity. It is hoped that establishing discount houses to act as dealers in these securities will promote much more secondary trading.

Of the government securities on issue, government bonds are the most important and, as shown in Table 6.32, in 1981 comprised 92.2 per cent of the government securities outstanding. Of the bonds outstanding, the Bank of Thailand holds the most (36.3 per cent of the total), the commercial banks are a close second (30.8 per cent) due to their reserve requirements and these securities' importance in lender of last resort financing. The GSB is third. As a rule, the low interest rates offered by these securities do not attract much private investment. In 1981, the government moved to encourage more government bond sales by requiring commercial banks wishing to establish new branches to purchase

TABLE 6.32   Thailand government domestic debt by holder (figures as at end February 1981, in million baht)

Government bonds	104470.2
Held by	
Bank of Thailand	37941.5
Commercial banks	32169.7
Government Savings Bank	25289.8
Other financial institutions	9069.2
IBRD loans participation certificates	427.0
Held by Bank of Thailand	
Treasury bills	8400.0
Held by	
Bank of Thailand	6398.0
Exchange Equalisation Fund	1362.0
Commercial banks	226.0
Government Savings Bank	30.0
Financial institutions	61.3
Other domestic sectors	322.7
Grand total	113297.2

Source: Bank of Thailand, *Quarterly Review* (March, 1981) pp. 32–3.

additional government bonds and attempt to resell these to the public.

Though Treasury bills comprise only a small portion of government borrowing, they constitute an important liquidity base for the local market. These securities are auctioned on a weekly basis, and since 1976 have been available in maturities of 7, 28, 63 and 128 days. At one time, the commercial banks and GSB purchased a major portion of these securities, but more recently, as was shown in Table 6.31, the Bank of Thailand (and, to a lesser extent, the Exchange Equalisation Fund) are now the major holders.

(iii) *Commercial paper market*

The commercial paper market has been the slowest sector to develop, despite a relatively early start. The Siam Industrial Credit Company, (a Siam Cement affiliate), for example, issued commercial paper in Thailand as early as 1966[31] and in 1969 the Thai Investment and Securities Company was the first to deal in domestic bills of exchange.[32] Even today, however, there is little secondary trading in these securities. The finance and investment companies have worked to develop this market, as well as trading in their own promissory notes, but progress has been slow and post-dated cheques (also seldom traded) are probably more popular overall.

(iv) *Certificates of deposit market*

In 1979, the Bank of Thailand established a study group to plan the introduction of bank CDs within the Thai financial system. On 15 July 1981, the Bank invited representatives from the Bangkok Bank, Thai Farmers' Bank, and Siam Commercial Bank to examine the legislation this group prepared, and it was amended accordingly. The issue of CDs will be controlled by the Bank of Thailand and banks will be prohibited from purchasing their own CDs prior to maturity. They can, however, purchase those issued by other banks, and these will count as deposits within any asset ratio requirements. While both bearer and inscribed certificates are envisaged, the former will probably trade primarily through the use of a depository system. The introduction of CDs are included as goal within the financial side of the government's fifth 5 Year Plan, and should be introduced in the near future.

(v) *'Unorganised' or informal market*

In addition to that portion of the money market involving institutions, there is also a substantial 'unorganised' or informal money market, largely operating outside effective government control. As the Bank of Thailand explained, it 'is quite large and plays a not insignificant role, especially in rural areas . . . transactions include lendings by private moneylenders, operations of the so called 'pia-huey' or 'rotating credit societies', savings with and borrowings from private, non-registered credit unions, borrowing and lending between private persons in general; etc.'.[33] Family companies, particularly ethnic Chinese interests, are also of importance. As another government publication pointed out, it is particularly important within some sectors of the market, since 'for the majority of rural farmers, small and medium business enterprises and urban households, the unorganised [financial] markets fulfil many needs which are not being satisfied elsewhere'.[34] Even the public sector was apparently involved in this market for on 5 May 1982 all government bodies and state enterprises were prohibited from accepting loans offered by private individuals or brokers.

While this 'unorganised' market does not involve the formal financial institutions directly, there is nevertheless more than just an interest rate relationship between the two. Indeed, they are a major reason for the black market's success. If a customer is refused a loan at a bank or finance company, for example, it is apparently not uncommon for the staff to recommend approaching a certain private lender for the money. If a loan results, the officer often receives a 'commission' for his efforts. Sometimes the more wealthy loan officers will even make such 'informal' loans on their own account.

These informal lenders both make loans and accept deposits at rates far above those available from regulated financial institutions and therefore attract substantial deposits; while the funds are much more expensive than a bank loan, they are often more readily available. The government monetary officials have tried to reduce the size of this market in favour of the regulated financial institutions, and no doubt the finance companies' money market activities have reduced the informal market's relative share. It nevertheless grows rapidly when the official sector's interest rates become unrealistic. Taxation is another important factor, and it is feared that the interest withholding tax on deposits with financial institutions – which came into effect in 1983 – will redirect substantial funds from the organised to the 'unorganised' market.

(b) The Securities Exchange of Thailand (SET)

Thailand's securities industry dates at least to 1946, when a group of Middle East businessmen unsuccessfully attempted to establish a local Stock Exchange centred on the commercial banks.[35] Nevertheless, interest in share trading subsequently developed, and eventually one auctioneer began holding special share auctions on a Sunday afternoon.[36] Eventually a more permanent market became warranted, and Thailand's first exchange, the Bangkok Stock Exchange, was finally established on 1 July 1962. It, too, was mainly associated with foreign interests and did not prove successful. From a trading peak in 1968–9 of 238 million baht, its annual turnover continued to decline until in its last full year of operations (1974) the trading volume accounted for only 26 million baht (the market's capitalisation then was over 2374 million). As one study described it 'the meeting was held in the secretary's office before a school-type blackboard located on one wall of the room. On the average about 10–12 conducted . . . their business between 2.45 and 3.15 p.m.'.[37] Another suggested that it operated 'more in the nature of a private club than a truly national market'.[38] Some members tried to change this and increase securities trading, but their efforts proved inadequate, and the Bangkok Exchange ceased operations on 7 March 1975.

Its closure was effected by the Securities Exchange of Thailand Act BE 2517 (1975) which established SET. The new Exchange began trading on 30 April 1975, with 30 members and 15 listed securities of 11 companies. As of 1981, SET had 30 member firms

TABLE 6.33   Securities Exchange of Thailand member firms, 1981

Adkinson Securities Ltd
Asia Credit Ltd
Ayudhya Investment and Trust Co. Ltd
Bangkok Tokyo Finance and Securities Co. Ltd
Bangkok Nomura International Securities Co. Ltd
Bangkok First Investment and Trust Ltd
Bara Investment and Securities Co. Ltd
Cathay Trust Co. Ltd
Dynamic Eastern Finance Co. Ltd
First Trust Co. Ltd
General Finance and Securities Corpn Ltd
International Finance and Consultants Co. Ltd
International Trust and Finance Co. Ltd
Mit Thai Europartners Finance & Investment Ltd
Multi-Credit Corpn of Thailand Ltd
National Finance and Securities Co. Ltd
Nava Finance and Securities Co. Ltd
Phatra Thanakit Co. Ltd
Poonpipat Finance and Securities Co. Ltd
Thai Finance Co. Ltd
Thai Financial Syndicate Ltd
Thai Financial Trust Co. Ltd
Thai – Oversea Trust Co. Ltd
Thai Securities Ltd
The Asia Financing and Trust Co. Ltd
The Book Club Finance and Securities Co. Ltd
The Siam Industrial Credit Co. Ltd.
The South East Finance and Securities Co. Ltd
Union Finance Co. Ltd
Union Securities Co. Ltd

Source: SET, *Annual Report 1981*, pp. 49–51.

TABLE 6.34 Securities Exchange of Thailand listings by industry type, 1981

Financial institutions	25
Commerce	9
Warehouse & silos	3
Interior furnishings	5
Cement	3
Plastics	2
Automotive	3
Hotel	2
Metal	2
Textiles & clothing	10
Mining	2
Food & beverage	5
Others	6
Unit trusts	6
Total	80

Source: SET, *Annual Report*, pp. 44–8.

and 80 listed companies: a listing of the former, and a breakdown of the latter by type of industry, are shown respectively in Tables 6.33 and 6.34.

Of these 80 companies, 76 are registered listings and four have an 'authorised for trading' status. To become a registered firm, the company must first have an authorised capital of at least 250 million baht, with 20 million fully paid; at least 300 ordinary shareholders with individual holdings not more than 0.5 per cent of the total paid-up capital and together comprising at least 30 per cent; not more than 100 baht par value Ordinary Shares bearing the name of the owner; a net profit for 2 or more consecutive years; a purpose socially and economically desirable for the Thai nation; no unusual restrictions on share transfer. The 'authorised' classification is slightly less rigorous: authorised companies need not be profitable; their authorised capital of at least 100 million baht need be only 10 million paid; they need only 200 ordinary shareholders, with individual shareholdings not more than 0.5 per cent of the total paid-up capital, which together comprise at least 25 per cent of the paid up capital. The other conditions are similar to those for the company 'authorised for trading'.

In addition to the corporate sector, there are some 85 government securities (primarily different series of savings, loan and investment bonds) also listed. In the early years government securities comprised the bulk of the SET's turnover volume as the share market initially declined, reaching a low of 75 in March 1976. But with the start of the boom market in 1977, corporate securities came to dominate the market. This trend continued until 24 November 1978, when the Book Club Stock Index hit a high of 232.54. A major decline started in January 1979, and neither the share prices nor trading volumes have recovered since. Government transactions thus again became important. As shown in Table 6.35, in 1981 they accounted for 12.99 per cent of the SET's volume: a marked increase over 1980's 0.15 per cent. As the market showed some recovery in 1982, corporate securities are likely to have increased again in relative importance.

TABLE 6.35   Securities Exchange of Thailand turnover value, 1975–81 (figures as at end year in million baht)

| | | % of total value | |
| | | --- | --- |
Year	Annual turnover	Corporate securities	Government securities
1975	1522.92	36.74	63.26
1976	1681.15	59.10	40.90
1977	26592.28	98.83	1.17
1978	57272.40	99.64	0.36
1979	22533.12	99.63	0.37
1980	6559.22	99.85	0.15
1981	2897.68	87.01	12.99

Source: Fact Book '82 (Bangkok: SET, 1982) p. 17.

One cause of the SET's long delayed recovery was the poor reputation it developed during 1979. Overspeculation, marketrigging, and many other questionable practices were not uncommon as the boom market continued and most SET member firms did little to stem these activities. In fact, they actively encouraged speculators by loaning funds based on the collateral of their shares, and in effect allowing them to pyramid their holdings. One of the more notable of these lenders was Raja Finance, an SET member finance and securities company, whose assets mushroomed from 21.6 million in 1977 to some 100 million in 1978 (to become the fourth largest finance company and the third largest SET listed firm in terms of capitalisation). By mid-July 1978, however, the share market's decline caused substantial bad debts for both Raja and other securities lenders, and in July 1979 the firm collapsed.

Another problem area for the SET is the Public Companies Act

BE 2522 (1979). It was intended to help break the family control of Thai business, and promote individual shareholding, by permitting only 'public companies' to sell shares to the public when they wished to increase capital. The conditions for registration proved too strict, and even most of the listed SET firms are ineligible. Probably the most difficult requirement is the ownership spread: companies must have at least 100 or more individual shareholders holding no more than 0.6 per cent of the shares; together, these shares must equal at least 50 per cent of the total shares issued. Any remaining shareholders may not hold more than 10 per cent of the shares outstanding.

The Thai government's other actions to promote public ownership have proved more successful; its actions in response to the 1979 crash were particularly impressive. These were designed to keep the finance and securities companies in operation, and included the Capital Market Development Fund (CMDF), the Krung Thai Fund, a liquidity fund and rediscounting support for the Bank of Thailand. They allowed the securities industry and the share market direct support through direct lending and share purchasing via repurchase agreements. The CMDF was one of the more important. It was established by the IFCT on 6 August 1979 with the assistance of the Thai government; the Bank of Thailand; the GSB; the SET; and commercial banks: 300 million baht was contributed by the government, 700 million by the GSB and private banks, a total of 1 billion baht (these funds are managed by the IFCT). The CMDF may later serve as the basis for Thailand's proposed Securities Finance Corporation, as well as assuming some unit trust functions.

In addition to financial support, the government has also tried to encourage new SET listings and share investment by a number of fiscal incentives. These include a corporate income tax rate of 30 per cent (compared to the standard 40 per cent level); there is also a lower tax on listed company dividends. One may, for example, elect to pay either a 15 per cent withholding tax at source and no further tax, or receive a tax credit of 35 per cent and include the payment within normal assessable income; the wealthier investors understandably chose the former option. In July 1982, the government also waived its former 0.1 per cent business tax on securities transactions to promote greater trading volumes.

While the SET has so far not been a major success, it has not been a failure either. The SET does operate; there is a growing secondary market for the major securities; and, since its foundation it has helped Thai companies raise over 12 million baht in new capital. More important, its performance must be viewed against Thailand's investment climate. Its opening on 1 April 1975 occurred on the same day as the fall of Saigon, and the subsequent problems in Kampuchea have hardly been encouraging to Thai investors. Thailand has suffered from the substantial increases in oil prices and often uncertain domestic political situations, the 3 day coup on 1 April 1981 being perhaps the best example.

(c) The Foreign Exchange Market

The foreign exchange business in Thailand is controlled by the Bank of Thailand through the Exchange Control Act BE 2485 1942. The business itself, however, is centred on the government's Exchange Equalisation Fund (EEF). The EEF was established in 1955 with an initial capital of 1.2 billion baht and a separate Board of Directors. In practice, however, it is managed by the Bank of Thailand, and operates as its foreign exchange trading arm. The EEF's main purpose is to stabilise the baht's exchange rates with other currencies.

On 20 October 1963, the baht was effectively pegged to the US dollar, and the EEF ensured a rate close to a parity of 20.8 baht to the dollar. When the US dollar devalued in 1971 and 1973, the baht followed suit. After the latter move, the value proved too low for government policy and on 15 July the baht was revalued to a new parity of 20 baht. Subsequent changes in the US dollar in relation to other currencies eventually caused the government (on 8 March 1978) to switch from a US dollar to a trade weighted 'basket' of linked currencies. The 'basket' includes the Japanese yen, the Singapore dollar, the Malaysian ringgit, the German mark, the British pound sterling, and the Hong Kong dollar, but the US dollar is the most important component and accounts for perhaps as much as 60 per cent of the total. This 'basket' is valued in gold, and expressed in terms of a US dollar rate. It was hoped that the new system would help develop the local foreign exchange market, and reduce the financial sector's dependence on the US dollar.

With the introduction of the 'basket', the baht remained relatively stable compared to most currencies from 1978–80. But in 1981, with a strong US dollar, the baht began to rise sharply against most other currencies. It soon became overvalued, and Thailand experienced a serious balance of trade and payments deficit. New capital inflow was also affected, and the official reserves declined. To offset this, the baht was devalued by first 1.08 and then by a further 8.7 per cent respectively on 12 May and 15 July 1981. The Bank of Thailand also introduced a special exchange rate protected 3 month swap facility from October 1981 until the end of the year, to encourage additional capital inflow. The government (both in its own right and through the Bank of Thailand) also arranged for a substantial level of foreign borrowings, and extended the exemption of the interest withholding tax on foreign borrowings.

The government's borrowing facilities have not been required to any great extent as the 1981 measures helped reduce Thailand's trade deficit to more manageable proportions. Capital inflow, when the effects of the swap facility are considered, has also shown improvement. Nevertheless some observers still feel the baht remains overvalued and that a weakening of the currency would afford many advantages: they predicted a devaluation (to a 25 baht to the dollar level) by the end of 1983.[39]

Since 1 November 1978, the EEF has set the exchange rate of the baht for seven currencies: the US dollar; Japanese yen; Deutsche mark; pound sterling; Malaysian ringgit; Singapore dollar; and Hong Kong dollar. Until July, 1981, the EEF in effect created the US dollar baht rate by buying or selling during the fixing session with the commercial banks while the other rates were determined without trading. Now, however, the EEF simply notifies the banks of the daily rates for all seven currencies. The commercial banks may then add up to a 0.05 baht margin on these rates when selling those currencies, or when buying or discounting more than 0.10 baht on sight bills or 0.4 on telegraphic transfers. This fixing system was initially introduced as part of the government's decision to float the baht, but as already indicated exchange rates are still very much government controlled.

The largest portion of the banks' foreign exchange business is conducted in US dollars. In March 1981, for example, commercial banks in Thailand traded 1717.188 million of US dollars (compared to £9.968 million. HK$ 145.94 million, and M$ and S$ 67.17 million).[40] Besides spot transactions, the banks also provide forward cover, and again this is dominated by US dollar business. In April 1982, baht–US dollar forward cover had a premium of 0.07 (a rate of approximately 3.6 per cent per annum).

ANALYSIS

The Thai financial system has expanded rapidly in the post-war period, and in the process become increasingly locally owned and controlled – particularly in the banking sector. While this expansion has been at the expense of the foreign controlled institutions, it is not necessarily an indication of the industry's service to local industry. Rather, it reflects the substantial restrictions placed on foreign owned banks and other institutions within the country. As in many countries, banks are not popular institutions within Thailand (it is worth noting that in the 1981 coup attempt, their nationalisation was one of the group's intentions). The problems are multifaceted, but basically relate to the banks not fulfilling the role desired by the government or public. Instead of assisting Thailand's agricultural and industrial development, the banks have retained their traditional emphasis on trade finance; agricultural loans are considered too expensive to administer and most banks, while reportedly encouraging rural lending, still direct substantial funds to the BAAC in order to fulfil their agricultural quotas. The handling of non-agricultural loans is also often criticised as being directed to businesses associated with the major shareholders or chief executives of these institutions. The Commercial Bank Act's public ownership requirements were introduced to a large extent to reduce this concentration and a 'Fund for the Development of Commercial Banks' (or the 'Fund for the Development of Financial and Industrial Establishment') has been proposed as a means to ensure the Act's success. It would buy up the required interest in the banks and finance companies (as well as shares in promising industrial companies) and redistribute them to the public through its own unit trust or mutual fund. Whether this fund is established remains to be seen, but its related proposals give some insight as to the banking sector's potential ownership problems.

This emphasis on the banking sector is understandable given that it accounts for close to 70 per cent of the financial sector's total assets, deposits and advances, but the importance of the major domestic banks in particular is at least partly a function of government limitation on new entry. If instead of the current 16 domestic banks, many of the finance and securities company joint ventures had been allowed a commercial banking licence, the present concentration would probably be much less. Instead foreign interests often combined with the major banking families in forming their local non-bank institutions, and in the process added to (not detracted from) the latter's overall power and control.

The government could similarly be criticised for the slowness with which it has permitted the development of new financial institutions and instruments, and the restraints it has placed on their operation. Certainly it has been the moving force behind the establishment of most of the country's more specialised institutions – the Bank for Agriculture and Agricultural Co-operatives (BAAC); Government Savings Bank; Small Industries Finance Office (SIFO); Government Housing Bank, Securities Exchange of Thailand, and Industrial Finance Corporation of Thailand (IFCT) – but it has been a rather slow moving force. Most of the basic studies for the new Stock Exchange were conducted in the late 1960s, but it took until 1975 for the SET to open its doors. Discount houses have been under discussion for years (and since 1979 subject to a number of serious proposals) but by 1982 with no result. Bank CDs seem subject to the same fate, and there are many more instituions and instruments whose establishment would aid the Thai economy.

A long term export promotion body has long been discussed, but it took until early 1982 for the Bank of Thailand, the Ministries of Finance and of Commerce, and the IFCT to announce their plans to form the Export Credit Guarantee Corporation of Thailand. The new body would expand on the Bank of Thailand's present export finance rediscounting scheme so that Thai exporters could compete more effectively on new markets. In late 1982, however, this body had yet to commence operations.

In the provincial areas, too, there seems some merit in establishing new financial institutions to meet specific rural banking needs rather than forcing the existing institutions to perform – rather ineffectively – that role. In the fifth National Economic and Social Development Plan, for example, a new type of banking institution – a regional bank – is suggested for just this purpose. It is envisaged as a locally owned public company operating only within specific provincial areas and raising and lending its funds locally. Besides improving the level of banking services in these areas, the proposed institution is seen as mobilising new savings for rural agricultural and provincial centre manufacturing development within its area. Initially four such banks have been suggested – one for the north, east, northeast and south – [41] but others could also be established for more specific areas.

Long term capital investment, despite the efforts of the IFCT and SIFO, also remains a problem, and its shortage is a major hinderance to Thai economic development – particularly in respect of export related manufacturing. The Bank of Thailand sent a team to Japan to study the operation of the Industrial Bank of Japan and other long term credit banks. It was thought that such an institution in Thailand might improve medium and long term financing.[42] No industrial bank has yet been established, and Thailand is somewhat remarkable among its neighbours for not having at least one development bank; a government sponsored (and probably government owned) institution seems likely in the future.

The problem that the lack of discount houses presents to the money market's development has already been discussed, as has the need to make more efficient utilisation of the country's provident funds for long term savings and capital investment. The insurance industry could also be used to more effect, both in terms of saving and investment, and the Stock Exchange capital mobilisation and secondary market roles could both be much improved.

The government's monetary authorities could equally make more effective use of market related instruments in implementing its monetary policy. In the past, the Bank of Thailand has traditionally relied heavily on direct control measures over certain institutions rather than attempting to influence the market as a whole. Strict control – either real or potential – has allowed these policies to be successful in curtailing money supply growth within the formal financial sector, but there is always the danger that unrealistic interest rate ceilings would shift funds to the 'unorganised' or black market: it was encouraging to see the Bank of Thailand raising interest rate ceilings when local conditions required, but not lowering them after the demand had peaked. The Bank of Thailand's government repurchase market window was another potential step toward more market orientated policies. Though slow in coming, the necessary infrastructure is gradually developing.

The Bank of Thailand, however, has begun to move somewhat more rapidly than in the past, and since the share market's problems in 1979 has been willing to play a much more central role in stabilising the local market. In 1981, for example, the Bank assisted in adjusting the baht's currency rate realignment through a series of interest withholding tax exemptions on short and other foreign borrowings, and introducing cover for such borrowings through special 3 month swap agreements.

When considering Thailand's financial sector, it thus appears that the government policymakers have at least identified most of the present problem areas, and (more importantly) have also proposed some tentative solutions. The problem that remains, however, is to prod what has been a traditionally slow, overly cautious, and very conservative Central Bank and Finance Ministry into taking appropriate action. The need for them to act soon is quite evident when the recent patterns of savings and investment are examined. As shown in Table 6.36, household savings is the only domestic sector to experience surplus in terms of savings during 1977–80, but it has not been sufficient to offset the economy's total requirements. Worse still, this deficit has been expanding rapidly, and has led to an increasing level of external debt and interest payments. The government's fifth National Economic and Social Development Plan calls for even greater foreign borrowings 'which may not be acceptable from the point of view of internal and external stability'.[43] To avoid such problems, as one economist recommended 'the government of Thailand should rely more on domestic savings, otherwise a shortage of capital will certainly cause the growth rate to fall'.[44] Thailand's financial institutions will play a key role in any attempt at improved mobilisation, and hence their successful operation will play an increasingly crucial role in the health of the Thai economy.

TABLE 6.36 Thailand resource gap analysis (figures as at end year, in million baht)

	1977	78	79	80
Government	−9.9[a]	−13.7	−18.5	−20.8
Public enterprises	−6.0	−8.2	−12.3	−25.7
Private business	−50.3	−58.4	−78.7	−78.0
Household	+44.1	+57.4	+67.8	+76.0
External	22.1	22.9	41.7	48.5

[a] Deficit (−) and surplus (+) matrix.

Source: Siri Garnjarevndee, 'Pattern of Household Financial Savings in Thailand Since 1960', Bank of Thailand, *Quaterly Bulletin* (March 1981) p. 16.

THE FUTURE

Balance of payments problems in 1979 caused Thailand to request World Bank assistance. The Bank prepared a dismal forecast for the Thai economy in its present state, and recommended a massive 5 Year structural readjustment programme to prevent future problems; this was launched in 1981 in conjunction with the government's fifth National Economic and Social Development Plan.

This Plan, which commenced on 1 October 1981, differs from the previous four in that it places more emphasis on resolving the country's social problems – particularly with respect to the distribution of income – and on restructuring both the economy and society, than on strictly economic growth. 'Growth' has not been discarded, but 'growth for growth's sake' is no longer accepted as a major goal. Instead the Plan promotes economic efficiency; reduced energy consumption; and more careful investment planning. Its overall objectives are addressed by a number of related programmes, including Poverty Eradication; Stabilisation; Economic Restructuring; Social Structure Adjustment; National Security Co-ordination; and Development Administration Reform. In regard to the financial sector, the Plan will require substantial funds to finance its objectives (during 1982–6, for example, it is estimated to need some US$17.5 billion in foreign capital). 7.5 billion will come from the World Bank; the ADB and various overseas government bodies will no doubt also provide much of the remaining funds, but there will still be a requirement for extensive private overseas borrowings.

Over a longer period (1981–2001), the Eastern Seacoast Industrial Development Project will also absorb a major portion of Thailand's domestic and foreign borrowing. The project is a heavy industry zone designed to utilise some of Thailand's 16.1 million cubic feet of natural gas reserves found recently in the Gulf of Siam. Among the various industrial projects planned are a natural gas separation/processing plant; an ethylene cracking (olefin) plant and petro chemical complex; an ammonia/urea fertiliser plant; and a rocksalt–soda ash and potash complex. These industries (in 1981 prices) are estimated to require at least 65000 million baht to construct, and another 3700 million in working capital. To support this industry, the government, too, must provide a wide range of infrastructure support – little of which is currently available: deep sea ports; railroads; water supplies; highways; electric power; telephones; housing; and other related services will require at least another 30500 million baht.

The public and private sector requirements then total some 102700 million baht in new investment and, as shown in Table 6.37, a large portion of these funds is to come from overseas sources. The exact proportion of commercially raised funding has yet to be determined, but the end amount should be substantial and very attractive to the international banker.

TABLE 6.37 Thai Eastern Seacoast Industrial Project: estimated funding requirements (figures in million baht at 1981 prices)

Funding Source	Funds required for investment		
	Foreign	Local	Total
Government loan	22000	23350	45350
Private sector			
Loan	38600	4700	43300
Equity	3100	10950	14050
Total	63700	39000	102700

Source: Eastern Seacoast Study, cited in 'Natural Gas and Oil – Their Impact on Thailand's Economy', Bangkok Bank, *Monthly Review* (September 1982) p. 395.

Thailand could, perhaps, raise most of its funding for the Industrial Project and the Plan on the international capital market, but given its recent balance of payment problems the Plan requires domestic saving to be a much higher percentage of GDP than in the past (27 per cent, compared to 23.1) in order to reduce the savings–investment resource gap from 6.3 to 4.1 per cent of GDP. To reduce this gap (and hence the foreign capital required), the Plan calls for improved savings mobilisation measures; improved stability and efficiency of financial institutions; and possible establishment of new institutions.

In conclusion, Thailand's recent natural resource discoveries (and lower international oil prices) have given its economy a much needed breathing space in which to resolve its difficulties. Plans have been made accordingly, and on the surface at least there seems cause for optimism. If successful, Thailand by 1986 will have joined Taiwan and South Korea in becoming a 'newly industrialised country'.

NOTES

1. Recent World Bank studies, for example, suggest that real incomes in the most affected north and northeast have not improved. See Ho Kwon Ping, 'Thailand's Broken Rice Bowl', *Far Eastern Economic Review* (1 December 1978) for a further discussion. Boonchu Rojanastien, 'The economy and national security', Bangkok Bank *Monthly Review* (March–April 1979) pp. 130–4 gives further insight into these problems.
2. *Thailand* (Hongkong and Shanghai Banking Corporation, 1982) p. 5.
3. Paisal Sricharatchanya, 'A guided revival', *Far Eastern Economic Review* (4 June 1982) p. 58.
4. The 'unorganised' or informal money market is unorganised or informal only to the extent that it is not government regulated. In theory, these activities should be subject to at least the interest rate ceiling set by the government for usury purposes. In practice, however, effective interest rates (if calculated on a per annum basis) can be as high as 280 per cent. Bangkok Bank *Monthly Review* (December 1979) p. 456.
5. Virach Aphimeteetamrong, 'The Contribution of Financial Institutions to Thai Economic Development': PhD thesis, University of Illinois, Urbana–Champaign campus (1980) p. 24.
6. Robert F. Emery, *The Financial Institutions of Southeast Asia: a country by country study* (New York: Praeger, 1970) p. 576.
7. The Bank was established by Prince Chaiyanantamongkhon as a result of his 1897 overseas tour to study European business practices. The initial choice of the name 'Book Club' rather than 'bank' is well explained in the Prince's letter to the King (19 January 1905): 'I was uncertain as to the outcome of the venture because although there were sure to be demand for payments, nothing was assured regarding the inflow of deposits. And if deposits were insufficient, it follows naturally that payments cannot be successfully executed. I have therefore called this office the Book Club. When a Thai hears the word, he will not know its meaning, while a foreigner will think it is a public library. And we shall do things in such a way as to make everything obscure, so as not to let it be known that a banking business is in operation, so that if the enterprise should fail it would not be considered a disgrace or make banking a miserable venture forever'.
   Fortunately the 'Club' proved a success and in 1905 it conducted a share offering to raise sufficient funds to establish a full service banking operation. The King gave his formal approval, which was announced in the Royal Gazette on 30 January 1906. The Bank considers this its official founding date. 'The Siam Commercial Bank', *Bangkok Post* (30 January 1979) p. 9.
8. Robert F. Emery, *Financial Institutions*, p. 567.
9. The Bangkok Bank has traditionally been the largest of the ASEAN domestic banks. It has only recently been surpassed by Malaysia's Bank Bumiputra. They were ranked 202 and 232 in *The Banker*'s 1982 'top 500' world banks' listing.
10. *Far Eastern Economic Review* (1 September 1978) gives a discussion of these family corporate group relationships.
11. Nukul Prachuabmoh, 'An address to the annual banquet of the Thai Bankers' Association 18 February 1981', Bank of Thailand *Quarterly Bulletin* (March 1981) p. iv.

12. Lee Sheng-Yi and Y. C. Jao, *Financial Structures*, p. 153.
13. Rob Salamon, 'Chin Sophonpuchi: the Bangkok connection', *Insight* (June 1978) pp. 7–18.
14. Nukul Prachuabmoh, 'An address to the annual banquet of the Thai Bankers' Association 18 February 1981', Bank of Thailand *Quarterly Bulletin* (March 1981) p. iii.
15. Paisal Sricharatchanya 'Divestiture hits a snag', *Far Eastern Economic Review* (12 March 1982) p. 110.
16. 'Banking on the German Model' *Euromoney* (Thailand Supplement) (December 1980) p. 2.
17. Paisal Sricharatchanya 'Book it in Thailand', *Far Eastern Economic Review* (15 January 1982) p. 54.
18. *Business Review* (August 1982) p. 64.
19. IFCT, *Annual Report 1981*, p. 1.
20. A full discussion of the finance and securities companies' development and operation can be found in Michael T. Skully, *Merchant Banking in the Far East*, 2nd edn (Thailand Ch.) (London: *Financial Times*, 1980).
21. Robert F. Emery, *Financial Institutions*, p. 588.
22. Robert F. Emery, *Financial Institutions*, p. 610.
23. More details on its operations can be found in 'Reinsurance: a great stride forward', Bangkok Bank *Monthly Review* (January 1979) pp. 15–16.
24. 'Failure in Thailand (Insurance)', *Asian Money Manager* (October 1977) p. 32.
25. Robert F. Emery, *Financial Institutions*, p. 610.
26. Bank of Thailand, *Quarterly Bulletin* (March 1981) p. 16.
27. There is some conflict concerning the first savings co-operative's establishment date. Emery, for example, suggests that the first consumer co-operative was established in 1938 and the first savings and credit co-operative was formed in 1949. The latter was a Pilot Project on which Thailand's modern credit unions are based: Robert F. Emery, *Financial Institutions*, p. 598.
28. 'Asia's Pawnbrokers still flourish' *Insight* (July 1978) p. 58.
29. Robert F. Emery, *Financial Institutions*, p. 608.
30. Paisal Sricharatchanya, 'Thai Discount Houses Proposal on the Launch Pad', *Asian Banking* (July 1981) p. 55.
31. Sydney M. Robbins, *A Capital Market in Thailand* (limited edn) (Bangkok: Bank of Thailand, 1970) pp. 15–16.
32. TISCO's initial involvement with three party paper – a payee, payor and acceptor – was so significant, especially as a paying agent, that the term 'TISCO acceptance paper' was commonly used for Thai Bills of Exchange. The situation followed the development of Bancom bills in the Philippines, and was introduced with the assistance of Filipino seconded staff while Bancom was a TISCO shareholder.
33. Bank of Thailand, cited in the *Far Eastern Economic Review* (21 September 1979) p. 101.
34. *Thailand into the 80s* (Bangkok: Office of the Prime Minister, 1979) p. 187.
35. P. Hunt and D. M. T. Gibson, *Bangkok Stock Exchange* (Board of Trustees, Leland Standford Junior University, 1965) p. 1.
36. Peter E. Basel (ed.), *Securities Exchange of Thailand: 1978–1979 Handbook* (Bangkok: Business Information and Research Ltd, 1979) p. 13.

37. Khanit Sethandha, 'Thailand Securities Exchange: Its Operations, Problems and Prospects': MBM thesis, Asian Institute of Management (1975) p. 73.
38. Alex A. Rozental, *Finance and Development in Thailand* (New York: Praeger, 1970) p. 342.
39. Bank of America, *Thailand: Economic Update* (14 October 1982) p. 6.
40. Bank of Thailand, *Quarterly Bulletin* (March 1981) pp. 10–11.
41. Viraphong Vachratith, 'Fear of the Big Stick Haunts Bankers', *Asian Finance* (15 February 1982) p. 12.
42. *Far Eastern Economic Review* (21 September 1979) p. 51.
43. Siri Garnjarerndee, 'Pattern of Household Financial Savings in Thailand Since 1960', Bank of Thailand *Quarterly Bulletin* (March 1981) p. 15.
44. Damrong Karishnamara, 'The Structure of Income and Savings Mobilization in Thailand', Bangkok Bank, *Monthly Review* (February 1981) p. 62.

Bibliography

GENERAL

A Study of Commercial Banks in ASEAN Countries 1979 (Manila: SGV Group, 1980).

Allen, G. C. and Donnithorne, A. G., *Western Enterprise in Far Eastern Economic Development* (London: George Allen & Unwin, 1954).

Allen, T. W., *The ASEAN Report* (Hong Kong: Dow Jones, 1979).

ASEAN: An Economic Profile 1978 (Manila: SGV Group, 1978).

ASEAN Banking Fact Book 1981 (Singapore: ASEAN Banking Council, 1981).

Asian Corporate Profile and National Finance 1978–9 (Hong Kong: Asian Finance Publications, 1979).

Bankers' Handbook for Asia 1982–3 (Hong Kong: Asian Finance Publications, 1983).

'Banking '79', *Far Eastern Economic Review* (6 April 1979).

'Banking '80', *Far Eastern Economic Review* (4 April 1980).

'Banking '81', *Far Eastern Economic Review* (27 March 1981).

'Banking '82', *Far Eastern Economic Review* (26 March 1982).

Banking Structures and Sources of Finance in the Far East, 3rd edn (London: *Financial Times*, 1980).

BIAC Report on Capital Market in South East Asia (Paris: Business and Industry Advisory Committee to the OECD, 1974).

Broinowski, A. (ed.), *Understanding ASEAN* (London: Macmillan, 1982).

Cameron, Rondo (ed.), *Banking in the Early Stages of Industrialization: a Study in Comparative Economic History* (New York: Oxford University Press, 1967).

Capital Markets in Asia's Developing Countries (Hong Kong: Business International, 1976).

Chia Siow Yue (ed.), *ASEAN Economic Cooperation: proceedings of the ASEAN Economic Research Unit* (Singapore: Institute of Southeast Asian Studies, 1980).

Compendium to BIAC Report on Capital Market in South East Asia (Paris: Business and Industry Advisory Committee to the OECD, 1974).

379

380   *Bibliography*

Davies, S. G., *Central Banking in South and East Asia* (Hong Kong University Press, 1960).
Drake, Peter J., 'Securities Markets in Less Developed Countries', *Journal of Development Studies* (January 1977).
Drysdale, Peter (ed.), *Direct Foreign Investment in Asia and the Pacific* (Canberra: Australian National University Press, 1972).
Emery, Robert F., *The Financial Institutions of Southeast Asia: A Country by Country Study* (New York: Praeger, 1970).
Garnaut, Ross (ed.), *ASEAN in a Changing Pacific and World Economy* (Canberra: Australian National University Press, 1981).
Goldsmith, Raymond, *Financial Structure and Development* (New York: Yale University Press, 1969).
Gurley, John G. and Shaw, Edward S., 'Financial Aspects of Economic Development', *American Economic Review* (September 1955).
——, 'Financial Structure and Economic Development', *Economic Development and Cultural Change* (April 1967).
——, *Money in a Theory of Finance* (Washington DC: The Brookings Institution, 1960).
Hall, D. G. E., *A History of South-East Asia*, 2nd edn (New York: Macmillan, 1966).
Highlights of the ASEAN Economy (Singapore: Singapore Airlines Ltd, 1977).
Ichimura, Shinichi (ed.), *Southeast Asia: Nature, Society and Development* (Honolulu: University Press of Hawaii, 1977).
Kim, Kil-Joong, 'Financial Intermediation in Economic Development': PhD thesis, University of Cincinnati (1980).
Kindleberger, C. P., *The Formation of Financial Centers* (Princeton: Princeton University Press, 1974).
King, F. H. H., *Money in British East Asia* (London: British Colonial Office, 1957).
Lee, Sheng-Yi and Jao, Y. C., *Financial Structures and Monetary Policies in Southeast Asia* (London: Macmillan, 1982).
Lim, Chong-Yah, *Economic Development in Southeast Asia* (Kuala Lumpur: Federal Publications, 1981).
Lo, Daniel Chin Chai, 'ASEAN Bankers' Acceptances': academic exercise for a Bachelor Degree, University of Singapore (September 1980).
Lowe, John W., 'Financial Markets in Developing Countries', *Finance and Development* (December 1974).
McKinnon, R. I., *Money and Capital in Economic Development* (Washington, DC: Brookings Institution, 1973).
——, (ed.) *Money and Finance in Economic Growth and Development* (New York: Marcel Dekker, 1976).
'Merchant Banking '78', *Far Eastern Economic Review* (22 September 1978).

'Merchant Banking '79', *Far Eastern Economic Review* (21 September 1979).

'Merchant Banking '80', *Far Eastern Economic Review* (19 September 1980).

'Merchant Banking '81', *Far Eastern Economic Review* (18 September 1981).

'Merchant Banking '82', *Far Eastern Economic Review* (24 September 1982).

Newlyn, W. T., *The Financing of Economic Development* (Oxford: Clarendon Press, 1977).

Ooi, Guat Tin, *The ASEAN Preferential Trading Arrangements (PTA): An Analysis of Potential Effects on Intra-ASEAN Trade* (Singapore: Institute of Southeast Asian Studies, 1981).

Patrick, Hugh J., 'Financial Development and Economic Growth in Underdeveloped Countries', *Economic Development and Cultural Change* (January 1966).

Rana, Pradumna B., *ASEAN Exchange Rates: Policies and Trade Effects* (Singapore: Institute of Southeast Asian Studies, 1981).

Roxas, Sixto K., *Managing Asian Financial Development* (Manila: Sinag–Tala Publishers, 1976).

Saw, Swee-Hook and Lee, Soo Ann, (eds), *Economic Problems and Prospects in ASEAN Countries* (Singapore University Press, 1977).

Senkuttan, Arun (ed.), *MNCs and ASEAN Development in the 1980s* (Singapore: Institute of Southeast Asian Studies, 1981).

Shaw, E. S., *Financial Deepening in Economic Development* (New York: Oxford University Press, 1973).

Sirisena, N. L., 'ASEAN Banking and Monetary Policies', in Saw Swee-Hock and Lee, Soo Ann (eds), *Economic Problems and Prospects in ASEAN Countries* (Singapore University Press, 1977).

Skully, Michael T., *ASEAN Regional Financial Cooperation: Developments in Banking and Finance* (Singapore: Institute of Southeast Asian Studies, 1979).

——, *Merchant Banking in ASEAN: A Regional Examination of its Development and Operations* (Kuala Lumpur: Oxford University Press, 1983).

——, *Merchant Banking in the Far East*, 2nd edn (London: *Financial Times*, 1980).

——, 'Prospects for Merchant Banking in the Far East', *Bankers' Handbook for Asia 1977–8* (Manila: Asian Finance Publications, 1978).

Tan Sri Ismail bin Mohamed Ali, 'The Role of the Central Banks in South East Asia's Financial Markets': paper to the *Financial Times'* Conference on 'The South East Asian Financial Markets – Present and Future' (7–9 July 1975).

10 Years, ASEAN (Jakarta: Association of South East Asian Nations, 1978).

Viksnins, George, J., *Financial Deepening in ASEAN Countries* (Hawaii University Press, 1980).

Wai, U Tun, *Financial Intermediaries and National Savings in Developing Countries* (New York: Praeger, 1972).

Wawn, B., *Economics of Asean Countries* (London: Macmillan, 1982).

Wong, John, *ASEAN Economies in Perspective: a Comparative Study of Indonesia, Malaysia, the Philippines, Singapore and Thailand* (London: Macmillan, 1979).

——, *The ASEAN Economies: Development Outlook for the 1980s* (Singapore: Economic Research Centre, University of Singapore, 1977).

Yenko, Aleth, *Exchange Rate Regimes of ASEAN Countries: A Critical Evaluation* (Singapore: Institute of Southeast Asian Studies, 1982).

BRUNEI

Ahmad, Hamzad, 'Oil and Security in Brunei' *Contemporary Southeast Asia* (September 1980) pp. 182–91.

'Brunei Hopes to Join ASEAN', *ASEAN Newsletter*, vol. 2, no. 1 (June 1981) p. 2.

Brunei Information Section, State Secretariat, State of Brunei *Annual Report 1976*.

Brunei State Chamber of Commerce, *Chamber Journal 1980–1: Jubilee Edition* (1981).

Bank of America, *Brunei: Economic Update* (7 July 1982).

Brown, D. E., *The Structure and History of A Bornean Malay Sultanate* (Brunei: The Brunei Museum, 1970).

Burley, T. M., 'Brunei: ASEAN's Reluctant Independence', *Insight* (December 1981) pp. 38–40.

Crosbie, A., 'Brunei in Transition', *Southeast Asian Affairs* (1981) pp. 75–82.

——, 'Brunei: The Constraints on a Small State', *Southeast Asian Affairs* (1978) pp. 67–79.

Das, K., 'Welcome to the Club (Brunei)', *Far Eastern Economic Review* (26 March 1982) p. 16.

Department of Trade and Resources, *Guide to the Market: Brunei* (Canberra: Australian Government Publishing Service, 1982).

Hamzah, B. A., *Oil and Economic Development Studies in Brunei* (Singapore: Institute of Southeast Asian Studies, 1980).

Hongkong and Shanghai Banking Corporation, *State of Brunei* (August 1980).

National Bank of Brunei Ltd, *Annual Report 1980*.

National Development Plan 1962–6 (Kuala Belait: Government Printer, 1962).

Tarling, Nicholas, *Britain, the Brookes and Brunei* (Kuala Lumpur: Oxford University Press, 1977).

Tasker, Rodney, 'Brunei: Nervously into the World', *Far Eastern Economic Review* (12 March, 1982) pp. 22–6.

——, 'Oh to be in Brunei Now That it is Free', *Far Eastern Economic Review* (12 March 1982) pp. 26–7.

——, 'When Oil is the Only Food for Thought', *Far Eastern Economic Review* (12 March 1982) p. 28.

Thambipilai, Pushpa, 'Brunei in ASEAN: The Viable Choice?', *Southeast Asian Affairs* (1982).

Wain, Barry, 'In Brunei, Sultan's New Palace Recalls Days of Glory', *Asian Wall Street Journal* (10 October 1982) pp. 1–2.

——, 'Independence Won't Change Brunei's Maverick Style', *Asian Wall Street Journal* (28 September 1982) pp. 1; 11.

Brunei Currency Board, *Annual Report 1980*.

INDONESIA

A Study of Commercial Banks in Indonesia (Manila: SGV Group, 1980).

Allen, G. C. and Donnithorne, A. G., *Western Enterprise in Indonesia and Malaysia* (London: Allen & Unwin, 1957).

Arief, Aritua, *Banking and Money in Indonesia: an Econometric Study* (Jakarta: Aritua Arief Associates, 1978).

Arndt, H. W., 'Banking in Hyperinflation', *Bulletin of Indonesian Economic Studies* (October 1966) pp. 45–70.

——, 'Monetary Policy Instruments in Indonesia', *Bulletin of Indonesian Economic Studies* (November 1979) pp. 107–22.

—— 'The Jakarta Dollar Market', *Bulletin of Indonesian Economic Studies* (July 1982) pp. 35–64.

Awanohara, Susumu, 'Stockmarkets: a Purely Domestic Issue', *Far Eastern Economic Review* (18 June 1982) pp. 88–90.

Bank Indonesia, *Report for the Financial Year 1980–1*.

Banking in Indonesia (Jakarta: Bank Bumi Daya, 1979).

Booth, A. and McCawley, P. (eds), *The Indonesian Economy During the Soeharto Era* (Kuala Lumpur: Oxford University Press, 1981).

Cole, D., 'New Directions in the Banking System', *Bulletin of Indonesian Economic Studies* (July 1969) pp. 60–9.

Corden, W. M. and Mackie, J., 'The Development of the Indonesian Exchange Rate System', *Malayan Economic Review* (April 1962).

Department of Trade and Resources, *Guide to the Market: Indonesia* (Canberra: Australian Government Publishing Service, 1982).

Dick, H., 'Survey of Recent Developments', *Bulletin of Indonesian Economic Studies* (March 1979) pp. 1–44; (March 1982) pp. 1–38.

Emery, Robert F., *The Financial Institutions of Southeast Asia: A Country by Country Study* (Indonesian Ch.) (New York: Praeger, 1970).

Ferris, George W., 'Recommendations for Accelerating the Growth of the Capital Market in Jakarta': paper presented in Jakarta (1978).

Fox, J. J. *et al.* (eds), *Indonesia: Australian Perspectives* (Canberra: Research School of Pacific Studies, Australian National University, 1980).

Garnaut, Ross and McCawley, Peter (eds), *Indonesia: Dualism, Growth and Poverty* (Canberra: Australian National University Press, 1981).

Gautama, S., Allan, D. E., Hiscock, M. E. and Roebuck, D., *Credit and Security in Indonesia: The Legal Problems of Development Finance* (St. Lucia: University of Queensland Press, 1973).

Geertz, Clifford, 'The Rotating Credit Association: a 'Middle Rung' in Development', *Economic Development and Cultural Change*, vol. x., no. 3. (April 1962).

Glassburner, Bruce, 'The Attempt to Foster Private Entrepreneurship in Indonesia', *Indian Economic Review* (1962) pp. 71–92.

—— (ed.), *The Economy of Indonesia* (Ithaca: Cornell University Press, 1971).

Grenville, S. A., 'Money, Prices and Finance in Indonesia 1960–74': PhD thesis, Australian National University (1976).

——, 'Survey of Recent Developments', *Bulletin of Indonesian Economic Studies 13* (March 1977) pp. 1–32.

Habir, Manggi, 'New Lease of Life', *Far Eastern Economic Review* (20 August 1982) p. 70.

Hasjim, Mohamad, 'Development and Insurance in Indonesia', *International Insurance Monitor* (November 1979) pp. 11–12.

Hensley, Roy J., 'Development Banks and Economic Development in Indonesia, *Economic Development and Cultural Change* (July 1964) pp. 392–415.

Higgins B. and Hollinger, W., 'Central Banking in Indonesia', in G. Davies (ed.), *Central Banking in South and East Asia* (Hong Kong: University Press, 1960).

Indonesia, *Laporan Direktorat Lembaga Keuangan Ke-xii Tentang Kegiatan Usaha Perasuransian Di Indonesia Tahun 1979* (Report of the Directorate of Financial Institutions no. xii Concerning the (Activities of the Insurance Industry in Indonesia in 1979), 1979.

Indonesia, *Undang-Undang No. 14 Tahun Ketiga 1979–80 – 1983–4* (Third 5 Year Development Plan).

Indonesia Research and Development Company, *Financial Directory of Indonesia 1980* (Jakarta: Karmanna, 1980).

'Indonesia: Special Report', *Asian Banking* (January 1982) pp. 59–89.

'Indonesia: The Awakening Giant', *Euromoney* (Supplement) (January 1979).

Jenkins, David, 'Creditworthy Credit Limits', *Far Eastern Economic Review* (8 April 1977).

Kanesa-Thasan, S., 'Multiple Exchange Rates – the Indonesian Experience', *IMF Staff Papers* (July 1966).

Legge, J. D., *Indonesia*, 2nd edn (Sydney: Prentice-Hall, 1977).

Liddle, R. W., 'The Politics of *Ekonomi Pancasila*', *Bulletin of Indonesian Economic Studies* (March 1982) pp. 96–103.

Lintong, Julianty, 'Some Administrative Factors to be Considered in the Reactivation of the Stock Exchange in Jakarta': MBA thesis, Asian Institute of Management (1975).

Liu, Kenneth, 'Indonesia: a Special Report', *Asian Banking* (January 1982) pp. 59–68.

Mackie, J. A. C., *Problems of the Indonesian Inflation* (Monograph Series, South-East Asia Project) (New York: Cornell University Press, 1967).

—— (ed.), *The Chinese in Indonesia* (Melbourne: Nelson, 1976).

McCawley, Peter, 'Some Consequences of the Pertamina Crisis in Indonesia', *Journal of Southeast Asian Studies* (1978).

——, *Industrialization in Indonesia: Developments and Prospects*: occasional Paper no. 13, Development Studies Centre (Canberra: Australian National University Press, 1979).

——, 'The Economics of *Ekonomi Pancasila*', *Bulletin of Indonesian Economic Studies* (March 1982) pp. 102–9.

McDonald, H., *Suharto's Indonesia* (Fontana: Blackburn, 1980).

McLeod, R. H., 'On Middlemen', *Malayan Economic Review* (1978) pp. 211–26.

——, 'Dualism in Financial Markets', in J. J. Fox *et al.* (eds), *Indonesia: Australian Perspectives* (Canberra: Research School of Pacific Studies, Australian National University, 1980) pp. 321–32.

——, *'Finance and Entrepreneurship in the Small-Business Sector in Indonesia'*: PhD thesis, Australian National University (1980).

Moon, Andrew, 'Leasing Firms Mushroom in Jakarta', *Asian Banking* (January 1982) pp. 88–9.

Mortimer R. (ed.), *Showcase State: the Illusion of Indonesia's 'Accelerated Modernisation'* (Sydney: Angus and Robertson, 1973).

Panglanykim, J., 'Financial Institutions in Indonesia', *The Indonesia Quarterly*, vol. 3, no. 1 (October 1974).

Panglaykin J. and Thomas, K., 'The New Order and the Economy', in *Indonesia* (Ithaca: Cornell University Press, 1967).

Papanek, G. F. (ed.), *The Indonesian Economy* (New York: Praeger, 1980).

Partadireja, Ace, 'Rural Credit: the Ijon System', *Bulletin of Indonesian Economic Studies 10* (1974) pp. 54–71.

Pauw, D., *Financing Economic Development: the Indonesian Case* (Illinois: Free Press, 1960).

Sargent, J. S., 'How BAT went public in Indonesia', *Asian Money Manager* (October 1980) pp. 2–3.

Sereh, J. A., 'Problems and Prospects of the Development of the Money and Capital Market': paper presented to the First Asian Securities Industry Forum, Philippines Village Hotel (10–16 November 1975).

Short, K., 'Indonesia: The Multinationals and the Future', in Skully, Michael T. (ed.), *A Multinational Look at the Transnational Corporation* (Sydney: Dryden Press Australia, 1978).

Sinclair, Jeffrey J., 'The Role of the Financial Institutions in the Indonesian Economy': paper presented at a seminar on money and capital markets, Jakarta (1 July 1975).

Skully, Michael T., 'Commercial Banking in Indonesia: an Examination of its Development and Present Structure', *Asian Survey* (September 1982).

——, 'Jakarta: Toward a Real Money Market', *Euromoney* (May 1977).

——, 'Jakarta's Two Horse Stock Race', *Insight* (August 1978) pp. 28–30.

——, *Merchant Banking in the Far East*, 2nd edn (Indonesia Ch.) (London: *Financial Times*, 1980).

'Survey of Recent Development', *Bulletin of Indonesian Economic Studies* (Canberra: Australian National University, all volumes).

Tan T. (ed.), *Sukarno's Guided Indonesia* (Sydney: Jakaranda, 1967).

The Development of Foreign Banks in Indonesia 1980 (Jakarta: Bank Bumi Daya, 1981).

The Jakarta Report (Palo Alto: SRI International, 1978).

Wiraatmadja, Rasjim, *Himpunan Peraturan Perbankan di Indonesia*, Jilid i, ii dan iii (Collection of Indonesian Banking Regulations, vols. i, ii and iii) (Bandung: PT Bank NISP, 1973; 1975; 1978).

Wong, Mark K. Y., 'Some Legal Aspects of Commercial Offshore Lending to Indonesia', *Singapore Banking and Finance 1979* (Singapore: Institute of Banking and Finance, 1979).

MALAYSIA

A Study of Commercial Banks in Malaysia 1980 (Kuala Lumpur: SGV–Kassim Chan Sdn Berhad, 1981).

A Study of Licensed Borrowing Companies in Malaysia 1980 (Kuala Lumpur: SGV–Kassim Chan Sdn Berhad, 1981).

A Study of Merchant Banks in Malaysia 1979 (Kuala Lumpur: SGV–Kassim Chan Sdn Berhad, 1980).

Allen, G. C. and Donnithorne, A. G., *Western Enterprise in Indonesia and Malaysia* (London: Allen & Unwin, 1957).

Anand, Sudhir, *Inequality and Poverty in Malaysia: Measurement and Composition* (Oxford University Press, 1982).

Ariff, M., 'Japanese Direct Investment in the Manufacturing Sector of Malaysia: Pattern in Perspective', in *Japan's Overseas Investment* (Tokyo: Institute of Developing Economies, 1976).

Aziz, Zeti Akhtar, 'Commercial Bank Portfolio Behavior in an Open Developing Economy: The Malaysian Case': PhD thesis, University of Pennsylvania (1978) (Ann Arbor, Michigan: University Microfilms International, 1978).

Bank Negara Malaysia, Annual Report 1981.

Bowring, Philip, 'Malaysia: Half-way to Maturity', *Far Eastern Economic Review* (10 April 1981) pp. 70–7.

'Breaking the Post Office Link at the Poor Man's Bank', *Asian Banking* (February 1981) pp. 71–3.

Browning, E. S., 'Malaysia Presses its Foreign Branches to go Local', *Australian Financial Review* (6 November 1981).

Chew, Alan, 'The Need for and Functions of Foreign Exchange Reserves in Malaysia 1960–70', *UMBC Economic Review*, vol. viii, no. 2 (1972) pp. 53–61.

Chung, Paul, 'A Note on Financial Development of Malaysia', *Malayan Economic Review* (April 1970).

'Commercial Banks Mount a Higher Plateau', *Asian Finance* (15 June 1981) pp. 60–7.

Cumming-Bruce, Nicholas, 'Mahathir of Malaysia Shakes up the Banks', *Euromoney* (July 1982) pp. 145–50.

——, 'Malaysia's Ethnic Bank Comes of Age', *Euromoney* (August 1981) pp. 139–42.

——, 'Time after Time, Malaysia Demands – and Receives', *Euromoney* (July 1982) pp. 140–3.

Department of Trade and Resources, *Guide to the Market: Malaysia* (Canberra: Australian Government Publishing Service, 1981).

Directory of Licensed Finance Companies in Malaysia (Kuala Lumpur: Association of Finance Companies of Malaysia, 1982).

Drake, Peter J., *Financial Development in Malaya and Singapore* (Canberra: Australian National University Press, 1969).

—— (ed.), *Money and Banking in Malaya and Singapore* (Singapore: MPH Publications, 1966).

Edwards, Clive T., *Public Finances in Malaya and Singapore* (Canberra: Australian National University Press, 1970).

Emery, Robert F., *The Financial Institutions of Southeast Asia: Country by Country Study* (Malaysian Ch.) (New York: Praeger, 1970).

Greenwood, John, 'Malaysia: Money Supply Growth Blights Management by Basket', *Asian Banking* (February 1981) p. 64.

'Islamic Banking Comes to Malaysia', *Asian Finance* (15 August 1982) pp. 22–3.

Koh, Frieda, 'Malaysia's Banking Reforms . . . Caught in the Act', *Far Eastern Economic Review* (17 September 1982) pp. 54–6.

Kong, Sik Hung, 'Borrowing Companies in Malaysia', *UMBC Economic Review*, vol. ix, no. 2 (1973) pp. 4–11.

Lee, Hock Lock, *Household Savings in West Malaya and the Problem of Financing Economic Development* (Kuala Lumpur: University of Malaya, 1971).

——, *Public Policies and Economic Diversification in West Malaysia 1957–70* (Kuala Lumpur: University of Malaya Press, 1978).

——, *Public Policies, Commercial Banks, and Other Deposit Institutions in Malaysia 1957–70* (Kuala Lumpur: University of Malaya Cooperative Bookshop Publications, 1981).

Lee, Sheng-Yi, *Monetary and Banking Development of Malaysia and Singapore* (Singapore University Press, 1974).

Lee, Sheng-Yi and Jao, Y. C., *Financial Structures and Monetary Policies in Southeast Asia* (Malaysian Ch.) (London: Macmillan, 1981).

Lee, Soo Ann, *Economic Growth and the Public Sector in Malaya and Singapore 1948–60* (Singapore: Oxford University Press, 1974).

Lim, Chong-Yah, *Economic Development of Modern Malaya* (Kuala Lumpur: Oxford University Press, 1967).

Lim, David, *Readings on Malaysian Economic Development* (Kuala Lumpur: Oxford University Press, 1975).

Lim, Mah Hiu, *Ownership and Control of the One Hundred Largest Corporations in Malaysia* (Kuala Lumpur: Oxford University Press, 1982).

Liu, Kenneth, 'Malaysia Tinkers With its Banking Machine, *Asian Banking* (December 1981) pp. 45–9.

'Malaysia: A Special Report', *Asian Banking* (February 1981) pp. 37–74.

'Malaysia '80', *Far Eastern Economic Review* (22 August 1980) pp. 33–56.

McBride, Jo, 'Malaysia: Drive for Fees Meets the Deadline', *Asian Banking* (February 1981) pp. 45; 48; 56.

McKenna, D., 'Financial Developments Since Independence', in Silcock, T. H. and Fisk, E. K. (eds). *The Political Economy of Independent Malaya: a Case Study in Development* (Canberra: Australian National University Press, 1963).

'Merchant Banking: New Horizons for the Wholesalers', *Malaysian Business* (January 1979).

Money and Banking in Malaysia (Kuala Lumpur: Bank Negara Malaysia, 1979).

Mukerjee, Dilip, 'Bank Negara Bares its Claws', *Asian Finance* (15 August 1981) pp. 14–17.

Peyman, Hugh, 'Tighter Money and a More Tranquil Time Ahead', *Far Eastern Economic Review* (27 March 1981) pp. 84–5.

Purcal, J., (ed.), *The Monetary System of Singapore and Malaysia: the Implications of the Split Currency* (University of Singapore, 1967).

Ridzuan Abdul Halim, 'The Three Challenges Facing Malaysian Commercial Banking', *UMBC Economic Review*, vol. xiv, no. 1 (1978) pp. 50–9.

Roy, Barun, 'Malaysia: Merchant Banks Get the Whistle', *Asian Finance* (15 June 1981) pp. 50–9.

Rudner, Martin, *Nationalism, Planning and Economic Modernization in*

Malaysia: the Politics of Beginning Development (Beverly Hills: Sage Publications, 1975).

Segal, Jeffery, 'Surgery at Bank Rakyat', *Far Eastern Economic Review* (9 July 1982) pp. 72–4.

Short, Broch H., 'Monetary Aspects of the Currency Board and Central Bank in Malaysia and Singapore 1951–66': PhD thesis, Cornell University (1970).

Sieh, Lee Mei Ling, 'Effects of Investment Incentives on Share Ownership Distribution in Malaysian Manufacturing Companies', *UMBC Economic Review*, vol. xvii, no. 1 (1981) pp. 44–54.

Silcock, Thomas H., *The Economy of Malaya: an Essay in Colonial Political Economy* (Singapore: Moore, 1954).

—— (ed.), *Readings in Malayan Economics* (Singapore: Eastern Universities Press, 1961).

Silcock, Thomas H. and Fisk, E. K., (eds), *The Political Economy of Independent Malaya: a Case Study in Development* (Canberra: Australian National University Press, 1963).

Singh, J., Allan, D. E., Hiscock, M. E. and Roebuck, D., *Credit & Security in West Malaysia* (St. Lucia: Queensland University Press, 1978).

Skully, Michael T., 'Malaysia's Merchant Banks: License Means Freedom – But With Conditions', *Asian Money Manager* (August 1979) pp. 31–5.

——, *Merchant Banking in the Far East* (Malaysian Ch.) 2nd edn. (London: *Financial Times,* 1980).

Smith, Patrick, 'Feeling the Pinch in a Worsening Situation' (Malaysian Banking), Far Eastern Economic Review (26 March 1982) p. 86.

Snodgrass, D. R., *Inequality and Economic Development in Malaysia* (Kuala Lumpur: Oxford University Press, 1980).

Soe, Myint, *A Source Book on Banking Law in Singapore & Malaysia* (Singapore: Institute of Banking and Finance, 1977).

Tan Sri Ismail bin Mohamed Ali, 'The Management of the Banking System': speech to the Malaysian Economics Association, Kuala Lumpur (17 October 1975).

10th Anniversary Commemorative Issue 1959–69 (Kuala Lumpur: Bank Negara Malaysia, 1969).

Tham, Soh Kum, 'Malaysian Commercial Banks' Contribution Toward National Development in the Seventies,' *UMBC Economic Review*, vol. xv, no. 2 (1979) pp. 32–8.

'The Base Erodes Under Finance Firms', *Asian Finance* (15 September 1982) pp. 22–3.

Verchére, Ian, 'Bank Bumiputra: Malaysia's Booming Bumi Bank', *Insight* (July 1978) pp. 45–8.

Walters, A. A., 'Monetary Policy and Economic Development in Malaysia', *Kajian Ekonomi Malaysia* (June 1970).

Wells, R. J. G., 'Commercial Banks and the Rural Financial Markets: The Malaysian Experience', *Asian Economies* (March 1981) pp. 70–87.

——, 'The Rural Credit Market in Peninsula Malaysia: A Focus on Informal Lenders', *Asian Economies* (December 1979).

Young, Kevin, Bussink, William C. F. and Hassan, Parvez, (eds) *Growth and Equity in a Multiracial Society: World Bank Country Economic Reports* (Baltimore: Johns Hopkins University Press, 1980).

Zielenzinger, David, 'Some Malaysians Hope Central Banker Will Retire', *Asian Wall Street Journal* (6 March 1980).

PHILIPPINES

A Study of Commercial Banks in the Philippines (Manila: SGV Group, 1981).

Alejandro, Ma. Elisa, Ruiz, Emma and Valoria, Alexander, *The Impact of Foreign Currency Deposit Units' Loans on Domestic Investment* (Quezon City: School of Economics, University of the Philippines, 1977).

Atienza, Wilfrido A., *Effects of Finance Companies on Consumption and Production of Consumer Durables with a Note on Finance Rates* (Quezon City: School of Economics, University of the Philippines, 1976).

Azurin, Agnes M., *A Study on the Impact of the Offshore Banking System* (Macro-economic Viewpoint) (Quezon City: School of Economics, University of the Philippines, 1979).

Balquin, Winifreda P., *The Role of the Social Security System in Capital Formation* (Quezon City: School of Economics, University of the Philippines, 1976).

Banking Structure and Sources of Finance in the Far East (Philippines Ch.), 3rd edn (London: *Financial Times*, 1980).

Barcelon A., Augusto M., 'Developments in the Philippine Banking, Financial & Economic Scene', *Singapore Banking and Finance 1978* (Singapore: Institute of Banking and Finance 1979).

Barrios, Victor S., 'The Evolution of Philippine Interest Rate Policy', *Philippine Review of Business and Economics*, x (1973).

Bautista, Carlos and Jevelino Villacastin, *A Study on the Lending Patterns of Philippine National Bank* (Quezon City: School of Economics, University of the Philippines, 1979).

Bernardo, P. N. L., 'The Feasibility of Underwriting the Cebu City Bond to Finance the Pasil Fish Market': MBA thesis, Asian Institute of Management (1976).

Besa, Emerito P. and Pecache, Glenn L., *The Financial Market After*

1970 (With Emphasis on the Government Securities and the Effects of the CBCI Flotation) (Quezon City: School of Economics, University of the Philippines, 1978).

Buenaventura, Elsa J., *A Study of the Operations of Stock Brokers with Seats in the Makati Stock Exchange* (Makati, Metro Manila: Asian Institute of Management, 1974).

Cabanilla, Nathaniel B., 'Money, Finance and Growth: an Empirical Inquiry into the Economic Development of the Philippines': unpublished PhD thesis, George Washington University (1979).

CBP, *Financing Company* (monograph) (Manila: CBP, no date).

——, *Fund Manager* (monograph) (Manila: CBP, no date).

——, *Investment House* (monograph) (Manila: CBP, no date).

——, *Lending Investor* (monograph) (Manila: CBP, no date).

——, *Rural Banking System in the Philippines* (CBP, *Annual Report 1981*) (Manila: CBP, 1982).

——, *Stockbroker* (monograph) (Manila: CBP, no date).

Chan, John, 'Offshore Banking in the Philippines', *Singapore Banking and Finance 1978* (Singapore: Institute of Banking and Finance, 1979).

Clemente, Irma P., *A Study of the Money Market in the Philippines* (Quezon City: School of Economics, University of the Philippines, 1975).

Collado, Geronimo M., 'Financing Dimensions of Philippine Agriculture: The Management of Institutional Credit Programs for Rice and Sugar Farmers': unpublished DBA thesis, Harvard University (1975).

Crisol, Alfredo B. and Gomez, Juli L. M., *The Offshore Banking System as Part of the Philippine Financial System: a Look into the Economic Efficiency* (Quezon City: School of Economics, University of the Philippines, 1977).

Cruz, Alfonzo M. and Olivar, Gene B., *The CBCIs and the Government Securities Market* (Quezon City: School of Economics, University of the Philippines, 1979).

Cruz, Cynthia M. and Dompor, Francis A., *A Probe into the Money Market Regulations and Their Impact on the Capital Market* (Quezon City: School of Economics, University of the Philippines, 1979).

Cruz, Ismael A., *The Philippine Stock Market: Some Theoretical and Empirical Results* (Quezon City: School of Economics, University of the Philippines, 1975).

Curabo, Jesus E. D., *Philippine Stabilization Policy Under the Floating Exchange Rate* (Quezon City: School of Economics, University of the Philippines, 1979).

De la Cruz, Angel G., 'The Philippines Investment Banking Industry': MBA thesis, Asian Institute of Management (1973).

De la Paz, Rolando M., *Some Implications of Exchange Control Policies* for *Resource Allocation and Growth: An Appraisal of the Philippine Experience* (Quezon City: School of Economics, University of the Philippines, 1970).

Department of Trade and Resources, *Guide to the Market: Philippines* (Canberra: Australian Government Publishing Service, 1981).

Domingo, Emilio R., *A Branch Establishment Scheme for a Filipino Comercial Bank* (Makati, Metro Manila: Asian Institute of Management, 1979).

Dosdos, Eulogio Y. (ed.), *Philippine Directory of Financial Institutions*, 5th edn (Manila: Sinag–Tala Publishing, 1982).

Duran, Maria S. and Japon, Alexander, *The Impact of the External Sector and Monetary Policy on Commercial Bank Lending Rates* (Quezon City: School of Economics, University of the Philippines, 1978).

Emery, Robert F., *The Financial Institutions of Southeast Asia: a Country by Country Study* (Philippines Ch.) (New York: Praeger, 1970).

Espiritu, O. V., 'The Interbank Call Loan Market' in Robert J. Manzano, *Investment Banking in the Philippines* (Makati: Media Systems, 1976).

Fookien Times Philippine Yearbook 1981–2 (Manila: The *Fookien Times*, 1982).

Gallardo, Joselito S., *The Structure of the Financial System of the Philippines, 1950–70* (Manila: CBP, 1972).

——, *The Structure of the Financial System of the Philippines, 1950–70* (report on research undertaken for the Joint IMF–CBP Banking Survey Commission) (Manila: CBP, 1972).

Garcia, Alfonso, Jr, *An Industry Study of the Private Development Banking System* (Makati, Metro Manila: Asian Institute of Management, 1981).

Getzelman, John C., 'Casting a Distinctive Role for Manila's OBUs', *Asian Banking* (July 1980) pp. 63–5.

Gonzaga, Leo, 'Banking: Floating With the Market', *Far Eastern Economic Review* (3 July 1981) pp. 56–7.

——, 'Banking: High Noon in Manila', *Far Eastern Economic Review* (19 March 1982) pp. 74–5.

——, 'Investment: Making of a Market Merger', *Far Eastern Economic Review* (28 November 1980) p. 66.

——, 'Investment: Propping up the Market', *Far Eastern Economic Review* (29 May 1981) p. 70.

——, 'Manila Adjusts its Strategy,' *Far Eastern Economic Review* (6 February 1981) p. 88.

——, 'Teeth in the Fine Print – the Philippines', *Far Eastern Economic Review* (18 June 1982) pp. 92–3.

——, 'Philippines: Unibanking – Recommended by IMF – is on its

Way', *Far Eastern Economic Review* (4 April 1980) pp. 93–4.

—— and Sacerdoti, Guy, 'Finance: Operation Cold Comfort', *Far Eastern Economic Review* (14 May 1982) pp. 86–8.

Hawkins, Edward K., *The Philippines: Priorities and Prospects for Development: World Bank Country Economic Report* (Washington, DC: World Bank, 1976).

'Helping Hand in Manila', *Far Eastern Economic Review* (3 April 1981), pp. 43–4.

Hooley, Richard W. and Moreno, H. A., *A Study of Financial Flows in the Philippines: IEDR Discussion Paper 74–6* (Quezon City: School of Economics, University of the Philippines, 1976).

Ibay, Rufino G., *Economics of Scale in Commercial Banking in the Philippines* (Quezon City: School of Economics, University of the Philippines, 1975).

Ibazeta, Henrietta T. and Legaspi, Angelica V., *Interest Rate Policies of the Central Bank and Their Effect on the Growth and Allocation of Funds Within the Financial Sector* (Quezon City: School of Economics, University of the Philippines, 1978).

IBRD East Asia and Pacific Regional Office, *The Philippines: Aspects of the Financial Sector* (Washington, DC: World Bank, 1980).

Josue, Macario P., *The Development of Non-bank Financial Institutions in the Philippines: Importance and Role* (Quezon City: School of Economics, University of the Philippines, 1971).

Laset, Rogelio C., *The Private Commercial Banking Industry: A Challenge for Corporate Planning* (Makati, Metro Manila: Asian Institute of Management, 1979).

Laya, Jaime C., *A Crisis of Confidence and Other Papers* (Manila: CBP, 1982).

Lee, Sheng-Yi and Jao, Y. C., *Financial Structures and Monetary Policies in Southeast Asia* (Philippines Ch.) (London: Macmillan, 1981).

Lim, Robyn, 'The Multinationals and the Philippines Since Martial Law', in Michael T. Skully (ed.), *A Multinational Look at the Transnational Corporation* (Sydney: Dryden Press Australia, 1978).

Lorenzo, Hilda Ong, *Response of Time and Savings Deposit to Changes in Interest Rates* (Quezon City: School of Economics, University of the Philippines, 1978).

McBride, Jo, 'The Philippines: a Special Report', *Asian Banking* (September 1981) pp. 46–73.

——, 'The Rise and Flight of Dewey Dee', *Asian Banking* (May 1981) pp. 43–97.

Magnaye, Cesar L., *A Study on Stock Prices and Money Market Rate Movement* (Quezon City: School of Economics, University of the Philippines, 1974).

Malloy, Michael T., 'Philippines to Lift Many Restrictions on Way

Domestic Banks do Business', *Asian Wall Street Journal* (26 February 1980).

Manzano, Robert J. (ed.), *Investment Banking in the Philippines* (Makati, Metro Manila: Media Systems Inc., 1976).

Maravilla, Josefa B. and Uy, Jo-Anne, *Private Domestic Commercial Bank Mergers: Its Evaluation and Implications* (Quezon City: School of Economics, University of the Philippines, 1979).

Mayoralgo, Alejo V., *A Study of the Financing Industry in the Philippines* (Makati, Metro Manila: Asian Institute of Management, 1979).

Morte, Lorna F., *The Development of Commercial Banks in the Philippines: Patterns, Sources and Implications* (Quezon City: School of Economics, University of the Philippines, 1979).

Muro, Vicente, *Philippines Financial Institutions* (Manila: Systems Publishing, 1976).

——, *How to Study & Finance Philippine Enterprises* (Manila: Alemar–Phoenix Publishing House, 1968).

Page, Francisco S., *Monetary Policy and the Commercial Banking Operations 1968–76* (Quezon City: School of Economics, University of the Philippines, 1979).

Patanne, E. P., 'Philippine Financial Changes Meet with Resistance', *Asian Business* (September 1981) pp. 45–8.

Philippine Financial System Fact Book (Quarterly) (Manila: CBP).

Power, J. H. and Sicat, G. P., *The Philippines: Industrialization and Trade Policies* (London: Oxford University Press, 1971).

Ranis, Gustav, *Sharing in Development: a Program of Employment, Equity and Growth in the Philippines* (Geneva: International Labour Office, 1974).

Ricasio, Vicente R. and Bermudez, J. L., 'The Market for Long Term Debt in the Philippines', in Manzano, Robert J. (ed.), *Investment Banking in the Philippines* (Manila: Media Systems Inc., 1976) pp. 38–50.

Roxas, Sixto K., *Managing Asian Financial Development* (Manila: Sinag–Tala Publishers, 1976).

Sacerdoti, Guy, 'Stockmarkets: Long and Winding Road', *Far Eastern Economic Review* (26 March 1982) pp. 148–9.

Sales, Emmanuel O., *The Primary Securities Market: Some Findings* (Quezon City: School of Economics, University of the Philippines, 1975).

Securities and Exchange Commission and Business Day's 1000 Top Corporations of the Philippines (1981 edn), (Quezon City: Business Day Corporation, 1981).

Skully, Michael T., *Merchant Banking in the Far East* (Philippines Ch.), 2nd edn (London: *Financial Times*, 1980).

——, 'Philippine Investment Houses After Filcapital', *Asian Business & Industry* (August 1977).

Stauffer, Robert B., *Transnational Corporations and The Political Economy of Development: The Continuing Philippine Debate* (Sydney: Transnational Corporation Research Project, 1980).

Tampi, Indar L., *Management Problems and Prospects of Islamic Banking in the Philippines* (Makati, Metro Manila: Asian Institute of Management, 1977).

Tan, Edita A., *Credit Measures and their Impact on the Development of the Financial Structure: IEDR Discussion Paper 76–6* (Quezon City: School of Economics, University of the Philippines, 1973).

——, *A Note on Central Bank Regulation of the Financial System: IEDR Discussion Paper 76–7* (Quezon City: School of Economics, University of the Philippines, 1976).

——, 'Philippine Monetary Policy and Aspects of the Financial Market: A Review of the Literature', in *PIDS Survey of Philippine Development Research I* (Manila: Philippine Institute for Development Studies, 1980).

Umana, Salvador C., *A Study of Saving and Monetization with Special Reference to the Philippines* (Ann Arbor, Michigan: University Microfilms International, 1971).

Williamson, Jeffrey G., 'Personal Savings in Developing Nations', in *Economic Theory and Practice in the Asian Setting* (New Delhi: Wiley Eastern Ltd, 1975).

Yu, Edward, *The 35 Percent Tax on Money Market Borrowings: an Appraisal* (Quezon City: School of Economics, University of the Philippines, 1977).

Yu, Natividad C., *Concentration in the Commercial Banking System* (Quezon City: School of Economics, University of the Philippines, 1979).

'The Philippines: a Fitter Shape for the Financial System', *Asian Banking* (September 1981) pp. 64–9.

The Philippines: Housing Finance (Washington, DC: World Bank, 1982).

'The Philippines: Into a New Economic Era', *Euromoney* (Supplement) (April 1982).

'The Philippines: the Economy That Came up Smiling' *Euromoney* (Supplement) (April 1979).

SINGAPORE

A Study of Commercial Banks in Singapore 1980 (and various issues) (Manila: SGV Group, 1980).

A Study of Finance Companies in Singapore 1980 (and various issues).

396 *Bibliography*

A Study of Merchant Banks in Singapore 1980 (and various issues).

Banking Structures and Sources of Finance in The Far East, 3rd edn (Singapore Ch.) (London: *Financial Times*, 1980).

Banks and Financial Institutions in Singapore Yearbook 1979 (Singapore: Consulton Research Bureau, 1979).

Chandiramani, Lachmandas P., 'Merchant Banking in Singapore': BBA academic exercise, Department of Business Administration, University of Singapore (1980).

Cheong, Hua Pak, *Elements of Banking in Singapore*, 2nd edn (Singapore: Institute of Banking and Finance, 1981).

Collins, Nancy and McBride, Jo, 'Singapore Institutions: Rules and Contenders in the Race for 1990', *Asian Banking* (July 1981), pp. 59–70.

Department of Trade and Resources, *Guide to the Market: Singapore* (Canberra: Australian Government Publishing Services 1981).

Drake, Peter, J., *Financial Development in Malaya and Singapore* (Canberra: Australian National University Press, 1969).

Edwards, C. T., *Public Finances in Malaya and Singapore* (Canberra: Australian National University Press, 1970).

Emery, R. F., *Financial Institutions in Southeast Asia* (Singapore Ch.) (New York: Praeger Publishing, 1970).

Fact Book '80 (Singapore: SES, 1981).

Geiger, T. and Geiger, F. M., *The Development Progress of Hong Kong and Singapore* (London: Macmillan, 1975).

Hou, Sui Sen, 'Development of Singapore as a Financial Centre'; speech by the Minister for Finance at the Singapore International Chamber of Commerce Luncheon (5 May 1972).

Hunt, J. C., 'The Impact of Other Financial Centres on Singapore', *Singapore Banking and Finance 1978* (Singapore: Institute of Banking and Finance, 1978).

Iau, Robert, 'CPF: Compulsory Savings Scheme for Workers', *Singapore Banking and Finance 1977* (Singapore: Institute of Banking and Finance, 1977).

Khor, Thiam Chye, 'The Singapore Money Market', *Singapore Banking and Finance 1976* (Singapore: Institute of Banking and Finance, 1976).

Koh, Kheng Lian, Allan, David E., Hiscock, Mary E. and Roebuch, Derek, *Credit and Security in Singapore: the Legal Problems of Development Finance: a Research Project of ADB and LAWASIA* (Manila: Asian Development Bank, March 1973).

Lee, Sheng-Yi, 'ASEAN Finance Corporation', Singapore–Chinese Chamber of Commerce and Industry, *Souvenir Magazine* for the Commemoration of 75th Anniversary (1981).

——, 'Finance Companies in Singapore', *Singapore Trade and Industry Yearbook 1973*.

Lee, Sheng-Yi, 'Insurance Can do so Much More', *Singapore Trade and Industry* (October 1973), pp. 31–3.
——, *The Monetary and Banking Development of Malaysia and Singapore* (Singapore University Press, 1974).
——, 'Ownership and Control of Local Banks', *Singapore Year book of Banking and Finance 1980–1* (Singapore: Institute of Banking and Finance, 1980–1), pp. 109–17.
——, 'Public Enterprise and Economic Development in Singapore', *Malayan Economic Review* (October 1976) pp. 49–73.
——, *Public Finance and Public Investment in Singapore* (Singapore: Institute of Banking and Finance, 1978).
——, 'Recent Development in Asian Currency Market and Asian Bond Market': occasional paper no. 32, Institute of Economics and Business Studies, Nanyang University (April 1979).
——, 'Recession, Inflation and the Asian Currency Market' *Securities Industry Review* (April 1976) pp. 21–30.
——, 'The Role of Financial Institutions in the Singapore Economy', *Business Times* (Banking Supplement) (24 February 1978) p. xx.
Lee, Sheng-Yi and Jao, Y. C., *Financial Structures and Monetary Policies in South East Asia* (Singapore Ch.) (London: Macmillan, 1982).
Lee, Sheng-Yi and Wee, Kenny, 'Liquidity and Growth: The Case of a Local Bank' *South Asian Journal of Social Science* (1975).
Lee, Soo Ann, 'Banking and the Asian Dollar Market', in *Highlights of the ASEAN Economy* (Singapore: Singapore Airlines Ltd, 1977).
——, 'Flow of Funds and Financial Markets' *Securities Industry Review* (September 1975) pp. 13–16.
Ooi, Grace, 'Shareownership Survey', *Singapore Stock Exchange Journal* (March–May; November–December 1976); *Securities Industry Review* (September 1977).
MAS, *Annual Reports 1970 – 1981–2* (various issues).
——, *Financial Structure of Singapore 1980*, 2nd edn (Singapore: MAS, 1980).
——, *Papers on Monetary Economics 1981*.
——, *Quarterly Bulletin* (which has been superseded by *Monthly Statistical Bulletin* since 1980).
Ng, Kok Song, 'The Asian Dollar Bond Market: Developments and Prospects', *Singapore Banking and Finance 1979* (Singapore: Institute of Banking and Finance, 1979).
Rasmussen, Eric, 'Financial Sector Leads Singapore Boom', *Asian Money Manager* (October 1981) pp. 9–12.
Sam, Elizabeth, 'The Central Bank and the Financial Centre': paper presented at the Seminar on 'Banking and Finance in the 1980s', organised by the Institute of Banking and Finance and the Association of Banks in Singapore (27–8 October 1977).

Saw, Swee–Hock, *The Securities Market in Singapore* (Singapore: Singapore Securities Research Institute, 1980).

Shimpi, A. T., 'Sources and Uses of Insurance Funds', *Singapore Banking* and *Finance 1976* (Singapore: Institute of Banking and Finance, 1976).

Sia, Yong, 'Finance Companies: Their Role in the Eighties and the 1967 Act', *Singapore Banking and Finance 1979* (Singapore: Institute of Banking and Finance, 1979).

'Singapore Institutions: Rules and Contenders in the Race for 1990', *Asian Banking* (July 1981 pp. 59–82).

Singapore Banking and Finance 1977 (Singapore: Institute of Banking and Finance, 1977).

Singapore Banking and Finance 1978 (Singapore: Institute of Banking and Finance, 1978).

Singapore Banking and Finance 1979 (Singapore: Institute of Banking and Finance, 1979).

Singapore Banking and Finance, 1980–1 (Singapore: Institute of Banking and Finance, 1981).

Sio, Tat Hiang, 'The Singapore Government Securities Market', in Saw, Swee–Hock and Lim, Choo Peng (ed), *Investment Analysis* (Singapore University Press, 1979).

Skully, Michael T., *Merchant Banking in the Far East*, 2nd edn, (Singapore Ch.) (London: *Financial Times*, 1980).

——, 'Singapore Banks Spawn New Ventures', *Asian Money Manager* (February 1979) pp. 23–6.

——, 'Singapore Grows as Major Money Centre', *Bankers' Handbook for Asia 1979–80* (Hong Kong: Asian Finance Publications, 1980).

Tan, Chwee Huat, *Financial Institutions in Singapore*, 2nd edn (Singapore University Press, 1981).

Teo, Anthony and Sim, Eric K., 'Prospects of Merchant Banking in Singapore', *Singapore Banking and Finance 1977* (Singapore: Institute of Banking and Finance, 1977).

The Financial Structure of Singapore (Singapore: MAS, June 1980).

The Post Office Savings Bank of Singapore: 100 years (Singapore: POSB, July 1977).

Wee, Cho Yaw, 'Growth in the Banking and Finance Industry: Problem Areas and Prospects', *Singapore Banking and Finance 1979* (Singapore: Institute of Banking and Finance, 1979).

Wilson, Dick, 'Singapore's Maturing Markets', *The Banker* (April/May 1980) pp. 125–7.

Wong, Kum Poh, 'Central Provident Fund: What is the Ultimate Destination?' *Singapore Banking and Finance 1979* (Singapore: Institute of Banking and Finance, 1979).

Wong, Paksong Michael, 'Singapore's Banking & Financial System: A Period of Change', *Journal of Business* (1972–3) pp. 35–8.

Wong, Paksong Michael, 'What the Monetary Authority Does', *Singapore Trade and Industry Yearbook 1973.*

THAILAND

A Study of Commercial Banks in Thailand 1980 (Bangkok: SGV, 1981).
A Study of Finance and Securities Companies in Thailand 1980 (Bangkok: SGV, 1981).
Aphimeteetamrong, Virach, 'The Contribution of Financial Institutions to Thai Economic Development': PhD thesis, University of Illinois, Urbana–Champaign Campus (1980).
Bank of America, *Thailand: Economic Update* (October 1982).
Basel, Peter E. (ed.), *Securities Exchange of Thailand: 1978–9 Handbook* (Bangkok: Business Information and Research Ltd, 1979).
Bouvier, Lucy, 'Divestiture Blues at Thai Banks', *Asian Banking* (January 1982) pp. 91–2.
'Challenge from Thai Farmers Makes for Shift in Bangkok's Top Three', *Asian Banking* (August 1980), pp. 59–60.
'Commercial Banks in the Seventies', Bangkok Bank, *Monthly Review* (August 1981) pp. 290–6.
Co-operatives in Thailand (Bangkok: Ministry of Agriculture and Co-operatives, 1979).
'Credit for Housing' (in Thai), Bank of Thailand, *Monthly Bulletin* (September 1978).
Donner, Wolf, *The Five Faces of Thailand: An Economic Geography* (London: C. Hurst, 1978).
Emery, Robert F., *The Financial Institutions of Southeast Asia: A Country by Country Study* (Thailand Ch.) (New York: Praeger, 1970).
Fact Book '79 (Bangkok: SET, 1980).
Finance Business and Securities Business in Thailand (in Thai) (Bangkok: Bank of Thailand, 1978).
Financial Institutions in Thailand (Bangkok: Bangkok Bank Ltd, 1982).
Financial Institutions in Thailand (Bangkok: Bank of Thailand, 1978).
Garnjarerndee, Siri, 'Pattern of Household Financial Savings in Thailand Since 1960', Bank of Thailand, *Quarterly Bulletin* (March; June 1981) pp. 15–20.
Girling, J., *Thailand: Society and Politics* (Ithaca: Cornell University Press 1981).
Harling, Joseph E. and Westphal, L. E., 'Financial Policy in Postwar Thailand: External Equilibrium and Domestic Development', *Asian Survey* (May 1968).
Hunt, P. and Gibson, D. M. T., *Bangkok Stock Exchange* (Board of Trustees, Leland Standford Junior University, 1965).

Ingram, James Carlton, *Economic Change in Thailand, 1850–1972* (Stanford: Stanford University Press, 1972).

'Insurance–Life has its Ups and Downs', *Business in Thailand* (August 1981) pp. 36–40.

'Insurance Business in Thailand 1970–7' (in Thai), Bank of Thailand, *Monthly Bulletin* (November 1978).

Kaocharern, Sukri, 'The Development of the Securities Exchange of Thailand', *International Journal of Accounting* (Fall 1976).

Kirakul, Suchada, 'Investment and Sources of Capital Funds', Bank of Thailand, *Quarterly Bulletin* (September 1981) pp. 33–43.

Karishnamara, Damrong, 'The Structure of Income and Saving Mobilization in Thailand', Bangkok Bank, *Monthly Review* (February 1981) p. 61.

Mousny, A., *The Economy of Thailand* (Bangkok: Social Science Association Press of Thailand, 1964).

Muscat, Robert J., *Development Strategy in Thailand: a Study in Economic Growth* (New York: Praeger, 1966).

Nananukool, Surask, 'Thailand's Money Market', Bangkok Bank, *Monthly Review* (December 1979) pp. 447–57.

Neher, Clark D., *Modern Thai Politics: From Village to Nation* (Cambridge, Mass.: Schenkman, 1979).

Panitchpakdi, Supachi, 'Financial Structure: Segmentation and Development' Bank of Thailand, *Quarterly Review* (March 1981) pp. 51–71.

'Pawnshops in Thailand' (in Thai), Bank of Thailand, *Monthly Bulletin* (in Thai) (May 1975).

Phombejara, Vichbituong (ed.), *Readings in Thailand's Political Economy* (Bangkok: Bangkok Printing Enterprise Co., 1978).

Prachuabmoh, Nukul, 'An address to the Annual Banquet of the Thai Bankers' Association 18 February 1981', Bank of Thailand, *Quarterly Bulletin* (March 1981) pp. i–v.

'Reinsurance: a Great Stride Forward', Bangkok Bank, *Monthly Review* (January 1979) pp. 15–19.

Robbins, Sidney M., *A Capital Market in Thailand* (limited edn) (Bangkok: Bank of Thailand, 1970).

Rozental, Alex A., *Finance and Development in Thailand* (New York: Praeger, 1970).

Sapcharoen, Seri, 'Raja Finance: An Awesome Legal Tangle', *WEEK* (2 June 1980) pp. 30–3.

Sachchamarga, Savaraj, 'A Study of the Determinants of the Money Supply in Thailand': PhD thesis, Texas A & M University (1977).

SET, *Annual Report 1978*.

Seshadri, T. K., 'Profile: Thailand', *Asian Finance* (15 November 1981) p. 79.

Sethandha, Khanit, 'Thailand Securities Exchange: Its Operations,

Problems and Prospects': MBA thesis, Asian Institute of Management (1975).

Setboonsarng, Sunantar and Srisilpavongse, Kanitha, 'Agricultural Credit: More 'Bread' for the Farmers', *Business in Thailand* (January 1982) pp. 48–51.

Silcock, T. H. (ed.), *Thailand: Social and Economic Studies in Development* (Canberra: Australian National University Press, 1967).

Sithi-Amnual, Paul, *Finance and Banking in Thailand: a Study of the Commercial Banking System, 1888–1963* (Bangkok: Thai Watana Panich, 1964).

Skully, Michael T., *Merchant Banking in the Far East*, edn (Thai. Ch.) (London: *Financial Times*, 1980).

Sondysuvan, Pratcep (ed.), *Finance, Trade and Economic Development in Thailand* (Bangkok: Sompong Press, 1975).

Sophastienphong, Kiatchai, 'More Bankers Want In – Foreign Bank Representative Offices in Thailand', *Business Review* (August 1982) pp. 62–4.

——, 'Where the Bears Live: The Securities Exchange of Thailand', *Business Review* (August 1982) pp. 18–23.

Sricharatchanya, Paisal, 'Cashing Out and In on the Thai Coup', *Asian Banking* (May 1981) pp. 50–1.

——, 'Nukul's Opening Gambit Gets Thai Money Moving Again', *Asian Banking* (March 1980) pp. 35–8.

——, 'Specialisation Needed in the Banking System and Financial Sector', *Far Eastern Economic Review* (24 September 1982) pp. 82–5.

——, 'Thai Discount Houses Proposal on the Launch Pad', *Asian Banking* (July 1981) pp. 55–6.

Srisilpavongse, Kanitha, 'The Government Housing Bank: Cleanup at the Top', *Business in Thailand* (October 1981) pp. 30–7.

Statistical Data on Commercial Banks in Thailand (Bangkok: Bangkok Bank Ltd, 1978).

Supachi, P., *Issues in Banking and Finance in Thailand 1975–80* (Bangkok: Marketing Media, 1980).

Thailand: Industrial Development Strategy in Thailand (Washington, DC: World Bank, 1980).

Thailand into the 80s (Bangkok: Office of the Prime Minister, 1979).

'Thailand: Pulling Together in Thailand, Inc.', *Euromoney* (Supplement) (December 1980).

Thailand: Toward a development strategy of Full Employment (Washington, DC: World Bank, 1980).

The Cooperative Movement in Thailand (Bangkok: Cooperative Marketing and Purchasing Federation of Thailand Ltd, 1974).

The Industrial Finance Corporation of Thailand: History and Operations, 1959–76 (Bangkok: IFCT, 1976).

Thepthana, Somchai, 'Government Expenditures, Taxes, and Income

Distribution in Thailand': PhD thesis, University of Kentucky (1979).

Trescott, Paul B., *Thailand's Monetary Experience: the Economics of Stability* (New York: Praeger, 1971).

Unakol Snoh, 'Thai Banks Spread to the Provinces', *Asian Money Manager* (April 1977) pp. 14–16.

Unphakorn, Puey, *Finance, Trade and Economic Development in Thailand* (Bangkok: Somprasong Press, 1975).

Wattanasiritham, Paiboon, 'Review of Existing Savings Institutions and Methods Used in Mobilizing of Small Savings in Thailand', Bank of Thailand, *Monthly Bulletin* (October 1974).

Wattanasiritham, Paiboon, 'Thailand's Financial Institutions: Brief Description and a Comparative Analysis of Their Roles in Mobilizing Savings and Providing Credit', Bank of Thailand, *Monthly Bulletin* (September 1974).

Wongvasu, Vichit, 'The Determinants of The Money Supply in Thailand': PhD thesis, University of Utah (1977).

Index

DATE DUE

PRINTED IN U.S.A.

GAYLORD